*Seventh Edition*

# *Introduction to Social Work*

**Rex A. Skidmore**

**Milton G. Thackeray**

**O. William Farley**
*University of Utah*

**Allyn and Bacon**
*Boston • London • Toronto • Sydney • Tokyo • Singapore*

*To our students,*
*who have raised the questions*
*and helped with the answers*

*Series Editor, Social Work:* Judy Fifer
*Editor in Chief, Social Sciences:* Karen Hanson
*Editorial Assistant:* Mary Visco
*Marketing Manager:* Quinn Perkson
*Editorial Production Service:* Chestnut Hill Enterprises, Inc.
*Composition Buyer:* Linda Cox
*Manufacturing Buyer:* Megan Cochran
*Cover Administrator:* Suzanne Harbison

Copyright © 1997 by Allyn & Bacon
A Viacom Company
Needham Heights, MA 02194
Copyright 1994, 1991, 1988, 1982, 1976, 1974 by Prentice-Hall, Inc.

**Library of Congress Cataloging-in-Publication Data**

Skidmore, Rex Austin
    Introduction to social work / Rex A. Skidmore, Milton G.
Thackeray, O. William Farley. —7th ed.
        p.    cm.
    Includes bibliographical references and index.
    ISBN 0-205-19341-2
    1. Social service.   2. Social case work—United States.   3. Social
service—United States.   I. Thackeray, Milton G.   II. Farley, O.
William, 1934– .   III. Title.
    HV40.S59   1997
    361—dc20                                                    93-7397
                                                                  CIP

Printed in the United States of America
10  9  8  7  6  5  4  3          01   00   99   98

**Photo Credits:**
Photo credits are found on page 402, which should be considered an extension of the copyright page.

# TRIBUTE

Professor Milton G. Thackeray died on March 24, 1996, just as we were editing the page proofs of this book.

Our friendship and collaborations in writing reach across many years. His contributions were insightful, pertinent, and challenging. In mental health and child welfare, he was recognized as a creative pioneer and authority.

The very heart of social work is the need to dignify the human process. Professor Thackeray's entire life was spent building, giving to, and loving people. He was a living example of William Menniger's memorable saying, "The essence of living is loving, and the essence of loving is giving, not getting."

May we always remember Milt for his kindness, gentleness, and positive appreciation of others. Milt contributed much to his students, colleagues, and the profession of social work.

Rex and Bill

# Contents

# *Preface*

The authors are pleased to present this seventh edition—thanks to the wide use of the sixth edition by students, social work educators, and practitioners. Many of their suggestions have been incorporated in this current version.

We live in a world with electrifying scientific wonders and achievements that excite the mind. Imagine simultaneously transmitting thousands of telephone conversations over a single strand of glass fiber no larger than a human hair! We live in an information age with messages coming from satellites thousands of miles away. Medical schools now offer departments of Medical Informatics that computerize each disease and make the information readily available to practitioners.

Since the first edition of this book, advancements in knowledge have exploded in nearly every field of human endeavor. Our high-tech/high-touch society opens swinging doors for communication and meaningful human relationships, but people are still having difficulty in communicating and in getting along with each other. For example, a person may be in a room mingling with others but feel abject loneliness for lack of ability to interact effectively with those present. Human relationships can bring satisfaction and joy, but also—for many people—suffering, insecurity, and other difficulties. Social work is one answer to challenges related to communication, feelings, and human actions.

The purpose of this book is to help students understand social welfare and social work. It presents a comprehensive, highlighted view of social work. It focuses on the *why,* the *what,* the *who,* the *when,* the *where,* and describes beginnings of the *how* of social work. The book is for (1) college undergraduate students who want to increase their general understanding about social welfare and social work, and (2) those who have a professional interest in social work. It can also be used in social work philosophy classes and as a reference on the graduate level.

Social welfare depicts human beings as the center of the universe. In their associations with others their lives are enriched, but they also encounter numerous problems. Social work is a professional attempt to help people solve and prevent problems in social functioning, strengthen their social relationships, and enrich their ways of living.

Social work is both a field *and* a method. This book presents an introductory, integrated, overall view of both. Special consideration is given to such perplexing problems as AIDS, youth suicide, drugs, battered women and children, as well as to improved methods in solving social problems through new developments in family home-based care, and other creative and effective social work practices.

The authors want to thank and acknowledge the many reviewers who have provided their thoughtful comments for this and previous revisions: Stephen M. Aigner, Iowa State University; William C. Berleman, University of Washington; Scott Burcham, Arkansas State University; Mary A. Dowery, Ball State University; Ginger Edwards, Charles Stewart Mott Community College; Charles E. Grenier, Louisiana State University; Martin Hope, Winthrop College; Joan M. Jones, University of Wisconsin–Milwaukee; Thomas D. Oellerich, Ohio University; and Paul Sanzenbach, Louisiana State University.

The 1995 editions of the *Encyclopedia of Social Work* (19th Edition), the *Social Work Almanac* (2nd Edition), and the *Social Work Dictionary* (3rd Edition) have been used extensively to update and enrich this book. Also, the new chapter on case management has been revised with current data and examples to increase understanding and skills. The chapter on business and industry has been retitled *Occupational Social Work* and refocused. Chapter 4, *Generalist Practice and Introductory Theory,* is entirely new.

Several additional unique areas are given special emphasis, with new materials and references on rural social work, drug abuse, minorities, prevention, enrichment, aging, professional social work, women in the workplace, and social work education. In one sense, this book encompasses the sociology of social work. Case glimpses and cases are used to illustrate traditional and innovative social work settings and services.

The authors deeply appreciate the caring support and encouragement of their wives, Knell, Farol, and Mary, who made many helpful suggestions and devoted their time and talents to reading, editing, and typing the manuscript.

Rex A. Skidmore
Milton G. Thackeray
O. William Farley

# Chapter 1

# What Is Social Work?

At 3:00 A.M. an ambulance pulled up to the medical center emergency room. Attendants rushed to get a 17-year-old Hispanic teenager into the hospital and onto life support systems. The teenager had desperately, but resolutely, driven his car into a solid brick wall.

The social worker on duty during those early hours was called to be there when the boy's parents arrived. The look of desperation on their faces told the whole story. This couple had come to the United States from Mexico some three years ago, bringing their boy and his three younger sisters with them. The language, the school system, and the entire community had created subtle barriers for this family. The father and mother both obtained low-paying jobs and tried to begin a new life.

The 17-year-old tried to fit in. His grades weren't bad, but he just didn't have friends. He couldn't get a sense of who he was. His dad saved some very hard-earned dollars to buy the young man a car. Perhaps the car would help his son find a place. It was that same car that now was a twisted wreck.

The boy died that night. The social worker tried to comfort the parents. Over and over again the social worker asked himself the questions, "Why couldn't this tragedy have been prevented? What can I do now to help this family?"

A second case glimpse illustrates community problems. Riots rocked Los Angeles after the acquittal, Wednesday, April 29, 1992, of four white police officers in the videotaped beating of a black motorist, Rodney King. In less than twenty-four hours mobs attacked police headquarters, motorists were dragged from their cars and beaten, and hundreds of businesses and homes were looted or burned in South Central Los Angeles. A night of arson, looting and gunfire killed nine persons. By the following Tuesday when life was "back to normal" the rioting had resulted in 55 dead and 5,500 fires. What might have been done to prevent such disaster? Can social work play a part in facing and helping to solve community problems?

We live in a challenging, fascinating world. We have learned how to travel to the moon and project a satellite around Mars, yet we often have difficulty reaching someone in the same room. We live in a fast-moving, push-button space age, yet we find that people are still the center of the world and its values. The rocks, the stars, and the moon are important; but humans are more important. As people live together, problems of relationship and interaction emerge. Personal problems, family problems, and community problems appear on the horizon of everyday living. Drug abuse, homelessness, crime, delinquency, mental illness, suicide, school dropouts, AIDS, and numerous other social problems abound at every turn.

Every day new scientific and technological discoveries enlarge our knowledge and skills. We not only travel in space and have space stations but also have one or more cars in the garage for personal travel. We carry tiny radios, cellular phones, laptop computers, and TV sets that bring instant news twenty-four hours a day, shrinking the world to a small community. Fifteen-second ads channeled into our homes are common. Wonder drugs are used by millions everywhere searching for peace of mind as well as for treatment. Genetically engineered foods are reaching dining tables for distinctive eating. Automatic cameras, VCRs, computer chips, Internet, CD Roms, and computer banking are altering our recreational, educational, and business endeavors at every turn.

Medical triumphs surprise the imagination with use of lasers and miniature instruments under high magnification to restore eyesight, use of an artificial arm that gives amputees lifelike dexterity, and test-tube babies.

On the negative side, all kinds of difficult situations exist. Terrorism is still rampant; no place on the globe is any longer free from attack. Single mothers are raising children in many women-dominated homes with no fathers around. Use of drugs is on the increase around the world, bringing bizarre, uncertain behavior into the lives of people, their families, and their communities. "Computer criminals" are on the scene. Movies, TV, radio, and current literature are continuing to increase in negativism and violence. The average child views TV about four hours a day. By the age of sixteen he or she has watched more than 200,000 acts of violence—50,000 of which are murders.

In this high-tech uncertain world personal, family, and community problems exist as never before. Emotional difficulties are rife. Teenage suicides are on the increase. There seems to be an overall ebb in meaningful human relationships—people enjoying people and helping each other.

When serious difficulties in human relationships arise, the question immediately becomes, "Can we get help?" The answer is usually, "Yes." Many professions, one of which is social work, are ready and eager to help. What is social work? What is social welfare? What part do they play in this satellite age?

Social work and social welfare are based on three premises: (1) that the person is important, (2) that he or she has personal, family, and community problems resulting from interaction with others, and (3) that something can be done to alleviate these problems and enrich the individual's life. An introductory glimpse of one particular case illustrates all three premises.

Joe had been in a state hospital for nineteen years, confined to one of the back wards. Those who had known him reported he was institutionalized because of severe emotional pressures due to a "shattered marriage." The attendants indicated he had talked to no one for several years and that he apparently lived in a world of his own.

Then came a change. As a part of experimentation in treatment, a social worker was assigned to meet with Joe for thirty minutes daily with the goal of bringing him back to reality. The worker explained to Joe that she was going to see him regularly and was genuinely interested in him. For the first two weeks, he uttered not a word. Then one day he surprised the worker by saying, "I like you."

The worker continued to spend about thirty minutes daily with Joe. She was sympathetic, interested in him, warm, friendly, and accepting. He responded steadily to her interest and efforts. Within six months, he was discharged from the hospital and had become established in his community. A follow-up several years later showed he had made a successful return to society and was an accepted, productive citizen.

When asked what had happened by a close friend, Joe eagerly replied, but with seriousness, "The worker was just like a magnet—drawing me out of my shell. I couldn't resist her."

## Social Welfare

The terms *social work* and *social welfare* are often confused and sometimes used synonymously. Actually, social welfare has a broader meaning and encompasses social work, public welfare, and other related programs and activities. Social welfare, according to Friedlander,[1] "is the organized system of social services and institutions, designed to aid individuals and groups to attain satisfying standards of life and health, and personal and social relationships that permit them to develop their full capacities and to promote their well being in harmony with the needs of their families and the community."

Social welfare, in a broad sense, encompasses the well-being and interests of large numbers of people, including their physical, mental, emotional, spiritual, and economic needs. Economically it is big business. For example, in August 1985, the Old-Age, Survivors, Disability, and Health Insurance (OASDI) program in the United States was paying $15.3 billion in monthly cash benefits to 36,787,000 beneficiaries. By August 1994 monthly benefits were sent to 42,632,141 beneficiaries. In September 1990 more than 11,794,000 individuals were assisted under the Aid to Families with Dependent Children (AFDC) program, which involved 4,092,876 families.[2]

A broad range of programs has been established by federal, state, and local governments in the United States to promote the welfare of individuals and families. These have expanded to the extent that in 1983 nearly one person in three was receiving U.S. benefits,[3] amounting to 66 million people, according to the Census Bureau. These included beneficiaries as follows: Social Security, 31,710,000; Medicare, 26,711,000; food stamps, 18,662,000; Medicaid 17,508,000; veterans aid, pensions, 4,622,000; and infants' nutrition, 2,429,000.

In 1970 according to the U.S. Bureau of the Census, there were 216,000 social workers in the United States—136,000 female and 80,000 male. In 1995 there were more than 500,000 social workers in the United States, two-thirds of whom were women.

Social welfare includes the basic institutions and processes related to facing and solving social problems—problems that affect large numbers of people and that require some kind of concerted group effort to resolve. In this sense, social welfare includes not only qualified social workers, but also untrained personnel employed in public welfare, probation, and other areas where social problems are being faced and resolved. Minimum traditional standards required a Master of Social Work degree for the professional social worker, with at least two years of work experience under adequate supervision.

However, action by the National Association of Social Workers, the Council on Social Work Education, and schools of social work has provided for recognition of undergraduate programs in social work; students who have completed these programs satisfactorily are recognized as the first level of "professional" social workers. Their training includes supervised field experiences as well as classes in methodology and basic knowledge. In addition, many two-year programs have been introduced in community and other colleges that provide two-year certificates in social services and training for paraprofessionals as social work technicians or aides to help people with problems.

A glance into the history of social welfare reveals that services have been provided across the centuries for disadvantaged persons and groups. Examples of such services include the care of the sick and the poor administered by the early Christian Church, and the provisions of the Elizabethan Poor Laws of the sixteenth and seventeenth centuries. Social services came first, and methods of social work developed out of social welfare. At the turn of the twentieth century, social work was becoming more formalized, and within the next several decades emerged into a profession—a specialized, modern segment of the totality of social welfare.

Social welfare is talked about today in the United States as it has never been talked about before. It is something that is of interest to political and religious leaders as well as citizens. The preamble of the Constitution of the United States includes the famous words to "promote the general welfare."

## Social Work

The next question that follows is, "What is social work?" An answer appeared in an editorial in the *New York Times:*

> A new profession has been growing to maturity under our noses. It is social work. Once thought of as basket-on-the-arm assistance to the poor, it now is a discipline, scientific in method and artful in manner, that takes remedial action on problems in several areas of society. It ministers to families in economic or emotional difficulty. It helps communities to bring their welfare and related services into good balance. It works in medical, group, and school situations. It seeks to correct the causes underlying delinquency and adult criminality.

A much-used definition of social work appears in the Curriculum Study sponsored by the Council on Social Work Education: "Social work seeks to enhance the social functioning of individuals, singly and in groups, by activities focused upon their social relationships which constitute the interaction between man and his environment. These activities can be grouped into three functions: restoration of impaired capacity, provision of individual and social resources, and prevention of social dysfunction."[4]

The underlying assumptions of social work are:

1. Social work like all other professions has problem-solving functions.
2. Social work practice is an art with a scientific and value foundation.
3. Social work as a profession came into being and continues to develop because it meets human needs and aspirations recognized by society. . . .

Social worker developing a relationship.

4. Social work practice takes its values from those held by the society of which it is a part. However, its values are not necessarily or altogether those universally or predominantly held or practiced in society.

5. The scientific base of social work consists of three types of knowledge: (a) tested knowledge, (b) hypothetical knowledge that requires transformation into tested knowledge, and (c) assumptive knowledge (or "practice wisdom") that requires transformation into hypothetical and thence into tested knowledge....

6. The knowledge needed for social work practice is determined by its goals and functions and the problems it seeks to solve.

7. The internalization of professional knowledge and values is a vital characteristic of the professional social worker since he is himself the instrument of professional help.

8. Professional skill is expressed in the activities of the social worker....[5]

The basic functions of social work—restoration, provision of resources, and prevention—are intertwined and interdependent. Restoration of impaired social functioning may be subdivided into curative and rehabilitative aspects. Its curative aspects are to eliminate factors that have caused breakdown of functioning, and its rehabilitative aspects, to reorganize and rebuild interactional patterns. Illustrations of restoration would include assistance in obtaining a hearing aid for a partially deaf child or helping a rejected lonely child to be placed in a foster home. The rehabilitative aspect might be helping the one child to psychologically accept and live with the hearing aid and supporting the other child as he or she adjusts to the new foster home.

Provision of resources, social and individual, for more effective social functioning may be subdivided into developmental and educational. The developmental aspects are designed to further the effectiveness of existing social resources or to bring to full flower personal capacity for more effective social interaction. An example would be the services of a Family Service Society that help Mr. and Mrs. X, through individual and conjoint interviews, to understand each other better and to open the channels of meaningful communication between them. The educational spectrum is designed to acquaint the public with specific conditions and needs for new or changing social resources. Again, this could be illustrated by public talks given by staff members of a Family Service Society, in which counseling services are described as a resource in alleviating marriage and family problems.

The third function, prevention of social dysfunction, involves early discovery, control, and elimination of conditions and situations that potentially could hamper effective social functioning. The two main divisions are prevention of problems in the area of interaction between individuals and groups, and second, the prevention of social ills. Premarital counseling would be an example of an attempt to prevent individual and social problems in relation to social functioning. It is hoped that through this process couples will be able to anticipate possible difficulties in marital interaction and, through adequate consideration and understanding, avoid the problems that might ensue otherwise. Prevention of social ills ordinarily falls within the area of community organization. An example of this function is the Community Services Council approach to the reduction of juvenile delinquency through the utilization of all community organizations and economic resources (for example, to build a new Youth Center and provide it with a professionally trained staff to work with boys and girls who are near-delinquent or who live in "delinquency areas"). An overall conclusion in the Curriculum Study states that "the focus on social relationships, however, is suggested as the *distinguishing characteristic* of the social work profession."

Harriet Bartlett claims that social work is "a configuration of elements none of which is unique but which, in combination, represent a contribution quite distinct from that rendered by any other profession."[6] The 1992 Curriculum Policy Statement of the Council on Social Work Education (CSWE) indicates that "the profession of social work is committed to the enhancement of human well-being and to the alleviation of poverty and oppression. The social work profession receives its sanction from public and private auspices and is the primary profession in the provision of social services." The 1995 edition of *The Social Work Dictionary* defines social work as "the applied science of helping people achieve an effective level of psychosocial functioning and effecting societal changes to enhance the well-being of all people."[7]

## A Current Definition

Social work may be defined as an art, a science, a profession that helps people to solve personal, group (especially family), and community problems and to attain satisfying personal, group, and community relationships through social work practice (see Figure 1.1). Social work practice today is often generic, involving all three of the traditional methods. The major focus is on reducing problems in human relationships and on enriching living through improved human interaction.

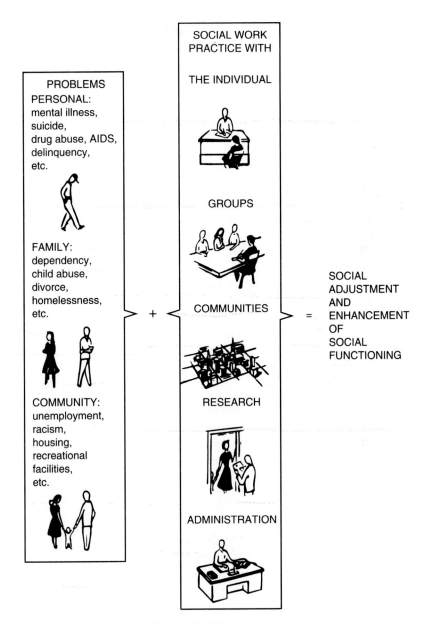

**FIGURE 1.1   What Is Social Work?**

Certainly the main focus of the social worker is upon helping people to improve their social functioning, their ability to interact and relate to others. On the other hand, there are many in the related helping professions who also assist with interactional problems. In addition, social workers sometimes help individuals to solve individual and personal problems. The social worker ordinarily works with clients on a conscious level, helping them to face realities and to solve problems without delving into the realm of the unconscious.

Social work is an art; it requires great skills to understand people and to help them to help themselves. It is a beginning science because of its problem-solving method and its attempt to be objective in ascertaining facts and in developing principles and operational concepts. It is a profession because it encompasses the attributes of a profession.

## *Distinguishing Characteristics of Social Work*

Comprehension of social work may be enhanced by consideration of its distinguishing characteristics that follow:

**1.** Focus is on the wholeness and totality of the person—encompassing the person, environmental factors, and behavior. Social work stresses the total person in the total environment.

**2.** Emphasis is on the importance of the family in molding and influencing behavior. Social workers attempt to understand the principles underlying family interaction and to work with the family as the basic unit for improving social functioning, recognizing that most social problems inhere in inadequate or imbalanced family relationships. The family is often regarded as the *case* in social work. Although the modern family is changing and many new forms of marital and family living have appeared, the family is still the basic institution in society and as such is a focal factor in social work.

**3.** Utilization of community resources in helping people to solve problems is very important. Social workers have a comprehensive knowledge of community resources and are able to tap them to meet the needs of their clients. They help to get "Mr. or Mrs. Jones to the clinic," to the agency that can help the most in the solution of his or her particular problems. Making referrals is a major service of social workers. They also make significant contributions to the larger community, utilizing their skills in planning and organizing, helping governmental and private organizations and agencies to be more effective.

**4.** Use of the supervisory process provides for guidance and direction of inexperienced workers and for continuing growth of the experienced. Both in academic study and in practice, social work provides supervision by qualified, professional personnel to help the worker to continue to grow professionally and to acquire increased understanding and skill. The supervisor is available regularly to help the worker do a better job and increase his or her understandings and skills in working with people. This process is particularly important because social workers themselves are the tools in helping troubled persons, and they need to grow professionally, keeping abreast of new knowledge and skills.

Patterns of supervision have been changing so they are less rigid today than previously. The general trend is toward more self-direction and less formalized supervisor-supervisee relationships. Participatory supervision, self-supervision, and peer supervision are being used extensively.

**5.** Social work has a unique educational program involving classwork and practical field work experience, which go hand in hand. To obtain a Master of Social Work (MSW) degree requires two years of graduate training—or its equivalent—in one of the 112 (1994) Master of Social Work Education programs in the United States. This program includes both academic classes and live field experiences in working with clients, which gives an integrated combination of theory and practice.

Provision has been made for undergraduate programs in social work and/or social welfare to be accredited by the Council on Social Work Education. Thus, graduates in these programs with a BSW (Bachelor of Social Work) degree are recognized as beginning social workers, qualified to start in professional practice.

**6.** Traditional social work emphasizes three basic processes: casework, group work, and community organization. Casework involves a close, face-to-face relationship—mainly on an individual-to-individual basis—in working with people and their problems. Group work utilizes the group as the tool to bring about desired changes in social functioning with troubled persons. Community organization is the intergroup approach toward facing and solving social pathologies. It aims to increase understanding of community needs and helps to provide for them. Social workers often play an advocate role to strengthen and improve community resources and bring desired social changes.

Some social workers claim there is only one social work process—that of problem-solving related to social relationships. They state that the method is basically the same whether working with individuals, groups, or communities.

**7.** Social work has distinctive professional bodies: The National Association of Social Workers (NASW) and the Council on Social Work Education (CSWE). NASW was established in 1955, after careful study, and brought together several smaller professional social work groups in a unified, dynamic organization. Its membership has increased rapidly, and in 1995 it enrolled more than 154,000 social workers. This organization is doing much to raise the standards of social work practice, to recruit qualified persons for professional training, and to interpret practice and values of social work to the public. CSWE, originated in 1952, is helping to improve training facilities, standards, and programs as well as helping with recruitment, public relations, and strengthening social work practice.

**8.** The *relationship* is the key in the social work process. Everything that is a part of the interview is important, but to the social worker, the feeling tones between the worker and client are particularly important. The social worker attempts to make it possible for the client to face and solve his or her problems by sharing knowledge and helping with understanding and acceptance in an emotionally supportive relationship.

**9.** Social work has an orientation in psychiatric concepts and places considerable stress upon understanding people. The social worker is particularly interested in how clients feel about themselves and their relationships with others. The social worker possesses considerable understanding of the basic knowledge and concepts of psychiatry and dynamic psychology that assist him or her in dealing with human behavior.

**10.** The *social* in social work emphasizes stress on social interaction and resultant social functioning and malfunctioning. Significant principles from sociology and social psychology, as well as from group dynamics, are woven into the artful fabric of social work, and are utilized in understanding relationships of people and in helping them to resolve their conflicts.

**11.** Social work recognizes that social problems and human behavior inhere to a considerable degree in the social institutions of humanity. To understand these problems and behavior, it is necessary to understand the institutions of humans. Social problems may be reduced by working with individual personalities or by changing social institutions. For example, a particular boy may be helped to turn from delinquent behavior through individual therapy; on the other hand, social work recognizes that perhaps thousands of delinquent acts may be prevented through sensible changes in political or economic institutions.

**12.** Most social workers are employed in agency settings. Although the number of social workers in private practice is increasing, most operate within the framework and policies of agencies; this gives them structural backing and support that strengthens their services in many ways. Supervision, consultation, and collaboration, inherent in agency settings, provide many positive resources for the workers.

**13.** The basic aim of social work is to help clients to help themselves or to help a community to help itself. Contrary to what many people believe, the social worker does not listen to a client and then prescribe a "social-psychological pill"—even though many clients ask for this. The social worker endeavors to help a person to improve his or her understanding of oneself and relationships with others and to tap his or her own and community resources in solving personal problems. The social worker operates under the premise that most people have the ego strength to solve their own problems when they really bring them out into the open and understand what they are. Whereas several professions are primarily concerned with pathological problems, social work endeavors to stress and utilize strengths—both individual and community—to effect desired changes. Social work also makes a major thrust to understand community resources and to help solve community problems, thereby bringing desired changes.

**14.** Because most social workers are employed in agencies and are on fixed salaries, fees are utilized for the welfare of the agency rather than for increased incomes for the workers.

**15.** Traditionally, social workers have provided services and therapy for individuals and families. Within the past two decades, prevention has received considerable emphasis, and recently a focus on enrichment in living, for all people, has surfaced.

**16.** A social worker is particularly effective in developing and using the team approach and in bringing about coordination of services and activities. Many professional workers regard the social worker as the catalyst who has the ability and responsibility to help the professional team work together and function in optimal fashion. The social worker often acts as coordinator and integrator for the team effort.

## *Sociology and Social Work*

How are sociology and social work related to each other? Admittedly, they share much in common but are also different in many ways. Sociology has been defined by early American sociologists as follows: by L. F. Ward as the "science of society," and by F. H. Giddings as "the scientific study of society." A. W. Small said that sociology "is the study of men considered as affecting and as affected by association."

Sociology and social work are both interested in people, their interactions, and understanding these interactions. The sociologist is particularly concerned about the *how, when,* and *why* people behave as they do in association with others. He or she aims to pinpoint the social problems, conduct research, and do everything possible to understand interaction in human associations. The sociologist is particularly interested in the *why* of human interaction.

The social worker is interested in understanding people and how they behave in association with others; but he or she is particularly concerned about helping these same people to solve the problems they have and to improve their social functioning. Whereas the sociologist generally spends most of his or her time in study and in ferreting out the facts, the social worker tries to understand the client or the community, to make an appropriate diagnosis, and to proceed with treatment, helping to solve the problems and change the situations to bring about better adjustment.

## Psychiatry and Social Work

The roles of the social worker and psychiatrist are different but are of coordinate status. The psychiatrist and the social worker are frequently both members of the same professional team and each has unique contributions to make.

The founding of the American Psychiatric Association, first known as the Association of Medical Superintendents of American Institutions for the Insane, took place in 1844. Great strides have been made during the intervening years, and today more than 36,000 psychiatrists practicing in the United States are making significant contributions in increasing understanding of the dynamics of family life, of human personality and how it functions, and in helping many individuals with various kinds of personal and emotional disturbances.

One psychiatrist states that the major difference between psychiatry and social work is that the psychiatrist deals with the treatment of illness and the medical model, whereas the social worker focuses on problems and strengths in human relationships. The psychiatrist places stress on intrapersonal dynamics, often delving into and handling unconscious motivation and related factors, whereas the social worker utilizes environmental and community resources, usually operating within the conscious level of behavior.

Psychiatry and social work have many things in common. Both professions involve work with people who possess personal and social problems. Both help people to improve their relationships with others, and both have considerable interest in, and sensitivity and ability to understand and direct feelings and emotions.

Several differences stand out between social work and psychiatry. The social worker tends to utilize the total community resources, sometimes tapping many material resources, economic and otherwise, in improving social relationships. The psychiatrist deals with patients on a medical basis, prescribes medication and hospitalization, if needed, and tends to focus on the unconscious, intrapsychic factors, working particularly with individual personality reorganization. With the advent of new drugs, drug therapy has become common to the psychiatrist in the treatment of the emotionally ill. The social worker often works with the marriage and/or family as a whole, rather than just the individual person. Ordinarily, serious mental disturbances are handled by the psychiatrist; yet social workers use psychiatric understandings in diagnosis and treatment, and sometimes work directly with seriously disturbed individuals and families.

Psychiatry tends to focus on pathology and the healing of illness; social work concentrates on strengths and the development of potential. The psychiatrist is particularly interested in the internal dynamics of individual and group behavior. The social worker is especially concerned about social functioning involving social and community factors and interactions.

## Psychology and Social Work

The psychologist and social worker are often members of the same professional team, particularly in treatment clinics and related settings. Nevertheless, many people raise questions about the overlapping and the differences between the two.

Psychology is the science of the mind; it seeks to study, explain, and change behavior of people. The psychologist is particularly interested in understanding the individual and his or her behavior.

Psychology and social work operate on some common grounds. Both are interested in the behavior of people, in their interactional patterns in particular, although the psychologist focuses mainly on individual behavior and the social worker on social functioning. They both seek the thinking and feeling processes of people.

In regard to differences, psychologists have an area entirely unto themselves in the field of testing and measurements. Psychologists study biological factors as well as social factors related to individual behavior. The psychologist is particularly interested in the individual attributes of people, and aims to understand their characteristics and behavior. On the other hand, some psychologists, particularly clinical psychologists, go beyond the study phase and work directly with people in the helping process. These activities overlap some with social work, and yet the focus seems to be different when considered as a totality. The psychologist usually works with individuals on a rather intensive basis and sometimes becomes a psychotherapist. Conversely, the social worker is particularly interested in the social functioning and relationships of clients and in utilizing community resources to meet clients' personal and social problems.

A clarifying tribute was paid to social work by a graduate student who reported:

It may sound naive, but I was most impressed by the philosophy underlying the principles used in social work. I am in psychology, and while I am certain psychology operates from the same philosophy, this had never been spelled out. What I am referring to is emphasis on human worth and dignity which would seem to stem from a Judeo-Christian ethic and also the belief in democratic processes and an attempt to make this work at the community level—not only in community organization, but in case and group work as well.

## Counseling and Social Work

Some people confuse the role and functions of the counselor with that of the social worker. There are many kinds of counselors, but only three are mentioned here: the school counselor, the marriage counselor, and the rehabilitation counselor.

The school counselor is usually trained in educational psychology. He or she ordinarily works with students on a short-term basis, helping them particularly with vocational choices and academic problems. The school counselor and the social worker share much in common. The social worker tends to be more intensive, works with the client longer, focuses more on the family constellation, and utilizes community resources. The school counselor also uses testing to advantage in many situations.

The marriage counselor may receive basic training from any of several graduate fields of study, only one of which is social work. He or she is then required to have clinical experience under supervision. In one sense, then, social work is a part of marriage counseling. In another sense, marriage counseling is one particular emphasis in social work. The differences arise across the variations in graduate training and professional experiences.

The rehabilitation counselor is one who usually is trained in educational psychology, is skilled in the use of testing, and focuses attention and abilities on the individual and his or her immediate problems of vocational rehabilitation. In situations where both a counselor and social worker are part of the team in rehabilitation, the counselor ordinarily helps with the testing, the short-term counseling, and related activities. The social worker usually assists with the emotional and/or family problems, has fewer cases, and works with clients more intensively.

## Social Work in the World Today

Social work is emerging as an important profession in the modern world. As we noted earlier, the National Association of Social Workers has 154,000 members. In December 1961, provision was made for professionally trained and experienced social workers to become members of the Academy of Certified Social Workers, which gave them additional professional status; more than 20,000 qualified. By 1995, some 58,000 were certified.

Social work today is utilized in a variety of settings and agencies. Some of the important ones are psychiatric, medical, marriage, and family counseling; the school; rehabilitation; corrections; public welfare; workplace; drug abuse; and child welfare. Schools of social work train a student to work in any agency, giving him or her the generic understandings, skills, and attitudes that make it possible to function adequately.

Social work is becoming more important because thousands of persons are benefiting from its services and are telling their friends and associates who have problems of its many values and services. People are not only being helped with personal and family problems but also with neighborhood, national, and even international difficulties. A prominent American, upon returning from a trip abroad, made the statement that what the United States needs most of all to improve its foreign policy and relations is to have trained social workers as State Department attachés where each of the official government representatives works and lives. Trained social workers in foreign countries would understand the people and work with them where they are, helping them to help themselves and interpreting the United States in a much more favorable light than in the past.

Current evidence indicates that social work is here to stay and that in the decades ahead it will likely grow and expand its services, helping more people with personal, family, and community problems, especially related to adequate social functioning.

# Summary

However fast-moving and uncertain today's world may be, people are still at its center and core. People have problems that invite professional assistance: personal, family, and community. Social welfare is an important aspect of the modern way of life. Social work is a profession that focuses particularly on helping people to solve their personal, family, and community problems through enhancing social functioning. It emphasizes human values and also the value of humans.

The basic functions of social work are: (1) restoration of social functioning, (2) provision of social services, and (3) prevention.

Social work shares some knowledge and skills with sociology, psychiatry, psychology, and counseling, but it possesses distinguishing characteristics that set it apart from these disciplines.

Social work is moving ahead as a progressive profession in the helping services arena.

# Selected References

BRIELAND, DONALD, "Social Work Practice: History and Evolution," in *Encyclopedia of Social Work,* 19th ed., Vol. III. Washington, DC: NASW Press, 1995, pp. 2247–2258.

COMPTON, BEULAH R., *Introduction to Social Welfare and Social Work: Structure, Function and Process.* Homewood, IL: The Dorsey Press, 1980.

FARLEY, O. WILLIAM, BOYD E. OVIATT, REX A. SKIDMORE, and MILTON G. THACKERAY, "Social Work—Professional Mediocrity or Maturation," *Social Casework,* 58 (April 1977), 236–242.

GARVIN, CHARLES D., and JOHN E. TROPMAN, *Social Work in Contemporary Society.* Englewood Cliffs, NJ: Prentice Hall, 1992.

HAGEN, JAN L., "Women, Work, and Welfare: Is There a Role for Social Work?" *Social Work,* 37 (January 1992), 9–13.

KLEIN, WALDO C., and MARTIN BLOOM, "Social Work as Applied Social Science: A Historical Analysis," *Social Work,* 39 (July 1994), 421–431.

NURIUS, PAULA S., and WALTER W. HUDSON, "Computer-Based Practice: Future Dream or Current Technology?" *Social Work,* 33 (July–August 1988), 357–362.

REESER, LINDA CHERREY, and IRWIN EPSTEIN, *Professionalization and Activism in Social Work: The Sixties, the Eighties, and the Future.* New York: Columbia University Press, 1990.

SKIDMORE, REX A., *Social Work Administration, Dynamic Management and Human Relationships,* 3rd ed. Boston: Allyn and Bacon, 1995.

# Notes

1. Walter A. Friedlander, *Introduction to Social Welfare,* 2nd ed. (Englewood Cliffs, NJ: Prentice Hall, 1961), p. 4; see also 5th ed., 1980, p. 4.

2. *Social Security Bulletin,* 54 (December 1991), 20, 64; 57 (Fall 1994), 109.

3. *U.S. News & World Report,* October 8, 1984, p. 12.

4. Werner W. Boehm, *Objectives of the Social Work Curriculum of the Future,* Curriculum Study I (New York: Council on Social Work Education, 1959), p. 54.

5. Ibid., pp. 41–42.

6. Harriet M. Bartlett, *50 Years of Social Work in the Medical Setting, Past Significance/Future Outlook* (New York: National Association of Social Workers, 1957), p. 24.

7. Robert L. Barker, *The Social Work Dictionary,* 3rd ed. (Washington, DC: NASW Press, 1995), p. 357.

*Chapter* 2

# The Evolution of Social Welfare and Social Work in the United States

*It was evening in the city. Couples were arriving at the theater to attend the opening night of a new musical. Crowds were pressing the box office, and ushers were busily engaged in tearing tickets and guiding the theater-goers to their seats. Not more than thirty steps from the well-lighted entrance was a blind man, with tattered clothes and wrinkled brow, playing a beat-up violin with a weathered plate before him. A few passersby stopped and dropped coins on the plate. Most glanced quickly and kept moving. In almost every storefront homeless individuals were setting up cardboard shelters to get some protection from the bitter cold wind. What systems do we have for taking care of those in need? Which are most effective?*

In 1962, for the first time in history, a president of the United States gave a message to Congress devoted solely to public welfare. President John F. Kennedy declared to the 87th Congress: "Our basic public welfare programs were enacted more than a quarter century ago. Their contribution to our national strength and well-being in the intervening years has been remarkable.

"But the times, the conditions, the problems have changed—and the nature and objectives of our public assistance and child welfare programs must be changed, also, if they are to meet our current needs."

President Kennedy, in his statement to Congress, stressed the importance of the family unit and its preservation. He indicated that a united attack needed to be made on the problem of family breakdown, and then continued, "unless such problems are dealt with effectively, they fester and grow, sapping the strength of society as a whole and extending their consequences in troubled families from one generation to the next."

Each president of the United States since Kennedy has taken messages to the Congress with recommendations and interpretations regarding social welfare programs for this country. These programs have varied philosophically and in regard to specificity, but most have

**15**

underlined a vital concern for the welfare of the American people. President Ronald Reagan proposed many curtailments and restrictions of social welfare programs while maintaining that those in need who could not help themselves would be given welfare. Subsequently there were many cutbacks and elimination of some social work services. In his inaugural address, President George Bush talked about a kinder nation, to "secure a more just and prosperous life for man on Earth," and the need for greater tolerance of "each other's attitudes and way of life."

At the inauguration of President Bill Clinton he emphasized the importance of change: "We must do what no generation has had to do before. We must invest more in our own people, in their jobs and in their future.... We must do what America does best: offer more opportunity to all and demand more responsibility from all." The 1994 Republican U.S. Congress came in to office with "Contract With America" commitments both to reduce the costs of public welfare services and to improve their effectiveness.

Inhabitants of the United States live in a land of freedom wherein democracy and democratic processes are prevalent. Stress is on the interdependence of people in society, and it is generally recognized that the well-being of one person affects the well-being of neighbors and others. The preamble of our Constitution, spelled out by the Founding Fathers, contains the immortal words, "to promote the general welfare."

The worth of the human personality and the importance of individual adjustment and well-being are significant aspects of the American way of life. The pages of American history, past and present, reflect that in a given society there are many disadvantaged persons. What has been done in the United States in the past to help them? What is being accomplished at present? Social welfare and, more recently, social work have arisen upon the American scene and provide some answers to these questions. Social Welfare, according to *The Social Work Dictionary,* is "a nation's system of programs, benefits, and services that help people meet those social, economic, educational, and health needs that are fundamental to the maintenance of society."[1]

## Echoes of the Past

The beginnings of social welfare were probably coexistent with the beginnings of human life and humans' association with others. It is not difficult to imagine that even in the days of the cave dwellers, neighborliness and helping one another with problems, both personal and family, were part of the daily living pattern. In all probability some of the wiser of these inhabitants had paths beaten to their dwellings by people seeking someone who would listen and help.

In primitive societies numerous kinds of plans and programs have often been in operation for helping people with social problems. Tribal customs and mores have provided for care of the sick, the aged, the deformed, and others who needed to be nurtured and given special attention. There has been a recognition of the necessity to help one another to promote the welfare of all.

In ancient civilizations various and sundry attempts were made to care for the destitute, the poor, the sick, the unfortunate, and the handicapped. Many of these were handled on a family, neighborhood, or religious basis.

Social welfare was rooted in the distant past.[2] In ancient China there were refuges for the aged, the sick, and the poor, free schools for poor children, free eating houses for weary laborers, associations for the distribution of secondhand clothing, and even societies for paying expenses of marriage and burial among the poor and destitute. In India, especially after the time of Buddha, considerable activity was related to giving to beggars. A saint with his bowl was one of the traditions of the Orient, and the emphasis in the religious teachings upon the obligation of almsgiving not only made the holy men of that country a nuisance but also encouraged imposters. The Greeks had no regular charitable organizations, but they did have institutions for the unfortunate and the sick. Gifts and assistance were publicly distributed at the time of the great festivals by men who were candidates for public office. There were asylums for wounded soldiers and for abandoned children; and in Athens a poor tax was levied and collected to help the destitute. The religion of the Hebrews laid great stress upon charity and helping those in need.

In the medieval period the Church played a significant role in giving relief and in helping distressed persons. Monks and monasteries provided services to care for the indigent, the lame, the halt, and other unfortunate individuals. The monasteries were utilized to provide food and housing for pilgrims, soldiers, and beggars, as well as medical and hospital facilities for those in need. Orphaned or deserted children were also cared for by the monks and nuns.

Across the centuries there has been a shift from individualism to collectivism in helping those in need. Mutual aid has come to the fore particularly as populations have increased and moved into concentrated areas, and there has been additional need for societal programs to aid the disadvantaged.

## European Roots

The roots of social welfare, and in a general sense of social work, reach a long way into the past. However, several significant developments in Europe have been particularly important in setting the stage and patterns for development of social welfare and social work in the United States. In 1536 a law was passed in England stating that alms collected by local authorities and by churches on Sundays were to help to relieve the sick and the poor. This act, which is often regarded as the beginning of the English poor law system, superseded the merely repressive measures of earlier legislation in an attempt to work out specific and definite provisions for relief To deter people from openly begging, the law stipulated that "the mayor of every town and the Church wardens of every parish were to collect alms every Sunday, holiday or festival in common boxes," which were then to be utilized by those in need. Accounts were to be kept of the money collected and dispersed. The income was to be allocated so that poor, sick, impotent, and diseased persons, not able to work, might be helped and relieved. This law marked the shift in poor relief from an ecclesiastical to a secular system. The act had several significant provisions, including the illegality of begging, responsibility of society to help, assistance by and through the local community, and voluntary alms, with clerical assistance, but under the direction of the state.

In 1572 overseers of the poor were appointed as civil officers. The Parliamentary enactment at this time provided for a direct public tax for the purpose of assisting the poor and destitute.

During the reign of Queen Elizabeth several laws were enacted that have been designated as the Elizabethan Poor Laws. Toward the close of the sixteenth century a civic sense of responsibility on a nationwide basis had developed in England. An act was passed in 1598 and revised in 1601 that provided a systematic plan for helping the poor and established a system of public responsibility implemented through local care. The main provisions of the law remained in operation basically until 1834, and have played important roles in the development of social welfare in Europe, in the United States, and elsewhere. The act of 1601 established legislation that differentiated three classes of the poor: the able-bodied poor, who were to be provided with work, or with punishment in prison or the stocks if they refused to work; the impotent poor, who were to be kept in almshouses; and dependent children, who were to be apprenticed unless parents or grandparents could support them. For the dependent children group, the boys were to be apprenticed until they were twenty-four years old and the girls until they were either twenty-one or married. Monies to finance these laws were provided by taxes levied on lands, houses, and tithes, from money left for charitable purposes, and from fines levied for the breaking of certain laws. To carry out the administration of the system, the justice of the peace appointed civil officers in each parish, although nominations for these positions were made at a meeting of the parish church.

Many other laws have been passed in England and on the Continent to help the poor, and to provide other services for children, families, and individuals in trouble. The industrial revolution of the eighteenth century, accompanied by urbanization, slums, and anonymity in living brought numerous situations resulting in many persons with problems that called for help. Begging, almsgiving, charity, workhouses, orphanages, insane asylums, and jails became part of the culture of the times. Attempts to help people in a dignified manner were instigated, and various programs, both public and private, came into existence.

The Elizabethan Poor Laws provided the basis for public social welfare in England with only minor changes until the Poor Law of 1834 was passed. This act provided for centralized administration with a pattern of uniformity throughout the country. It established a central authority consisting of three Poor Law Commissioners, who were given regulatory powers over the local authorities. They could divide the country into districts, which were called Poor Law Unions, to replace the parishes as units of administration. Each unit was a district with an elective Board of Guardians with salaried officers who were responsible for the administration of relief. The law also stipulated that the Guardians of each district were authorized to build or provide at least one workhouse, and all relief to able-bodied persons outside the workhouse was abolished.

In England in the 1860s, there was a considerable increase in the number of applicants for aid that focused attention on welfare and helping the poor. As a result there was revived concern in social reform, and some individuals became interested in bringing about innovations and change. Such persons as Octavia Hill and Edward Denison pioneered in social welfare at this time. As a result of their efforts and those of others, a new type of social work organization emerged. In 1869 the "London Society for Organizing Charitable Relief and Repressing Mendicancy" was established and has generally been referred to as the London Charity Organization Society. The name of the organization is descriptive of its purpose—the organization of relief rather than its creation or multiplication. It proposed, in other words:

(1) the coordination of the work of the various charitable societies in London so as to prevent duplication; (2) an acquaintance by each of the work of other agencies; (3) a bureau of registry for all cases; (4) personal service to promote independence of spirit rather than the giving of material aid; and (5) a devotion to measures for the prevention of pauperism.[3]

## Beginnings in the United States

No attempt is made here to give a historical coverage of social welfare in the United States. Nevertheless, some highlights and examples of such developments are considered.

In colonial days in America the basic pattern for assisting the poor and unfortunate followed the poor laws and activities of the mother country. Town and local governments provided services somewhat similar to those that had been instigated in the homeland. "Outdoor relief" was administered to the poor in their own homes initially. Placement or boarding out of dependents was also utilized both for children and adults. Almshouses were established as a means of "indoor relief." Extreme examples of the "farming out" procedure involved public auctions where orphans, neglected children, or disabled individuals were passed on to those who were willing to support them at the lowest cost to the community. The first almshouse for the care of the poor and indigent was established in Massachusetts in 1662. In 1685 it began to function both as an almshouse for the disabled and as a workhouse for the able-bodied poor. Another indication of community interest in providing services for the poor and needy was the establishment in 1644 of the Boston Latin School, which was supported in part by a land grant from that town. This was the beginning of free or charity schools in this country, and was the foundation underpinning free public education, which developed decades later. In 1691, in Boston, the town leaders appointed the first "overseers of the poor," which was an initiatory step toward governmental centralization in the care of the destitute.

Beginnings in the child welfare movement go back many years. In 1729 in New Orleans an institution was established by the Ursuline Sisters for children of parents massacred by Indians. In 1790 an orphanage was begun in Charleston, South Carolina, for children who had no living parents. By 1817 a school for the education of the "deaf and dumb" was in operation in Connecticut.

In early nineteenth-century America people who were mentally ill were treated harshly, inhumanly, and often regarded as persons who had no sense of feeling either mentally or physically. In March 1841, the famous Dorothea Lynde Dix by chance visited the East Cambridge, Massachusetts, jail and was shocked at the deplorable treatment of the insane inmates. She visited other jails and almshouses throughout the state and found all kinds of brutalities being practiced within them. On the basis of these experiences, she devoted the rest of her life to improving services for those who were mentally ill. She gave speeches, wrote letters, and contacted community and political leaders and others at home and abroad. As a result of her relentless campaign many state hospitals for the insane were established or enlarged and great improvements in treatment in poorhouses and jails took place. Through her activities and those of other dedicated leaders, the treatment of the mentally ill has shifted so that now they are more respected as other persons who are ill, and attempts are made to treat them and return them to their families and to society as quickly as possible.

Likewise, in the area of the treatment of the juvenile delinquent and the criminal, the pages of history show significant developments related to social welfare and social work. In the latter part of the eighteenth century, in the very shadows of Independence Hall in Philadelphia, a new system of prison discipline, called the Pennsylvania System, was established. This innovation provided for individualized attention and treatment of prisoners accompanied by housing in separate cells. Prior to this time inmates were held in congregate rooms, sometimes twenty or thirty or even forty of them, day in and day out, often both men and women confined together. The new philosophy and practice was an attempt to treat and rehabilitate rather than merely to punish or seek retribution.

With the depression of 1873, after the Civil War in the United States, came chaos and many personal, family, and community problems. The charity organization movement in America was started, patterned in the main after European innovations. Across the decades this movement has resulted in the establishment of numerous private agencies and community welfare councils in most of the large population centers of this country. These councils, increasingly staffed by competent social workers, attempt to understand community needs, involve community leaders in studying these needs, make plans regarding them, and bring these plans to fruition.

The first Charity Organization Society in the United States was established in Buffalo, New York, in 1877. The coordinating function of this type of agency was urgent because of the numerous independent welfare agencies that were springing up and mushrooming in the population centers. In 1909 in Pittsburgh and Milwaukee the first community welfare councils—called Councils of Social Agencies—were established. These have grown and developed so that today one such council in a large metropolitan area has thirteen full-time people working in research—collecting and interpreting information pertinent to community needs, problems, and solutions.

The charity organization movement in the United States was a significant one because it provided for private agencies that were interested in finding ways and means of organizing help to the poor through individualized services. These services included investigation of need, a registration bureau for charitable agencies for clearance to avoid duplication, friendly visiting, and other related activities.

Closely allied to the community welfare council movement has been the one for federated drives, collecting money for several agencies at one time. Historically the first such drive took place in Liverpool, England, in 1873, and the original one in the United States occurred in 1887, spearheaded by the Associated Charities in Denver. The latter involved twenty-three agencies, which joined together and raised a total of $20,000. After World War I federated drives in this country were organized under the name of the Community Chest. By 1950 more than 1,400 such organizations existed in this country. In the last forty years the trend has been toward establishment of united fund agencies (now called United Way in many communities), which have been organized on a broader base than Community Chests, the aim being to bring together as many of the local and national health and welfare agencies as possible in the collecting of funds.

Another significant development in social services in America has been that of the social settlement house. The first American settlement was organized in New York City in

1886; and three years later the most famous one, Hull House, was established by Jane Addams in Chicago. Similar neighborhood centers were instigated in many of the large cities in this country. Today these centers play a significant role in providing for the recreational, health, and welfare needs of boys and girls, youth, men, and women, particularly in deprived areas. They are also being used by the total citizenry, including the middle and upper classes, as centers for providing social experiences, for taking care of recreational needs, and for solving personality problems.

There have been several pioneers in this country in social welfare. Many of these people have come from the upper classes and many have devoted their lives to helping disadvantaged people.

Jane Addams was such a person. She was born in Cedarville, Illinois, in 1861 and died on May 21, 1935. She traveled extensively in Europe, where she was impressed with Toynbee Hall in England. She decided to establish a similar settlement house in this country, which was located on Chicago's west side. Hull House provided many educational opportunities and social services for those with limited economic means and was patronized by immigrants who had come to make this country their homeland. This settlement was established particularly for the working people and those in meager circumstances. Jane Addams was also a leader in international women's and children's movements and wrote extensively. Two of her best known books were *Democracy and Social Ethics* (1902) and *Twenty Years at Hull House* (1910).

Social welfare services have developed so that today they reach out to practically every personal, family, and community need. As a result, research in welfare is being sponsored as never before.

## Public Assistance and Social Welfare Emerge

Almost from the beginning of the colonization of America there have been various attempts to provide governmental assistance to the poor and needy. For example, following the patterns of the Dutch, and later the English, New York City had a city physician for the poor as early as 1687. Various other programs were established by towns and local communities in colonial America to provide for those who required different services.

Later laws were passed in states of the Union helping to provide financial and other services for the indigent, poor, destitute, and those with personal and family problems.

With the financial collapse of 1929 and the Great Depression that followed, numerous attempts were made to assist the poor and the unemployed and to bolster the economy. The Federal Emergency Relief Administration (usually known as ERA), the Works Progress Administration (WPA), the Civilian Conservation Corps (CCC), and other federal programs were established to provide work and assistance for millions. Social workers played an important role in the creation of some of these agencies and in their implementation. Many men and women gained their first interest in social work during those difficult times.

On the federal level the monumental Social Security Act of 1935 altered the total plan of helping persons in need. For the first time the federal government assumed a major role and responsibility in assisting the needy. The major provisions of the original act are summarized as follows:

1. A national old-age insurance system (OASDI), to be supported through taxes on payrolls, equally shared by the employers and employees. The survivorship provision was instituted in 1939.
2. A federal-state unemployment insurance system, to be financed by a federal tax on payrolls. Liberal provisions were offered that encouraged the states to become partners in this system, and all states adopted unemployment acts soon after the law was passed.
3. Grants-in-aid to the states for old age assistance, aid to families of dependent children, and aid to the blind.
4. Services for aiding maternal and child health, crippled children, child welfare, vocational rehabilitation, and public health measures.

Through increased federal services, children, families, and adults have been aided in many ways. Indicative of this situation is the fact that during April–June 1984, the average number of recipients of money payments under the program of Aid to Families with Dependent Children (AFDC) was 10,924,000 people. Average monthly cash payments amounted to $1,193,612,000 and 3,746,000 families were being assisted.[4] By September 1990 the number of families had increased to 4,092,000 and the monthly cash payments amounted to more than $1,455,000,000.

Major significant changes were made in social security legislation in the enactment of Public Welfare Amendments of 1962—Public Law 87-543. For the first time the importance of preventive, protective, and rehabilitative services in public welfare was significantly recognized by a new formula that provided 75 percent of the costs of such services from federal funds.

As President Kennedy said when he signed the legislation, "This measure embodies a new approach—stressing services in addition to support, rehabilitation instead of relief, and training for useful work instead of prolonged dependency. . . . Our objective is to prevent or reduce dependency and to encourage self-care and self-support—to maintain family life where it is adequate and to restore it where it is deficient."[5]

A major development in social welfare began on July 1, 1966, when the health insurance program for the aged under Title XVIII of the Social Security Act went into effect. Commonly called Medicare,[6] it provided a compulsory hospital insurance plan and a voluntary supplementary medical insurance. This program helps to provide economic security and protection against the high costs of hospital and medical care for the elderly. It is for everyone aged sixty-five or over who is entitled to social security or railroad retirement. Others over sixty-five may enroll by paying monthly premiums.

The 1972 amendments expanded Medicare to extend the coverage to certain disabled workers, disabled widows and widowers, and childhood disability beneficiaries.

Medicaid, medical care for low-income people, was enacted under Title XIX of the Social Security Act. Administered by the states, it provides direct payments to providers of services. Persons who qualify for assistance under the federally financed income maintenance program are eligible for assistance. Medicaid may be used to provide hospital and medical care for people who have no regular income from employment and for others whose income is so low that they are unable to provide payments for medical and health care for themselves and their families.

On the volunteer level, two programs were developed that have been significant in the areas of education and social welfare. The Peace Corps, established under President Kennedy, invited persons, particularly the young, to enlist for a two-year period to provide much needed services, particularly in underdeveloped countries throughout the world. The Volunteers in Service to America (VISTA) program was established to use volunteers to help their own country and citizens in disadvantaged areas—educationally, economically, vocationally, and otherwise—to improve their situations in life.

Policies and programs regarding welfare continue to shift. Rigid resident requirements are no longer in operation for persons who ask to qualify for assistance and need. State barriers have been removed in public assistance.

In 1972 there was a basic separation between maintenance and social services provided in public welfare and by divisions of family services. Many social workers were shifted from helping with maintenance into the specific areas of social services that are attempting to assist individuals and families with personal, family, and community problems.

Hansan[7] observes that social welfare has expanded rapidly in the United States so there are 1,030 federal domestic assistance programs, administered by 55 federal agencies, and that "federal spending for what the Social Security Administration defines as 'social welfare purposes,' rose from $14 billion in 1950 to nearly $175 billion in 1975." By August 1994 Social Security benefits (OASDI) alone provided more than $25 billion in monthly benefits to beneficiaries.

In the last two decades there has been a major development among social workers individually and in agencies to become more concerned about protecting the rights of clients, being advocates for them, and also in helping to alter our basic institutions, to provide better aid for the poor and the needy. Social workers as never before are using a two-edged approach: helping individuals and families clinically and focusing on improving society's institutions and programs.

A historic event took place on May 4, 1980, with the creation of a cabinet level U.S. Department of Education, taken from the parent Department of Health, Education, and Welfare (HEW). The health and welfare sectors of HEW are now called the U.S. Department of Health and Human Services; the change has been accepted positively by social workers and others who believe this dual partnership may prove advantageous to both areas and the United States as a whole.

The 1983 and 1988 amendments to the Social Security Act were particularly significant. Ozawa suggests the 1983 amendments reflected that the country is willing to face the challenge of meeting social security's enormous financial crisis, and reported, "Through a complex, sweeping, reform package, Congress established an actuarial balance between the cost rate and the income rate in social security for the coming seventy-five years."[8] For recent amendments and policy changes see Chapter 12.

## Services of Volunteers

Over the years many dedicated and interested individuals have provided their time and money to help people in need. They have done this as individuals or as families rather than as citizens in a city, state, or federal community. These services have increased so that today thousands of volunteers are assisting in social welfare services in almost every kind of setting.

Examples of volunteer services include the following:

Twenty-five members of a Junior League in a middle-sized city spend half a day a week in assisting with activities in the local Comprehensive Mental Health Center. They provide their own cars and transport clients to and from the center. They "care" for the children in the waiting rooms and also spend time with some of the clients, on a friendship basis, helping them with routine problems and decisions.

The Medical Wives Auxiliary in a small city invites its members to spend half a day at one of the local hospitals performing a variety of kinds of tasks that facilitate total services. They work on telephone switchboards, care for children, and perform multitudinous other helpful services.

Volunteers from churches and religious groups minister to the sick, the poor, the destitute, and unfortunate in numerous ways. They cooperate with the professional disciplines to bring total, effective services.

Working as a volunteer is characteristic of the American way of life. From the young to the old, volunteers help other people through various social work and welfare agencies and on an individual basis. In 1965 the U.S. Department of Labor estimated that 16 percent of persons over fourteen years of age, or 22 million individuals, made contributions to some health, education, or welfare service on a volunteer basis. More than half of these persons were in the twenty-five to forty-four age group. In 1974 some 37 million men and women, one of every four Americans over age thirteen, did some form of volunteer work.[9]

Social worker and two children doing art work.

In 1973 the United Way of America made a quantitative study of volunteer activities. It revealed that United Way and its member agencies average an estimated 2.4 billion volunteer person-hours per year and that the largest percentage of volunteer activities (over 80 percent) is in the area of direct program activity rather than in setting policy and raising funds.[10] In the 1978 United Way campaigns more than 32 million people made contributions to help others. The nation's 2,200 United Way campaigns, in 1985, collected a recordbreaking $2.33 billion, a gain of 9 percent over 1984. Giving in the United States was on the increase and United Way was not the only philanthropy enjoying a boom in giving. In 1980 total giving in the United States stood at $49 billion; in 1985 total giving was more than $75 billion—up more than 50 percent over 1980.[11] In 1988 contributions to voluntary organizations in the United States exceeded $100 billion, and 80 million people volunteered a total of 14.9 billion hours, worth at least another $150 billion.[12] By 1995 it was reported that more than a third of the U.S. population—89 million people—were participating in voluntarism.[13]

## Social Workers Appear

In the eighteenth and nineteenth centuries, with industrialization, greater mobility, and the increase in population and the accompanying social problems, it became apparent that both public and private social services needed to be increased if the problems and needs of the public were to be met.

Social welfare has developed slowly over several centuries. It is only within the past few decades, however, that social work has entered the scene as a major aspect of social welfare. In the latter part of the nineteenth century humanitarians and other dedicated persons, especially women, devoted their time and talents to helping the underprivileged, and began to lay the groundwork for the development of social work as a profession. In 1898 education for social work was initiated in a summer training course given by the Charity Organization Society of New York. This was a beginning impetus toward providing trained social workers. This course developed into a one-year program in 1904 within the New York School of Philanthropy. Other schools of social work developed and before long many men and women were calling themselves *social workers*. These were people who had obtained special training and experience to help people to help themselves. By 1921 the American Association of Social Workers was established, the first major professional social work body. In 1955 the National Association of Social Workers was created based on the amalgamation of seven smaller specialized social work associations. This professional body has grown in stature and in numbers so that it now enrolls 154,000 members. In 1995 NASW celebrated its 40th anniversary and recognized it had made many contributions to social work but still had many challenges ahead.

Social workers today are employed in every kind of setting of social welfare. They are given, ordinarily, the more difficult tasks to perform and many gravitate to administrative and supervisory positions. They are also used as consultants in helping to guide the work and activities of less trained social welfare aides and associates. Numerous county and state welfare departments now have many on their staffs who have received baccalaureate or Master of Social Work degrees, and the work being accomplished in these agencies is taking on a professional demeanor that was unknown in the past.

In 1974 the Council on Social Work Education approved the accreditation of the undergraduate programs in social work or social welfare with the understanding that they would be upgraded and would provide the first level of practice in social work. At the other end of the continuum is the increasing number of doctoral programs being offered by schools of social work aimed at developing leaders in the top echelons of social work and social welfare.

## Summary

*The American way of life with its democratic emphasis has been conducive to the initiation and development of social welfare services. The pages of history reflect that, almost from the beginning of the colonization of this country, humanitarian men and women, both in public and private agencies and situations, have been interested in establishing and supporting services and activities to help distressed and unfortunate individuals and families.*

*The roots of social welfare in America had their beginnings in Europe, particularly related to the Elizabethan Poor Laws of England. Towns and local communities assumed responsibilities for aiding the unfortunate and disadvantaged.*

*Most of the other beginnings in social welfare were private in nature and involved philanthropic programs and activities. Gradually, civic-minded individuals and leaders proposed welfare programs financed by the tax dollar. Various state programs were started.*

*In 1935 the Social Security Act was passed in the United States, revolutionizing the total social welfare scene. The act provided public assistance, social insurance, unemployment insurance, aid to dependent children, aid to the blind, and other special services.*

*In 1962 major modifications were made in the Social Security Act. These provided for additional federal participation, for liberalization of grants, and for safeguarding the rights of children and families. They also placed considerably greater emphasis on rehabilitation and preventive social welfare.*

*Medicare, which encompasses a compulsory hospital insurance plan and a voluntary supplemental medical insurance, and Medicaid, which provides medical care for low-income people, were both established in 1965 as amendments to the Social Security Act and are forming a foundation for an expanding medical and health care system in the United States.*

*A major step in the development of social welfare has been the rise of the profession of social work. Since the turn of the twentieth century the number of trained social workers has increased rapidly. Social work now has a central professional body, the National Association of Social Workers, and a national educational body for setting standards, the Council on Social Work Education.*

## Selected References

ABBOTT, EDITH, *Some American Pioneers in Social Welfare.* Chicago: University of Chicago Press, 1937.

GARVIN, CHARLES D., and JOHN E. TROPMAN, *Social Work in Contemporary Society.* Englewood Cliffs, NJ: Prentice Hall, 1992.

GILBERT, NEIL, and HARRY SPECHT, *The Emergence of Social Welfare and Social Work.* Itasca, IL: F. E. Peacock Publishers, Inc., 1976.

HART, AILEEN F., "Clinical Social Work and Social Administration: Bridging the Culture Gap,"

*Administration in Social Work,* 8 (Fall 1984), 71–78.

KLEIN, WALDO C., and MARTIN BLOOM, "Social Work as Applied Social Science: A Historical Analysis," *Social Work,* 39(July 1994), 421–431.

MANDELL, BETTY REID, and BARBARA SCHRAM, *Human Services: Introduction and Interventions.* New York: John Wiley & Sons, 1985.

MORRIS, ROBERT, *Social Policy of the American Welfare State,* 2nd ed. New York: Longman, 1985.

PATTI, RINO J., "Managing for Service Effectiveness in Social Welfare Organizations," *Social Work,* 32 (September–October 1987), 377–381.

REID, P. NELSON, "Social Welfare History," in *Encyclopedia of Social Work,* 19th ed., Vol. III. Washington, DC: NASW Press, 1995, pp. 2206–2225.

RESNICK, HERMAN, and RINO J. PATTI, eds., *Change from Within: Humanizing Social Welfare Organizations.* Philadelphia: Temple University Press, 1980.

SKIDMORE, REX A., *Social Work Administration, Dynamic Management and Human Relationships,* 3rd ed. Boston: Allyn and Bacon, 1995.

TRATTNER, WALTER I., *From Poor Law to Welfare State: A History of Social Welfare in America,* 4th ed. New York: The Free Press, 1989.

## Notes

1. Robert L. Barker, *The Social Work Dictionary,* 3rd ed. (Washington, DC: NASW Press, 1995), p. 357.

2. For a highlighted description of historical developments, see James H. S. Bossard, *Social Change and Social Problems,* rev. ed. (New York: Harper & Row, Publishers, 1938), pp. 673–678.

3. Ibid., p. 697.

4. U.S. Department of Health and Human Services, *Quarterly Public Assistance Statistics* (April–June 1984), 1, 14.

5. Wilbur J. Cohen, "The New Public Welfare Legislation," News Release, U.S. Department of Health, Education, and Welfare, September 24, 1962.

6. See Chapter 12 for details.

7. John E. Hansan, "Social Planning, Governmental: Federal and State," *Encyclopedia of Social Work,* II (Washington, DC: National Association of Social Workers, 1977), 1443.

8. Martha N. Ozawa, "The 1983 Amendments to the Social Security Act: The Issue of Intergenerational Equity," *Social Work,* 29 (March/April 1984), 131.

9. Violet M. Sieder and Doris C. Kirshbaum, "Volunteers," *Encyclopedia of Social Work,* II (Washington, DC: National Association of Social Workers, 1977), 1583.

10. United Way of America, *A Study of the Quantity of Volunteer Activity of United Way and Its Member Agencies* (Alexandria, VA: United Way of America, 1974), p. iv.

11. *The Wall Street Journal,* December 24, 1985.

12. Brian O'Connell, "Our Open Hearts and Open Wallets," *Deseret News,* January 26, 1989.

13. *Deseret News,* May 14, 1995.

# Chapter 3

# Education for Social Work

*From his Pacific island home, Luis applied to one of the 112 accredited graduate programs of social work offering the MSW degree in the United States. In that year he was one of 33,212 successful applicants. Why was Luis accepted as a student? Would he be a good social worker? What did the admissions committee find in his application to put their stamp of approval on him? His autobiographical sketch contains material schools look for. Luis wrote: "In the Jesuit high school I attended, religion classes were often spent in discussing the condition of the slum dwellers on our island, and what we could do to help them. I belonged to clubs that were encouraged to work with the poor, the elderly, and juvenile delinquents. In high school I was a volunteer with social service agencies.... In my first year in college I trained in the juvenile justice system, and* *for the next several years I combined full-time work as a counselor with my night classes at the University.... For the past three years I have worked in the prevention division of a substance abuse agency. My efforts have been directed at developing an educational curriculum in the schools as a drug abuse prevention approach. I have observed that young people who have positive self-esteem, who can communicate with their peers and their elders, and who have problem-solving skills are less likely to turn to drugs and other self-destructive practices.... I intend to return to my Pacific island home upon completing my degree in social work, and I hope to acquire the skills to plan and implement programs that will meet the unique cultural needs of my people, and at the same time help me realize my full human potential."*

Social work education is a phenomenon of the twentieth century. Social work's prominence among the professions results from community demands for trained staff to administer a multibillion dollar human service system. Society has declared that the work of helping people with personal and social problems must be handled with professional competence and subjected to rigorous tests of accountability.

The first agencies trained their own staffs in the "fundamental theory and practice of charity." The early schools of social work, the outgrowth of pressures and demands from agencies for competent personnel, were sponsored by the agencies themselves. Classwork was practice-oriented and intended to prepare staff for work in particular agencies.

Through the efforts of the Charity Organization Society of New York, the first course of instruction was established in 1898 with thirty students enrolled for three months. This summer school of "philanthropic workers" continued until 1904, when the course was recognized on an eight-month basis to become the New York School of Philanthropy, now the Columbia University School of Social Work.

At the turn of the century, an Institute of Social Science was established as a part of the Extension Division of the University of Chicago. In response to efforts of practicing social workers, the institute became an independent School of Civics and Philanthropy and was later incorporated into the University of Chicago and the School of Social Service Administration. In Boston a school was established jointly by Harvard and Simmons College, and in Pennsylvania the Philadelphia Training School for Social Work was begun. These institutions have become schools of social work at Simmons College and at the University of Pennsylvania.

An Association of Training Schools for Professional Social Work was formed through which schools could "gain recognition and exchange views and experience." The association was a forerunner of the American Association of Schools of Social Work and the present Council on Social Work Education. Membership in the first association was open to any school that maintained a course of training covering at least one academic year with substantial fieldwork and classwork. A minimum curriculum, adopted by the schools in 1932, was association policy until 1944 and set forth the standard for one year of training.

Graduate social work students in computer lab.

During the Great Depression new demands were made upon the social work profession, and opportunities were offered by the social legislation enacted to meet the growing needs of society. To meet these demands, social work education was greatly expanded.

Early schools trained workers for jobs in specific agencies. But in a mobile society, social work graduates are on the go, and their education needs to be applicable to all situations. Mobility places a premium on flexibility and the free exchange of personnel, intelligence, knowledge, and skill. In planning curriculum, schools take into consideration the fact that their graduates will be employed in agencies widely dispersed throughout the country, representing not one, but many fields of practice. Fortunately, because of the timely and forward-looking action on the part of schools, graduates completing their training have the assurance that their professional skills can be utilized. Moreover, it is possible for graduates who receive part of their training in one school to transfer to another school.

## Social Work Education

Social work education provides excellent opportunities for students in undergraduate, master's, and doctoral programs. Community colleges also offer course work in human services.

The master's degree has been acclaimed in the past as the basic professional social work degree. Programs for this degree are the heart of education for social work and are among the best in American universities. Doctoral programs, developed by an increasing number of schools, have taken their place among the strong professional schools of the country.

In response to mounting pressures for manpower in the human services, practice degree programs have been instituted at the bachelor's degree level. These programs have been given official recognition and sanction by the profession as the first professional practice degree in social work. Undergraduate social work programs have become very popular, and the number of programs has increased dramatically. Today there are some 382 baccalaureate social work programs in the United States.

In May 1982 the Board of Directors of the Council on Social Work Education (CSWE) adopted a new curriculum policy statement for both the MSW and BSW programs. This policy statement was the first time that the BSW education program's expectations were included in this seminal document.

In July of 1992, the Board of Directors of CSWE adopted a revised curriculum policy statement that defined the premises underlying social work education. Some of the core elements are:

M3.1 The purpose of social work education is to prepare competent and effective social work professionals who are committed to practice that includes services to the poor and oppressed, and who work to alleviate poverty, oppression, and discrimination.

M3.2 Social work education is based upon a specific body of knowledge, values, and professional skills. It is grounded in the profession's history and philosophy. Education for the profession promotes the development and advancement of knowledge, practice skills, and services that further the well-being of people and promote social and economic justice. Social work education is responsible for the production and application of research and scholarship aimed at advancing social work practice.[1]

The preparation of effective social work professionals is expected at both the baccalaureate and master's level. The baccalaureate programs prepare students for generalist social work practice while the master's programs prepare students for advanced social work practice in a specific concentration. The concentration can be in a social work method, such as direct practice or community organization and planning, or in a field of practice such as mental health, family services, health and child welfare. When attempting to differentiate between the baccalaureate and master's programs, CSWE states:

> These levels of education differ from each other in the depth, breadth, and specificity of knowledge and skill that students are expected to synthesize and apply in practice."[2]

While the focus and theoretical depth may be different between the BSW and MSW level, the following material from the 1992 Master's Degree Curriculum Policy Statement gives the basic parameters of the foundation areas:

### Social Work Values and Ethics

M6.5  Programs of social work education must provide specific knowledge about social work values and their ethical implications, as well as opportunities for students to demonstrate their application in professional practice. Students must be assisted to develop an awareness of their personal values and to clarify conflicting values and ethical dilemmas. Among the values and principles that must be infused throughout every social work curriculum are the following:

> M6.5.1  Social worker's professional relationships are built on regard for individual worth and dignity, and are advanced by mutual participation, acceptance, confidentiality, honesty, and responsible handling of conflict.

> M6.5.2  Social workers respect the individual's right to make independent decisions and to participate actively in the helping process.

> M6.5.3  Social workers are committed to assisting client systems to obtain needed resources.

> M6.5.4  Social workers strive to make social institutions more humane and responsive to human needs.

> M6.5.5  Social workers demonstrate respect for and acceptance of the unique characteristics of diverse populations.

> M6.5.6  Social workers are responsible for their own ethical conduct, the quality of their practice, and seeking continuous growth in the knowledge and skills of their profession.

## *Diversity*

M6.6 Professional social work education is committed to preparing students to understand and appreciate human diversity. Programs must provide curriculum content about differences and similarities in the experiences, needs, and beliefs of people. The curriculum must include content about differential assessment and intervention skills that will enable practitioners to serve diverse populations.

Each program is required to include content about population groups that are particularly relevant to the program's mission. These include, but are not limited to, groups distinguished by race, ethnicity, culture, class, gender, sexual orientation, religion, physical or mental ability, age, and national origin.

## *Promotion of Social and Economic Justice*

M6.7 Programs of social work education must provide an understanding of the dynamics and consequences of social and economic justice, including all forms of human oppression and discrimination. They must provide students with the skills to promote social change and to implement a wide range of interventions that further the achievement of individual and collective social and economic justice. Theoretical and practice content must be provided about strategies of intervention for achieving social and economic justice and for combating the causes and effects of institutionalized forms of oppression.

## *Populations-at-Risk*

M6.8 Programs of social work education must present theoretical and practice content about patterns, dynamics, and consequences of discrimination, economic deprivation, and oppression. The curriculum must provide content about people of color, women, and gay and lesbian persons. Such content must emphasize the impact of discrimination, economic deprivation, and oppression upon these groups.

Each program must include content about populations-at-risk that are particularly relevant to its mission. In addition to those mandated above, such groups include, but are not limited to, those distinguished by age, ethnicity, culture, class, religion, and physical or mental ability.

## *Human Behavior and the Social Environment*

M6.9 The professional foundation must provide content about theories and knowledge of the human bio-psycho-social development, including theories and knowledge about the range of social systems in which individuals live (families, groups, organizations, institutions, and communities). The human behavior and social environment curriculum must provide an understanding of the interactions among human biological, social, psychological, and cultural systems as they affect and are affected by human behavior. The impact of social and economic forces on individuals and social systems must be presented. Content must be provided about the ways in which systems promote or deter people in maintaining or achieving optimal health and well-being. Content about values and ethical issues related to bio-psycho-social theories must be included. Students must be taught to evaluate theory and apply theory to client situations.

### Social Welfare Policy and Services

M6.10 The foundation social welfare policy and services content must include the history, mission, and philosophy of the social work profession. Content must be presented about the history and current patterns of provision of social welfare services, the role of social policy in helping or deterring people in the maintenance or attainment of optimal health and well-being, and the effect of policy on social work practice. Students must be taught to analyze current social policy within the context of historical and contemporary factors that shape policy. Content must be presented about the political and organizational processes used to influence policy, the process of policy formulation, and the frameworks for analyzing social policies in light of principles of social and economic justice.

### Social Work Practice

M.6.11 The professional foundation prepares students to apply a generalist perspective to social work practice with systems of all sizes. Foundation practice content emphasizes professional relationships that are characterized by mutuality, collaboration, and respect for the client system. Content on practice assessment focuses on the examination of client strengths and problems in the interactions among individuals and between people and their environments.

Foundation practice content must include knowledge, values, and skills to enhance the well-being of people and to help ameliorate the environmental conditions that affect people adversely. Practice content must include the following skills: defining issues; collecting and assessing data; planning and contracting; indentifying alternative interventions; selecting and implementing appropriate courses of action; using appropriate research to monitor and evaluate outcomes; applying appropriate research-based knowledge and technological advances; and termination. Practice content also includes approaches and skills for practice with clients from differing social, cultural, racial, religious, spiritual, and class background, and with systems of all sizes.

### Research

M6.12 The foundation research curriculum must provide an understanding and appreciation of a scientific, analytic approach to building knowledge for practice and for evaluating service delivery in all areas of practice. Ethical standards of scientific inquiry must be included in the research content.

The research content must include qualitative and quantitative research methodologies; analysis of data, including statistical procedures; systematic evaluation of practice; analysis and evaluation of theoretical bases, research questions, methodologies, statistical procedures, and conclusions of research reports; and relevant technological advances.

M6.13 Each program must identify how the research curriculum contributes to the student's use of scientific knowledge for practice.

### Field Practicum

M6.14 The field practicum is an integral component of the curriculum in social work education. It engages the student in supervised social work practice and provides opportunities to apply classroom learning in the field setting.

M6.15 Field education at the master's level requires a minimum of 900 hours in the field practicum.

M6.16 Each educational program must establish standards for field practicum settings that define their social work services and practices, field instructor assignments and activities, and student learning expectations and responsibilities. Individual programs may organize their practice in different ways but must ensure educationally directed, coordinated, and monitored practicum experiences for all students....[3]

In addition to the foundation areas, the MSW program offers students the opportunity to select concentrations. Each graduate program determines which areas it will make available to students. The following concentration frameworks are outlined in the Curriculum Policy Statement:

### Concentration Curriculum

M6.20 The central purpose of the master's curriculum is to prepare students for advanced social work practice in an identifiable concentration area. Each program must clearly explicate for each concentration the (1) conceptualization and design, (2) expected educational outcomes, and (3) content.

### Conceptualization and Design

M6.21 A concentration provides a context within which advanced practice skills and knowledge are acquired. A conceptual framework, built upon relevant theories, shapes the breadth and depth of knowledge and practice skills to be acquired.

Programs have the freedom to establish concentrations within an organizing framework that is consistent with the purpose of social work and its traditional values. The organizing framework for concentrations must have curricular coherence and logic, and must be anchored in the liberal arts and the professional foundation. The program must have sufficient resources to support the concentrations offered. Frameworks and perspectives for concentrations that are frequently offered by programs include fields of practice, problem areas, populations-at-risk, intervention methods or roles, and practice contexts and perspectives. Combinations of concentrations are permitted.[4]

## The Master's Program

There has been an increase in the number of schools offering the master's degree. There were 63 schools in 1963 compared with 112 in 1992. The number of MSW students graduating in 1994 was 12,856, which exceeded the record high of 10,080 MSW students who graduated in 1979.

The pattern for the master's degree had been a two-year program of class and field instruction. However, in 1971 the board of directors of the Council on Social Work Education adopted standards that provided for advanced standing for students, making it possible for schools to opt for a master's degree to be completed in one year.

The master's program prepares students for professional service and leadership. Curricula include diversified bodies of knowledge, professional skills, and value orientations as requisites for practitioners to serve individuals, families, small groups, communities, and organizations. Master's programs provide opportunity for mastery of concentrations as can be seen in Table 3.1 and Table 3.2 in selected social work methods and social problems.

**TABLE 3.1   Master's Degree Students Enrolled on 11/1/94, by Primary Methods Concentration***

| Methods | Concentration Framework | | | | | | | |
|---|---|---|---|---|---|---|---|---|
| | Methods Only | | Methods Combined with Field of Practice or Social Prob. | | Field of Practice or Social Problem Only (No Methods) | | Total | |
| | # | % | # | % | # | % | # | % |
| Direct Practice | 4,168 | 51.9 | 12,056 | 56.1 | — | — | 16,224 | 53.8 |
| Community Organization and Planning | 169 | 2.1 | 397 | 1.8 | — | — | 566 | 1.9 |
| Administration or Management | 378 | 4.7 | 666 | 3.1 | — | — | 1,044 | 3.5 |
| Combination of Direct Practice with C. O. and Planning or Administration or Management | 189 | 2.4 | 1,195 | 5.6 | — | — | 1,384 | 4.6 |
| Combination of C. O. and Planning with Administration or Management | 167 | 2.1 | 233 | 1.1 | — | — | 400 | 1.3 |
| Generic | 1,729 | 21.5 | 2,226 | 10.4 | — | — | 3,955 | 13.1 |
| Other | 238 | 3.0 | 730 | 3.4 | — | — | 968 | 3.2 |
| Not Yet Determined | 986 | 12.3 | 3,975 | 18.5 | — | — | 4,961 | 16.5 |
| None (Field of Practice or Social Problem Only) | — | — | — | — | 643 | 100.0 | 643 | 2.1 |
| Total | 8,024 | 100.0 | 21,478 | 100.0 | 643 | 100.0 | 30,145 | 100.0 |

*Column totals may not correspond among tables within this report due to variance in response rates.

Source: *Statistics on Social Work Education in the United States,* 1994 (Alexandria, VA: Council on Social Work Education, 1994), p. 34. This article was first published by the Council on Social Work Education, and is reprinted here with the permission of the Council on Social Work Education.

TABLE 3.2    Master's Degree Students Enrolled on 11/1/94, by Primary
Field of Practice or Social Problem Concentration*

| Type of Concentration | # | % |
|---|---|---|
| Aging/Gerontological Social Work | 646 | 2.1 |
| Alcohol, Drug or Substance Abuse | 522 | 1.7 |
| Child Welfare | 2,131 | 7.1 |
| Community Planning | 186 | 0.6 |
| Corrections/Criminal Justice | 230 | 0.8 |
| Family Services | 2,599 | 8.6 |
| Group Services | 128 | 0.4 |
| Health | 2,239 | 7.4 |
| Occupational/Industrial Social Work | 225 | 0.7 |
| Mental Health or Community Mental Health | 3,514 | 11.7 |
| Mental Retardation | 131 | 0.4 |
| Public Assistance/Public Welfare | 88 | 0.3 |
| Rehabilitation | 60 | 0.2 |
| School Social Work | 883 | 2.9 |
| Other | 1,353 | 4.5 |
| Combinations | 313 | 1.0 |
| Not Yet Determined | 6,873 | 22.8 |
| None (Methods Concentration Only) | 8,024 | 26.6 |
| Total | 30,145 | 100.0 |

*Column totals may not correspond among tables within this report due to variance in response rates.

Source: *Statistics on Social Work Education in the United States,* 1994 (Alexandria, VA: Council on Social Work Education, 1994), p. 35. This article was first published by the Council on Social Work Education, and is reprinted here with the permission of the Council on Social Work Education.

Education is structured to provide opportunity for the application of skills and knowledge acquired in the classroom to actual social work situations through an integrated field-work experience.

Students are also given opportunities to participate in school governance, to involve themselves in school policy and procedure formulation and implementation, and to engage in all dimensions of the learning process.

Social work education is an open system with different patterns of education encouraged. Illustrative of schools' conceptions of what is to be achieved by their training programs are the following educational objectives, assumed to have been attained when students:

1. Understand and incorporate the basic values, concepts, and methods of social work, recognizing some significant variations by method and field of practice.
2. Acquire and utilize understanding of human behavior and the social environment, of social policy and services, of institutional reconstruction, and of forces shaping public policy.

3. Achieve competence and basic skill through study and practice in one method, or in a combination of related methods by which services are provided.
4. Understand the unique features of minority and disadvantaged peoples, the significance of their problems, and of their contributions to the resolution of issues in effecting social change.
5. Acquire mature and sensitive attitudes toward one's self and others, which result in becoming an accountable and a disciplined helping person.
6. Develop a commitment to the spirit of inquiry and to research methods through which inquiry can be pursued in advancing professional knowledge and practice.
7. Establish an identification with the profession of social work and the need to integrate knowledge, feeling, and responsible action in becoming a professional person.
8. Become oriented to the contribution of the professional social work association and develop a conviction that the student will carry responsibility for specifying the dimensions of its concerns and practices.
9. Gain the ability to work with and support other professional disciplines, volunteer, and paraprofessional groups in the belief that many of the social and personal ills of our time can be overcome by intelligent and cooperative intervention.

### *Admission to the Master's Program*
Candidates admitted to the master's program have received their undergraduate degrees and possess the requisite qualifications for practice in the profession of social work. Men and women who can meet the personal and academic qualifications are accepted for training irrespective of race, creed, or color. Qualifications usually include:

1. Evidence of superior ability, character, and personality.
2. Academic credentials attesting above-average scholarship and satisfactory completion of four years of college work with a baccalaureate degree from an accredited college.
3. Suitable undergraduate background in the arts and sciences with some emphasis in the social sciences—sociology, psychology, political science, social ethics, anthropology, economics, education.
4. A bachelor's degree from an approved undergraduate college or university.

The policy of schools of social work, which is reflected in their admission procedures, is to select only those college graduates who combine native endowment, relationship capacity, maturity, imagination, industry, motivation, and such other physical, social, emotional, and spiritual qualities that lend themselves to excellence in helping others.

Numbers of students are admitted from foreign countries representing cultures radically different from American communities. Special problems often ensue in the training of foreign students, and this matter has received searching study from the profession, which has guidelines for schools admitting and training students from other countries. The profession is jealous of maintaining and improving its public image. It is constantly upgrading and seeking to improve the quality of its services to the public. Schools of social work are often the vanguard of this striving and have made notable advances in their educational contributions.

## The Baccalaureate Program

In 1970 CSWE initiated a plan to "approve" undergraduate educational programs whose objective included the preparation for practice in the field of social work. Since that time baccalaureate degrees have been awarded to an increasing number of students who are considered professional and are employed in social welfare positions. In addition, students enroll in the programs to enrich their general education, to prepare for graduate social work study, or to prepare for graduate study or employment in one of the other human service occupations.

Of the 382 undergraduate programs reporting in November 1994, a total of 24,536 junior and senior students were matriculated with 10,511 having graduated the previous school year of 1993–1994. Enrollment has been increasing in recent years.

In 1974 the council began "accrediting" programs that met their standards, which specify that the school will provide an educational program that prepares for beginning professional practice by demonstrating that it:

1. builds on, and is integrated with, a liberal arts base that includes knowledge in the humanities, social, behavioral, and biological sciences;
2. provides content in the areas of (a) social work practice, (b) social welfare policy and services, (c) human behavior and social environment, and (d) social research.
3. requires educationally directed field experience with engagement in service activities for at least 300 clock hours, for which academic credit commensurate with the time invested is given.[5]

Building upon the broad base of prerequisite course requirements, individualized study programs, and careful coordination of required and elected social work courses, students are assured of a foundation in the liberal arts, research, human behavior and social environment, social welfare policies and services, social work practice skills, and practical experience in the field.

The practice portion of the curriculum makes possible not only the opportunity for students to integrate and internalize their understandings into practice skills, but also allows field- and campus-based faculty a chance to evaluate and determine whether the educational content given to students is being developed, utilized, and translated into practice. A learning atmosphere can be created in which a student can share any inadequacies, fears, or an experiencing of an educational gap.

In many undergraduate programs the field seminar and practice sequence classes are limited in numbers of students enrolled to encourage the kind of in-depth exchange and resultant learning that can occur within the context of a supportive group. Built into the curriculum is the provision for ongoing, individualized educational direction for accomplishing the program's educational objectives with each student.

Undergraduate programs include the following desired educational goals:

1. Analytic and research skills that enable students to evaluate critically the complex social problems and issues that confront America today, including knowledge and

understanding of the resources and strategies that have been used—or may be used—to meet these problems and issues in the future.

2. Basic knowledge, skills, and values related to problem-solving in social work practice regardless of the particular position a student may occupy upon graduation. These include an understanding of:

   **a.** the philosophical values that underlie practice in the field of social welfare;

   **b.** social welfare institutions and their relationship to other institutional structures in society;

   **c.** social welfare policies and the ways in which they are developed;

   **d.** social work as a profession;

   **e.** individuals in society, including an understanding of human behavior and development; and

   **f.** basic social work treatment techniques and skills employed in working with individuals, groups, and communities, including educational opportunities to participate directly in service programs through field experience.

Students are exposed liberally to the many disciplines and professions concerned with the welfare and behavior of people. Social work courses, whenever possible, serve to integrate and to apply concepts learned in the related basic sciences and disciplines to the field of social welfare and the profession of social work.

### *Admissions*

Students are admitted into social work undergraduate programs under procedures compatible with those of the parent institution. The first interview with students is given particular emphasis, with the faculty member pointing out the requirements and helping students to assess their motivations, interests, and abilities to perform successfully in this profession. These interviews are part of an ongoing advisement process, which allows for periodic evaluation of the students' performance.

A fieldwork placement center is necessary for each student, and this often places a limitation on the number of students who can be accepted into the program. Fieldwork instructors and supervisors are necessary to maintain the close liaison between faculty and students. Imaginative faculty, cooperating with fieldwork placement centers, often are able to create field placements that offer opportunities to the students and fill a need for the community.

An example of involvement of undergraduates in field placement is in foster care of children. Students work with small groups consisting of a set of natural parents, the child in placement, and the foster parents. This gives an opportunity for the natural parents to share as equal partners in the planning for their child, and to meet and relate to the foster parents on a basis of respect and mutual admiration. Students plan for conferences of foster parents and assist in the program planning. In an analysis and building program dealing with foster care, the information gained by the students may produce a composite picture of foster children, natural parents, and foster parents. Students can review the strengths as well as gaps in the social service delivery system. This provides an experience in operational research when they present the material to the agency involved.

Other students work through YWCAs and YMCAs to develop volunteer programs for various groups, such as women at state prisons, minority youths, or divorced women.

These programs help a student to become tuned in to personnel and human needs, and to realize the potential for help in creating a better society.

## The Doctoral Program

The doctoral program in social work has as its primary objective the preparation and development of selected professional social workers for leadership positions. In offering this advanced degree, the 55 available schools are responding to the need for qualified social work educators, researchers, social planners, and administrators. Requirements for admission to the program are usually the MSW degree, with some practical work experience. In 1994 approximately 294 students received doctoral degrees.

The aims of the doctoral program are to enable students to: (1) develop and demonstrate their capacities as social work scholars and to acquire the requisite knowledge, background, and skill to teach, conduct research, write, and speak with authority about social work; and (2) achieve an advanced understanding of the methods employed in social work practice and of the broad range of social welfare services, and to study the social and behavioral sciences and to assess their relevance to social work practice.

### Curriculum

Schools vary in the curriculum offered, but typically there is emphasis on continuing scholarship, with students expected to develop their abilities in organizing, extending, testing, communicating, and applying knowledge of the field of social work and social welfare. Study centers on social work theory and practice, research and statistics, social and behavioral science theory, social welfare policy and planning, and educational theories and methodologies.

To enrich the educational program, courses from other departments of the university are usually recommended. There also is opportunity for the pursuit of individualized interests.

## Continuing Education

With the vast accumulation of knowledge in the social work field, workers continually need to re-evaluate their habits of thought, concepts, values, and methods of practice. Those who say, "That's it! I'm educated," when they receive a degree are only saying, "I have stopped learning."

Continuing education (CE) is an essential part of social work education, designed to qualify practitioners to meet the demands of an ever-changing social service kaleidoscope. It prepares workers to accept change. It is recognition by the profession that degree-producing programs can provide only entry-level qualifications for practitioners.

The point of entry of community college workers, with no previous practice, demands knowledge and underpinning. Seeking professional identity to provide direction and purpose to their practice, they look to continuing education provided by social work schools and professional associations.

The bachelor's degree practitioner looks ahead to movement along the continuum. Moving up the ladder of practice, meeting new challenges, developing new skills, and building a knowledge base are imperatives. CE is an important means for fulfilling these demands.

The master's degree holder who understands the knowledge explosion, who increasingly relates to practice in collaboration with prestigious disciplines and the decision-makers, and who reads the professional literature, ensures against obsolescence by continuing education.

Continuing education makes it possible for workers to update their knowledge and skills, acquire new knowledge, advance on the job, and to prepare for new roles and responsibilities.

Social work is an open and ever-changing system. It is constantly being renewed, added to, and improved. Continuing education is a major component of social work education, serving all curricular sequences and all levels of practice through sharing of research, empirical findings from practice, and new knowledge from the sciences and humanities. It is an essential part of the continuum, an imperative in a rapidly developing profession.

Continuing education is a network of learning associations, arrangements, and resources designed to improve practice and the quality of services. It aids in the formulation of ideas, keeps the mind alert to new and exciting developments in social work and related disciplines, and helps one become a "wise man" as defined by André Gide, the French novelist who won the Nobel Prize for literature in 1947: "The wise man is he who constantly wonders afresh."

## Student Participation in Social Work Education

In the 1960s students often complained of powerlessness, that their views were not heard, and that the schools served not students, but the faculty and the Establishment. Education, they said, was not relevant.

Students in the 1990s have become more involved and identified. They are serving on the board of directors of the National Council on Social Work Education and as members of the House of Delegates, where they participate in policy formulation and decision making. They are appointed to national committees and commissions. In the universities they are elected or appointed to college councils, and to executive and policy-making committees, including the important curriculum and student review committees.

In these positions students not only offer a student point of view, but have voting power and impact decisions having to do with their education. In some universities they serve on university-wide committees and participate in university government.

Students in social work in many ways are the architects of their learning, and they contribute to the system as they take from it.

## Stipends and Scholarships

Financial assistance is available to qualified students at all levels of training. Students planning to attend school may contact the school of their choice for detailed information on stipends, scholarships, and work-study arrangements administered by the educational institutions and social agencies. A list of accredited colleges and universities for training social workers may be obtained from the Council on Social Work Education.

### Faculty in Schools of Social Work

In 1994 faculty teaching social work at the undergraduate and graduate degree levels numbered 5,571. Because of the strong affirmative action programs in social work education, 22.7 percent of the faculty in graduate and joint graduate-undergraduate programs and 26.7 percent of the undergraduate faculty were ethnic minorities.

The inclusion of nonwhite faculty added an important dimension to schools of social work in the 1970s and 1980s, strengthening their offerings by adding cultural input to the curriculum and important role models for students.

## Council on Social Work Education

Schools guided by the Council on Social Work Education have improved their offering to students by raising their standards of training, tightening admission requirements, and shifting to a common core, concentrations, some specialties, and a continuing emphasis on basic principles, values, and philosophy.

The CSWE reviews the programs of schools and accredits training. It also actively assists colleges and universities in implementing their programs, and offers consultation services to both undergraduate and graduate programs.

It assists with curriculum studies, student admission procedures, rights and responsibilities, and with faculty recruitment and development.

An important part of its function is to publish informational materials, including statistics and research findings on all phases of social work education at all levels, and distribute them to students, faculty, administrators, and agencies. It also selects and publishes teaching materials for use in schools and in staff development programs.

Moreover, CSWE sponsors an annual meeting attended by faculty members and by leaders of voluntary and government agencies at local, state, and national levels.

Colleges and universities are the source of well-educated social workers to meet the needs of agencies concerned with the many social problems of the country. The CSWE helps schools to maintain standards, so that a social worker graduating from an accredited school will be able to function in his or her role in working with those who need social services.

## Summary

Social work education is a phenomenon of the twentieth century and resulted from the nation's demand for trained staff to administer a multibillion-dollar human service system. It has moved from practice-oriented, agency-focused training to colleges and universities having status with other professional schools and academic colleges.

Curricular models have been developed for professional education at the doctor's, master's and bachelor's degree levels. All programs have enjoyed significant growth, but the bachelor's level programs have increased their numbers dramatically.

The Council on Social Work Education, the only official accrediting body, addressed itself to the important problems of structure and quality in social work education. Because of the complexity of modern society, CSWE has required schools on all levels to stress generalist practice and a generalist perspective. The social worker needs to understand and be able to work with the interaction of multiple human systems.

Continuing education has developed on a broad front in recognition of the need for practitioners to keep current in the rapidly expanding and changing field of practice.

## Selected References

ANDERSON, JOSEPH, *Foundation of Social Work Practice.* New York: Springer, 1988.

COMMISSION ON ACCREDITATION, *Handbook of Accreditation Standards and Procedures,* 4th ed. Alexandria, VA: Council on Social Work Education, 1995.

CONSTABLE, ROBERT T., "Social Work Education: Current Issues and Future Promise," *Social Work,* 29 (July–August 1984), 366–371.

HOKENSTAD, MERL, C., JR., "Curriculum Directions for the 1980's: Implications of the New Curriculum Policy Statement," *Journal of Education for Social Work,* 20 (Winter 1984), 15–22.

HOWERY, VICTOR I., "Continuing Education: Program Development, Administration, and Financing," *Journal of Education for Social Work,* 10 (Winter 1974), 34–41.

KOLEVZON, MICHAEL S., "Conflict and Change Along the Continuum in Social Work Education," *Journal of Education for Social Work,* 20 (Spring 1984), 51–57.

MILEY, KARLA KROGSRUD, MICHAEL O'MELIA, and BRENDA L. DUBOIS, *Generalist Social Work Practice.* Boston, MA: Allyn and Bacon, 1995.

NORTON, DOLORES G., *The Dual Perspective.* New York: Council on Social Work Education, 1978.

PAYNE, MALCOLM, *Modern Social Work Theory: A Critical Introduction.* London: Macmillan, 1990.

RIPPLE, LILLIAN, *Report to the Task Force on Structure and Quality in Social Work Education.* New York: Council on Social Work Education, 1974.

RUBIN, ALLEN, PETER J. JOHNSON, and KEVIN L. DEWEAVER, "Direct Practice Interests of MSW Students: Changes from Entry to Graduation," *Journal of Education for Social Work,* 20 (Spring/Summer 1986), 98–108.

RUSSELL, MARY NOMME, *Clinical Social Work: Research and Practice.* Newbury Park, CA: Sage Publications, 1990.

TICE, KAREN, "Gender and Social Work Education: Directions for the 1990's," *Journal of Social Work Education,* 26 (Spring/Summer 1990), 134–144.

## Notes

1. Commission on Accreditation, *Handbook of Accreditation Standards and Procedures,* 4th ed. (Alexandria, VA: Council on Social Work Education, 1995), p. 134.

2. Ibid., p. 136.

3. Ibid., p. 139–142.

4. Ibid., p. 143.

5. Lillian Ripple, *Report of the Task Force on Structure and Quality in Social Work Education* (New York: Council on Social Work Education, 1974), p. 12.

# *Chapter 4*

# *Generalist Practice and Introductory Theory*

*Jimmy was failing in school; his sister, May, was in and out of correctional homes; their father never seemed to be able to keep a job; and the mother was always "sick." The family got by—they lived mostly on public assistance—but they never had enough money. Food stamps helped. Neighbors and the local church unit had tried, but this family was "undeserving"—they just wouldn't try to help themselves. Actually, the entire family didn't perform, or performed poorly at best, all their various social roles. The parents failed at parenting; the children failed in school; parents and children were failing as a family.*

*Multiproblem families epitomize family disorganization and breakdown, and in their failure to perform in their various roles, they illustrate problems of social functioning, or more appropriately, the failure to function. Functioning or dysfunctioning individuals, families, or communities in their many socially determined roles become the objects of the social work profession.*

Because of the complexities of modern society, the profession of social work has chosen to emphasize the generalist practice perspective. The profession was actually founded on a generalist premise that social workers needed to consider and work with both the individual and the environment as they attempted to improve the life quality and functioning of individuals, groups, and communities. This basic premise compelled the profession toward a holistic and comprehensive knowledge base that honors diverse value systems and possesses a wide range of professional skills.

Over the years the social work profession partially left the commitment to generalist principles in an effort to specialize and develop specific methodologies designed to work in "direct practice" (i.e., individuals, families, and groups) or "indirect practice" (i.e., community organization and administration). The Council of Social Work Education suggested in its 1992 curriculum policy statement that the undergraduate program teach a strong generalist practice core and that graduate programs also teach a generalist perspective, combined with an advanced concentration of some type. The advanced concentration could be in working with individuals, groups, or communities or in a field of practice such as mental health or child welfare. Schools of social work were encouraged to develop their curriculum in a flexible way within basic guidelines.

One of the strong basic themes of all social work education today is the generalist conceptualization. Miley et al. offer the following definition:

> Generalist social work provides a contemporary approach for meeting the purpose of social work. This view moves beyond the confines of individually focused practice to the expansive sphere of intervention with multiperson systems. Broadly defined, generalist social work considers the interplay of personal and collective issues and works with a variety of human systems—societies, communities, neighborhoods, complex organizations, formal groups, informal groups, families and individuals—to create changes which maximize social functioning.[1]

When a person comes into a social worker's office requesting help or when the social worker visits an individual in a homeless shelter, the purpose of the meeting is to enhance the person's well-being or social functioning. Also, when the social worker meets with a state legislative committee or a local school board, the professional purpose is to help them design programs that will alleviate poverty and oppression and meet basic human needs. The professional social worker is expected to perform difficult and complex tasks. In order to help conceptualize the role of social workers, the Council of Social Work Education defined the purposes of social work in the 1992 curriculum policy statements for both the baccalaureate and master's programs as follows:

> M4.1 The profession of social work is committed to the enhancement of human well-being and to the alleviation of poverty and oppression. The social work pro-

Social worker reaches out to troubled youth.

fession receives its sanction from the public and private auspices and is the primary profession in the provision of social services. Within its general scope of concern, professional social work is practiced in a wide variety of settings and has four related purposes:

M4.1.1 The promotion, restoration, maintenance, and enhancement of the social functioning of individuals, families, groups, organizations, and communities by helping them to accomplish tasks, prevent and alleviate distress, and use resources.

M4.1.2 The planning, formulation, and implementation of social policies, services, resources, and programs needed to meet basic human needs and support the development of human capacities.

M4.1.3 The pursuit of policies, services, resources, and programs through organizational or administrative advocacy and social or political action, to empower groups at risk and to promote social and economic justice.

M4.1.4 The development and testing of professional knowledge and skills related to these purposes.[2]

## Need for a Theoretical Framework

Because of the inclusive professional purpose statements, the wide variation of client groups, and the intense interaction among and between these groups, the profession of social work has struggled to develop a theory base that would provide an adequate foundation for the knowledge needed to carry out its mandate. The profession of social work has borrowed heavily from academic disciplines dealing with human biological, social, psychological, and cultural systems. Theories stressing the impact of economic forces on individuals and communities have added another important dimension in understanding how systems promote or deter people from achieving optimal health and well-being. The study of political processes and policy formulation has recently been incorporated into the social work knowledge base.

In order to address the wide-ranging theories from other academic disciplines and to help make these theories understandable to social work practitioners, the Council on Social Work Education has required that schools of social work teach a series of classes under the title of Human Behavior and the Social Environment. The council has defined the HB and SE sequence as follows:

M6.9 The professional foundation must provide content about theories and knowledge of human bio-psycho-social development, including theories and knowledge about the range of social systems in which individuals live (families, groups, organizations, institutions, and communities). The human behavior and the social environment curriculum must provide an understanding of the interactions between and among human biological, social, psychological, and cultural systems as they affect and are affected by human behavior. The impact of social and economic forces on individuals and social systems must be presented. Content must be provided about the ways in which systems promote or deter people in maintaining or achieving optimal health and well-being. Content about values and ethical issues related to bio-psycho-social theories must be included. Students must be taught to evaluate theory and apply theory to client situations.[3]

The HB and SE sequence has been a basic mechanism to help the professional focus on the dual perspective of the person and the environment with a proper understanding of the important interaction that goes on between people and the context in which they live. The dual perspective has assisted social workers to incorporate theories into practice that explain how individuals grow and develop socially, biologically, and emotionally. Also, the dual perspective has encouraged an understanding of social structures, systems, and cultural norms that play such an important part in the lives of all people.

In the early days of social work the dual perspective was evidenced in the Charity Organization Societies (COS) and the Settlement House Movement (SHM). The COS focused on changing the individual, while the SHM chose to change social systems. There was an important shift toward more emphasis on the individual with social work's adoption of Freud's psychodynamic model. However, as different theorists broke away from Freud, the environmental perspective began to again claim more prominence. The profession of social work accepted theoretical constructs from such theories as ego psychology, behavioral and cognitive models, humanist and existential models, social psychological, and communication models. Since the 1970s, the profession has added the systems and ecological models as a way of again stressing the importance of balancing the focus of social work practice between the "person" and the "environment."

The systems and ecological models also give the social work practitioner theoretical constructs to thoughtfully analyze interactions between and among social systems and to visualize how these interactions influence people's behavior.

Systems theory addresses the impact that organizations, policies, communities, and groups have on individuals. Individuals are thought of as being involved in constant interaction with various systems in the environment. The aim of social work is to improve the interactions between clients and systems. Barker defines a system as follows:

> A combination of elements with mutual reciprocity and identifiable *boundaries* that form a complex or unitary whole. Systems may be physical and mechanical, living and social, or combinations of these. Examples of social systems include individual families, groups, a specific social welfare agency, or a nation's entire organizational process of education.[4]

Ecological theory is a subset of systems theory that makes some important contributions to social work. One contribution of this theory is the definition of three levels of systems in the following:

1. **Micro:** This system refers to an individual and incorporates the biological, psychological, and social systems that impact on the individual.
2. **Mezzo:** This system refers to small groups that impact the individual such as the family, work groups, and other social groups.

3. **Macro:** This system refers to groups and systems that are larger than families. Four important macro systems which impact individuals are organizations, institutions, community, and culture.

Both systems theory and ecological theory have assisted the profession by giving the practitioner an organizing framework to analyze the ever-shifting, volatile interaction of people in their environments. Also, these two theoretical constructs facilitate the process of linking concepts from traditional theories such as "psychodynamic" and "behaviorism" together, enabling practitioners to visualize the human process as an eclectic whole. After the linkage has been established, practitioners can then sort out the concepts they subscribe to and utilize them in their practice in an organized and disciplined fashion.

## Introductory Inner and Outer Forces Paradigm[5]

The following paradigm has been developed to introduce the dual perspective of social work to students who anticipate becoming social work practitioners. The paradigm is simple and straight-forward, and yet it incorporates elements of systems and ecological theory. The paradigm is basic, but it allows for additions of the more sophisticated theories of human behavior.

The inner and outer forces paradigm attempts to explain why people seem to act at times in strange and unpredictable ways. Some people get excited thinking about a golfing vacation, while others prefer the ocean. Some like to work with their hands, and others enjoy paper work behind a desk. The reasons behind the selection of mates, too, have often been a great mystery.

While there is seemingly no chance in the foreseeable future to fully explain and predict the human drama, the authors propose a conceptual model to assist the social worker in bringing some kind of order to the human scene. The basic assumption in the inner and outer forces model is that there are forces developed both within the person and from the person's environment that cause him or her to behave in certain ways. The real origin of the forces may never be identified, but the recognition that the forces exist and continually interact to produce behavior is significant.

The authors have chosen the terms *inner* and *outer* to identify the two major forces that shape human behavior. An example of the inner and outer framework can be observed when a child begins to walk. One important inner force is created by the neurological development of the child that produces a force which incites the child to try to walk, as well as creates the capacity to walk. The important outer force of mother's rewarding the child with pleasant smiles and hugs further encourages the continuation of this new behavior. Thus, the child's walking is a product of the interaction of inner and outer forces.

Figure 4.1 illustrates the inner and outer forces model in a simplified format. The arrows indicate that force is being exerted on the individual from within and without, which produces a resultant behavior.

Social workers can utilize the inner and outer forces framework in several ways. The framework can assist in assessing and treating problems of a troubled person. The following case history illustrates the assessment and treatment use of the model.

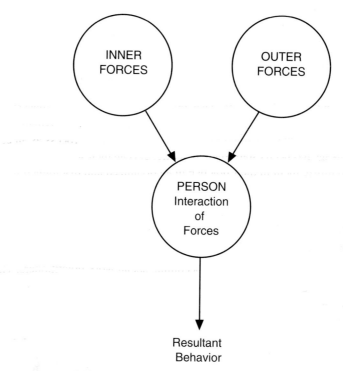

**FIGURE 4.1**

John, a 17-year-old high school student from a small rural community, was referred to the mental health center because he was continually fighting, had received numerous speeding tickets, was doing poorly in school, and had beaten up his stepfather. As John described his problems, it was apparent to the worker that the outer forces in John's life were overpowering him. The school officials seemed to be set on removing him from the school and the local police watched constantly for him to drag Main Street so they could give him a ticket. John's stepfather, an aggressive, anxious person, was trying to help John by, in his words, "tightening the screws" to make him perform better.

While the worker was able to recognize the outer forces precipitating the present referral, consideration was also given to the inner forces influencing John's life. John admitted that he felt insecure because he had no plans for earning a living. He felt he was a failure in so many areas that he was almost panicked. These feelings of inferiority and insecurity were strong inner forces that required attention from the social worker.

Recognizing that the outer forces needed to be relieved before anything could be done to work on John's inner forces, the worker called meetings with school officials, police personnel, and John's family. After the worker explained the great negative pressure brought to bear on John by the outer forces, all the people involved agreed to work toward the goals of realistically reducing the outer pressure on him. Teachers set up tutorials for him and gave him positive support. The policemen agreed to overlook the fact that sometimes John drove two miles over the speed limit on Main Street. This was the same consideration they gave to boys who weren't in the "troublemaker" category. The stepfather, too, relaxed his controls on John.

As the outer forces were reduced, John's behavior began to change. He functioned better in the community. The worker then helped him work on some of his negative inner forces, such as feelings of inferiority, and brought about additional changes. John completed high school and opened an auto body shop.

The inner and outer forces model utilized in John's case is shown in Figure 4.2.

The social worker reduced the negative outer forces and increased some positive inner forces, producing more functional behavior in John. The inner and outer forces framework helped the worker assess John's problems and suggest a successful treatment course.

Another use of the inner and outer forces framework is in prevention. If the worker can recognize what impact outer forces have on people, it will be possible to remind communi-

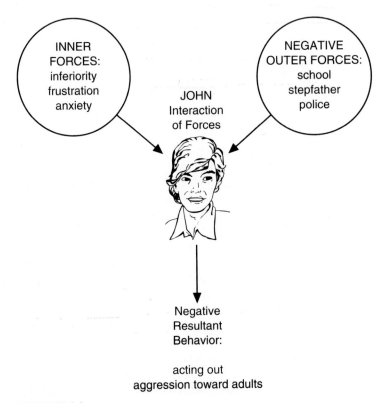

**FIGURE 4.2**

ties and other social systems of the effect they have on the behavior of people. There is a growing recognition in all systems of our society that meaningful planning has to be done to help the social systems create positive outer forces. Recently there has been a push in industry to recognize and work with the outer forces created in the important area of employment.

A third use the social worker can make of the inner and outer forces framework is creating a classification system for the new theories that are developing in the area of human behavior. The worker can place the new theories from sociology, psychology, social work, psychiatry, and anthropology in the inner and outer forces framework, thus helping the learning process and increasing the understanding of those in the field of social work.

## Additional Model Definition

In order to be more specific, the inner and outer forces have been divided into the micro, mezzo, and macro systems. It should be recognized that these systems overlap and are not all-inclusive. With the expanded definition (see Figure 4.3) of the inner and outer forces model, the social worker can sharpen assessment abilities. The following case illustrates the use made of the micro, mezzo, and macro designations.

> George, an 18-year-old high school senior, was referred to the social worker because of his refusal to do any work in class. He presented himself in a belligerent, negative fashion, stating that he did not enjoy school and did not want to work.
>
> In the initial interviews the social worker explored along the lines of the micro, mezzo, and macro systems. There were no problems in the macro system. George and his family had lived in the same community for many years and had

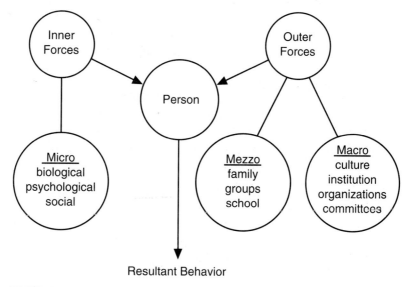

**FIGURE 4.3**

accepted the mores of the group. In the micro and mezzo systems, however, there were problems: George did not feel good about himself and had aggressive impulses that he couldn't control; and school personnel were pressuring him to make sure he would graduate. The worker discovered what he considered the most difficult problem, however, in the micro system. George was suffering from a learning disability and couldn't read. His inability to perceive and organize the written word was striking. George had struggled through all his classes in a small rural school not having the capacity to read.

The social worker proceeded to help George understand his reading problem as a biological failure and one that was not due to his laziness. Teachers were asked to modify their teaching techniques to allow George to do more verbal work than the rest of the class. The science teacher refused to go along with the social worker and continued to try to force him to read several chapters a day. George was hopeless in the class and responded with aggressive behavior. After intervention by the principal and the social worker, George was transferred into another class where the teacher was willing to cooperate.

George graduated from high school, although he still could not read. However, because of the efforts of the social worker and the school personnel, he felt less ashamed of himself and had less need to fight the world. The social worker discovered that the most important force in this young man's life at this particular time was his learning disability; the worker used the inner and outer forces model, focusing on the micro system of the inner force classification.

## The Life Cycle and the Inner and Outer Forces Model

An important addition to the inner and outer forces model is the life cycle concept. Theorists in behavior recognize that there are stages of human development that seem to be universal. One simple developmental classification is childhood, adolescence, adulthood, and old age. Erik Erikson who adapted his formulation of a life cycle from basic Freudian theory, developed an eight-stage classification that he felt identified the main life crises or stages, which are: (1) trust (0–1 years); (2) autonomy (1–3 years); (3) initiative (4–6 years); (4) industry (7–11 years); (5) identity (12–17 years); (6) intimacy (18–22 years); (7) caring (23–45 years); and (8) integrity (45 + years). The age ranges appearing next to the stages have been added to give the reader an approximation of the person's age at a given stage of development. Erikson's formulations are especially useful when combined with the inner and outer forces model in Figure 4.4.

The representation of Erikson's eight stages of life, utilizing the step configuration, gives one a sense of climbing and also moving ahead one step at a time. The step diagram is used to illustrate Erikson's epigenetic approach.

With the superimposition of the life stages diagram on the inner and outer forces model, the social worker can consider a person's problem from an organized, total approach. For instance, a child in the third grade is reported to be daydreaming too often and not completing her assignments. The child has been referred to the social worker. Utilizing the model, the worker can ask the following questions.

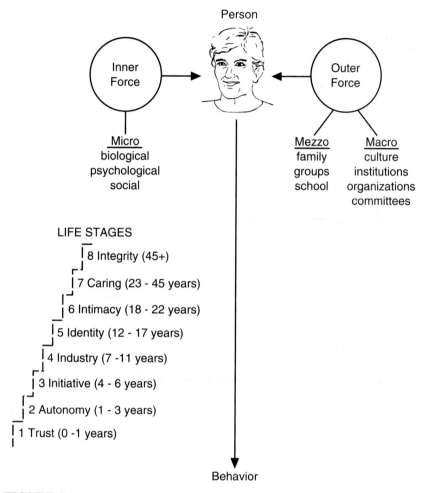

INNER AND OUTER FORCES MODEL

**FIGURE 4.4**

1. What stage of life is the child in? What are the most important developmental tasks for the child at this time?
2. Is it an inner or an outer force that seems to be causing the problems? Is there a combination of pressure from both inner and outer forces?
3. If it seems to be the inner forces, is the main problem in the psychological or biological area within the micro system? Does the child have feelings of inferiority that prevent her from working or does she have something wrong with her eyes that prevents her from reading?
4. If the problem is mainly in the outer force area, is it in the mezzo or macro system? Perhaps the child has been having trouble in the family because of tremendous conflict

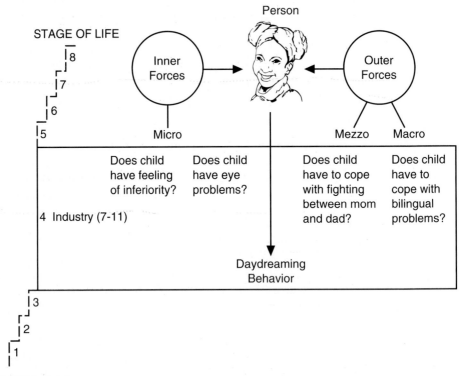

**FIGURE 4.5**

between her mother and father. In the cultural area it could be discovered that the child's Hispanic parents speaking Spanish in her home makes it difficult to relate to class material written or spoken in English.

The above series of questions that a social worker could ask about a client can be represented in Figure 4.5. Stage four, Industry, is highlighted. As the diagram is followed horizontally, the main systems of inner and outer forces are considered. This diagram can help social workers assess the problems in a logical fashion. Also, it can assist the worker in looking across the individual's total experience, i.e., micro, mezzo, or macro.

## *Social Functioning*

The "inner" and "outer" forces framework is a tool to help the social worker explain some of the reasons why individuals may not function well in their environment. The behavior that is produced by the inner and outer forces can be defined as being on a continuum from functional to dysfunctional.

The intervention and aid of social work are indicated when people unaided cannot cope with social obligations and commitments, and when problems interfere with relationships that exist within the family, at school, on the job, or in other social groupings. The aim of social work is to improve and enhance social functioning.

During the history of social work, many attempts have been made to describe its nature and purpose and to differentiate social work from other helping professions. Social work has determined that "social functioning" is its central purpose. Intervention by social workers is to give prominence to the restoration, promotion, and enhancement of social functioning.

## Levels of Social Functioning

In their various roles—in the home, on the job, and in the neighborhood—individuals are not always at their best. Social workers have long since learned that individuals differ in their role performances, from moment to moment, and from other individuals. Nevertheless, the functioning of some people can be so grossly impaired as to preclude their doing anything for themselves.

A group—for example, a family—may be said to function in a rewarding and functional manner when its several members have more or less agreed-upon goals; the transmission of ideas among members is clear and unclouded; individuals reciprocally contribute to their own needs and to the interests of each other; activities are mutually supported with an adequate resource base; and disorganizing influences from the outside are effectively checked and held to a minimum. A community, or social system, is functional or dysfunctional depending on how responsive or unresponsive it is to the needs of the people who created it. For example, a school system that is constructively educational for *all* the children of all the people can be described as a functional system. Conversely, one that consistently records a 50 percent dropout rate and does not promote the curiosity and mental growth of pupils is dysfunctional to some degree.

All professions take cognizance of the *wholeness* of individuals. However, because life is complex and science is specialized, each profession must confine itself to some aspect of the human condition. Medicine, except for the fields of public health and preventive medicine, confines itself largely to work with those who are ill. Education is focused on teaching methods, learning theory, motivation, and other aspects of pedagogy. The rites and ordinances of the church and scriptural exposition are functions of the ministry.

Social work places its primary attention on an individual's relationships with other human beings. It focuses on how and with what effectiveness the person performs various social roles. Threats to, or actual impairment of, role function are the situations to which the profession addresses itself. The social worker analyzes the social relationships, works with clients to find solutions to the factors that interfere with social functioning, and also gives direction to the enrichment of human association.

A typical example of a problem is an illness causing inability of the wage earner to work or to work efficiently. Illness can result in loss of employment and income for the family, and in breakdown in family as well as employee-employer relationships. Social work, when called upon to intervene, concerns itself with the fact of unemployment, rehabilitation of the wage earner, the family's income-maintenance needs, and the shift in role relationship within the family due to the individual's illness.

A second illustration involves a mother suffering from "nervous exhaustion." She spent several days in a hospital. In a few weeks following her release, her symptoms reappeared, and it was necessary for her to be readmitted. A social study disclosed that her home was literally making her sick, and that her marital and family relationships would have to improve before she could derive any lasting benefit from medical treatment.

Social work is an enabling profession that helps with problems of living and human relationships, and with the dysfunctional complexities of various social institutions. Social work assumes humanity's worth and preeminence and takes the position that people inherently have the potential for dealing with their problems. However, at times and under stressful circumstances, people often need help. Social work addresses itself to this need and has systematically developed a helping philosophy and the knowledge and skill to implement this philosophy.

Social work is not antiseptic. It does not aim to make life free from stress-producing problems or to relieve people of their responsibilities. Problems can be building blocks. Crises are frequently the mainspring of adaptive behavior.

Generally, people struggle successfully, often with imagination and ingenuity, with their everyday concerns. Many people learn to cope with stress and to take minor crises in stride. Some, spurred on by handicaps, rise to great heights. In other situations, however, people are faced with problems they cannot solve by themselves. Some of these are personal, resulting from weak egos or poor native endowment; some are family induced and conditioned; and others result from community pressures and failures.

Abandoned, neglected, and deprived children may be incapable of functioning independently. As people grow old, many rely on their families or society to meet their basic needs. No age group, economic class, or society is ever completely free of difficulties that interfere with the role performance of some of its members.

## A Base for Generalist Social Work Practice

The dual perspective or "inner" or "outer" forces paradigm can be a basis for generalist social work practice. Generalist social work practice requires the worker both to be able to explain human behavior and to decide on a course of intervention to improve social functioning. The paradigm assists the practitioner to continually assess behavior across the micro, mezzo, and macro systems and to understand the tremendous forces that are brought to bear on the individual by these systems. The paradigm also utilizes the notion of systems theory, which recognizes the continual interaction of the systems and helps the worker understand the constant reconfiguration of the systems.

Since the generalist social worker must work with the micro, mezzo, and macro systems, it is important that each new social worker be grounded in the traditional social work methods. The rich history and methodology of social work practice with individuals, groups, and communities should be understood by the generalist social work practitioner. The following three chapters define each of the traditional social work methods that offer the generalist practitioner a base upon which to build a practice.

In addition to the three traditional methods, the social work profession has always been interested in the methodology of administration. Because of social work knowledge, skills, and values, most social workers become administrators in their agencies. Also a profession is required to develop its knowledge base, and there has been an increased effort by social work to stress the importance of research. Social workers must evaluate their own practice to see if they are doing effective work and to improve their skills. Recently, the public has been pressuring for more accountability in all areas of social services. This text includes a chapter on administration and research, since these basic processes are so important for the beginning generalist practitioners to understand.

## Summary

*The social work profession is emphasizing the generalist perspective to deal with complexities of modern society. The generalist perspective helps the social work practitioner deal with multiperson systems and gives direction in assessing the interplay of personal and collective issues with a variety of human systems. Both baccalaureate and master programs are focusing their curriculum on generalist practice.*

*The "inner" and "outer" forces paradigm is an introductory framework that helps generalist practitioners both explain behavior and plan meaningful intervention. The paradigm is based on social systems and ecological theory. It also includes a developmental component that places the human growth process in perspective.*

*Social work is an enabling profession that helps with problems of living and human relationships and with dysfunctional complexities of individuals and social institutions. The profession has*

*determined that "social functioning" is the central purpose of its existence and sets about to enhance or restore social functioning of individuals, groups, or communities.*

*Since the social work generalist practitioner works with individuals, groups, and communities, the person who chooses this profession should know and understand the traditional social work methods as well as the overall generalist perspective. The traditional methods of working with individuals, groups, and communities have a rich history and have provided the means of helping many people. Administration and research have also played a major role enabling the development and maintenance of the profession. The remaining chapters of this book offer the new generalist practitioner and others an overview of traditional social work methods and fields of practice.*

## Selected References

GARBARINO, JAMES, *Children and Families in the Social Environment,* 2nd ed. New York: Aldine De Gruyter, 1992.

EDWARDS, RICHARD L., ed., *Encyclopedia of Social Work,* 19th ed., 12. Washington, DC: NASW Press, 1995.

MILEY, KARLA KROGSRUD, MICHAEL O'MELIA, and BRENDA L. DUBOIS, *Generalist Social Work Practice.* Boston, MA: Allyn and Bacon, 1995.

NORTON, DOLORES G., *The Dual Perspective.* New York: Council on Social Work Education, 1978.

PAYNE, MALCOM, *Modern Social Work Theory: A Critical Introduction.* London: Macmillan, 1990.

ZASTROW, CHARLES, and KAREN K. KIRST-ASHMAN, *Understanding Human Behavior and the Social Environment,* 3rd ed. Chicago: Nelson-Hall, 1994.

## *Notes*

1. Karla Krogsrud Miley, Michael O'Melia and Brenda L. Dubois, *Generalist Social Work Practice* (Boston, MA: Allyn and Bacon, 1995), p. 10.

2. Commission on Accreditation, *Handbook of Accreditation Standards and Procedures,* 4th ed. (Alexandria, VA: Council on Social Work Education, 1995), p. 135.

3. Ibid., pp. 140–141.

4. Robert L. Barker, *The Social Work Dictionary,* 3rd ed. (Washington, DC: NASW Press, 1995), p. 385.

5. Some of the following material is adapted from Milton G. Thackeray, Rex A. Skidmore, and O. William Farley, *Introduction to Mental Health: Field and Practice* (Englewood Cliffs, NJ: Prentice Hall, 1979), pp. 155–66.

# Social Work Practice with Individuals

*After Henry and Rita Van Orman's only child drowned in a home swimming pool, guilt and accusations caused their previously "good" relationship to deteriorate rapidly. Soon they were no longer communicating or understanding each other. The marriage counselor, a social worker, assigned them to read the poem "Home Burial" by Robert Frost and discussed it with them in a subsequent interview. This discussion proved to be a turning point with the Van Ormans, for they discovered they could talk about the couple in "Home Burial" when they were unable to discuss their own feelings. "Home Burial," a dialogue between a man and his wife following the death of their baby, mirrored the Van Orman's grief. Talking about the couple in the poem opened the door for them to express their grief and find new dimensions of understanding. Each person handles grief in a different way, and Rita began to understand this as she studied the poem. When she read the lines spoken by the husband,*

> *"A man must partly give up being a man with women-folk ..."[1]*

*she realized that she, like Frost's character, wanted Henry to react as she thought he ought to react. Henry felt a kinship with the husband who spoke these lines:*

> *"My words are nearly always an offense. I don't know how to speak of anything so as to please you. But I might be taught I should suppose ..."[2]*

*His efforts to console Rita had been continually rebuffed, and now in seeing the social caseworker, he wanted to save his threatened marriage.*

## Work with the Individual—A Generalist Approach

Social work with individuals is one of the main parts of a generalist approach to social work practice. From its inception the profession has been vitally interested in helping individuals to help themselves.

In the main, traditional methods are frequently combined in practice. A worker may work basically with individuals, as in clinical practice, and set goals that may also include a *group* or *community* effort. A generalist is knowledgeable and skillful in the application of all methods. A worker may choose to practice with (1) the individual; (2) the group; (3) the community; or (4) with a combination of all methods.

This chapter, *Social Work Practice with Individuals,* focuses on an approach commonly recognized in clinical social work* and one basic to casework. The worth and dignity of people, and the singular importance of the individual and family—valued philosophical assumptions—chart the course of modern social work practice. Esteemed goals of self and group realization are embedded in the theory and practice of social work, exemplified by the traditional social work method, social casework.

The term *social casework* appeared rarely in the literature before 1920, and the practice of casework was at such a low ebb near the turn of the century as to prompt Mary K. Sinkovitch to declare at the conference on Charities and Corrections in 1909, "I believe that this paper will interest nobody, for I think that the modern emphasis is so strongly on preventative work of a social character, that casework is secretly, if not openly, despised. . . .The general feeling is that casework is a small affair, unimportant, a necessary evil, a depressing piece of business, a practically hopeless job."

In the 1990s casework is virtually the antithesis of Sinkovitch's earlier characterizations. Its emphasis is not on prevention, although the authors would welcome a stronger preventive, nonclinical mode. Casework is not despised, although most people would like to see a diminution or disappearance of social problems addressed by caseworkers. The literature attests to support—from weak to strong—for casework among clientele receiving services. An assortment of public institutions support casework. It is viewed as essential, but not as a "necessary evil" on any grand scale. Depressing? Sometimes, because of the nature of the problems it deals with. It has an upbeat side and institutions training caseworkers attract superior students in large numbers.

A great deal of back and forth jockeying takes place among professionals on the issue of effectiveness. This subject is tested and researched and most will agree that casework practice needs ongoing validation. Social workers insist that practice be subjected to critical review. They believe that practitioners should be held accountable for what they do and for their social work competence. Presumably their effectiveness will turn, in part, on whether they use the knowledge, values, theory, method, and principles of practice in treatment modalities determined as valid by the profession.

Social casework is a method of social work employed by tens of thousands of social workers in a wide variety of social service and other institutions. Whatever its limitations, work with individuals and families is widely used in social work practice. In a sense, it is the mother of methods. The authors of this text have chosen to use the term *social casework* because of the excellent definitions developed over the years and because the term is indigenous to the practice of social work.

Knowledge and skill derived from social casework have wide application in the several methods of social work. In a society of rapid change and shock, casework is a mitigating influence for individuals who experience anomie and isolation.

*There are those in practice who believe casework to be *the* method of clinical social work. The term *casework* widely used in the beginnings of social work has more recently been broadened and titled *work with individuals.* In the view of some, *social work* and *social casework* are synonymous. The methods of *group work* and *community work* were differentiated and developed later. The terms *micro, mezzo,* and *macro* are also descriptions of practice approaches.

## Social Casework Defined

Social casework is "The orientation, value system, and type of practice used by professional social workers in which psychosocial, behavioral, and systems concepts are translated into skills designed to help individuals and families solve intrapsychic, interpersonal, socioeconomic, and environmental problems through direct face-to-face relationships."[3]

Social casework is a method of helping people solve problems. It is individualized, scientific, and artistic. It helps individuals with personal as well as external and environmental matters. It is a method of helping through a relationship that taps personal and other resources for coping with problems. Interviewing is a major tool of casework. Change in attitudes and feelings is affected by the dynamics of the casework relationship. The possible need for the person to obtain help from one or more community services, facilitated by the casework process, is explained and interpreted. It is neither environmental manipulation nor preoccupation with wholly subjective considerations; it combines psychological and social elements and is psychosocial.

## History of Social Casework

Stereotyping, making broad generalizations about individuals and situations, is the antithesis of social casework; yet the past has been punctuated with efforts to lump categories of individuals together for convenient classification, if not for study and favorable attention. The "workhouse test" and the "less eligibility" clauses of the infamous English Poor Laws are based, in part, on naive and unfounded general assumptions, namely that *all* the poor are poor because of ignorance, willful refusal to work, shiftlessness, and depravity; that assistance to all of them should be made noxious, given in small amounts, extended for short periods of time, and only for emergencies. For only in this way can *poor* people be made to work, sense their responsibility, and be protected from the evils of relief.

The Association for Improving the Conditions of the Poor (AICP), founded in America in 1843, approached the problem of poverty individually. The aims of the AICP were to "visit the poor at their homes, to give them counsel, to assist them when practicable in obtaining employment, to inspire them with self-respect and self-reliance, to inculcate habits of economy, industry and temperance, and whenever absolutely necessary, to provide such relief as should be suitable to their wants."[4]

The Charity Organization Society (COS) established in the United States in 1877 gave additional impetus to individualization and casework. The main plan of this organization included an investigation of applicants to determine need, central registration, recording, relief-giving, and the use of the volunteer family visitor.

It was probably through the efforts of the family visitor that the concept of *scientific charity* evolved, and the seeds of social casework were sown. The visitors discovered that all poor people are not alike and that they should not be treated in the same manner. Various papers presented at the National Conference of Charities and Corrections during this period enunciated the principle of individualization. They affirmed that the aim of the COS was to reach the individual, and that its broad purpose was restoration of function, not detection of imposters on relief. "The poor, and those in trouble worse than poverty, have not in common any type of physical, intellectual or moral development, which would warrant an attempt to group them as a class."[5]

With the development of schools of social work at the turn of the century, *visitors in training* received instruction in methods of investigation, diagnosis, and treatment from experienced social workers. Developing out of the COS movement the first family welfare association was organized in 1905. Pioneered by Mary Richmond and Frances H. McKlean, family service societies, numbering over 300, offer specialized casework services to thousands of clients. *Social Casework,* journal of the Family Service Association of America, grew out of the efforts of this great pioneer movement.

Preoccupation with social conditions external to the individual was characteristic of casework during the early part of the twentieth century. Finding work for families in distress, getting all children to school, placing children in institutions when abused, neglected, and abandoned were natural products of this type of *manipulative* therapy. The thinking was that if the environment could not be changed, the individual should be removed from the environment, even if it meant separating families.

A shift in emphasis from external *sociological* factors to the individual's conscious social attitudes marked an important step in the development of social casework. Problems were considered as the outgrowth of real life experiences, such as neglect and rejection, and dealt with at the conscious level. This shifting of emphasis posed a need for new knowledge about the individual, and it was at this time that the impact of dynamic psychology and psychoanalysis was felt. Dynamic psychology shed new light on the importance of instinctual drives as part of psychobiological growth, as opposed to life experiences and the part played by repression and the unconscious in personality makeup and problems.

## Contributions of Freud and Psychoanalysis

G. Stanley Hall, who invited Sigmund Freud to this country in 1910, and William White, who later presented Freud's work, paved the way for the introduction of psychoanalytic theory and *depth*[*] psychology into the casework movement. This was the mental hygiene and psychiatric era of social work. In the decade following World War I, the psychosocial component of the problem-solving method in social casework was focused. There had been a decided shift in interest from sociological improvements to those in which psychology predominated, placing the individual and inner forces squarely in the center of the stage.

Deluged with psychoanalysis and *depth psychology,* caseworkers struggled to retain their social work identity in the twenties; nevertheless, it was during this period that individual therapy came into its own. Whereas the friendly visitor of the prepsychoanalytic era more or less intuitively relieved the patient's feelings in the last five or ten minutes of the interview, by "dwelling upon hopeful and cheerful things," the caseworker consciously handled anxiety, helped the client to help him- or herself, and used relief as a tool of treatment. Emotions, attitudes, repressed conflicts, and the struggle within the unconscious became an integral part of social casework understanding and method.

[*]By "free association" and "dream analysis" Freud learned that certain ideas, mental images, and emotions hidden away in the unconscious were often driving forces of behavior. By helping patients become aware (making conscious) of these "depth" elements, the individual could often learn to deal with disturbing intrapsychic forces.

The social and economic needs of the Great Depression refocused sociological and reality considerations for social work and compelled action on the part of the federal government. This was the period of the many work programs such as the Federal Emergency Relief Act, the Works Progress Administration, and Public Works Administration, and the Civilian Conservation Corp, culminating in the Social Security Act of 1935. The depression resulted in a healthy turnaround from emphasis upon psychological causation to the renewed study of economics, budgets, and environmental factors. Actually the pendulum swung from one extreme to the other, and over the years the two have come closer together.

According to Helen Perlman:

> A growing rapproachment between the social sciences and dynamic psychiatry has yielded a number of ideas of potential usefulness for caseworkers. Consonant with casework's focus upon the social environment are concepts such as these: role performance, as index of social functioning and as cause as well as effect of personality disturbances; culture identifications as affecting personality, behavior, interpersonal conflicts, caseworker-client relationships; class differences in behavior standards and values, as determinants of responses to given situations; social stability in its relation to personal stability; and so on. Practice has yet to test the actual value and import of these ideas for casework.[6]

There has also developed a renewed interest in the family, family dynamics, and the interaction of family members with the result that families are "better understood today and therefore potentially better dealt with. . . .Thus 'family diagnosis' and 'family treatment' are theoretical and methodological problems in casework today" and there is a greater interest than ever before in the "hard-to-reach" individual and family, in efforts to conceptualize practice, in research and evaluation.

The problem-solving method widely applied in social work today, combining work with individuals, small groups, and organizations, marks a shift from the traditional casework approach. However, the scientific base, the search for new knowledge, and philosophical assumptions regarding the worth and value of the individual remain.

## The Practice Framework

Purpose, values, sanctions, knowledge, and methods are at the heart of social work practice with individuals and families. Purpose is the *raison d'être* of practice. Values determine worker attitudes and approaches. Sanctions are society's mandates and provisions of social work expressed in structural arrangements, the law, and policy statements. The knowledge base provides the facts, concepts, and principles for practice. Method is both the science and art of applying theory to practice.

### Purpose

The purpose of social work practice is to prevent or cure the breakdown of a healthy relationship between an individual and his or her family or other associates. It helps people to identify and resolve problems in their relationships or, at least, to minimize their effects. In addition, social work seeks to strengthen the maximum potential in individuals, groups, and communities.

## Social Work Values

Social work assumes the inherent worth and importance of the individual and the interdependence between the individual and society. In the democratic tradition, powers not delegated are reserved to the individual and to the people. Social institutions are the creation of people, acting as individuals or with others, and are subordinate to their desires and wishes. They were formed by individuals and exist to serve them. They can be changed, constantly renewed, allowed to decay or even dismantled; but the individual remains and enjoys a certain supremacy. Emphasis is placed on the importance of respect for the dignity of the individual, and on his or her ability to make important decisions.

Basic assumptions about people profoundly influence professional practice. The following value postulates are examples of influences in the practice of social work and social work with individuals.

### Value Assumption on Individual Worth and Capacity

A "worth" value places the individual in a position of eminence. He or she is above objects and institutions, worth caring for because he or she is an individual. This is one of the entitlements a person does not have to deserve. Others include respect, dignity, and opportunities to express individuality.

The value of "worth" suggests that the individual has the ability to guide his or her actions, and the potential for determining goals and their achievement. The person's worth is validated equally by his or her decision to achieve potential or to permit it to lie unused, by a decision to achieve or merely vegetate.

### Uniqueness Value

Belief in the individual's uniqueness and individuality suggest a casework approach of acceptance and the view of differences as assets. Strength in role relationships is viewed as coming from differences. Marriage, for example, is enhanced by the contributions of husband and wife who combine their separate qualities of mind, feeling, and performance. Enhancement in human associations is recognized as deriving from differences organized for the good of the group. The perception of uniqueness, as a part of the social worker armamentarium, guides the application of the casework process.

### The Value Postulate of Self-Determination

As applied to the casework process this value concept clearly recognizes that the client is his or her own person. Whether to accept or decline a service is the client's decision. The client, not the worker, makes the choice among alternatives. In the casework process the worker may discuss and consider options, elaborate these, and help weigh their pros and cons. The worker may suggest preferences and cite evidence for them, but still retains awareness of what he or she is doing and clearly communicates that these are the client's prerogatives.

Self-determination means that the client will decide whether or not to engage in the casework process. Self-determination is affirmed, explicated, and implemented at the beginning, in the middle, and at the end of the process. It is part of each component and guides the interaction from moment to moment. Self-determination implies questioning and answering questions. It implies giving and taking, struggle, risk, pain, suffering, failing, and self-fulfillment. In all stages of service delivery the client remains free to withdraw or to continue.

The social worker remains effectively and mentally neutral, but may share ideas, feelings, experiences, along with expressing interest, concern, sympathy, and empathy.

Impositions that remove free choice and self-determination may damage the relationship and weaken the client's problem-solving resolve and capacity. Furthermore, they are likely to be perceived as unwelcome intrusions. The social worker applies knowledge, understanding, and skill, with discipline and intelligence and with the basic value assumption that the individual has the need and the right to make his or her own choices and decisions.

## *Sanctions*

Work with individuals and families, except for private practice, is under the auspices of various governmental and private agencies that receive their sanction from the people. Governmental agencies are intended to express the will of the people. Private voluntary associations are also mandated by the people to serve human needs. The authorization for services is provided by law, or by policy-making bodies in bylaws and constitutions of agencies reflecting the wishes of the people who support the services of the agencies.

The working definition of social work practice states:

> Social work has developed out of a community recognition of the need to provide services to meet basic needs, services which require the intervention of practitioners trained to understand the services, themselves, the individuals, and the means for bringing all together. Social work is not practiced in a vacuum or at the choice of its practitioners alone. Thus, there is a social responsibility inherent in the practitioner's role for the way in which services are rendered. The authority and power of the practitioner and what he represents to the clients and group members derive from one or a combination of three sources:
>
> 1. *Governmental agencies* or their subdivisions (authorized by law).
> 2. *Voluntary incorporated agencies,* which have taken responsibility for meeting certain of the needs or providing certain of the services necessary for individual and group welfare.
> 3. *The organized profession,* which in turn can sanction individuals for the practice of social work and set forth the educational and other requirements for practice and the conditions under which the practice may be undertaken, whether or not carried out under organizational auspices.[7]

## *Knowledge*

The theory underpinning for casework is derived basically from the profession of social work and from casework practice. Research contributes to the knowledge base and appears to be growing in sophistication and importance.

The profession continues to recognize the contributions from the behavioral and natural sciences. Among the more important contributing disciplines are: dynamic psychology, ego psychology, and the various theoretical developments in sociology, social psychology, psychiatry, and cultural anthropology.

Derived from dynamic psychology are theories of personality and personality development, structure, and function. Changes have occurred in relation to personality theory and are reflected in casework theorists' view of the nature of man and individual behavior:

> Thus concepts of conflict-free areas in ego development and function, of autonomy, and of drive for mastery and competence are included—although with varying degrees of emphasis and detail—in most, if not all, of the dynamically oriented practice theories. . . .
>
> In addition, these aspects of ego psychology may serve as the basis for the development of specific principles of operation for the general treatment tenet that social case-work treatment is allied with the "healthy" aspects of the personality or with the "healthy" defenses. A thorough integration of these ideas from ego psychology may, perhaps, continue the development of a model for social case-work assessment and treatment that is realistically balanced to take into account health, illness, and the wellsprings of strength in most people. Finally, understanding and integration of concepts of ego autonomy, drive for mastery, and competence may aid in the development of specific ideas and principles that will rescue the elusive doctrine of individual self-determination from its limbo between philosophy and psychology to take its place in the real world of principles of operation in social casework, and, indeed, in social work.[8]

Pavlovian and Skinnerian psychology is one of the newer strains of theory introduced into casework practice. Behavior modification does not use a theory of personality. It proceeds from assumptions about operant behavior and practice focused on observable behavior that can be researched and explicated.

Social casework practice applies role theory to casework practice. Role theory illuminates understanding of people using the services of social agencies, who frequently believe they have failed in one or more of their social roles or in society's expectations of them. Caseworkers understand that social roles are culturally ascribed or achieved. Everyone chooses from among many roles within the group or culture to which he or she belongs. The performance or behavior of the individual in these roles, with some leeway, can be fairly accurately predicted. Social role becomes a determinant of behavior and cuts across a wide variety of situations in which individuals find themselves. Knowledge about these forces and their culturally determined influences support practice with the individual.

Learning theory, adult socialization, small group and cognition theory, systems theory, and discoveries in biology and endocrinology are other strains that have been adapted for use in social casework practice and help to broaden the theory base of practice.

Although social work "borrows" from psychology, sociology, and from the biological sciences, the profession itself orders, arranges, adapts, and determines the emphasis it will make of these contributions. Theories of ego psychology are integrated into the several models of casework practice. Theory applied becomes practice theory. Theory from the disciplines becomes less and less biopsychological-social-cultural and more social work practice theory. The contribution of social work to the integration and adaptation of theories takes on a dimension of major proportions and of itself is a major contribution to theory building.

Knowledge of the various services of the community is basic to the practice of social casework. Knowledge from social work about social service agencies—legally mandated agencies sanctioned by the community, their organization and function—is an important part of the knowledge base of social casework. The function and purpose of agencies and referral procedures, and increasingly the legislative process, all provide essential underpinning for the casework process.

Services require community sanction and support. Laws when implemented by administrative policy become the framework in which a particular program operates. Knowledge of the constitutions and bylaws of voluntary organizations, and agency policy statements, serve a similar purpose for these organizations and are binding upon the directors and administrative officers. They must be understood for sound social casework practice.

## Methods of Social Casework

Methods of working with individuals and families have remained open. In the 1950s there was much discussion of the diagnostic and functional methods of casework. Many models of casework have been identified: psychosocial, functional, problem-solving, behavior modification, family group treatment, crisis-oriented brief treatment, and adult socialization. One of the newer models is task-oriented casework.

Social workers tend to be guided in practice by the theories of one or another model, by a method that combines principles from several theories and their own individual styles—which, in some particulars, may bear little resemblance to any of the existing models. New theories and new models of practice develop in response to the experience of practitioners to the many situations they encounter. Thus, theory building continues and practice is enriched by diversity, as differences of method are validated and guided by the values of the profession.

The trend in the 1990s appears to be what has been appropriately labeled *selective eclecticism:* (1) a greater utilization in practice of elements from a variety of theories and a blending of models, (2) selective interventions that are empirically grounded, (3) coping *skill* orientation with less of a focus on the inner problems, (4) direct practice embracing more than casework, and (5) a greater utilization of interventive approaches that can be measured and validated.

Brief mention is made of several models of casework practice. The *psychosocial* model was one of the first models to be developed and applied to the practice of social casework. Its psychological origins date back to the 1920s when psychoanalytic principles and theory were incorporated into the then largely sociological approach to casework. Conceptualizations, and refinements, of the psychosocial model are based on the pioneering work of Gordon Hamilton and her associates at the New York School of Social Work, now known as the Columbia University School of Social Work. Professor Hamilton referred to her work as an organismic approach to casework. Cause and effect relationships are identified between the individual and environment. Ego psychology and the behavioral sciences provide important underpinning for practice. Essentially this model has a Freudian theory base modified and adapted for use in social work practice.

The *functional* model was developed at the Pennsylvania School of Social Work in the 1930s. Emphasis was on the relationship, the dynamic use of time, and the "use of the agency" function. The psychology of Otto Rank provided underpinning as adapted for use by proponents of the functional school. Diagnostic categories have tended to be avoided as having limited usefulness in social work practice. For instance, how does one reconcile the concept of individuality and uniqueness with a pigeonholing of individuals into several classifications?

The *problem-solving* method is identified with the work of Perlman at the Chicago school. This model is formulated and made articulate in *Social Casework,* written by Perlman and published in 1957. A few characteristics of the problem-solving method include the identification of the problem by the person, subjective aspects of the person in-the-situation, the centrality of the person with the problem, the search for a solution to the problem, decision making, and action. The purposes of the process are to free the client for investment in tasks related to the solution of the problem, involve the client's ego in work designated to deal with the problem, and to mobilize inner and outer forces in the service of satisfactory role performance.

The *behavior modification model* is Pavlovian and Skinnerian, and it began to be incorporated in the social work literature in the 1960s. Practice applying to this model lends itself to research since behavior to be modified is observable. This may be one of the chief values of behavior modification.

Behaviorists agree that symptoms are the same as other responses in that the behavior is mainly respondent or operant. It was learned through the processes of conditioning and reacts in the same way to laws of learning and conditioning as does "normal" behavior. It can be modified by applying what is known about learning and modification.

*Task-centered casework,* a "general service model" developed at the University of Chicago, first appeared in publications early in the 1970s. Designed to solve specific psychosocial problems of individuals or families, this model is a short-term, time-limited form of practice. Together the caseworker and client reach an explicit agreement on the particular problems to be worked on, and also the probable duration of treatment. Organized around problem-solving actions developed collaboratively by the caseworker and client, the tasks assigned will state a general direction for the client's action, or a specific behavior the client is to follow. By concentrating his or her effort in helping the client follow the program, the caseworker makes use of various interventions.

The psychosocial approach, the functional approach, and the problem-solving model have been said to be schools of thought. Other approaches are identified as *family therapy, crisis intervention,* and *adult socialization.* These developments seem to be treatment approaches with an increasingly strong theoretical base. They are options of treatment, in different developmental stages, and have been tested in practice long enough to emerge as theoretical positions. They are examples of theory building in process and what happens to them in the future will depend on what use is made of them in practice. Social work is a profession of practice, and theory is always subjected to application.

## Problems in Social Casework

Social casework addresses itself to the solution of problems that block or minimize the effectiveness of the individual in various roles. Problems within the family that interfere with or prevent the discharge of the family's social and economic obligations are of paramount concern to the caseworker, as are those that block communication and free expression.

Problems preventing the maximum use of the opportunities offered by the school are pinpointed by the school social worker. In the clinic or hospital, of concern to caseworkers are those problems that militate against the effectiveness of treatment, the relationship of patients to their families and their physicians, their feelings about treatment and income maintenance.

Difficulties in classification of problems are immediately apparent when viewed in relation to the discrete needs of individuals. Nevertheless, some grouping appears desirable and can be justified. Obviously, problems related to income need and to social change are basically external to, and may be outside, the control of the individual. Problems of interpersonal relationships can be identified and clearly recognized. Typical, for example, are stressful and disturbed marital relationship problems that center in the marriage itself. Intrapsychic conflicts, trait disturbances, and other personality disorders are still another broad classification of problems with which casework is concerned. Some problems are environmental and sociological; some interpersonal and familial; some strictly personal and intrapsychic; and most contain both social and psychological elements.

Social workers are frequently confronted with situations in which the casework objective may be that of helping a client use a service. Problems related to attitudes toward accepting and using social services are often among the most difficult, although, paradoxically, these problems only exist for clients in relation to their decisions to do something about their problems.

## The Casework Process

Study, assessment, intervention, and termination are main divisions of the casework process (see Figure 5.1).

### Study

In the study phase, the client is engaged in presenting the problem. The key is engagement. Frequently, clients seeking help have the expectation that the agency or the caseworker will take over. This is an erroneous conception of the casework process, which may have resulted from the client's previous life experiences—with doctors, lawyers, the clergy, educators, and others whose help-giving models tend to be that of prescribing for, preparing briefs for, performing marriages for, and teaching by telling students what they are to learn. Engaging the client meaningfully begins with the study phase. It is one of the threads of the process that will continue to be interwoven throughout. Interaction and client participation are emphasized, not because of their special relationship to the beginning phase, but for their importance throughout the process as a setting for the process.

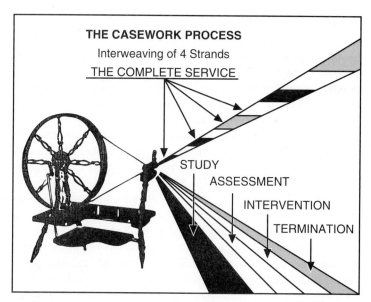

**FIGURE 5.1**

In the study phase, the client makes the important decision of whether to enter treatment. If the decision is not to accept the service, the initial contacts should be constructive and not diminishing experiences. The worker's attitude is an important controlling factor in what the client decides. Respect for the worth and dignity of the client and his or her right to self-determination will be communicated by interested concern, listening to statements of the problem, and by assurances that the views of the client are of paramount concern. Guided by social work values in each phase of the process, the worker will optimally develop a helping relationship by cooperation and collaboration in addressing the problem and the tasks associated with it.

The emphasis on the interaction is on the here-and-now and on the problem not as might be perceived by the worker, but as experienced at the moment by the client. The problem, as presented in the initial phase, is either *the* problem for which help is sought or that part of it the client chooses at the moment to focus upon. In later phases, as the relationship is tested by the client and proved to be sustaining, other aspects of the problem and possibly other problems will be focused. The client's view and the worker's view remain fluid in the study phase.

Data-gathering and history-taking concentrate on relevance. There is no requirement for a complete longitudinal history. A sufficiency of facts may be required to satisfy the demands of the agency. If so, this consideration should be communicated to the client. Of greater importance, data and feelings as these are communicated in the interview provide important clues regarding the problem, the client's perception of the problem, and the way in the past he or she has handled the problem. Such data are useful for assessment purposes and for decisions on treatment goals. Data-gathering is not an end but a means and is justified only as it serves the purposes of assessment.

Assessment and intervention are phases that sometimes are mistakenly believed to occur in a fixed time frame, namely, following the study or initial phase. Actually, "hunching" on a problem begins in the study phase, often with the making of appointments or in the contacts with the referral source. Contacts during the initial phase may be among the most dynamic of the entire process. During this phase the client is likely to feel most helpless and vulnerable, and hence most available to the helping process. At this point of crisis, sympathetic listening, demonstration of acceptance, reassurance, demonstration of confidence in ability, and judicious stroking can all be powerful tools in the hands of the skilled worker and can be highly therapeutic. The interventive potential of early encounters is inestimable. In fact, beginning social workers often underestimate the dynamic healing qualities of early encounters and misinterpret client's "dropping out of treatment" as rejection of the worker or the services when actually he or she has already received the help needed for a crisis.

The study-assessment-interventive phases blur and may proceed simultaneously. However, there tends to be an emphasis in time on one or the other, and although discrete stages are not the rule it seems helpful in discussing the processes to recognize their separateness.

Evaluation and termination are also phases of the casework process, which, although receiving an emphasis near the end of the process, are introduced in the study phase, during the period of assessment, and in the interventive process itself. In each interview, the worker will ask him or herself, and the client, to consider the importance of that interview in relation to goals. Also, terminal considerations are given as to how the client will function with greater satisfaction and self-reliance as a result of the interview and the steps taken to implement the problem-solving process. Transferability of gains in the interview to real life situations is always uppermost in the process at the beginning, in the middle, and at the end. Termination occurs when the client has gained the strength, the understanding, and the problem-solving know-how necessary for successful coping with problems and life situations.

## *Assessment*

Assessment provides a differential approach to treatment based on individual differences and needs. It clearly recognizes the uniqueness of every situation, the importance of treatment planning related to a particular problematic situation, area of family dysfunction, system breakdown, or trouble within a life situation. Defining the problem is clearly a way of individualizing the person.

Assessment is fluid and dynamic. It is ever-changing, beginning at intake and continuing to termination. It is likely to be the emphasis of the worker-client effort to understand the problem in the situation. Assessment begins with a statement of the problem by the client. It is guided by what is indicated by the client to be the major problem and may penetrate a range of somatic, psychological, social, cultural, spiritual, and environmental forces. Assessment results in an understanding of the problem. It includes initial impressions that are confirmed, modified, or even rejected in the light of additional information as the case moves from moment to moment. There is a circular quality about assessment. It never ceases during the casework process. It includes judgment about the strength and limitations of the individual in coping with the situation. Assessment addresses itself to strengths, capacities, limitations, motivation, and opportunity. Treatment planning and treatment itself are guided by assessment.

The functioning person, the person with mastering ego capacity, can be expected ordinarily to say what brings him or her to the agency. This becomes the point of intersection between the worker and the client. The worker will apply his or her knowledge of forces, knowledge of life situations, problem-producing stresses, and understanding of people to the helping role by questions, comments, and in many nonverbal ways. He or she will help to achieve elaboration of the problem as may be required for treatment. Because of the ever-changing diagnostic nuances, this may be repeated during the process. Assessment and diagnostic work do not result in the main in categorization of individuals, or in the application of labels to their problems, particularly when labels are likely to be misused and create a static situation where fluidity is called for. Social workers use psychosocial classifications but with a tentativeness that recognizes the dynamic and changing life situation. There is mutual agreement of the worker and the client in assessment. Goals must be congruent with the client's needs and the availability of services. These goals are respected, supported, and reinforced.

## Intervention

Intervention or treatment begins with the first contact. The study process *is* treatment when it helps the client to clarify the problem for him- or herself, and to make changes in his or her life situation resulting from this understanding. Interventive goals are determined by the client and the worker together. Intervention is determined by the client's need, and when the agency does not provide the service indicated the worker has the responsibility to help the client tap other sources.

The relationship is the mainspring of social work with individuals and families, with the possible exception of those who follow the behavior modification model. Warmth, genuineness, and congruence have been identified as essential qualities the worker must bring to the relationship. Combined with interviewing skills, the worker helps the client tell his or her story and to make a partial approach to treatment so as not to be overwhelmed.

Interventive skills include interviewing, recording, letter writing, referrals to other agencies and services, and helping the client to use personal and other resources. Interventive efforts support and strengthen the client's ego through emotional catharsis, reassurance, clarification of the problem, and sympathetic listening. Intervention, geared to the worker-client relationship, is guided by such basic principles as:

1. The client's right to determine his or her own course of action within the limits of his or her capacity to make sound choices. The client may have no more ability than to button a shirt or blouse; nevertheless, the decision to function to the limits of his or her capacity, or to button the shirt or blouse, is respected and encouraged, with the worker knowing that one small achievement can be the mainspring of an expanding capacity to achieve.
2. Acceptance of a client as is, implying acceptance of his or her capacity to change, and that he or she can and will utilize his or her resources to improve. In a nonjudgmental way, social work seeks to understand the individual or family, the reasons for their behavior, and to help them develop their potential for more satisfying social and personal adjustments.

3. Social work traditionally relates to strength rather than to pathology. Limitations are recognized and handled realistically, but the worker seeks to assess and develop strengths within the individual and his or her family.
4. The social worker seeks to understand the person and to help him or her plan for constructive change. He or she collaborates with the client on goal-setting and assessment, and supports the values of society.
5. Knowledge about the client's family and its situation is used responsibly for the welfare of the family and society. This permits sharing pertinent information wherever possible and appropriate and with the knowledge and consent of the client.
6. The family worker has a professional responsibility for the welfare of the total family. Social work is constantly evaluating the effect of treatment of one member of the family upon other members. A family-centered focus is maintained where intervention is carried out through work with one or several family members or through individual or joint interviews.
7. The family worker is responsible not only to the client but to oneself, the agency, the community, and the profession.
8. Innovations of professional activities, determined for the worker by various principles and concepts, must be consistent with casework goals.
9. As mobilizers of material, environmental, and psychological resources, family workers array themselves with efforts to develop, improve, change, and strengthen services, and facilitate their constructive use by the client in need.

## *Termination*

A decision to accept a "case," to intervene professionally, to provide help to an applicant (an individual, or to a family) needing help, carries with it the assumption that at some point in the process the intervention will end. *Termination* as used in social work means the ending or limiting of a process that was commenced when the agency (worker) agreed to enter into the interventive process aimed at delivering a service to a client with a problem. The processes of study, assessment, and intervention do not continue forever. Terminal plans need to be considered, and these should be understood alike by the worker and the client.

Termination can be a dynamic of change and growth, a time when the client can look back with satisfaction on what has been accomplished. Most often initiated by the worker, termination that outlines realistic goals will affirm the importance of what the client can do and is expected to do in resolving problems and in achieving goals. Termination in effect signals that the worker has confidence in the client's ability to learn to cope with situations and to grow, and that the role of the worker is enabling; he or she will serve as a resource for the client in the present situation.

Termination planning will avoid the fostering of crippling dependence and the false hope by some clients that in some magical way there can be a shifting of responsibility to the agency or to the worker. Termination, understandably, will receive the greatest emphasis as the ending of the relationship nears and will be a summation of gains made in the interventive process. This summation will be more than a recitation of the worker's observations; it will be a process entered into by both the worker and the client and includes self-assessment mainly, as well as worker contributions. Reassurance of the client's readiness to function more effectively will highlight this phase of the interventive process. When there are doubts and fears, these can be allayed by a review of realistic accomplishments, and the readiness of the client to perform his or her various roles with greater self-assurance and adequacy.

### Case Examples

The three case examples that follow are illustrative of three aspects of the casework process—the interweaving phases of study, assessment, and intervention as related to psychosocial model; task-centered casework; and the behavior modification model.

## Psychosocial Model

**Study.**   Such factors as the following, revealed in the initial interview, are noted and taken into consideration for assessment and intervention:

Mary, the only daughter in a family of six children, grew up having her parents always protecting her, limiting and controlling her activities, and often thinking for her. Even though she was married with three small children, not much had changed in her relationship with her parents since she was a child. They continued to be over-solicitous of her welfare, gave her money and gifts so that she wouldn't have "to go without anything."

Mary liked to receive gifts, and the money always came in handy, but she didn't like the strings the parents attached to their generosity. Mother always called Mary for help if she was ill, or if she needed someone to run an errand. Mother also took it for granted that Mary would do her ironing and her weekly cleaning. Father was sure Mary would love to do the bookkeeping for his small business. When Mary did not volunteer her services to her parents, they would ask her to do what they wanted.

**Assessment.**   Mary, excessively dependent upon her parents, resented this dependency, and wanted to break out of the box she felt she was in. She also was resentful of the demands of her own children, even though this dependency was age appropriate. Much of the time she was angry with her husband because he didn't take more responsibility with the children and because he took her for granted. She complained that he assumed how she felt, what she liked and didn't like, and made decisions for her. She became furious when he said, "Come on, you'll like it," when he wanted to make love. She wanted to decide matters that affected her, although she admitted to indecision and being unable to make up her own mind.

Her feelings of helplessness in social situations, with her children, her husband, and sometimes with neighbors and friends, appeared to be referable to the long period of time when the choices she made in myriads of family matters were minimal.

**Intervention.**   The goal was to support Mary in efforts to become more self-reliant and to help her become less dependent. She was encouraged to make decisions affecting her life. She was helped to question her relationship with her mother. She was aided to understand why she resented her children's dependency and how to cope with this by encouraging them to be self-reliant. She learned, for example, that it was not necessary to continue to tie the shoelaces for their five-year-old, but that she could teach this skill to the child.

She was helped to understand her dependency and how to handle her relationships with others without feeling helpless and rejected. She was supported by the caseworker in the positions she took with her parents. For example, she was helped to say "no" to them when they asked for favors in return for the money they gave, and to refuse the gifts if this meant that she couldn't be her own person.

## Task-Centered Casework

**Study.**    Betty, a 17-year-old pregnant girl, sought help at the Children's Service Society, a child placing and adoption agency.

She told the social worker that she was three months pregnant, frightened, and didn't know what she wanted to do. Although her parents were extremely upset, they were concerned about her, and had urged her to come to the agency.

In interviews with the girl and her mother, the following list of significant options surfaced; Betty listed the options in terms of priorities approximately as follows:

1. Have the baby and give it up for adoption. She preferred to keep the baby, but realized that she was not ready to be a parent.
2. Have the baby, keep it, and marry the father when he was released from the army in two years. She was willing to get married, but the putative father was not, and for a variety of reasons her parents were adamantly opposed to the marriage.
3. Continue in high school while she was pregnant and prepare for graduation. She had one year to complete her high school work. An "A" student, she was highly motivated in academic studies and extra-curricular activities. She sang in the school's chorus, played the violin, and participated in school plays. She definitely wanted to finish high school and go to college.
4. Have an abortion. Her mother opposed this on religious grounds. Betty, somewhat opposed to this, was not as strong in her view on abortion as her mother. Nevertheless, abortion was low on the list.

**Assessment.**    The problem was planning for an unwanted pregnancy. From the standpoint of the caseworker, the problem was one of assisting a young, immature woman make a decision about an unborn child, and possibly helping the girl's parents accept her decision. Betty's feelings about what to do were mixed—she would like to keep the baby, but questioned her readiness to care for a child. She first thought of getting married, but discovered that the father was not ready for this step. She needed practical help, such as where to live, where to get a job so she could have some income, medical care including hospitalization, and a chance to finish high school.

**Intervention.**    Specific interventive tasks that were addressed:

1. Betty was helped to make the decision to have her baby.
2. Arrangements were made for her to live in a foster home, in a city where she was unknown, and in a school district where she was permitted to attend school.
3. She was scheduled for regular clinic check-ups with an obstetrician who worked with the society.
4. She was paid a wage for light housekeeping in the foster home.
5. Provision was made for her to discuss her plans for the baby with the caseworker. Betty learned the policy of the society, and was assured that as far as possible her wishes regarding the baby would be respected.
6. The putative father was included and he helped financially and in other ways to assist Betty in her decision and with her plans.
7. At the end of six months, she was terminated and returned home to her family, where she finished high school and started to make plans for college.

The above list of tasks is illustrative only of what specifically was done to solve a psychosocial problem. This outline fails to show the skill and technique employed to accomplish these and related tasks. It fails to indicate the sustaining nature and importance of the relationship between the worker and the client. Nor does it begin to suggest the support provided by an agency and its staff to the girl and her parents that made it possible for her to make sound decisions and choices.

We have attempted to illustrate in an oversimplified manner something of the nature of a casework approach that is time limited, problem focused, and organized on the basis of a specific task to be accomplished. The caseworker role in carrying out the tasks is more implied than explicated in the outline, and the way the client and the worker collaborate is not fleshed out. Caseworkers can be expected to use an array of interventive, often eclectic modes, including tangible sociological reinforcers—a place to live, provisions for income, medical care, hospitalization, and transportation.

## *Behavior Modification*

**Study.** In behavior modification, study, as one aspect of the casework process, is problem focused, and involves the observation of the behavior to be changed. Jacques had a behavior problem whose most objectionable aspects were hitting the other children, kicking various objects in the classroom, and swearing when the other children hit back, or when the teacher corrected him.

**Assessment.** The caseworker[9] didn't look for the underlying causes of Jacques' behavior, or try to get at the why's of it. Taking a "social history" was not the object of the caseworker's efforts. Much more important was the charting of Jacques' behavior to determine its frequency and severity. During the observation period, it was noticed that the attention and response of the teachers and his classmates maintained Jacques' behavior. The way they conveyed attention was reinforcing.

**Intervention.** The following brief statement by the caseworker describes her effort to change Jacques' behavior:

> The expression "pay no attention" is perhaps closest to what must be done to discourage the patient's behavior. When we say "do not reinforce a behavior" we are actually saying "ignore the behavior." That is what I did. Every time Jacques would say crude words, kick the blocks around or express any form of aggressive behavior, I would ignore that behavior. I felt social reinforcement would be very important in modifying Jacques' behavior. Children repeat behavior if it is rewarded and avoid behavior if it is punished or ignored.
>
> Continuous social reinforcement was given to Jacques for any approved activity that took the place of his aggressive behavior. For example, prior to treatment, Jacques would kick and throw the building blocks when asked to clean up his mess, and was reinforced by peers laughing when the teacher scolded him. After the treatment was started, I would ignore Jacques' aggressive behavior and socially reinforce the other children who were cleaning up their blocks by saying "Thank you, Bobby, for being such a good helper; your blocks look so straight and nice." Soon all the children were trying to get praise by putting away their blocks. After a while no one paid any attention to Jacques and he started participating in the cleanup. I would reinforce him verbally as I did the other children.
>
> By using behavior modification I was able to perform my therapy with a direct application of conditioning principles and techniques, which can be used to alter or remove specific undesirable, maladaptive, or abnormal behavior.

Behavior modification, as is true of other approaches discussed in this chapter, has been treated somewhat superficially. Anyone wanting to use the approaches now extant will want to avail him- or herself of detailed and excellent texts on the subjects.

In the case of Jacques one might observe that quality reinforcers will affect the increase or decrease of behaviors and the performance of other behaviors, that one or more of these would likely be used as reinforcers of behavior that was not disruptive, as soon as it occurred. Abused children sometimes ask for further abuse because this is the only attention they have been getting, and that they know. Also they may continue to accept abuse rather than tell on their parents for fear of being removed from their families. The case of Jacques is a good example of a beginning student's use of "inattention" that in this instance seemed to work.

## The Multisystems Approach

Several traditional methods and "approaches" of working with the individual have been identified. More recently a multisystems approach[10] has been mentioned in such fields as child welfare and mental health. As the name implies, this approach affirms the interrelationships of the individual to an interlocking network of systems each influencing the other.

Treatment using this approach takes into consideration the importance of the systems—the individual, family, school, neighborhood, welfare institutions—impacting and being impacted by each other. Treatment may and often does enlist the support of others for the purpose of bringing about desired change in the individual. A multisystems approach is not a method but an *approach* and will need study and research for refinement. This approach is a far cry from an era when the theoretical view was that only understanding intrapsychic dynamics by the therapist and client was needed to bring about a cure.

Social work methods and approaches need to be proven and validated. Fortunately, social work is developing an effective and sophisticated evaluation and research base for guiding practice.

## Summary

*Intrapsychic forces, the psychodynamics of behavior, interpersonal relations, and the impact of family, small groups, school, and the work place are identified with the practice of social work with individuals.*

*The roots of casework are deep and date back hundreds of years to society's efforts to help people with relationship problems. Casework has evolved. It is not a* road *but an* inn.

*Psychoanalysis and Freud have contributed theories of personality and intrapsychic determinants of behavior that radically brought about a shift of emphasis from outer to inner forces of behavior. Current practice combines both inner and outer forces (see Chapter 4).*

*The knowledge base of practice includes the scientific work of a wide variety of disciplines, social work's adaptations of this knowledge, and its own theoretical and scientific formulations and findings.*

*The processes of social casework embrace study, assessment, intervention, and termination. The application process is designed to aid the client in the discovery of what is dysfunctional and to lead to solutions of personal, family, and other problems.*

*Brief examples provide clues to the application of such theories of practice as the psychosocial theory, functional theory, problem-solving theory, behavior modification, and to a multisystems approach.*

## Selected References

DAVIS, LARRY, and ENOLA PROCTOR, *Race, Gender and Class: Guidelines for Practice with Individuals, Families, and Groups.* Englewood Cliffs, NJ: Prentice Hall, 1989.

DORFMAN, RACHELLE A., ed., *Paradigms of Clinical Social Work.* New York: Brunner/Mazel, 1988.

EWALT, PATRICIA, and NOREEN MOKUAU, "Self-Determination: A Pacific Perspective," *Social Work,* 40 (March 1995), 168–175.

FARLEY, O. WILLLAM, KENNETH A. GRIFFITHS, REX A. SKIDMORE, and MILTON G. THACKERAY, *Rural Social Work Practice.* New York: The Free Press, 1982.

GARVIN, CHARLES D., and BRETT A. SEABURY, *Interpersonal Practice in Social Work: Process and Procedures.* Englewood Cliffs, NJ: Prentice Hall, 1984.

GILBERT, NEIL, HENRY MILLER, and HARRY SPECHT, *An Introduction to Social Work Practice.* Englewood Cliffs, NJ: Prentice Hall, 1980.

HEPWORTH, DEAN H. and JOANN LARSEN, *Direct Social Work Practice: Theory and Skills.* Chicago: The Dorsey Press, 1986.

LANTZ, JAMES E., *An Introduction to Clinical Social Work Practice.* Springfield, IL: Charles C. Thomas, 1987.

MAAS, HENRY S., *People and Contexts: Social Development from Birth to Old Age.* Englewood Cliffs, NJ: Prentice Hall, 1984.

SATIR, VIRGINIA, *Conjoint Family Therapy.* Palo Alto, CA: Science and Behavior Books, 1983.

THOMAS, EDWIN J., *Designing Interventions for the Helping Professions.* Beverly Hills, CA: Sage Publications, 1984.

THYER, BRUCE A., ed., *Behavioral Family Therapy.* Springfield, IL: Charles C. Thomas, 1989.

ZASTROW, CHARLES, and KAREN K. KIRST-ASHMAN, *Understanding Human Behavior and the Social Environment,* 3rd ed. Chicago: Nelson-Hall, 1994.

## Notes

1. From "Home Burial," *The Poetry of Robert Frost,* p. 70, edited by Edward Connery Latham, Copyright 1930, 1939, 1969 by Holt, Rinehart and Winston. Copyright 1958 by Robert Frost. Copyright 1967 by Lesley Frost Ballantine. Reprinted by permission of Holt, Rinehart, and Winston, Publishers.

2. Ibid., p. 70.

3. Quoted from Memorial of Robert M. Hartley in Virginia P. Robinson, *Changing Psychology in Social Casework* (Chapel Hill: University of North Carolina Press, 1930), p. 4.

4. Robert L. Barker, *The Social Work Dictionary,* 3rd ed. (Washington, DC: NASW Press 1995), 351.

5. Proceedings of the National Conference on Charities and Corrections (Boston: George H. Ellis, 1886), p. 187.

6. Helen Perlman, "Social Casework," *Social Work Year Book,* 1960 (New York: National Association of Social Workers, 1960), p. 538.

7. William E. Gordon, "A Critique of the Working Definition," *Social Work,* 7 (October 1963), 6.

8. Robert W. Roberts and Robert H. Nee, eds., *Theories of Social Casework* (Chicago: University of Chicago Press, 1972), p. 365.

9. JoAnna Jones was a volunteer worker in a Head Start program. The material is adapted from an unpublished recording of her work.

10. Rocco A. Cimmarusti, "Family Preservation Practice Based upon a Multisystems Approach," *Child Welfare* (May–June 1992), 241–254.

Chapter *6*

# Social Work Practice with Groups

*Patients from the mental health center summarized their perception of the benefits of group therapy. Sue had learned to express her feelings. Anne, not unscathed, was glad that members honestly told her what they thought of her. Joe and Ed learned that ultimately they had to take responsibility for their own lives; that blaming others, or dependency on others for a sense of direction, ended in being "driven and tossed." The discovery that they shared "kooky" ideas with others, that their own diffidence and malaise was shared, was reassuring. Bill was especially helped to* *learn that he really was obnoxious to others, though he was pained by this disclosure. Having others accept the unacceptable in themselves helped them to be less self-critical. For Jim, having the leader respond with understanding when he was attacked by the group seemed to open the door for Jim to take a second look at his real enemies. Almost all members of the group benefited from the chance to handle anger, to experience the relief from saying what bothered them, and to learn that one does not always have to hold back to be accepted.*

Over the years social workers have understood the power of the group process in helping individuals improve their social functioning. The generalist practitioner can utilize group work methodology in many productive ways. One only has to observe the number of support groups prevalent in our society to see the importance of group dynamics and methodology.

People are gregarious, and the more they discover themselves, the more they discover the group and society. They do not live by themselves; they are not islands. Their welfare, in fact, their existence, is tied to the success or failure of other humans, and to an ever-growing number of group associations.

There was a time when people's interests were mainly self- and family-centered; the clan, the tribe, and then the nation, in succession, received the spotlight of concern. But today the world is the stage and people are the center of it. Their existence on this globe can be secured depending upon how well the lesson is learned that human beings are social and must learn to live in society regardless of ethnic origins, national ties and loyalties, or even personal preferences.

To his daughter, Thomas Jefferson wrote:

> I am convinced our own happiness requires that we should continue to mix with the world, and to keep pace with it as it goes; and that every person who retires from free communication with it is severely punished afterwards by the state of mind into which he gets, and which can only be prevented from feeding our sociable principles.... From 1793 to 1797 I remained closely at home, saw none but those who came there, and at length became very sensible of the ill effect it had upon my own mind, and of its direct and irresistible tendency to render me unfit for society and uneasy when necessarily engaged in it. I felt enough of the effect of withdrawing from the world then, to see that it led to an anti-social and misanthropic state of mind, which severely punishes him who gives into it; and it will be the lesson I shall never forget.[1]

Science has made the discovery that infants who are isolated from other human beings, however well cared for otherwise, succumb to inattention. Children find loneliness intolerable. Psychologists have observed that learning can actually be enhanced by association with others. A parent can tell whether his teenage son or daughter has been driving the family car—the radio begins to play the moment the key is turned on; for youth is impatient with solitude, and the human voice, albeit on radio, is a welcome intrusion.

It is a well-documented fact that many of the physical and mental illnesses of people are caused by social and emotional malaise and that social needs bring people to the office of marriage counselors and social workers.

People not only need to be loved, they need to know that they are wanted and understood. A patient, about to be discharged from a mental hospital, voiced anxiety about leaving because the hospital had become "my home" and she was not sure that the future she faced in the community would be friendly. In talking to the social worker, she was reassured as she remembered that, "Mrs. Jones will be my neighbor. I can talk to her and she will understand." Anne Frank wrote in her diary, "A person can be lonely even if he is loved by many people, because he is still not the 'One and Only' to anyone."[2]

A patient who was a registered nurse hospitalized in a mental hospital, when greeted perfunctorily, "How are you?" defended her delusion by falsely claiming that she had been *asked* to come to the hospital to head the nursing services—thus affirming self-importance and worth. The fear of being unloved and devalued exists in the mind of the psychotic along with yearning for intimacy and friendship. The behavior of delinquents, the handicapped, shut-ins, and many others may be marked by social dysfunctioning and failure.

Isolation may not be physical. One knows that one can be lonely in the midst of a crowd. Members of families, living under the same roof, sometimes become isolated one from another. No sense of loneliness is more painful than that which exists between friends and loved ones because they are unable to communicate. The poet, Matthew Arnold, captured this universal dilemma with the words:

> Alas, is even Love too weak
> To unlock the heart and let it speak?
> Are even lovers powerless to reveal
> To one another what indeed they feel?

I knew the mass of men conceal'd
Their thoughts, for fear that if reveal'd
They would by other men be met
With blank indifference, or with blame reproved:
I knew they lived and moved
Trick'd in disguises, alien to the rest
Of men, and alien to themselves—and yet
There beats one heart in every human breast.[3]

Human relations are blocked by many influences—physical disability, illness, racial prejudice and discrimination, religious intolerance, class superiority and preference, and others.

Human beings are strongly dependent on interactions with other humans. Almost everything that is done in life is done in the context of groups and group interaction. Social work practice with groups builds on the important impact of groups on individuals and utilizes group processes to accomplish individual and group goals, as Toseland and Rivas state:

> . . . as we prepare to become effective social work practitioners, it is important for us to realize the impact that groups have on our lives. It is not possible to be a member of society without becoming a member of numerous groups and becoming familiar with others. Although it is possible to live in an isolated manner on the fringes of groups, our social nature makes this neither desirable nor healthy.
>
> Groups provide the structure on which communities and the larger society are built. They provide both formal and informal structure in the workplace. But more important, they provide a means through which relationships with significant others are carried out. Participation in family groups, peer groups, and classroom groups helps members to learn acceptable norms of social behavior, to engage in satisfying social relationships, to identify personal goals, and to derive a variety of other benefits that result from participating in closely knit social systems. Experiences with social groups, church groups, scouting, sports teams, and work groups are also important in the development and maintenance of people and society.[4]

## Historical Developments

Group work began as a form of *social service* with various kinds of activities under the auspices of the church. In the 1855–65 decade, the YMCA and YWCA were organized and became formalized, independent associations that provided group programs, activities, and opportunities.

During the latter part of the nineteenth century the settlement movement developed. The Industrial Revolution had brought considerable social disorganization and the breakdown of the primary group in many situations. Dedicated leaders believed that social improvement could be accomplished by having members of the more fortunate classes live or visit among and with the underprivileged groups, sharing their ideas and ways of life. Certain philanthropists donated money as well as time to help sponsor settlement houses in the underprivileged districts, especially in the large cities.

Toynbee Hall was established in London in 1884 in an attempt to help, with a group program, the underprivileged in that huge, milling city. The Neighborhood Guild was established in 1886 in the United States and was the first settlement house in this country. Jane Addams's Hull House, begun in Chicago in 1889, and other settlement houses were not long in developing and have become part of the American tradition. The basic aim of these settlement houses was to provide a place for the underprivileged to go and, through the two-way process of association and interaction, to develop their personalities and enrich their living.

Many group work agencies have developed in the twentieth century, including the Boy Scouts, the Girl Scouts, Camp Fire Girls, 4H Clubs, and others. Each one of these originated and has acquired many members through its stress on one particular group and activity. Today there are millions of boys and girls, youths, and adults who belong to organizations that operate on a group interactional basis.

In 1935 a group work section of the National Conference on Social Work was established to give additional emphasis and focus to this rapidly developing movement. In 1936 the National Association for the Study of Group Work was organized, with a representative coordinating committee of about 100 from all sections of the United States and an executive committee of 10. The association was established to further the interest of group work practice and to help in recruiting and getting more people professionally trained. In 1939 its name was changed to the American Association for the Study of Group Work.

In 1955 several different professional associations of social workers joined together to create a single professional organization, the National Association of Social Workers. The American Association of Group Workers, formed in 1946 as the successor to the American Association for the Study of Group Work, joined with the new organization, declaring itself an integral part of the new, unified social work professional organization.

In addition to the developments in areas of service, there have been several significant developments in regard to training of people interested in social work practice with groups. Apparently it was in the United States that the first major emphasis on training in group work was established. The first systematized class in a school of social work was offered in the School of Applied Social Sciences of Western Reserve University in the 1920s.

By the early 1930s the words *social group work* were used to distinguish it from social casework, the other main social work practice method. The National Conference of Social Work in 1935 included group work as a division at its annual program meeting, and several people joined together in sharing their thinking about this relatively new development. In 1939 a committee concerned with professional education began a study of the courses in group work offered by the schools of social work on both graduate and undergraduate levels. As a result of this study, an official statement, "Professional Education for Group Work Practice," was accepted by the American Association of Group Workers in 1947.

During the 1940s the American Association of Schools of Social Work encouraged and recommended the inclusion of group work courses in the graduate curriculum of its member schools, of which less than half offered a sequence in group work. Today all schools of social work offer one or more classes or curriculum units in working with groups, and several of them offer a basic sequence or concentration including class, field instruction, and related experiences in the group method. To illustrate, in 1962 there were 448 students enrolled in group work sequences in the schools of social work in the United States and Canada. Of the 30,145 master's degree students enrolled in training in 1994, nearly 67 percent were listed in "direct practice" or "generic"—both of which include group work methodology and skills as part of their expertise.

## *Group Work Defined*

Group work is a method of working with people in groups (two or more people) for the enhancement of social functioning and for the achievement of socially desirable goals. Group work is based on the knowledge of people's needs for each other and their interdependence. Group work is a method of reducing or eliminating roadblocks to social interaction and for accomplishing socially desirable purposes. Helen Northern gives the following definition of group work:

> Within the general purpose of the profession, social work with small groups may be directed toward helping the members to use the group for coping with and resolving existing problems in psychosocial functioning, toward preventing antic-

Social worker in fieldwork with children.

ipated problems or maintaining a current level of functioning in situations in which there is danger of deterioration. Further, it may be directed toward developing more effective patterns of group and organizational functioning and removing environmental obstacles.

With any group, the specific outcomes sought vary with the desires, needs, capacities, and situations of the members who comprise the group and with the purpose and nature of the group itself. . . .[5]

Konopka explains that "group work is an approach consciously directed toward developing the individual's greatest capacity while relating him to the group and learning when he has to contribute and when he has to withdraw."[6]

Toseland and Rivas define group work as follows:

Goal-directed activity with small groups of people aimed at meeting socioemotional needs and accomplishing tasks. This activity is directed to individual members of a group and to the group as a whole within a system of service delivery.[7]

Toseland and Rivas suggest their definition is broad and functional in that it allows for both generic and specialized group work practice:

This definition describes group work as goal-directed activity, which refers to planned, orderly, worker activities carried out in the context of professional practice with people. Goal-directed activity has many purposes. For example, group workers may aim to rehabilitate members, to educate them, to help them socialize, or to help them grow. Workers may also help members of a group develop leadership skills so that they can take increasing responsibility for the group's development. At the same time, workers should enable their groups to change the social environment. This includes helping members gain greater control over the organizational and environmental systems that affect their lives.[8]

Almost all social service agencies use group work. Group work is being utilized in fields of practice areas such as creating cohesion in new step families[9] and bereavement groups for inner-city children,[10] and with parenting groups for recovering addicts.[11] Zastrow reports that:

Every social service agency uses groups, and every practicing social worker is involved in a variety of groups. Social work with groups is practiced in adoption agencies, correctional settings, halfway houses, substance abuse treatment centers, physical rehabilitation centers, family service agencies, private psychotherapy clinics, mental hospitals, nursing homes, community centers, public schools, and many other social service settings. To effectively serve clients in human service systems today, social workers in generalist practice positions must be trained in group methods. Often, social workers serve as leaders and participants in myriad groups requiring skills ranging from the simple to the complex. The beginning social worker is likely to be surprised at the diverse groups in existence and excited by the challenge of practicing social work in such settings.[12]

The social group worker uses his or her knowledge of group organization and functioning to affect the performance and adjustment of the individual. The individual remains the focus of concern, and the group the vehicle of growth and change. Enhancement of social functioning through the use of the group is the primary aim of group work. Programs and facilities are used as dynamics of interaction and change. Because of the importance of the individual in all group work, the worker equips him- or herself with the knowledge of the individual. Glasser and Mayadas believe that group work will continue to grow. They state:

> The stream of practice developed around use of groups for treatment purposes will continue to grow, for the individual casualties of a fast-paced, changing society are heavy and the group treatment milieu has great utility. . . .[13]

Barker has summarized several theoretical paradigms of social group work in the definition he included in the 1995 *Social Work Dictionary.* He states that social group work is:

> An orientation and method of social work *intervention* in which small numbers of people who share similar interests or common problems convene regularly and engage in activities designed to achieve certain objectives. In contrast to *group psychotherapy,* the goals of group work are not necessarily the treatment of emotional problems. The objectives also include exchanging information, developing social and manual skills. changing value orientations, and diverting antisocial behaviors into productive channels. Intervention techniques include but are not limited to controlled therapeutic discussions. Some groups also include education and tutoring; sports; arts and crafts; recreational activities; and discussions about such topics as politics, religion, sexuality, values, and goals. Whereas social group work draws on the theoretical perspectives of *existential theory, learning theory, psychoanalytic theory,* and *social exchange theory,* its major theoretical perspective is *social systems theory* to describe group functioning. This orientation provides workers with a way to conceptualize about the effect of group dynamics and interrelationships outside the group.[14]

## Group Work Models

Humans are richly endowed with the potential for high achievement. Group work is a method and a process developed to assist people to improve the quality of their lives and to maximize their potentials. Applied skillfully, with imagination and intelligence by a competent, caring person, the group method can assist the group: (1) in achieving mutually determined goals, (2) in achieving desirable change for individuals experiencing personal, family, occupational, and adjustment problems, (3) in developing self-enhancement and individual enrichment, and (4) by using a combination of treatment, self-enhancement, and personal fulfillment.

Social work group work is especially relevant for many individuals who find themselves disempowered by our society. Gitterman and Shulman state:

Social workers in practice today deal with profoundly vulnerable and disempowered populations. People with such life conditions and circumstances as AIDS, homelessness, sexual abuse, and community and family violence are overwhelmed by oppressive lives, circumstances, and events they are powerless to control. Their problems often appear intractable because they are chronic and persistent, or acute and unexpected. They become overwhelmed by their overwhelming problems. When they lack community and family supports, they are often at risk of physical, psychological, and social deterioration. Moreover, when as well as lacking social resources, their internal resources are impaired, they become extremely vulnerable to social and emotional isolation. The group modality offers a powerful counterforce, a potential to empower vulnerable populations. A group mutual support system has the inherent potential to help members acquire a sense of greater personal, interpersonal, and environmental control over their lives.[15]

Group goals and objectives, or purposes, will determine the group work model employed. Three such models have been pioneered by Papell and Rothman: (1) the social goals model, (2) the remedial goals model, and (3) the reciprocal goals model.[16]

## Social Goals Model

Groups serving the social goals model are formed, and continue, because of socially determined interests, which, if attained, bring about important social gains for the group. This model is closely identified with the group interest and effort. It is likely to address itself to problems within communities, and is practiced in settlement houses, P.T.A. organizations, and community service and neighborhood councils. More recently this model has been used in addressing social problems accompanying community development and growth. Principles guiding practice involving the social goals model include:

> ...Clarification of agency policy, positive use of limitations, identification with agency goals, determination of appropriate issues for collective action, and the weighing of alternatives for action and their consequences.
> ...The principles of democratic group process that are fundamental to this model have become the hallmark of all social group work practice. Every practitioner, regardless of his theoretical loyalty, tends to work toward the adoption and institutionalization of democratic procedures in small groups.[17]

## The Remedial Model

The remedial model, a model of treatment, tends to be clinically oriented. The group is used as an agent of change. The group worker facilitates the interaction among members of the group to achieve change for the individual. He or she applies knowledge and skill in helping individuals gain self-awareness and improve social functioning. The group supports the member, encouraging new, more appropriate modes of functioning. Intervention is reality focused and addresses the problem of dysfunction in the group and within the full range of the individual's relationships. The treatment group is widely used in mental hospitals, correctional institutions, family service organizations, counseling services, schools, health care facilities, and in many other agencies.

## Example 1

Group process was initiated to improve a disturbed child-parent relationship. A mother noticed that her boy took greater interest in his schoolwork and was more responsive to the family after he became a member of a Boy Scout troop. What she did not fully realize was that her attitude about her son had changed as a result of *her* membership in a group, and that this was an important dynamic of improvement in her son's behavior. She recalled her tears of joy at a court of honor, when she said, "It is wonderful to have my boy do something good for once, rather than something for which he is always getting into trouble." The change in him was brought about because of his activity in the troop and because, for the first time, he had his mother's approval and acceptance.

## Example 2

A group of overweight adults wanted to lose weight. The approach that proved effective in bringing lasting results for most members consisted of medical information, diet, exercise, a system of rewards and punishments, greater self-awareness, and the support from the group. Similar results were obtained by a treatment approach with cardiac patients in adhering to a salt-free diet, exercise, rest, and in accepting the medical regimen. The group provided the means for diagnosing emotional problems related to physical difficulties, which were then approached by the group and individuals.

## *The Reciprocal Model*

The reciprocal model serves both the individual and society. It sees the individual largely as an abstraction that can be studied, understood, and treated only in relation to the many systems and subsystems of which he or she is a part. It views the individual as being created, influenced, and modified by his or her relationships, social institutions, and the interdependency between society and the individual. Papell and Rothman have written:

> The reciprocal model presupposes an organic, systemic relationship between the individual and society. . . This interdependence is the "focus" for social work and the small group is the field in which individual and societal functioning can be nourished and mediated. . . .
>
> Unlike the remedial model, the reciprocal model does not begin with a priori prescriptions of desired outcomes. However, it does conceive of an ideal group state, namely a system in mutual aid. Such a system is not dependent upon the specific problem to be resolved by the group but is a necessary condition for problem solving. To state it in still another way, the reciprocal model has no therapeutic ends, no political or social change programs to which it is addressed. It is only

from the encounter of individuals that compose a reciprocal group system that direction or problem is determined. Emphasis is placed on *engagement* in the process of interpersonal relations. It is from this state of involvement that members may call upon each other in their own or common cause.

The reciprocal model views the individual primarily in terms of his motivation and capacity for reciprocity....Diagnostic considerations or structural descriptions of the individual are not regarded as significant predictors of behavior in the group. Therefore they do not serve as a basis for selection of members for a group or assessment by the worker.

The image of the worker projected by this model is that of a mediator or enabler to the needs system converging in the group. The worker is viewed as a part of the worker-client system both influencing and being influenced by it. In the terminology of social work, he neither does *to* the client nor *for* him, but *with* him."[18]

Theoretical sources of this model come from systems theory, field theory, social psychological theories of behavior, and the practice principles that are a part of generic methodology for social work.

In the example to follow, the group had no preconceived purpose. The outcome of the association was not a major concern. Their emphasis was on engagement. The leader would influence the group behavior and be influenced by it.

---

Organized in a YWCA, the "Young Mothers" learned that it was good mental health to bring their children to a well-staffed nursery to be cared for while they joined others in a morning swim, an hour of "slimnastics," a few hands of bridge, an arts and crafts program, in a discussion of foods, fashions, child-rearing, or in talking to those who had similar worries, concerns, and problems with their young families.

Their program usually included refreshment or lunch arranged by their committee. Young Mothers provided an outlet for social contacts and relieved the stress and strain of caring for the children.

One mother who was receiving Aid to Families with Dependent Children (AFDC) was helped to make an adjustment to divorce. The group assisted her to find new purposes in life, to accept and enjoy her children rather than to see them as a burden. Before joining the group she thought there was nothing to look forward to but dirty dishes, soiled diapers, and runny noses. By talking to others who were also going through periods of adjustment she drew strength from them, and at the same time contributed her talents to the group.

---

A group of seven- and eight-year-old boys, formed for an engagement group, became a socialization tool under the leadership of a group worker.

---

The group was reconvening in the group room from an out-of-doors activity. Calvin pushed Stephen as they entered. Stephen retaliated and a brief fistfight ensued. The group worker separated the boys and stated that it was hard to wait for a turn through the door. Calvin did not say anything, but Stephen said, "It was all his fault. He pushed me first." Calvin looked at the floor, and Stephen added that he didn't like Calvin. The worker indicated that sometimes when we get in fights we really don't like the person at that particular time. Calvin looked up and caught Stephen's glance and then looked back down again.

The group worker asked, "What do we do when we have problems, or fights, or disagreements with one another?" The entire group got involved and offered ideas and suggestions about what happens in the process of fighting. Their focus was on resolving the immediate conflict. The group worker continued to discuss what happens when people fight and how difficult it often is for people to say, "I'm sorry," or "I didn't mean to do that."

Both boys were looking up and the worker asked Calvin how he was feeling. He said he had been really mad at Stephen, but it wasn't that important, and he wished he could learn how to prevent fights from happening. (This was one of his problems, and he had discussed it before.) The group talked about ways in which they could handle their enthusiasm and energy and have positive experiences and ways in which they could handle their feelings when a fight did occur. The worker asked for suggestions about how to make up, and the group members wanted Stephen and Calvin to shake hands immediately. The boys thought about it, jumped up, and shook hands.

Without a therapeutic goal or program for social change a group of adolescents was helped to evolve a method of mutual aid.

The girls came to the group individually. Everyone that day was very quiet and nonresponsive. The group worker tried a number of ways to get them to share their thoughts. No one wanted to say anything. The worker asked if something had happened outside the group. No one responded. She asked if there were problems about which anyone wanted to talk. No one spoke. When she commented that it was going to be a very quiet session a few girls nodded. After approximately five minutes of silence, the worker stretched out on the floor and said, "Some days it helps if you can just relax. Anybody wanting to relax on the floor may do so." One by one the girls relaxed on the rug, and gradually began to talk about some of their feelings and the problems they were having with schoolwork, pressure from parents and teachers, and general nonachievement. At the end of the period the girls were responding with greater effect and understanding.

## Formation of Groups

Groups come into being in a variety of ways. The existence of a social problem or need will often result in groups forming almost spontaneously to solve the problem. Social workers in treatment centers organize groups from their case loads and from the clientele of the agency. Lonely people who want friendship, those on weight-watching diets, and parents troubled by the behavior of their children actively seek group membership.

Regardless of the reason for a group forming or the mechanics of bringing people together, the agency, group member, and worker goals are at the heart of the process.

## Agency Goals

Agency goals, having to do with social consciousness and public concern for social welfare, are likely to reflect community interest. Usually they are related to identified needs, are likely to be fairly general, and often are given public utterance at the time the agency or new service mode comes into existence. The goals of agencies should be systematically reviewed for relevance, especially in times of rapid social change.

## Group Goals

Group purposes are often general in nature. However, they must be explicated for individual group members. Group purposes will ordinarily incorporate (1) the agency's purpose, (2) the goals of the group members, and (3) the goals and objectives of the group worker. In addition to being realistic and clearly definable they must be within the reality of attainment. They should be transferable to other social situations in which group members would be expected to function.

## Member Goals

Member goals are defined as those wishes and desires of each member that motivated the attainment of group member status. These are not to be confused with worker goals, and a distinction between the two is necessary.

The group worker in an agency should be aware that members join groups in order to achieve goals that may be secondary to the purpose for which the agency was established. An example: a member may join a group because he or she wants to participate in "fun" activities or test his or her reasoning ability with others of similar age and circumstances. The attainment of social skills and acceptance of differences in others, which are group purposes, become important to the individual only as he or she finds fulfillment of personal needs and is influenced by the group and the worker to consider meaningful reasons for participation.

The group is enhanced considerably when members and workers share compatible goals aimed toward the members' resolution of personal difficulties, the attainment of problem-solving skills, or personal improvement. This mutual agreement is often referred to as a "contract," and it identifies goals and purposes as well as methods to achieve objectives. The group worker commits him- or herself to responsibility for the group process, and members commit themselves to an investment in goal achievement.

## Worker Goals

The group worker goals include the plans, methods, means, and programming developed and used to help members accomplish their goals and purposes. Unless the worker is clear about group purposes and member goals, he or she will be ineffectual and unable to validate group success. Only when goals and purposes are clearly explicated, understood, and accepted can the process of attainment be actualized. The group worker is responsible for the organization, the treatment process, and termination. He or she must be engaged in a continual process of self-evaluation and understanding to avoid "hang-ups" that would mil-

**TABLE 6.1   Group and Worker Goals**

| Group Goals | Worker Goals |
|---|---|
| Improve self-image. | Provide opportunities for successful experiences in sports, arts, crafts, or discussions. |
| Expand self-awareness and understanding. | Provide leadership experiences. |
| Achieve a group status. | Encourage expressions and opinions related to self with opportunities for analysis for each individual and other group members. |
|  | Encourage looking at behavior and feelings and coming to terms with weaknesses and strengths. |
|  | Develop research proposals to evaluate the program. |
| Improve peer relationships. | Offer experiences in sharing, give-and-take considerations of others. |
| Accept peers as individuals. | Provide social experiences at appropriate levels. |
| Develop friendship-building skills. | Encourage practicing of skills. Reinforce goal attainment, tangibly and with praise when appropriate. |
|  | Provide role model identification and opportunities for discussion of friendship roles, expectations, rewards, satisfactions, and responsibilities. |

itate against group process. Clarity of purpose, goal formulations, and purpose are essential in group process.

The examples in Tables 6.1 and 6.2 illustrate group, member, and individual goal explication for a treatment group of 13-year-old boys.[19]

**TABLE 6.2   Worker and Member Goals**

| Worker Goals | Member Goals |
|---|---|
| Discuss the expectations of appropriate behavior. | Bobby wants to be accepted as a member of the group without scapegoating; wants to be liked by both boys and girls. |
| Provide support and reinforce other member's support of him. | |
| Supply casework as necessary to maintain him in the group until he can function more appropriately on his own. | |
| Determine with help of speech therapist speech limitations. | Joe wants to learn how to express himself without stuttering. |
| Provide support. | Wants to belong and feel more at ease in a group. |
| Recognize feelings of difficulty and achievement. | Wants to find out who he is and where he fits in. |
| Plan activities and short discussions around Joe's interest and previous experience. | Wants friends. |
| Help him present an activity to the group providing individual help with preparation as necessary. | |
| Verbalize understanding of his feelings and difficulties. | Ben wants to eliminate his "scapegoat" and "playboy" image. |
| Call his attention to reactions of the group. | Wants to improve his vocabulary and eliminate crude and rude remarks. |
| Place limits on offensive behavior. | |

*continued*

**TABLE 6.2**    *Continued*

| Worker Goals | Member Goals |
|---|---|
| Program for areas of his interest and strengths, such as swimming and hiking. | Wants to settle down to accomplish important activities and tasks. |
| Support his abilities. | |
| Discuss his lessened need to act as a playboy. | |
| Increase attractiveness of group by programming activities of interest. | Willey wants acceptance for his identification as a nonconformist. |
| Allow discussion of present group. | Would like to expand his friendship to include others outside his gang. |
| Bring members of his gang if the group can tolerate them. | Would like to bring members of his gang to group meetings. |
| Increase skills in areas other than current interest. | |
| Avoid criticism of dress, but encourage discussion thereof. | Wants to identify with good workers. |

## Selection of Group Members

How are individuals selected for groups? There has been much written on this subject, some controversial material, and some that has been generally accepted. Common threads run through the writings, and in essence the following are a few of the factors and principles that guide group selection.

**1.** *Age.* Chronological age seems to be less important in the early age group than the maturity of the individual. However, in adolescence, where age enjoys greater status and additional freedom privileges, it may be extremely important to strive for homogeneity of age in the group. With young adults and adult groups age seems much less important than other social or economic factors.

**2.** *Value System.* Some differences in value system can be tolerated and stimulate discussion in interaction. If the differences are too great, however, they may present problems. A group with more or less common values can work together, whereas a group with extremely diverse values can be expected to run into difficulty and to lose cohesion because of the differences. For example, in a group of girls who had been placed together to assist each other with an adjustment problem, some very destructive things occurred because the girls were physically attacking each other across a different value system.

**3.** *Common Problems.* Sometimes children who have common problems are grouped together. Children carry over from family groups to other groups their home relationship patterns, which have previously met their needs. A child who has been allowed great freedom in the home in the overt expression of hostile feelings may present a real difficulty to the youngster who has been considerably curtailed in the expression of his feelings.

**4.** *Enjoyment Patterns.* Common interest, while not always of the greatest importance, can help to bring about groupness among individuals. Groups find a common interest in activity. The base of interest can always be broadened and used to assist in better social adjustment in peer groups and in proper male and female identification.

**5.** *Intelligence.* Intellectual differences do not appear to be of prime importance, but where the extreme is great, difficulty may be encountered unless this factor is considered.

**6.** *Tolerance of Structure.* Sometimes groups do not congeal simply because the members of the group are unable to accept the structure or the leader. Treatment does not take place when clients are not interacting or relating to one another. There is nothing very therapeutic about listening to the "gastric rumbles of the other members of the group." In other words an important part of skill is to foster therapeutic relationships that will result in integration.

**7.** *Sex.* The sex of the members is less important in younger age groups. However, coeducational groups have been quite successful in working with certain problems of adolescence. Adolescents and adults have been most successful when some work is done separately with each sex group and then the groups are brought together to integrate what has been considered separately. Marriage counselors, social workers in schools, and those who work with parent groups and alcoholics, have recognized in single sex groups a greater freedom for intimacy in the discussion and greater support and encouragement around expression of common problems.

**8.** *Ego Strengths.* There is almost unanimous agreement that group members must have sufficient ego strengths to stand exposure, since group reactions cannot be controlled in the same way individual work is controlled.

Other variables might be considered but those touched upon briefly here seem to be of the greatest importance and are more or less recognized by most workers in the field.

## *Preparation of Group Members*

Principles to be applied to the preparation of members are directly related to (1) the purposes for which the group is established, (2) the goals of the members and the workers, (3) the reason for the agency's existence, and (4) the knowledge, skill, and individual preferences of the worker.

The worker will usually become acquainted with the members of the group in individual interviews. This may be a shared experience with the member and the worker learning about each other. Special knowledge, interest, skill, experience, and caring for the members are the worker's main contributions to the group.

In preparatory sessions, a working relationship will be achieved among the members and between them and the group worker. The group will define its purpose and continue the diagnostic and goal-setting process. Preparation will also be facilitated by the use of information prepared by the group leader with important input from group members.

Some groups will not predetermine their objective except in a tentative way. In their views of the ever-emerging quality of the human condition, they see the group as an experience in becoming. For groups who feel the excitement of anticipation, "the road is better than the inn." They exist to explore and to discover their potentials. Preparation includes setting the stage and creating a climate for discovery within the framework of democratic values and agency goals.

## Structuring the Group

Structuring aspects of the group process include: the setting, group size, rules and norms, open or closed groups, time limits, meeting days and times, male, female, or mixed groups, leadership, and the first meeting.

### The Setting

The setting is related to purpose. For children with limited self-control, activities in a gymnasium or on a playground do not provide essential boundaries for group programming. Lounges may not be conducive to activity groups. However, in some agencies one may have to learn to do with less and to help the members work within the available areas. Furnishings should not be so comfortable or formal as to detract from a "working" atmosphere. Privacy should be provided; the group should not disturb others. The use of a table may represent a psychological barrier to interaction for some groups, but for groups serving refreshments, a table may be helpful.

### Group Size

Seven to nine is thought to be an optimal number for adult treatment groups. A day camp for emotionally disturbed or socially inadequate children requires a small group. A group of ten or more may be difficult to manage where the focus is on recreation. It is important to keep the group small enough to maintain optimal member-worker relationships. Awareness of what is going on is enhanced when the group is small, and limited as it becomes larger. The recommended size for educational groups is larger and varied according to purpose. These groups may be as small as twelve or as large as thirty.

### Group Rules

A group that makes its own rules is more likely to abide by them and to apply sanctions as needed to enforce them. Individual beliefs and values should be considered in relation to group rules. Religious days, respected by some members of the group even though meaningless to others, need to be considered. Rules should not apply sanctions to norms of behavior peculiar to an individual member. Rules should be few in number and include only those deemed essential to achieve the purposes of the group. If they are appropriately chosen and enforced, they lead to the establishment of group norms. Capricious rules and those that make no sense will have little support from the group.

Some members may attempt to impose inappropriate rules on the group. The worker will need to remain active to avoid situations where coercion is attempted to meet the power needs of individuals at the expense of group cohesiveness.

### Open or Closed Groups

Designations of "open" and "closed" pertain to the timing of admission to the group. Open systems take new members at any time during the group's existence. Closed groups include only those members selected at the group's formation. In closed groups, a modus operandi is set up at the beginning. Group purpose, individual goals, and group norms tend to be established early. Open groups are like a slice of life—birth, separation, marriage, and death. Open systems tend to simulate reality and provide transferability to real life situations. Decisions related to this area are determined by the purpose and goals of the group.

## Short-Term or Long-Term Groups

Adults and mature adolescents usually can accept a time limit on the number of meetings to accomplish their goals. Youngsters who have experienced repeated rejections may see time limits negatively and try to negotiate for more sessions rather than invest themselves in the area of goal attainment.

## Meeting Days and Time

The day and time of meetings will be adapted to the needs and wishes of the members as part of initial planning. It is unrealistic to expect members radically to alter their patterns of living to participate in the group. Consideration should be given to distances, travel expenses, and the need for babysitters. For the mentally retarded and very young children, arrangements may need to be made for transportation.

Groups usually meet weekly for one or two hours. Groups living in institutions may meet more frequently, "Marathon" groups may literally continue around the clock for days. Nothing is magical about "once-a-week," and experimentation is encouraged. One meaningful encounter can have lasting influence and be the dynamic for a succession of changes.

Flexibility of time and meeting days as well as duration of the group seem warranted. As goals are achieved, as members successfully transfer learning from structured group meetings to practical everyday experiences, meetings can be tapered off.

## Male, Female, or Mixed Groups

Many young children, older adolescents, and adults may be members of male-female groups. They can be expected to work cooperatively toward the attainment of their goals. Older children and younger adolescents often prefer all-male or all-female groups, especially when they are working toward the acquisition of skills or tasks related to the male or female image. The group worker should be aware of the meaning that membership in the single sex or a mixed group has for the individual members. Will these feelings contribute to the attainment of goals and objectives?

## Leadership

Many group workers advocate the development of leadership ability in all group members. Most do not recommend a system of elected leaders at the beginning of the group's origin, for they are often chosen more for their initial display of power than for leadership ability. Some workers advocate a revolving leadership system, particularly in activity groups with children and adults.

Group workers continually must assess the leadership development of their group as well as the members' ability to share leadership functions and participate as both leaders and followers.

## The First Meeting

In the first meeting the group worker sets the stage for meetings to follow. It is, therefore, essential that the group worker takes time to identify the purposes of the group. He or she should clearly commit oneself to those actions and procedures the worker considers to be the group worker's role. The members need to know what they can expect the group worker to do, and to be, during the group experience and to reiterate their commitments.

## Programming for Goal Attainment

The use of resources should be geared to objectives and goals. If plans include discussion on health, or problems of children, a health nurse may be invited. If dealing with obesity, someone who has solved a weight problem may be helpful. The group worker will have knowledge about resources in programming a particular activity. The worker should be concerned with the following: (1) the components of the activity to be emphasized, (2) the competence of the group to handle the program, (3) the needs of the group, (4) the developmental stage of the group (groping, griping, grasping, and grouping), (5) the physical, social, emotional, and intellectual development of group members, (6) the rewards and threats involved in participation, and (7) the overall effect on group and member goal attainment.

Programming is the means of goal attainment. It includes games, crafts, discussions, tours and field trips, and all activities the group engages in during their group sessions. Appropriately developed, the program will stimulate and free individuals to behave and release their feelings in acceptable ways.

In discussion groups, themes reoccur. Adolescents frequently discuss unfair parents, bad teachers, drug use, poor peer relationships, body image, sexual development, and boy-girl relationships. Minority groups may discuss poverty, dislike for middle- and upper-class people, hunger and disease, and the futility of their present existence. Married couples often discuss their parents' unresponsiveness, undependability of mates, or lack of good parent-child relationships. The group worker needs to be aware that these themes are representative of many basic questions. His or her knowledge is essential to the facilitating of the activity of the group.

## Recording, Evaluation, and Termination

Individual and group files should be maintained. Records are a valuable tool for the group leader when used as an assessment tool and for purposes of accountability. The records are confidential.

Process recording is an effective teaching tool but a costly one. Summary types of recording are generally recommended and serve adequately to keep the experienced worker current on developments. Audio and video taping can be used by the worker to evaluate activities of the group, and to help members observe the way they handle situations in developing social and group skills.

Evaluation is an important and continuing part of group meetings. Members participate in reviews of sessions as well as goals and objectives for both the group and individuals. Evaluation begins with the formation of the group and does not end until the group is terminated. Just as emphasis in the beginning sessions will be on identification of problems and defining of goals, evaluation tends to be emphasized toward the end of the activity. It needs to take into consideration the gains made by members of the group and their readiness to function with greater independence within various life situations. The effectiveness of the group participation should not be determined only at the end of the group's existence, but should continue in each of the sessions.

Preparation for termination should begin with the first session. Time is a dynamic. Members knowing that only so many weeks are provided for the achievement of their goals tend to focus on those goals and make the maximum use of their time. Members need to find ways within the group to function effectively when they can no longer get help from the group. A group member or the leader may be available for support after termination, but members need to be prepared to function without the help of the group.

## Group Work Settings

### Traditional Settings

The YMCA and YWCA are examples of agencies that focus on the use of group process in helping youth. The YMCA had 2,000 units in the United States in 1992, with a registered membership of 12.8 million who utilized various programs and facilities. In 1992 the YWCA had over 400 associations, which delivered services in 4,000 locations and served some 2,000,000 women.

Groups in the YWCA are guided by the goals set at the 1979 national convention in Dallas, Texas. These goals indicated that in the 1980s programs would be developed by the National Board and member YWCAs to "assist women in transition and/or crisis, emphasizing services to displaced homemakers, battered women and their children, rape victims, women questioning their sexual identity, teen and adult women in trouble with the law, victims of crime, the wife in a mobile family, grieving women, to support the family unit and to help solve some of the problems that cause families to separate, and to assist the needs and concerns of handicapped women."

Again, residential accommodations are provided for women and girls in crisis situations as well as for those who need temporary living facilities.

Mildred came from a home broken by divorce. She felt alone in the world and left a small village to take a job in the "big city." She fortunately arranged to stay at the YWCA. There she mingled with other girls in their teens, some of whom had similar problems. She became an active member in one of the girls clubs sponsored by the "Y." This club, although organized primarily for recreational activities, planned and accomplished many other worthwhile things. Once a week it had meetings of intellectual and spiritual interests. Guest speakers were invited and there was a social worker who assisted in organizing and supporting the club and its activities. After several lecturers had been asked to make presentations, one evening the members informally decided to have some group discussions limited entirely to themselves and their social worker to discuss some of their own problems and questions about life.

These group sessions were most interesting and effective. Mildred shared with the other girls some of the emotional hurts that she had experienced. She discovered that other girls had problems and psychological scars also. As they shared these experiences, and particularly feelings regarding them, many of the emotional hurts were lessened, and Mildred, in particular, changed from a frightened, uncertain girl, bewildered by the perplexities of life and social interaction, to a girl who felt more comfortable in her daily living and more secure in her associations with others. Frank, informal discussions, on an intimate group basis, had unlocked some of the fears, uncertainties, and anxieties that had welled up within her. The group process had opened the door to a new outlook and perspective on life and to new patterns of behavior.

Another well-known organization that utilizes group workers is the Girl Scouts of the United States of America. This organization, established in 1912, had a membership in 1991 of 2,561,000 girls and 822,000 adults, some of whom are professionally trained social workers. Membership is open with no restrictions regarding race, creed, or color to girls aged 5 through 17 and to adults over 18. The purpose of the organization is to "inspire girls with the highest ideals of character, conduct, patriotism, and service that they may become happy and resourceful citizens." This program provides group activities for girls, planned democratically and carried out in accordance with a code of ethics embodied in the Girl Scout Promise and Law. It offers a variety of kinds of practical training opportunities for service to others in such fields as agriculture, arts, crafts, community life, health and safety, homemaking, international friendship, literature and dramatics, music, dancing, nature, out-of-doors, sports, and camping.

Mary, a girl of twelve, was not only shy, but did not have the ability to share with others. Through encouragement and support of her parents she joined the Girl Scouts. Gradually, through the various camping and social activities of this organization, she began to think more of others, to share her ideas and personality with friends. With the support and understanding of a group worker, she developed her personality in many ways, gaining confidence and an improved self-image. After two years' association with the Girl Scout group, she was elected, by vote, as one of the leaders. People who knew her before and after her membership in this organization could hardly believe the changes that had taken place. Group association, with understanding, interested leadership, had offered encouragement and opportunity for her to alter her personality and her ability, in particular, to associate effectively with other girls of her own age—to give as well as to receive.

Numerous other youth organizations also provide group work activities, including Boys' Clubs of America, Girls' Clubs of America, Camp Fire Girls, The Catholic Youth Organizations, Jewish Community Centers, and Young Men's and Young Women's Hebrew Associations (YMHAs and YWHAS). These agencies, and others, offer various recreational, health, and welfare opportunities, many of which are related to group endeavors.

## *Group Services in Host Agencies*

Group process is being used considerably in the field of corrections. The influence of group action is illustrated in this case glimpse from a juvenile correction facility. A new boy who had just been introduced to a group in a delinquency center was questioned by his peers. He was in legal trouble for stealing. They asked why he stole and he said "to get even with my dad." He had taken a gun and killed a goat belonging to his father. They asked him why he did this, and he again replied, "to get even with my old man." The boys questioned him further, and it was apparent that they were helping him to bring out some of his feelings as well as their own. Through these group discussions the youths shared with each other what they had done, why they had done these things, how they felt about their behavior and society, and what they thought they should do in the future.

In hospitals social workers often help patients in groups understand some of their medical and emotional problems. To illustrate, a small group of elderly cardiac patients met together to discuss their heart conditions, their feelings about their health, and the reaction of their families to their medical problems. As they shared their fears and anxieties, the social worker was able to guide their thinking to ways they could solve some of their problems. After a few sessions together their total adjustment to both medical and psychological conditions improved.

In psychiatric hospitals groups of patients join together on a group basis under the guidance of a group leader. They meet once or twice a week and discuss themselves, their difficulties, their hopes, their aspirations, and their plans. In one such hospital, the patients were even given the opportunity and responsibility to discuss and help with the planning of group members regarding their leaving the institution. The doctor who reported this experience said that the patients did an effective and fair job in helping people to plan for and to carry out departure from the hospital. In other words, through the use of the group as a tool, many patients were influenced and assisted in planning for release.

Many school districts utilize group process in working with boys and girls who have various kinds of personal and family problems. Under guidance of a qualified social worker, eight to twelve boys and/or girls meet together regularly. They discuss themselves, their problems, adjustments, relationships in school, family situations, and help each other to understand their difficulties and that effective action can be taken regarding them. Many boys and girls today are adjusting well in school because the group has been utilized as a tool to assist them to understand themselves better, to face personal and family problems, and to actively work toward improvement. The group has helped to free them of the problems that have shackled them and kept them from achievement in school.

Group process is used in the areas of marriage and family relations. John and Mary Smith were having serious marital difficulties which involved lack of affection and the inability to communicate. After individual interviews at a family service society they were invited to join a group of six couples who had similar or related difficulties. The worker who directed the sessions helped the group share their problems, hopes, and plans. Through this interaction they developed an understanding of themselves, of each other, and their marital relationship. After several sessions John and Mary discovered they were communicating on several levels, and they also became aware that each had become more affectionate.

An example of a newer service utilizing group process is that of Joe Jones, a nineteen-year-old who had been using drugs for three years and had decided he wanted to quit. He went to a residential drug treatment center. He paid $50 a month and lived there for six months. During that time, he was helped to become aware of other people's needs as well as his own and was assisted back to meaningful relationships with others. The group process was utilized as a major tool in achieving these goals.

Joe belonged to a group of about thirty who were living in the residential center and who shared meals and other living experiences. He joined with the total group in management and other discussions almost on a daily basis. He also participated at least weekly in small group discussions, in which there were five to eight members and one or two group workers. In these meetings they shared and discussed their own feelings, needs, plans, decisions, and hopes. These weekly conferences ordinarily lasted about ninety minutes. Occasionally Joe participated in a marathon, again involving a small group of five to eight, in which there was a deeper kind of group process utilized to help him and the others become more aware of their own needs, the needs of others, and to return to meaningful interpersonal relationships.

A third kind of group experience included recreational activities where the residents of the center became active in the local "Y," attended sports events, or participated in other recreational activities. The power of the group was effective in helping to bring about changes in Joe, in his attitude, his philosophy of life, and way of living. At the end of six months he walked out the front door of the living center with a firm conviction that use of drugs was a thing of the past for him.

---

In recent years group treatment has been emphasized in the area of spouse and child abuse. Groups have been formed to assist victims of childhood sexual abuse, perpetrators of sexual and physical abuse, and neglectful parents.

## Summary

*Everyone soon discovers social needs, interests, and imperatives basic to the individual's effort to survive. Social hungers are the common lot of mankind. People need association with other human beings, to be nurtured, loved, wanted, and understood.*

*Group work is based on the assumption that individuals have a need for each other. Personality enhancement and social functioning are tied to considerations related to the group. Group work is a method of working with the individual, of treating him or her, of helping him or her to adjust, to achieve his or her potential through the vehicle of the group, and of helping the group as a whole toward achievement of goals approved by society.*

*The social worker uses the knowledge of the individual and group association to effect change, and uses program and various media such as crafts, games, and other creative activity to produce change within the individual.*

*As an open system, the group process is identified with several models of practice including the social goals model, the remedial model, and the reciprocal model. Goals and purposes of the group determine the model to be used.*

*Selection of individuals for the group is determined by such factors as age, sex, common interests, common problems, ego capacity, and the level of tolerance members have for the group.*

*In planning group process, consideration is given to group size, composition, rules, meeting time and place, leadership, and whether the group is to be open or closed.*

*Group work, one of the basic social work processes, is utilized in providing services both in traditional group work agencies and in various host and treatment centers. It is being used effectively to help individuals and families to face their problems and to solve them through utilization of the power of the group and group interaction.*

*The principles of group work include recognition of the fact that it is an enabling function based upon scientific knowledge and understanding. It is guided by such principles as the use of* relationship, use of self, use of the agency, acceptance, starting where the group is, individualization, personal involvement and responsibility, and the use of verbal and nonverbal techniques for

achieving communication. Principles of group selection lead to more effective results in working with groups.

## Selected References

ALISSI, ALBERT S., *Perspectives on Social Group Work Practice.* New York: The Free Press, 1980.

BALGOPAL, PALLASANNA R., and THOMAS V. VASSIL, *Groups in Social Work on Ecological Perspective.* New York: Macmillan, 1983.

BEAVER, MARION L., and DON A. MILLER, *Clinical Social Work Practice with the Elderly,* 2nd ed. Belmont, CA: Wadsworth Publishing Co., 1992.

BROWN, ALLAN, *Groupwork,* 2nd ed. Brookfield, VT: Gower Publishing Co., Ltd., 1986.

COREY, GERALD, *Theory and Practice of Group Counseling,* 2nd ed. Monterey, CA: Brooks/Cole Publishing Co., 1985.

GARVIN, CHARLES D., *Contemporary Group Work.* Englewood Cliffs, NJ: Prentice Hall, 1981.

GITTERMAN, ALEX, and LAWRENCE SHULMAN, eds., *Mutual Aid Groups and the Life Cycle.* Itasca, IL: F.E. Peacock Publishers, Inc., 1986.

KONOPKA, GISELA, *Social Group Work: A Helping Process.* Englewood Cliffs, NJ: Prentice Hall, 1972.

NORTHERN, HELEN, *Social Work with Groups,* 2nd ed. New York: Columbia University Press, 1988.

REID, KENNETH E., *Social Work Practice with Groups: A Clinical Perspective.* Pacific Grove, CA: Brooks/Cole Publishing Co., 1991.

SUNDEL, MARTIN, PAUL GLASSER, ROSEMARY SARRI, and ROBERT VINTER, eds., *Individual Change Through Small Groups,* 2nd ed. New York: The Free Press, 1985.

TOSELAND, RONALD W., and ROBERT F. RIVAS, *An Introduction to Group Work Practice,* 2nd ed. Boston: Allyn and Bacon, 1995.

YALOM, IRVIN D., *The Theory and Practice of Group Psychotherapy,* 2nd ed. New York: Basic Books, 1975.

ZASTROW, CHARLES, *Social Work with Groups,* 2nd ed. Chicago: Nelson-Hall Publishers, 1992.

## Notes

1. John Day, *Jefferson Profile* (New York: John Day Company, Inc., 1956), pp. 136–137.
2. Anne Frank, *Diary of a Young Girl* (New York: Doubleday and Company, Inc., 1952), p. 139.
3. Frederick William Roe, ed., *Essays and Poems of Arnold* (New York: Harcourt, Brace & World, Inc., 1934), p. 411.
4. Ronald W. Toseland and Robert F. Rivas, *An Introduction to Group Work Practice* (New York: Macmillan, 1984), p. 3.
5. Helen Northern, *Social Work with Groups,* 2nd ed. (New York: Columbia University Press, 1988), p. 4.
6. Gisela Konopka, "Group Work: A Heritage and a Challenge," *Selected Papers in Social Work with Groups* (New York: National Association of Social Welfare, 1960), p. 8.

7. Toseland and Rivas, *An Introduction to Group Work Practice,* p. 12.
8. Ibid., p. 12.
9. Lynn T. Billenberg, "A Task-Centered Preventive Group Approach to Create Cohesion in the New Step Family," *Research on Social Work Practice,* 1 (October 1991), pp. 416–433.
10. Robert F. Schilling, Nina Koh, Robert Abramanitz, and Louisa Gilbert, "Bereavement Groups for Inner-City Children," *Research on Social Work Practice,* 2 (July 1992), pp. 405–417.
11. Beatrice Rogoff Plasse, "Parenting Groups for Recovering Addicts in a Day Treatment Center," *Social Work,* vol. 40, 1 (January 1995), 65–74.
12. Charles Zastrow, *Social Work with Groups,* 2nd ed. (Chicago, IL: Nelson-Hall Publishers, 1992), p. 4.

13. Paul H. Glasser and Nazneen S. Mayadas, *Group Workers at Work* (Totowa, NJ: Rowman and Littlefield Publishers, 1986), p. 20.

14. Robert L. Barker, *The Social Work Dictionary,* 3rd ed. (Washington, D.C.: NASW Press, 1995), p. 353.

15. Alex Gitterman and Lawrence Shulman, eds., *Mutual Aid Groups, Vulnerable Populations and the Life Cycle,* 2nd ed. (New York: Columbia University Press, 1994), p. XI.

16. Catherine P. Papell and Beulah Rothman, "Social Group Work Models: Possession and Heritage," *Journal of Education for Social Work* (Fall 1966), pp. 66–77. Reprinted with permission of the Council on Social Work Education.

17. Ibid., pp. 69–70.

18. Ibid., pp. 74–75.

19. Case examples and ideas on group formation adapted from unpublished papers by Margie E. Edwards, Professor of Social Work, Graduate School of Social Work, University of Utah.

# Chapter 7

# Social Work Practice with Communities

In a western city juvenile delinquency was rampant. Boys and girls in their early years were getting into trouble with the law, and both youths and adults were becoming apprehensive about being out on the streets at night. Newspapers reported robberies, burglaries, drug abuse, rapes, and occasional murders. What should be done? Could the citizens band together to do something?

Various citizens and community leaders began to think seriously about their local situation. Leaders in the Community Welfare Council met and discussed this social problem. A committee was appointed in the council under the direction of a social worker who was skilled in community organization to make a study and recommendations. From several months of study the committee ascertained that juvenile delinquency and youth violations had definitely been on the increase in this locality during the previous decade and warranted concerted action by citizens and community leaders. Another committee was appointed by the council to formulate plans and recommendations for alleviating this problem. This committee devised an overall plan with many recommendations for action. Members invited some of their youths to serve on the plan-

ning and action committees. The teenagers presented many ideas the adults had never thought about. Together they formulated sound plans and began to put them into operation. These plans called for informing the public about juvenile delinquency on a local level and inviting their cooperation in facing this problem. Professionally trained social workers were hired to work with the street-gang groups and to use their abilities in other ways. Paraprofessionals were also drafted. Local clubs and organizations, after discussing the problem of delinquency and the plans of action, gave support to the positive program for reducing antisocial behavior. Two recreational centers were established in temporary quarters to provide more opportunities for youths in their leisure-time hours.

What was the outcome? Within two years the amount of delinquency in this community was reduced by one-half. Parents and youths were communicating with each other and helping each other. Why had the change come about? Simply because people within a community faced a problem and worked together, helping each other to confront and reduce it.

## *What Is Community Organization?*

Working with the community requires the generalist practitioner to be able to assess community functioning and design specific intervention techniques. Community work can be very satisfying if the generalist worker understands both the knowledge and process variables needed to be effective in this area.

Community organization has been recognized for many years as one of the main methods of social work. In fact, the Curriculum Policy Statement of the Council on Social Work Education, issued in 1962, included community organization, along with casework and group work, as the three major methods of social work.

The 1982 Curriculum Policy Statement no longer listed specific methods but provided for concentrations. Several schools of social work now offer a concentration in community social work, and the variety of titles include community organization, social development, locality development, and social planning.

Currently many schools have chosen the term *macro practice* to refer to the more traditional term of *community organization*. Macro practice is still based on such basic theoretical concepts as social action, social planning, and locality development. There is considerable debate regarding which direction macro practice should take in the social work profession. Zastrow states:

> National and world politics have changed since the three traditional methods of community organization were enthusiastically espoused. Resources continue to shrink and hard decisions must be made regarding where they should be focused. Many postulate that macro practice today is substantially different than it was a few decades ago.
>
> Macro practice, which involves effective interventions with large systems and organizations on behalf of people, is still a major thrust of generalist social work. Systems and their policies need changes and improvement. Oppressed populations need advocacy on their behalf. The focus of change must not be limited to changing the behavior of individual clients or client groups. Rather, there is a cluster of macro practice skills that social workers can use to effect change. Today most macro practice takes place within an organizational context.
>
> The basic concept of community is no less important now than it was years ago. It remains just as critical to focus on the benefits of large groups of people, their overall well-being, their dignity, and their right of choice. The community concept provides a global perspective with which social workers can view the world, assess problems, and set goals.[1]

Dunham suggests that community organization is "a conscious process of social interaction and a method of social work concerned with any or all of the following objectives: (1) the meeting of broad needs and bringing about and maintaining adjustment between needs and resources in a community or other area; (2) helping people to deal more effectively with their problems and objectives, by helping them develop, strengthen, and maintain qualities of participation, self-direction, and cooperation; (3) bringing about changes in community and group relationships and in the distribution of decision-making power."[2]

Brager and Specht indicate that community organization is "a method of intervention whereby individuals, groups, and organizations engage in planned action to influence social problems. It is concerned with the enrichment, development, and/or change of social institutions, and involves two major related processes: planning (that is, identifying problem areas, diagnosing causes, and formulating solutions) and organizing (that is, developing the constituencies and devising the strategies necessary to affect action.)"[3]

Kettner, Daley, and Nichols[4] define community organization in the context of a planned change model. The three components of their model include the change process, arenas for practice, and types of interventive effort anticipated. The change process includes the following nine steps:

1. Identifying the change opportunity.
2. Analyzing the change opportunity.
3. Setting goals and objectives.
4. Designing and structuring the change effort.
5. Resource planning.
6. Implementing the change effort.
7. Monitoring the change effort.
8. Evaluating the change effort.
9. Reassessing and stabilizing the situation.

The two arenas for practice in this model are defined as organizations and the community itself. In other words, the community organization social worker may be asked to provide new or better services to people by helping to change the organization or the community. In terms of intervention, Kettner and colleagues state that: "Approaches or types of interventive effort are the creation or modification of policy, the creation or modification of a program, or the initiation of a project."[5] Thus, the community organization social worker must have an understanding of how policy guides human service programs—both in organization and communities—and must be able to change those policies and programs to be more responsive to human needs.

Certain basic factors underpin a definition of community social work practice. The community is the client. The needs of the community are paramount. These needs are spelled out in problems that affect large numbers of people. The resources of the community are taken into consideration and are tapped. Casework stresses the individual-to-individual relationships. Group work uses the group as the tool to help bring about personality development and to solve personal and family problems. Community organization is the intergroup process that utilizes community agencies and resources to ferret out its social problems and take appropriate action to remove them. Fellin states:

> Competent practice at both micro and macro levels requires that the social worker understand communities as a major element of the social environment. Knowledge about communities is needed for assessing the impact of the environment on

Social work community planning.

the individual's development and behavior. The social worker must know about resources located in the various communities to which the client relates (such as national helping networks), and about community conditions which might constrain an individual's personal and social opportunities. . . .[6]

Social work practice with communities is sorely needed in our society today. The 1992 riots in Los Angeles are a grim reminder that many of our communities are fragmented and in serious disarray. As Rivera and Erlich state:

> There is little doubt that the struggle to bring about significant social change at the community level is a Herculean task. Despite widely-heard political rhetoric to the contrary, the gates to social justice are sliding further shut—not open. Increasing numbers of people of color continue to be thrown into disadvantage and poverty—homeless, drug addicted, alcoholic, imprisoned, AIDS-infected, underemployed and unemployed, pushed out of deteriorating schools without marketable skills.
>
> Community organization and development with people of color offers one small vehicle for battling to reverse this trend. The editors join the authors in the belief that organizers can make a difference. The work is not lucrative and is rarely romantic, but it can be critical in helping to meet people's needs. Perhaps above all it is about empowerment, an empowerment that organizer and community can share.[7]

## Beginnings of Community Social Work

The first attempts to coordinate community activities and actions stemmed from the London Charity Organization Society, begun in 1869, which tried to eliminate duplication and fraud in relief administration. Its aim was to improve total services in the community through better cooperation and coordination. The first organized attempt to coordinate and systematize social services in the United States was made in 1877 with the establishment of the Buffalo Charity Organization Society. The need was great because many private agencies had been established and this brought about much duplication, with many gaps in total services, as well as unnecessary competition.

In 1909 in Pittsburgh and Milwaukee, the first community welfare councils in the United States were established. They were called Councils of Social Agencies. They have since spread and been extended so that most of the larger population centers now have community welfare councils. There are over 450 of them in the United States today. A few have developed to the extent that they have several persons on their staffs who spend full-time in research, helping to locate and interpret information that will be of value to the community.

These councils, organization-wise, generally focus on three main areas: health, welfare, and recreation. Most of them have a council delegate body representative of all of the agencies in the community that join the council. This membership body is the basic authority for carrying out the council's activities. Usually a board of directors, elected by the delegate body, is the operating authority. The board of directors appoints various administrative committees, which consider such matters as membership, personnel, and budgets. It also sponsors project committees or task forces that deal with particular problems; for example, a committee to work on the problem of transients, services to the aged, drug abuse, or school dropouts. Social policy and action committees often play important roles.

Historically the development of federated financial drives was also an important aspect of community social work. Originally private social service agencies conducted individual drives for money to maintain themselves and their services. As additional agencies came into being, various leaders suggested that it might be best to join hands to collect money and then divide it among the several agencies. In 1873 in Liverpool, England, the first such federated drive took place. In 1887 the first federated drive in the United States originated under the auspices of the Associated Charities in Denver. Twenty-three agencies joined together and raised a total budget of about $20,000. After World War I the name Community Chest became popular in designating federated fund driving. Expansion has taken place in these drives to the extent that in 1958 United Funds and Community Chests in 2,100 American communities raised $427,262,622 for the support of services of the 27,700 participating agencies during 1959. These united campaigns enlisted the efforts of 3,300,000 volunteers and secured 26,700,000 contributions.

Dunham[8] reported the following estimates for 1970 campaigns, which presented a vivid picture of the scope, involvement, and reach of United Fund campaigns:

Number of United Way Campaigns    2,250
Number of Health and Welfare Councils    450

Number of Chest and United Fund Agencies   31,500
Number of Families Served   28,400,000
Number of Contributors   33,800,000
Number of United Fund-Raising Volunteers   4,200,000
Amount Raised for 1969 (estimated)   $755,000,000

The 2,300 independent and autonomous United Ways in the United States in 1978 received pledges of over $1.3 billion. About 32 million people, or about one out of every three persons employed in the United States, gave through their United Way. In 1991 there were approximately 2,100 United Way Campaigns in the United States, and they collected $3.3 billion.

Community organization has been the last basic social work method to emerge. Casework gained status and recognition in the 1920s, as group work did in the 1930s. In 1909 the first section meeting of a national conference, The National Conference of Charities and Corrections, was held on the theme "Neighborhoods and Civic Improvement." This appears to be the beginning of specific interest in community organization in social work. In 1939 significant discussions on community organization as a field and method were held at the National Conference of Social Work. In 1944 the curriculum for the schools of social work included community organization as one of the "basic eight." By 1946 enough interest had developed in community organization so that, at the annual meeting of the National Conference of Social Work in Buffalo, the Association for the Study of Community Organization was founded. Its purpose was "to increase understanding and improve professional practice of community organization for social welfare." From its beginning until it merged with six other associations in 1955 to form the National Association of Social Workers, it had a membership that varied from about 500 to 1,000 individuals.

In 1950 representatives at the National Conference of Social Work at Atlantic City presented several papers on community organization topics and agreed that community organization was one of the basic processes in social work. In 1950 there were about 100 fieldwork placements in community organization in some sixteen of the accredited schools of social work. On November 1, 1962, there were 116 students in training in community planning services in the United States and Canada.

On November 1, 1994, there were 2350, or 7.7 percent, of the total of 30,145 full-time or part-time master's degree students who were taking community organization as a separate concentration or in combination with administration and planning.

The 1962 Curriculum Statement of the Council on Social Work Education reaffirmed the importance of community organization in both training and practice by specifying it as one of the basic methods of social work.

The 1982 Curriculum Policy Statement gives broad guidelines pertaining to social work practice and lists community organization under both the professional foundation and concentration areas. In other words, the Council of Social Work Education is recommending that every social work student should have some understanding of the knowledge, values, and skills of community organization practice and that some students should have the opportunity to pursue a community organization concentration.

The 1992 Curriculum Policy Statement recommends that all concentrations, including community organization, must include the following:

Programs have the freedom to establish concentrations within an organizing framework that is consistent with the purpose of social work and its traditional values. The organizing framework for concentrations must have curricular coherence and logic, and must be anchored in the liberal arts and professional foundation. The program must have sufficient resources to support the concentrations offered. Frameworks and perspectives for concentrations that are frequently offered by programs include fields of practice, problem areas, populations-at-risk, intervention methods or roles, and practice contexts and perspectives. Combinations of concentrations are permitted.[9]

Social work educators are beginning to reaffirm the necessity for all social workers to understand the interconnectedness between micro and macro practice. By definition, the social worker needs to understand and work with both the individual and the environment. Netting et al. summarize the need for a connecting link between micro and macro as follows:

Social work practice is broadly defined and allows for intervention at the micro (individual, group, or family) level, and at the macro (organization and community) level. Given this division of labor, some professional roles require that the social worker be involved full-time in macro practice. These professional roles are often referred to by such titles as *planner, community organizer, manager,* or *administrator.* The direct service worker or clinical social worker, however, also bears responsibility for initiating change in organizations and communities. The direct service worker is often the first to recognize patterns indicating the need for change. If one or two clients present a particular problem, the logical response is to deal with them as individuals. However, as more persons present the same situation, it quickly becomes evident that something is awry within the systems in which these clients are interacting. It then becomes incumbent upon the social worker to help identify the system(s) in need of change and the type of change needed. The nature of the system(s) in need of change may lead to community-wide intervention or intervention in a single organization.

Given these statements, practitioners may begin to feel overwhelmed. Is it not enough to do good clinical work? Is it not enough to listen to a client and offer options? Professional practice focusing only on an individual's intrapsychic concerns does not fit the definition of social work. Being a social worker requires seeing the client as part of multiple, overlapping systems that comprise the person's social and physical environment. If the social worker is not willing to engage in some macro-practice types of activities relating to these environments, then he or she is not practicing social work.

Similarly, social workers who concentrate in macro practice must understand micro practice, which may be defined as intervention directed primarily at the individual or group level. Without this understanding, macro practice may be carried out in the absence of an adequate grounding in the nature of client needs. MBA and MSW administrators would act similarly in all situations, and cost alone—rather than an understanding of client need balanced with cost—would drive community planning. The interconnectedness of micro and macro roles is the heart of social work practice. In short, it is as important for social workers in macro-practice roles to understand the importance of individual and group interventions as it is for social workers in micro-practice roles to understand the importance of organizational, community, and policy change.[10]

## *Underlying Principles in Community Organization*

It is important to understand some of the underlying principles in community organization before looking at the specific processes involved. McNeil, in a pioneering effort, observes that there are several principles that seem universally applicable:

1. Community organization for social welfare is concerned with people and their needs. Its objective is to enrich human life by bringing about and maintaining a progressively more effective adjustment between social welfare resources and social welfare needs.
2. The community is the primary client in community organization for social welfare. The community may be a neighborhood, city, county, state, or nation. Rapidly, too, there has emerged the international community. . . .
3. It is an axiom in community organization that the community is to be understood and accepted as it is and where it is. . . .
4. All of the people of the community are concerned in its health and welfare services. Representation of all interests and elements in the population and their full and meaningful participation are essential objectives in community organization.
5. The fact of ever-changing human needs and the reality of relationships between and among people and groups are the dynamics in the community organization process. Acceptance of the concept of purposeful change and John Dewey's philosophy of the "ever-enduring process of perfecting, maturing, refining" as goals in community organization is basic.
6. Interdependence of all threads in the social welfare fabric of organization is a fundamental truth. No single agency can usefully "live unto itself alone," but is constantly performing its functions in relation to others.
7. Community organization for social welfare as a process is a part of generic social work. . . .[11]

Community social work is based on and related to certain fundamental assumptions. Ross epitomizes these as follows:

1. Communities of people can develop the capacity to deal with their own problems.
2. People want change and can change.
3. People should participate in making, adjusting, or controlling the major changes taking place in their communities.
4. Changes in community living that are self-imposed or self-developed have a meaning and a permanence that imposed changes do not have. "Man, insofar as he acts on nature to change it, changes his own nature," says Hegel.
5. A "holistic approach" can deal successfully with problems with which a "fragmented approach" cannot cope.

6. Democracy requires cooperative participation and action in the affairs of the community, and people must learn the skills that make this possible.
7. Frequently communities of people need help in organizing to deal with their needs just as many individuals need help in coping with their own individual needs.[12]

## Community Social Work Processes

Although there are various classifications and descriptions regarding the processes utilized in community social work practice, those most commonly discussed and utilized are presented in the following pages.

### Research

Social research is the process of obtaining facts regarding social phenomena, social problems, and their solutions. Scientific research is regarded as basic to community social work. For example, a community recognizes that it has a problem in juvenile delinquency. The newspapers report a sensational account of a young girl being attacked in a dark alley. What can the community do about it? What does it do about it? How much delinquency is there? Where are the areas of greatest delinquency? These and other questions can be answered by capable and properly trained individuals ferreting out the facts, studying the total situation.

Various research methods are utilized in community social work practice. Statistical studies, surveys, and case studies are used in particular. The underlying idea is that a community, to act wisely and fairly, must know what the realities are and what the facts do show.

### Planning

Planning is purposeful formulation of future action and ways of procedure. In community social work it is used extensively. It is usually carried out by representatives of various community groups meeting together and making decisions regarding social difficulties and their solutions.

In a southern community a canal in an old dilapidated part of the city was wide open, with no fencing or protection. Several children had wandered to the banks of the canal, fallen in, and drowned. What happened? Finally, enough parents and irate citizens voiced their opinions to the extent that the community welfare council studied this problem. Representatives from various professions and organizations met many times and formulated plans for alleviating the problem. Through careful planning and other activities, they proposed to the city fathers that an allocation be made for fencing the dangerous areas. With support of the community welfare council, the press, radio, and TV, enough momentum was gathered so that the desired action was accomplished.

### Coordination

Coordination is the process of working together to avoid unnecessary duplication, effort, and conflict. On the positive side, it is the joining of people, agencies, and forces to support and strengthen each other, making possible increased effective services that surpass what could be done unilaterally. This process is easily exemplified by federated drives for financing, such as those accomplished by united funds. It is also illustrated by activities of community welfare councils, which have as one of their basic aims the avoidance of unnecessary duplication of social services in a community as well as alleviating service deficits.

Coordination is more than cooperation. Cooperation is a working together to accomplish a given end. It is usually utilized positively to bring about effective activities. Ordinarily, it involves a specific, single goal. Coordination generally encompasses a combination of goals and affects several people or groups. In community organization it means that various peoples and agencies in the community join hands to support each other, and help each other to attain better individual and mutually shared goals.

## *Organization*

Organization is the process of establishing a structure to accomplish certain goals. In community social work it is the method of formulating a structure to consider community needs, resources, and the utilization of the resources to satisfy the needs. Various kinds of organizations exist in this area. United funds, community welfare councils, coordinating councils, community information services, state conferences on social welfare, and national and international agencies are established to understand social problems and to help meet them. A formal organization usually gives substance to a movement. Without it, activities, even though some are significant, often take place on a hit-or-miss basis. (See Figure 7.1.)

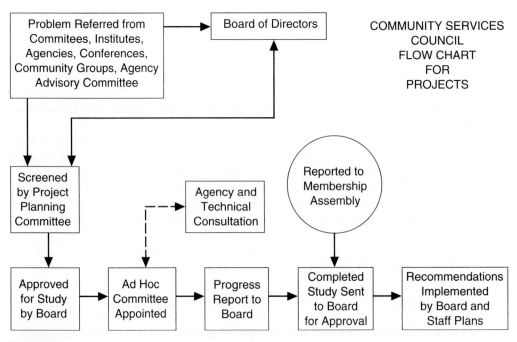

**FIGURE 7.1**

An example of an organization that is effective in relation to community problems is a state-formed association of citizens. It was organized to bring together representative individuals to become well acquainted with social problems in the state, study them, talk about them, and attempt to make specific recommendations to legislative bodies to do something about them. This association was organized as an action group. It has helped to bring about many worthwhile changes in its particular state. The organization has been a tool that has opened one avenue to accomplishing social goals.

## Financing

Financing is the process of collecting, budgeting, and spending funds in relation to community needs and resources. Collection is usually carried out by a combination of professional persons and volunteers. United Way drives are examples of this kind of activity. Millions of dollars are collected each year. Appeals are made to touch the heartstrings as well as the minds of people.

Most united funds, welfare councils, and other community social work bodies have committees on budgeting. These committees try to study the needs and make proper allocations so that the total community welfare is best served. This most challenging aspect of community organization requires dedication and careful thought and consideration.

The spending part of this process is done by the specific agencies, most of which have finance committees. These committees prepare budgets prior to fund drives and then work out detailed plans for the best use of the money that is available after the annual allocation has been received. Again, this process is a challenging one requiring careful consideration and planning. Frequently the trained social worker on the staff can be most helpful in assisting the finance committee to work out a fair and appropriate budget, with specific listings of expenditures.

## Administration

Social work administration can be defined as the process of transforming social policy into social services. It is the process of carrying out plans, implementing the actions upon which decisions have been reached. It is a particularly important process in community organization.

Effective administration includes all the staff, not only the executive, but the janitor, the assistant secretary, and the board. Where all staff members are a part of the total venture and make suggestions and contributions to the total effort, the best results ensue. In the next chapter, we will present a more detailed discussion of administration.

## Committee Operation

Committee operation is the essence of social work community practice. Through committees most of the planning and action takes place, decisions are made, and ideas and feelings are brought into the open, making it possible for appropriate action to follow. The social work community processes are effective when committees function on a democratic basis; otherwise complications arise. For adequate committee operation there needs to be adequate representation for all of the groups that may be interested and involved in relation to a particular project. Committees do most of the planning for community action. Ordinarily it is best for committees to be small, otherwise they bog down and become ineffective. Experts in the field recognize that it is difficult for a group of more than ten to fifteen to work together effectively. Usually even smaller groups are better.

Committee members should be selected for their interest in a given problem, for their knowledge and abilities to help with a problem, and for their willingness to use their time and talents in working on the problem to bring about appropriate action. Ordinarily, it is not best to pressure people into accepting committee assignments; rather it is more effective to appeal to their civic pride and to stress that their services are needed for important tasks ahead.

Within the work of the committee, the community organizer has to know how to resolve conflicts through negotiation. A good record must also be kept of the actions of the committee as a reminder of the thinking and planning of the past and as a tool for opening the door for appropriate action in the present and the future.

### Advocacy and Social Action

One of the significant developments in community social work has been the increasing emphasis on client advocacy. Earlier only a few social workers went "all out" to back up and champion their clients and groups of disadvantaged persons, trying to bring about social action and social change to help fulfill their needs and improve society. Today advocacy and the social action model of community organization are a well accepted part of social work practice. Examples of social action can be seen in the Civil Rights Movement, the Grey Panthers, and the National Association for the Mentally Ill. These movements were able to create action in our society because they generated "power" by forcefully educating our country about their legitimate problems. As a result of the efforts of the National Association for the Mentally Ill, every state was bound by law to have a case management plan for each chronically mentally ill person in the state by 1991. This case management law is designed to ensure that the chronically mentally ill will have a coordinated and comprehensive service delivery system to help them cope and maintain their human dignity.

Advocacy and social action in social work practice and education are gaining momentum. Many social workers in community settings and agencies are assisting their clients with support and guidelines in facing social problems and in trying to change strong debilitating situations and patterns. Social workers must be willing to learn and use principles of advocacy when they encounter dehumanizing conditions or abusive treatment within service agencies or societal institutions.

### Roles of the Community Organizer

Social workers in community organizations should have good technical skills and be able to get along well with people. Much of community organization is done to change systems, and many times the system resists change. The resistance usually comes in the form of anger or hostility from people who are going to be affected by the change. The community organizer needs to be able to systematically apply a relevant body of knowledge which is guided by social work values. Rubin and Rubin have defined four key roles in community organization as follows:

### Organizers as Teacher

Consistent with the ideal of community-development, it is fundamental for a community organizer to believe in the objectives of increasing human capacity. One way of doing so is through the creation and encouragement of local leadership, that is, the activation of potential partisans into roles in which they directly confront authorities. Building capacity is teaching people that they can be leaders....

### Organizers as Catalysts

A community organizer is also a catalyst, a person who stimulates actions in others. Organizers start community organizations by finding common problems that community members feel to be important, bringing together people who may not know each other, or working to create a sense of community that can become the basis for organizing. Organizers try to target initial actions so that they bring about victories to keep people interested and active. Organizers gradually enlarge people's vision of what is possible and thereby get them active on a range of issues.

### Organizers as Facilitators

Community organizers do more than start people on solving a problem; they also act as facilitators. Too often, community actions fail because members lack the experience or patience to keep an organization going. Probably, more organizations fail from lack of follow-through than from lack of original enthusiasm. The community organizer facilitates keeping an organization going and ensures the follow-through....

### A Linking Role

The fourth role often played by organizers is in bridging the gap between the organization, its members, and the community. There are many ways in which linking is accomplished.

Sometimes, linking involves a broad search for information: What is the political climate? How much support will the group receive for its cause? At other times, linking is limited to a very specific task. For example, one person in a woman's rape counseling center may work as a liaison with police to discuss testimony, protection, or training police to deal with victims....[13]

The community organizers should have the ability to relate to people, to analyze problems, to locate resources, to see potential for change, and to be able to create effective structures for problem solving. These abilities combined with skill in the roles of teacher, catalyst, facilitator, and a creator of linkages are essential for community organization effectiveness.

## Case Summaries

Current action in community social work is illustrated by the two case summaries that follow:

### Older Citizens' Center

Concern for problems of and services for older citizens prompted the Community Services Council to appoint a representative committee of aging to consider what needed to be done in the community. Based on a study of need made by the department of sociology of the university and information from other communities, the committee surveyed the community resources and existing programs for senior citizens. These responses indicated that many organizations and agencies were interested and that several had projects underway. However, the survey results revealed that, for the most part, these activities were fragmentary in nature and sorely in need of coordination and direction with respect to the overall needs of older persons in the community.

In developing its plan, the committee agreed that it would be most effective if the various programs were developed one by one, as resources and support became available. Several factors contributed to the selection of leisure-time services as the first area of focus by the committee. These included (1) the recognition that leisure-time activities represented a major need for older persons, (2) the need for a focal point around which a number of activities might be supplied, (3) the lack of a coordinated leisure-time program, and (4) identification of the inadequacies of facilities and program in the largest recreation program in the county, the County Recreation Department.

The committee involved others in its next steps. Census material was studied. Program experience was sought from other communities. A visit was made to the Los Angeles area to see developments first hand. Out of this investigation came the recommendation for a new facility in a central location. The story of need was presented to the county commissioners, who agreed to erect the building if the city would supply the land. The city commission asked the committee to recommend a location and considerable effort was expended in listing possible spots and an ideal location. Finally, after some disagreement in the community, the location was agreed upon and the building program set into motion. Result is that a new senior citizens' center has become a reality.

### Protective Services

At a meeting of the Community Services Council, representatives of several community agencies expressed concern over the large number of child neglect complaints that regularly came to them. It was reported that many children who were waiting for possible placement in foster homes were lodged in the county detention home, which was considered unsatisfactory and undesirable from the standpoint of both child and agency.

In discussing the situation, several questions were raised: How many complaints of child neglect were received by the agencies? What was the nature and source of such complaints? How many agencies were offering protective services? How adequate were the services? What constitutes a sound protective service program? As a result of the discussions a committee was formed to find answers to these questions based on an agreed upon definition of protective services.

Questionnaires were distributed to agencies to gather information concerning agency protective service activities during the previous year and protective service complaints. During the year the committee studied the responses and deliberated on a proposed plan of procedure. It was finally recommended by the committee and approved by the council's board of directors that a unit of protective services be established in the county department of Public Welfare's Child Welfare Division. Negotiations with the state and local departments culminated in the unit being established with the provision that the council cooperate in appointing an advisory committee to aid in getting the program underway, and in helping set up a plan of procedure and referral system with the other agencies. As a result, the State Conference on Social Welfare adopted "protective services" as the theme of its annual conference a year after the program was started, and other counties have requested assistance of the council in organizing such a service.

## Summary

*Community social work is one of the main approaches in social work. It is the intergroup process that attempts to help communities to understand social problems that exist, and to utilize available community resources to bring about solutions that will strengthen the total community and enrich the lives of its members.*

*Community social work is one of the newer thrusts in social work, and one that has great potential for preventing and solving social problems.*

*Many of the principles basic to community organization are shared with casework and group work, but there are several that are unique.*

*Basic processes in community social work practice include research, planning, coordination, organization, financing, administration, committee operation, and advocacy.*

*The four main roles of the community organizer are teacher, catalyst, facilitator, and a person who creates linkages between organizations and communities. These roles must be carried out with skill and an understanding of the importance of human relationships.*

## Selected References

AUSTIN, MICHAEL J., and JANE ISAACS LOWE, eds., *Controversial Issues in Communities and Organization.* Boston, MA: Allyn and Bacon, 1994.

BOULDING, KENNETH, *Three Faces of Power.* Beverly Hills, CA: Sage Publications, 1989.

BRAGER, GEORGE, and HARRY SPECHT, *Community Organizing.* New York: Columbia University Press, 1973.

DAFT, RICHARD L., and RICHARD M. STEERS, *Organizations: A Micro/Macro Approach.* Glenview, IL: Scott, Foresman & Co., 1986.

FELLIN, PHILLIP, *The Community and the Social Worker.* Itasca, IL: F. E. Peacock Publishers, Inc., 1987.

GOTTLIEB, BENJAMIN, *Marshaling Social Support: Formats, Processes and Effects.* Newbury Park, CA: Sage Publications, 1988.

GRIEFER, JULIAN L., ed., *Community Action for Social Change: A Casebook of Current Projects.* New York: Praeger Publishers, 1974.

KETTNER, PETER, JOHN M. DALEY, and ANN WEAVER NICHOLS, *Initiating Change in Organizations and Communities.* Monterey, CA: Brooks/Cole Publishing Co., 1985.

MONDROS, JACQUELINE B., and SCOTT M. WILSON, *Organizing for Power and Empowerment.* New York: Longman Publishing Group, 1993.

NETTING, F. ELLEN, PETER M. KETTNER, and STEVEN L. MCMURTY, *Social Work Macro Practice.* New York: Longman Publishing Group, 1993.

RIVERA, FELIX, and JOHN L. ERLICH, *Community Organizing in a Diverse Society.* Boston: Allyn and Bacon, 1992.

RUBIN, HERBERT J., and IRENE RUBIN, *Community Organizing and Development.* Columbus, OH: Charles E. Merrill Publishing Co., 1986.

SZILAGYI, ANDREW D., JR., and MARC J. WALLACE, JR., *Organizational Behavior and Performance,* 2nd ed. Santa Monica, CA: Goodyear Publishing Co., Inc., 1980.

TAYLOR, ELEANOR D., *From Issues to Action: An Advocacy Program Model.* Milwaukee, WI: Family Service of America, 1987.

ZEY-FERRELL, MARY, *Dimensions of Organizations: Environment, Context, Structure, Process, and Performance.* Santa Monica, CA: Goodyear Publishing Co., Inc., 1979.

## *Notes*

1. Charles Zastrow and Karen K. Kirst-Ashman, *Understanding Human Behavior and Social Environment,* 3rd ed. (Chicago, IL: Nelson-Hall Publishers, 1994), p. 39.

2. Arthur Dunham, *The New Community Organization* (New York: Thomas Y. Crowell Co., 1970), p. 4.

3. George Brager and Harry Specht, *Community Organizing* (New York: Columbia University Press, 1973), pp. 27–28.

4. Peter Kettner, John M. Daley, and Ann Weaver Nichols, *Initiating Change in Organizations and Communities* (Monterey, CA: Brooks/Cole Publishing Co., 1985), p. 25.

5. Ibid., pp. 25–26.

6. Phillip Fellin, *The Community and the Social Worker* (Itasca, IL: F. E. Peacock Publishers, Inc., 1987), pp. 2–3.

7. Felix G. Rivera and John L. Erlich, *Community Organizing in a Diverse Society* (Boston: Allyn and Bacon, 1992), p. 25.

8. Dunham, *The New Community Organization,* p. 471.

9. Council on Social Work Education, *Curriculum Policy Statement for Master's Degree Programs in Social Work Education* (Alexandria, VA: Council on Social Work Education, 1992), pp. 11–12.

10. F. Ellen Netting, Peter M. Kettner, and Steven L. McMurty, *Social Work Macro Practice* (New York: Longman Publishing Group, 1993), pp. 4–5.

11. C. F. McNeil, "Community Organization for Social Welfare," *Social Work Year Book,* 1954 (New York: American Association of Social Workers, 1954), p. 123.

12. Murray G. Ross, *Community Organization, Theory, Principles, and Practice,* 2nd ed. (New York: Harper & Row, Publishers, 1967), pp. 86–93.

13. Herbert J. Rubin and Irene Rubin, *Community Organizing and Development* (Columbus, OH: Charles E. Merrill Publishing Co., 1986), pp. 45–47.

Chapter *8*

# *Administration and Research*

*The supervisor sent a cutting memo to Ron, a caseworker with three years' successful experience in a mental health agency. The supervisor was incisive, blunt, and critical of Ron's work and his reports. Ron responded with a retaliatory memo, stating he resented what had been written and asking for a chance to see the director. The supervisor sent another memo, avoiding talking with Ron in person; then the sparks really flew. Finally, the agency administrator heard of the conflict that had begun to divide the staff and invited the two workers to her office.*

*The director asked each one to state what he thought the situation was and what should be done about it. Although differences were wide, as they discussed their ideas and feelings, changes began to emerge. The director encouraged them to get together more often to discuss their work, with understanding and acceptance. Gradually they learned to communicate with each other and carry out their assignments with effectiveness and satisfaction.*

Traditional methodology in social work has encompassed social casework, group work, and community organization, with administration and research as enabling processes. Generalist practice today provides an integrative approach with these processes intertwined and utilized to help provide a perspective and focus that is comprehensive and effective in bringing about appropriate changes in individual and group behavior. Generalists need basic knowledge of the administrative process as well as its skills in utilizing its facilitative resources.

Generalist practice reaches for increased knowledge about human behavior, especially social relationships, and recognizes the essential need for more scientific research. Again, social workers need an introductory knowledge of significant research and an ability to read and understand research literature. This chapter considers briefly the administrative and research processes that are vital to the social work profession.

**119**

## Administration

Some social work educators have advocated that the administrative process is the very heart of social work education and practice. For example, the University of Chicago's graduate school of social work was named the School of Social Service Administration when it was established at the turn of the century.

Administration is one of the major aspects of social work practice. Certainly every agency program requires an able administrator to be effective.

The demand for trained workers for administrative positions is definitely on the increase. Salarywise, many attractive opportunities exist for social work administrators.

Historically, administration has been utilized through the centuries, but has not been recognized in a formal way as it is today. More than 2,500 years ago a poem, written by Laotse in the *Book of Tao,* illustrated goals for leaders:

> A leader is best
> When people barely know that he exists . . .
> But of a good leader, who talks little,
> When his work is done, his aim fulfilled,
> They will say, "We did this ourselves."

At the meeting of the Council on Social Work Education in Detroit in 1958, a study was reported that indicated only 1 percent of full-time students in graduate schools of social work in 1957 were majoring in administration; yet 54 percent of the men suggested that within 10 years they hoped to be in administrative positions. In 1960 about one-third of all social welfare workers in practice in the United States were performing as administrators, either as supervisors or executives.

Today most master's graduates move into administrative positions upon graduation or within a few years of practice. They become supervisors, assistant executives, consultants, or directors of agencies.

In 1962 there were only twenty-four students enrolled in administration in graduate schools of social work in the United States, representing eight schools. In 1974 there were 604 students enrolled in a concentration of "administration, management, social policy," representing twenty-eight schools of social work. In November 1979, there were 309 first-year master's students and 619 second-year students enrolled in the "administration, management, social policy" concentration, amounting to 3.8 percent and 6.7 percent of their respective groups. In 1994 there were 1,044 MSW students enrolled in the administration and management concentration. In addition, there were 1,384 MSW students enrolled in a concentration involving a combination of direct practice with community organization and planning or with administration or management.[1]

A study of NASW members by Chess, Norlin, and Jayaratne[2] presented a positive statement about social work administration. A significant finding of this study was that between 1981 and 1985 the percentage of practitioners in social work administration increased from 27.8 to 36.5 (see Table 8.1). These authors concluded that "given the economic and political climate and its implications for the practice of social work administra-

TABLE 8.1    **Practice Method of NASW Members Employed Full Time, 1981–1985**

| Category | 1981 | | 1985 | |
|---|---|---|---|---|
| | **Number** | **Percent** | **Number** | **Percent** |
| Casework | 280 | 41.1 | 168 | 29.4 |
| Group Work | 13 | 1.9 | 5 | .9 |
| Community Organization | 8 | 1.2 | 7 | 1.2 |
| Administration | 189 | 27.8 | 209 | 36.5 |
| Supervision | 70 | 10.3 | 49 | 8.6 |
| Case Management | | | 29 | 5.1 |
| Policy Analysis | | | 9 | 1.6 |
| Teaching | | | 28 | 4.9 |
| Other | 121 | 17.8 | 68 | 11.9 |
| Total | 681 | 100.0 | 572 | 100.0 |

*Source:* Wayne A. Chess, Julia M. Norlin, and Srinika D. Jayaratne, "Social Work Administration, 1981–1985: Alive, Happy and Prospering," *Administration in Social Work,* 11 (Summer 1987), 68.

tion, the data presented here are generally quite positive. In short, these data suggest that social work administration in 1985 is alive, happy and prospering."[3]

## *Definition*

John Kidneigh states that social work administration is "the process of transforming social policy into social services... a two-way process: (1) ... transforming policy into concrete social services, and (2) the use of experience in recommending modification of policy."[4] This definition, of course, encompasses the idea that administration is the process of implementation, of translating policies into action programs. Stein defines the concept of administration as a "process of defining and attaining the objectives of an organization through a system of coordinated and cooperative effort."[5]

*The Social Work Dictionary,* 1995 edition, defines administration in social work as "methods used by those who have administrative responsibility to determine organizational goals for a *social agency* or other unit; acquire resources and allocate them to carry out a program; coordinate activities toward achieving selected goals; and monitor, assess, and make necessary changes in processes and structure to improve effectiveness and efficiency. In social work, the term is often used synonymously with management."[6]

Skidmore summarizes the various definitions of administration as follows: "... social work administration may be thought of as the action of staff members who utilize social processes to transform social policies of agencies into the delivery of social services. It involves executives—the leaders—and all other staff—the followers or team members. The basic processes most often used are planning, organizing, staffing, directing, and controlling...."[7]

That administration is relatively new in social work is illustrated by the fact that it was only in 1946 that the National Conference of Social Work sponsored a section on administration for the first time in its seventy-two years. This program included consideration of the following: process of administration, dynamics of leadership, salaries, job classification, boards, public relations, organized labor, civil service, program development, and retirement planning.

In the early days of social work, administration was not thought of as distinct from direction of services and functions. By 1914 a course in administration was established in at least one school of social work and the content was borrowed mainly from adjoining fields. World War I, the Great Depression, and World War II—with their numerous problems and tensions—gave considerable focus and emphasis to interest in the administrative process. Technical literature began to appear. For a while the Cooperative Committee on Administration was in operation. Further interest in administration was developed through a special department in the magazine *The Survey,* and through the activities of leaders in the YWCA, YMCA, and Family Welfare Association of America, whose organizations were beginning to set standards for their administrators. In 1944 the Curriculum Committee of the American Association of Schools of Social Work included social welfare administration as one of the *Basic Eight* for training students.

The 1962 and 1969 curriculum statements did not emphasize administration as a specific required methodology. Nevertheless, these statements provided flexibility and opportunity for emphasis in this area. Administration is included as a possible concentration in the 1982 curriculum policy statement. The guidelines state: "Practice Roles and Interventive Modes: Practice with individuals, families and groups, consultation, training, community organization, social planning, program planning and development, administration, policy formulation, implementation, and analysis, and research."[8] Several schools now have a concentration in administration or in an administration focus related to social planning or other aspects of social work practice. By 1977 interest in social work administration had developed to the extent that a new journal appeared, *Administration in Social Work,* a quarterly, "devoted to the theory and practice of management and administration in social work and related human services fields." In 1978 the Council on Social Work Education issued a communication that indicated administration in social work was being given "high priority." Currently, many social workers are being hired as administrators in large social service systems such as state hospitals and state divisions of family services. This trend is likely to continue.

## Basic Assumptions and Principles

One of the basic principles in administration is that all levels of staff participate in the administrative process. This includes executives, subexecutives, supervisors, consultants, caseworkers, group workers, community organizers, secretaries, attendants, and others. Traditionally, people have thought of administration only as involving those at the helm, the directors or the executives. Today, if we are to be realistic, it is essential to recognize that all staff members are involved, directly or indirectly, in the administrative process. It is also apparent that some of the major contributions toward improving administration come from persons in the lesser status categories of staff.

Spencer, in the pioneering *Curriculum Study,* suggests that several underlying assumptions should be kept in mind in relation to administration:

1. Administration of social agencies is the process of securing and transforming community resources (human and financial) into a program of community service. This process involves active participation of the board, executive, staff, and volunteers or constituency in varying degrees.
2. Administration in social work is concerned in a major way with enterprise determination, which includes goal formation. This means that the agency itself has the primary responsibility for the creation and control of its own destiny and community planning bodies exercise only a secondary role.
3. Administration in social work is concerned in a major way with "provisioning" the service. It has to do with the logistics of the program and activities of the particular agency.
4. The executive is not a neutral agent. This means that creative leadership is needed in all phases of the agency's operation.
5. The executive's functions within the agency combine the following: (a) to provide a seeing-the-enterprise-as-a-whole quality, (b) to participate in a leadership capacity and policy formulation, (c) to delegate, coordinate, and control the work of others to promote and enhance the work of board and staff, (d) to provide for board, staff, and community an executive who represents in personal attitudes, abilities, and activities a person with whom they can identify positively.
6. Administration is involved with the creative use of human resources—board, staff, and volunteer. The social agency is a group enterprise.
7. The parts of the enterprise are interrelated and interacting. This principle is basic to the operation of a social agency and means that a part of the executive function is to establish roles, relationships, rules, and regulations that will produce the optimum of good effects and the minimum of bad effects.
8. What one does not do has effects as well as what one does do.[9]

Within the past few years, social work administration has incorporated many of the principles and approaches utilized in business, particularly in improving efficiency and effectiveness in the delivery of social services.

Newman and Turem indicate that accountability is an issue of high visibility, high priority, and considerable controversy in the social work profession. At the same time, they describe the need for understanding what accountability is and for utilizing it to advantage for social work. They suggest:

> A sound system of accountability goes beyond honesty and is based on results. The techniques oriented to relationships and processes, which are the heart of the social work profession, are the most "soft" and most in need of being put in proper perspective. If credible professional accountability is to occur, casework and group work must be viewed as inputs that may or may not reduce the incidence of definable social problems, and the profession must develop a new orientation based on outputs that can be measured objectively.[10]

It is suggested by Rapp and Poertner that "not to monitor client outcomes substantially and use that data to improve operations is tantamount to managerial irresponsibility, incompetence, and unethical conduct."[11] Doueck and Bondanza represent the attitude of present-day administrators in social work, as well as most political and community leaders, that we live in an era of accountability and diminishing resources and "it becomes increasingly important for human services agencies to demonstrate the efficacy of their programs."[12]

## Supervision

Supervision, a major part of social work administration, is concerned with helping staff to *use* their knowledge and skill in getting the job done efficiently and well. In the etymological sense, the word *supervision* means "oversight, control, surveillance." In social work it is more commonly used to define the function that one individual, the supervisor, assumes in relation to another, the supervisee. Supervision can be thought of as an administrative process that assists staff development and performance. The agency will function with the optimum of efficiency, conserving human values in work with clients, when the staff responsible for the operation of the agency is qualified, and when its capacity to render service is aided by effective agency policy and procedures that emphasize the preeminence of the worker in the helping process. Supervision focuses upon the acquisition and use of knowledge and the application of skills to practice. It is a teaching-learning situation, educational as well as administrative and enabling.

In the public and private welfare agency the position of supervisor enjoys status and respect. The qualified and competent supervisor is a key person in a staff organization with responsibility for both administration of services and staff development.

Supervision in social work is a response to the needs of clients and the mandate of the community to relieve suffering and to restore people to greater usefulness. Social problems are always a challenge and decisions aimed at relieving stress and rehabilitation are among the most difficult on the spectrum of human experience. The supervisor's role is one of support, encouragement, the imparting of information, and of listening to the worker, particularly to the new and inexperienced staff. Supervisors point out knowledge gaps and deficiencies in skill and assist workers to control their biases. They give psychological support by allaying anxiety and by their interest and understanding; they are professional models for new workers and a bridge to the agency for the experienced worker new to the particular job or agency.

### Supervision Is Teaching

Supervision is essentially a teaching job, and its theory is derived from education as well as social work. Some of the important educational principles of supervision are mentioned in the following paragraphs.

The supervisee participates actively in his or her own learning. He or she is involved in the planning for his or her function in the agency and not a receptacle of a "ready-made, hand-me-down plan" devised by someone else. This person must think through and make decisions relative to clients, which will be implemented in his or her interviews and social study. Supervision is based on the assumption that the worker learns best when taking responsibility for one's own learning. Hence, the supervisor resists the temptation, however great, to impose personal standards, values, and methods of helping. He or she encourages, gives information, and even offers advice, but will not preempt the learning role. The supervisor would agree with Emerson that "Nothing is ... sacred but the integrity of our own mind."

The assumption is that the worker learns by doing. This individual must be given the opportunity to carry responsibility for the work performed in the agency. If mistakes are made, they will be viewed as learning opportunities and used by the supervisor to call attention to better ways of doing things. They will not be an excuse for the supervisor to take over the service function. In a VA psychiatric hospital, a social worker was promoted to supervisor, but continued his direct service function until supervisees objected because they were not permitted to do their work. One learns by doing, in part through identification. A worker, however, may be driven by fear to identify with his or her supervisor and to accept that which is imposed from without. When this occurs, learning may not be integrated, only falsely imitated, used ambivalently, and later rejected.

The worker learns by using his or her whole self. Learning is more than an intellectual exercise. It involves the integration of feelings, intellect, and performance. Frequently, learning fails to take place because of a worker's excessive anxiety, which often results in stereotyped behavior, excessive dependency, passivity, submission, and intellectualization. A friendly working atmosphere and acceptance of a supporting relationship with one's supervisor are safeguards to performance and a protection against immobilizing anxieties. Feeling and intellect are one in learning in social work.

The worker-supervisor relationship is the main dynamic in learning. It is predicated on the greater knowledge and skill of the supervisor, his or her regard for the worker, willingness to share, and on the capacities and desires of the worker. Positive learning takes place through a positive relationship. When the relationship is negative and destructive, learning is resisted or occurs under conditions inimical to good practice. The relationship can be facilitated by the supervisor who has confidence in the worker, who believes in the worker's capacity and worth. He or she builds on the worker's strengths and emphasizes those qualities that make for competence and efficiency on the job. He or she freely acknowledges the superiority of the worker in those situations where it is demonstrated. Honesty and integrity must characterize the relationship if the purpose of the agency is to be served.

One beginning worker, whose relationship with the supervisor was one of mutual respect and trust, was heard to say that she had been enhanced by (1) the knowledge her supervisor shared with her, (2) the kind of a caring person the supervisor was, and (3) in knowing that if she needed help, her supervisor was available.

### Techniques of Supervision

Records of supervisory conferences are used for teaching purposes, for improving practice, and to point up areas of need in the armamentarium of the worker. Evaluations are also dynamic, continuous, and are discussed freely in worker-supervisory conferences that may be regularly scheduled.

Evaluation conferences at times reveal fear on the part of the worker of his or her ability to control the situation, a loss of self-esteem, a threat to the worker's self-image, and fear of punishment. Evaluations, too, become sources of satisfaction when used realistically to appraise and assess the performance of the worker by his or her superior.

The supervisor too, has feelings about evaluations. If the person lacks self-confidence and has a desire to be liked it may lead him or her to cover up the worker's weaknesses and inadequacies. To avoid conferences too charged with feeling the supervisor keeps in mind that the evaluation is a means of promoting the supervisee's learning and self-awareness and a process in which the supervisor and the worker both participate.

The subject matter of evaluation is the worker's feelings about people, his or her method of handling feelings, understanding of behavior in social situations, as well as ability to express oneself. He or she will be helped to relate to the client's needs and to the *what* and *how* of resources, and will be taught to participate in the agency's program for staff development—institutes, classes, workshops, and regularly scheduled staff meetings.

One caution needs to be kept in mind—the danger of too much supervision. Some leaders in social work suggest that their supervisory system makes the inexperienced workers too dependent on the administrators arid senior workers. Certainly care should be taken so this does not happen. A basic goal in supervision should be the helping of a worker to become independent in the planning and implementation of the worker's practice.

Basic to successful supervision are enabling qualities of personality that make it possible for the worker and for the supervisor to be essentially giving persons. Supervisors need to bring to their jobs a readiness to live beyond themselves and a concern for people. Giving and a regard for people, combined with a trained and disciplined mind, make supervision a constructive and dynamic force in the life of the learner, enabling him or her to meet obligations to the client and the agency.

## Consultation

Another important part of administration is consultation, which is the means by which agencies are able to extend and improve their services to clients. Consultation is an interaction between professional persons who explore a problem to find a solution that will best serve the needs of a client.

As a process, consultation is a technique for improving and expanding services. This method provides specialized help and technical information from a variety of disciplines by bringing together competent persons in an exchange of information, making it possible to provide greater service to troubled individuals and families.

Consultation is not the province of any one discipline. The knowledge, skill, and the scientific base it rests upon is that of the professional discipline of the consultant. Social work consultants derive their competence from social work.

Consultation is predicated on three main assumptions:

1. That the consultant has a greater knowledge than the consultee in the areas of agency and worker needs, which can be communicated in usable form.
2. That the consultant can help the consultee to improve upon the use of his or her skills, or to acquire new ones for the better performance of the job.
3. That the consultee can use the process to enhance his or her caretaking function by clarifying thinking, elaborating his or her own ideas, and defining treatment goals and purposes. Consultation may result in the confirmation of the soundness of what the consultee is doing and identify gaps and weaknesses in his or her efforts. Psychological support, selective testing of the worker's thinking, and the results of creative interaction of professional people when goal-focused are important products of the consultation process.

### *Principles of Consultation*

The consultant organizes and arranges knowledge and skill for a specific consultation purpose, namely, that of helping someone else to do the job that he or she is hired to do, and to do it better.

Consultation is a helping process involving the use of technical knowledge and a professional relationship with one or more persons. This is a relationship of mutual respect and confidence, which the consultant develops, enhances, and maintains by the employment of sound principles of social work. These include beginning where the client is, the use of a nonjudgmental approach, emotional support, acceptance, defining the situation, role clarification, and confidentiality.

Essentially, the consultant has a conviction that the consultee can do the job he or she is assigned to do. The egocentric person who attaches a magic quality to his or her own self fails in consultation for the reason that the consultant must be an enabler of others. The consultant does not evaluate or make judgments about the work of the consultee.

The consultant-consultee role is task-oriented and is concerned with only certain aspects of the consultee's function. The consultant helps with problems experienced by the consultee, although he or she may recognize that the main problem is something other than that for which help is requested. In the process of clarification the consultant may assist the consultee to encompass the broader, more vital elements of the problem. Unless this is done, however, no shift is made in the area identified by the consultee.

The consultee must be free to accept or reject the services of the consultant. The consultant never carries the force of administration and the consultation role is destroyed when the consultant tries to prescribe the use that will be made by the consultee of the service offered. The confidentiality of communication between the consultant and the consultee is the cornerstone of consultation. Consultation is facilitated when the worker's relationship with the consultant is one of trust, and when he or she knows that the consultant does not evaluate personnel or report conversations to administration.

The heavily laden consultee, burdened by the pressures of the job, responds to the emotional support that comes from intelligent listening and understanding of his or her problems.

It has been generally observed that a crisis in life can serve as an impetus toward getting things done. Crises may mobilize individuals, families, and even larger groups to more thoughtful, creative behavior, and to action that may lead to constructive change and progress. Thinking behavior can be the product of crises.

Major and minor crises occur in the lives of all people and the staffs of social agencies are often confronted with crises in the lives of their clients. Sometimes workers, unaided, are powerless to give effective help in a crisis; but it is a known fact that a crisis can motivate the worker to seek and use the help of a consultant. Sometimes the inadequacies of the worker result from feelings of helplessness stemming from the magnitude of the task to be accomplished, and sometimes because of gaps in training or lack of preparation and experience. Regardless of the reality, when a need exists the worker who can mobilize independently to array the various forces at his or her disposal to meet the demands of the situation is particularly favorable at that moment for consultation.

Social agencies and their workers have long recognized the benefits resulting from the contributions of psychiatrists, psychologists, cultural anthropologists, sociologists, and others who have been retained by agencies in consultant capacities. Social workers confronted with difficult and perplexing social and personal situations have been among the first to recognize and to use the knowledge of the specialist. In turn, social workers serve as consultants to other professions and on staffs in the fields of health and welfare in local, state, regional, and national offices. Services to clients are thus improved and extended. Consultation often can be particularly helpful in the schools where social workers help teachers understand human behavior and child growth and development. In addition, they help teachers develop skills in dealing with children and in evaluating their behavior.

The use of social work consultants by other helping professions and by administrators of health and social service departments and units is increasing. Their knowledge and skills related to human behavior and practice skills in helping persons with personal, family, and community problems are being utilized as never before. Also, they are often asked to provide a gestalt view of problems and solutions that is helpful to professional workers outside the social work arena.

## Collaboration

Collaboration is a device for making treatment as total and as effective as possible by a wide and discriminating use of resources, and by combining professional competences. At its best, collaboration is an orchestration of agency services, professional talents, and client needs.

Collaboration in the social service system becomes a shared experience in which the knowledge of professionals, paraprofessionals, and indigenous workers is shared in the various processes of service delivery.

Interagency collaboration is achieved formally and informally by cooperation and community planning, communication of information, by case conferences, and referral of clients. Agencies are only loosely federated. Collaboration among them results from their common purpose of relieving suffering and restoring clients to more helpful and satisfying ways of functioning. Thus, a hospital, for example, may, through proper use of medication, nursing care, and rest, succeed in relieving a patient of distressing symptoms that are due to severe stress situations in the patient's home environment. Knowing this, the hospital, through its social work department, refers a client to a family agency for counseling, helps with family finances, and aids in the budgeting of the family income. Or again, an adoption agency whose program is to provide food, shelter, clothing, and casework services to unwed mothers, refers these mothers to their own physicians for obstetrical care and uses the hospital services available in the community. If the agency takes relinquishment from the natural mother and makes plans to adopt the baby, the adopting parents are directed to lawyers who handle the legal technicalities of adoptions.

The clinic team is the best known of the formal arrangements for collaboration. It is a closely knit working group in contrast with the looseness of the organization of a community of agencies. A more rounded service is available to the client when the knowledge, skill, and training of several disciplines are pooled in deciding objectives, building programs, and planning services.

The clinic team functions under one administrator. It has a common budget. It shares the same office and work space with clients whose needs can be served by the efforts of the team working individually or in concert. Historically, the team created by the child guidance movement was somewhat proscribed. The social worker did the social study and worked with the parents, generally the mother, with a parent-child focus. Representing other disciplines were the psychiatrist, who treated the child, and the psychologist, who did the testing. These somewhat arbitrary divisions of labor have been relaxed in the child guidance clinic and community mental health center, and team concepts have been modified and adapted to a rather wide variety of clinic settings and agencies.

### Teamwork Concepts

Teamwork derives its meaning and validity from the democratic tradition; it is incompatible with an authoritarian ideology. The authority is largely that of knowledge and competence, which asserts itself at each encounter with the client, or of the work to be done in the agency at that moment when it is needed.

A team is a cooperative democratic group of professional individuals who work together to provide diagnosis and treatment. They think and contribute as a whole, and no important action is taken without the consent of the group.

The team is a fellowship of people and ideas. The bond that unifies a clinic team is a bond of service—each member of the team has and shares a common purpose, a common objective, and each is desirous of providing a maximum of service for the individual who comes to the agency for help.

The team is a union of interdependent inquiry. Different team members approach the problem from the standpoint of their particular disciplines and from the framework of their body of knowledge, their philosophy of working with individuals, and their skill; yet at the same time they respect the independence, the skill, and the competence of other team members. Respect and regard for the competences of others is a cornerstone of successful teamwork. The common denominator of a team is the conception of man as a product of a biological, psychological, social, and spiritual continuum, and the method pervading the efforts of the team is that of scientific inquiry jointly pursued, or of collaboration.

Teamwork is predicated on the individuality of the participating disciplines. It derives its strength through the preservation of differences. For social work this implies that before one can become a useful clinician he or she must first have established identity as a social worker. It is true, however, that individuals on the team surrender some of their independence. Team members are obligated not only to deliver their professional functions, but also to be aware of what is going on in other phases of treatment. In addition, a member must keep others on the team informed about his or her own progress, for other professions depend upon him or her for the success of the case.

Teamwork does not just happen. It is a process. It develops from the discovery of self and others. It is a dynamic process. It implies a capacity for growth and change.

There must be conviction at the administrative level of the validity of the common purpose. There must be executive conviction that the team purpose is as important as any other. Teamwork cannot exist by administrative decree alone and structure cannot make a team. The administration should acquaint other services with, and define responsibility for, each service. The chief of the individual service defines his or her service and explains how it is given. This individual is responsible for the standards of performance and the quality of services given.

To illustrate the importance of teamwork, Skidmore has coined the term "teamship." He explains the concept as follows:

Considerable emphasis has been placed on the importance of leadership in the administration process. However, teamship, or lack of it, is also vital. Teamship means teamwork plus the ability to work effectively in a joint endeavor. *The New Twentieth Century Webster's Dictionary* states that teamwork is "joint action by a group of people, in which each person subordinates his individual interests and opinions to the unity and efficiency of the group; co-ordinated effort."

The ability of staff members to work together effectively is part of teamship. A total team effort in social work practice, involving leaders and workers, is particularly significant since social work involves people, their relationships and their feelings. Competent leadership and supportive teamwork can make a major difference in the services offered.

The contributions of individual staff members to an agency can equal more than the sum of their efforts. They can be synergistic, with joint efforts and combined actions enhancing the significance of individual efforts. Staff members working cooperatively together can bring results that surpass in quantity and quality the mere addition of the contributions of each. When they do not work together, the results may be negative or diminished. As in football, cooperative, unified action brings the team's efforts and forces together; individual competition, inaction, or showing off by players may do the opposite.[13]

Overall collaboration of team members is a continuous process. Collaboration begins with a group leader, the one who coordinates all services in the setting, who must recognize the positive and negative feelings that he or she brings to the collaborative process. Such an individual must value oneself as a professional person and be clear about the way in which the service entrusted is to be offered. In social work, stress is placed upon the need for the individual to be clear about individual responsibility and relationship to the patient. Unity of purpose within the organization is basic and can be reached best through the planned conference, the formal method by which the team is put together and comes into existence. However, there are informal methods through which team work is enhanced, and the informal methods are often equal in importance to the more formal ones.

## Shifting Power in Social Work Administration

Traditionally, social work administration included an agency director at the top with considerable authority and jurisdiction. Assistant directors and supervisors had authority to direct staff and provide services. Planning and decisions were made mainly by the administrators. Clients had little opportunity for input, to offer suggestions or raise questions.

There has been considerable shifting taking place, allowing for redistribution and sharing of administrative power. Three groups are involved in agency services: executives, staff, and clients. Today the leaders share more power with their staffs and with clients. In one sense, symbolically, this move leaves an authoritative power triangle behind, shifting to an open circle, which allows for interaction and sharing of ideas, feelings and actions among all three groups. Joint discussions and decisions are common. Participatory administration is gaining momentum among staff and clients.

# Research

Research is an enabling process in social work, one that is being stressed more in practice. Social workers are recognizing the need for scientific answers to numerous questions. They need to know why people behave as they do, particularly in their social functioning, and, also, what happens when various skills and techniques of the social worker are applied in helping disadvantaged people. Social workers recognize that they can ask many more questions than they can answer; thus research is needed as never before.

## Definition

What is social research? Webster's *New International Dictionary* states that research is "careful or critical inquiry or examination in seeking facts or principles; diligent investigation in order to ascertain something." *The Encyclopedia of the Social Sciences* explains that research is "the manipulation of things, concepts or symbols for the purpose of generalizing to extend, correct, or verify knowledge, whether that knowledge aids in the construction of a theory or in the practice of an art." Stated briefly, social research is systematic inquiry regarding social situations and problems, the process of obtaining social facts, or methodical inquiry into social phenomena.

Social research is related to two or more people, or situations involving such people, and their interactions. Much social research is focused on social problems of people who live together.

There is a difference between pure research and applied research. Social workers are particularly interested in applied research, which is for utilitarian purposes contrasted with pure research, which is conducted for its own sake. Nevertheless, more social workers today are developing an interest and practice related to pure research as well as applied research.

As explained previously, social problems exist in society and cause pain, unhappiness, and difficulties to millions of people. Crime and delinquency, for example, cost the United States more than $3

00 billion each year. Even more important than the financial burdens are the individual and family heartaches and emotional scars that result. What causes crime? How can it be reduced? Can social work help to prevent it? These and related questions are open challenges to social workers on the present scene. Such problems as mental illness, physical handicaps, and many others open the door to similar questions and the need for research.

People have many false ideas and superstitions regarding the behavior of others, their social functioning, and their social problems. Millions of dollars are spent each year on charlatans who give questionable answers and guidance to people with personal and family difficulties. Scientific research is sorely needed to help provide data for social planning, improving society, and aiding people on an individual, family, and community basis.

## Social Work and Research

Many social workers believe that "Common sense is enough in working with people." This is not so. Facts are needed if we are to accomplish the goals of professional social work.

Many values of research attach to social work. Accurate observation is basic to both research and other aspects of social work. Students and practitioners who develop abilities to do research enhance their abilities to work with people in other ways. A healthy skepticism of statistics is needed by social workers and is usually acquired by research study.

Social workers need to keep abreast of current investigations and to obtain access to the new facts, techniques, and skills that are developing. Social workers are more and more called upon to participate in social research activities. Many of them are now hired on a full-time basis with their professional energies going into research. Social workers need to utilize the objective techniques of science and research in all that they do. This does not mean that they abolish or eradicate their personal warmth and interest in people, but it does mean that they bring into operation scientific attitudes and techniques that can help them to come closer to the realities of life and to the solutions of problems.

Briar reaffirms the growing importance of research in the following statement:

Research is becoming accepted as an integral part of the social work profession. As we know, research was, of course, a part of our profession from its earliest beginnings, but more often than not we regarded research as a less than welcome intruder whose presence we ignored, avoided, and even openly rejected.

Such attitudes toward research stemmed, in part, from two beliefs. One idea was that research was somehow incompatible with the human elements central to our profession (especially social work practice)—the feelings, emotions, and intense relationships that are an inherent part of the social worker's daily practice. The other source was the belief that what social workers do, what their practice objectives are, and even the nature of problems that social workers deal with are

Administrative unit of a social work agency.

too complex and elusive to be studied and measured by "scientific research techniques." These beliefs were widespread among social workers until quite recently.

We have discovered that research can generate findings (knowledge) that have a direct and immediate use for us. The skepticism about research among social workers was not unfounded. Little of the social work research that had been conducted produced data that we could find useful in practice. In recent years an increasing number of research findings have appeared that have direct, useful, and constructive application to social work practice. As this trend continues, social workers can be expected to look to research findings (and actually engaging in research studies) for solutions to practice problems. Also, the emergence of research methods and techniques makes it more feasible for social workers to conduct research on their own practice and in their own agencies. This development, which makes possible the incorporation of research techniques into the normal routine of practice, provides the necessary foundation not only for the generation of a body of knowledge based on practice research but also for the use of research techniques by social workers to solve their practice problems.[14]

The 1992 curriculum policy statement developed by the Council on Social Work Education emphasizes the importance of research in social work education and practice. The curriculum guidelines for the MSW programs include the following:

M6.12 The foundation research curriculum must provide an understanding and appreciation of a scientific, analytic approach to building knowledge for practice and for evaluating service delivery in all areas of practice. Ethical standards of scientific inquiry must be included in the research content.

The research content must include qualitative and quantitative research methodologies; analysis of data, including statistical procedures; systematic evaluation of practice; analysis and evaluation of theoretical bases, research questions, methodologies, statistical procedures, and conclusions of research reports; and relevant technological advances.

M6.13 Each program must identify how the research curriculum contributes to the student's use of scientific knowledge for practice.

Grinnell has identified the following three research roles for social workers:

*The Consumer of Research:* The first professional role is that of the consumer of research. This role stems from the conviction that social workers have an obligation—to self, to society, and to the recipients of services—to base their efforts on knowledge in the field. . . .

*The Disseminator of Knowledge:* The second professional role is that of a disseminator of knowledge. Social workers have a responsibility to initiate and participate in systematic efforts to determine effective practice methods for social work problems. The results of such efforts are then communicated to other social workers in ways that will be useful to them. . . .

*The Contributing Partner:* The third professional role is that of a contributing partner, This means joining with others to broaden the knowledge base of our profession. This means joining with others who have similar tasks and problems to rank the importance of gaps in knowledge and to determine appropriate ways of filling them.[15]

Research has a vital role in social work education. The knowledge of the research process enhances professional practice by helping the social worker become both a consumer and producer of research.

A current example of significant developments in social research in social work comes from the National Institute of Mental Health (NIMH), which in 1994 funded 49 research programs, 19 of them new, with social work faculty and practitioners as directors or codirectors, with total funding amounting to $12.5 million. "These research projects rely on collaborations between practice settings and schools of social work. They produce knowledge to make a difference in people's lives. They provide a training ground for the investigators of the future."[16]

## *Major Steps in Research*

Social workers need to have a knowledge of basic research technology. Because of the complexity of human problems, social workers often forget or neglect to utilize the scientific method in evaluating their own practice.

All research efforts, regardless of how complex they may seem, are—based on the scientific method—a logical guide to thinking that helps the scientist study and explain problems. The scientific method has been formulated into the following paradigm by Polansky.

1. A researchable problem is located, sharpened, and related to theory (conceptualized); since this is an applied field, its practical significance is also stated;
2. The logic by which conclusions will be drawn is specified (study design);
3. Potential subjects of the study are identified (sampling design);
4. Instruments for collecting information from or about the subjects are borrowed from others or created (method of data-collection);
5. Data are collected (study execution);
6. The data are analyzed statistically and/or qualitatively (analysis of results);
7. Results are compared with the problem originally posed so that conclusions may be drawn;
8. Larger implications for theory and for practice are inferred;
9. The significant elements of the whole process are summarized into an intelligible report to be disseminated to colleagues.[17]

Actually social workers apply the scientific method in all of their practice efforts. Both practice and research require an orderly thought process, beginning with a problem and working toward a solution. Social work practitioners base their conclusions on careful observation, experimentation, and intelligent analyses.

## *Main Kinds of Research for Social Workers*

Several methods and techniques are utilized in social work research. *Experimental research* that encompasses statistical methodology is being used considerably and involves study of a number of cases. These cases are generally arranged and classified into two groups, a control group and an experimental group. The control group proceeds in normal fashion and the experimental group has some new facet or interactional relationship introduced, which theoretically will bring about the hypothesized change or alteration. Statistical techniques and procedures are utilized to show relationships and correlations between different sets of data. Most schools of social work require one or more classes in statistical knowledge and research procedures. They also specify the preparation of a thesis or participation in a research project, either individual or group, or "research lab" experiences, which helps the student to learn about the importance of research and provides a beginning knowledge regarding research methodology and techniques.

A second approach utilized by social workers is the *case study* method. This process is basically an intensive study of one or a few cases, keeping in mind that an understanding of a specific case may be helpful in acquiring knowledge of human behavior and social functioning. Case studies may be accomplished by the social worker through examining records or by interviewing a client or clients. They may be obtained through the *own story* technique, which provides an opportunity for a person to write about his or her experiences and his or her reactions to them. Not only are the details of a case important, but the feeling and implications are particularly significant to social work practice.

Another method utilized by social workers is the *social survey*. This is an attempt to study on a broad basis a given neighborhood or community and to attempt to understand the underlying foundations and principles related to social problems, the behavior of people within these localities, and the total social milieu. Ordinarily, control groups are not utilized but rather an attempt is made to give an overall descriptive view of a community or other segment of society. This kind of research has been sponsored in particular by community welfare councils and coordinating councils in an attempt to find out the facts of given communities descriptively.

The *human ecological* approach is also used in studying social phenomena. This emphasizes the spatial distribution of human behavior and attempts to explain why there are differentials, geographically speaking, in regard to social conditions and problems. An example of this would be a study in a given community that would result in a geographical map showing the actual distribution by residence of the homes of the delinquents handled by the police or courts. Generally, such a map depicts certain clusterings and concentrations. Using this information, social planners attempt to understand the differentials and to do something to prevent and control delinquency, particularly in the areas of high concentration of antisocial behavior.

Another useful method in social work is the *historical* approach. This attempts to give perspective from the past for understanding present issues, problems, and plans of action, and to help in improving situations. Historical research can be accomplished through library study, interviews, viewing original documents of various kinds, and through objective study, comparison, and contrast of various materials.

One of the newer methods is *evaluation research*. This is an approach to assess program effectiveness—in social work, particularly social programs designed to improve the welfare of people. Weiss suggests that in evaluation research "the tools of research are pressed into service to make the judging process more accurate and objective. In its research guise, evaluation establishes clear and specific criteria for success. It collects evidence systematically from a representative sample of the units of concern. It usually translates the evidence into quantitative terms (23 percent of the audience, grades of 85 or better), and compares it with the criteria that were set. It then draws conclusions about the effectiveness, the merit, the success, of the phenomenon under study."[18]

Some researchers indicate a need to improve methodology in program evaluation. Grasso and Epstein observe that the traditional approach based on a retrospective quantitative focus is inadequate even though it may result in statistical indicators such as number of units of service delivered or the number of cases closed. They recommend a developmental approach that includes five primary stages of client-agency involvement which evaluation can address: referral, intake, intervention, program completion, and program follow-up. Grasso and Epstein conclude that:

> Developmental program evaluation relies on both qualitative and quantitative data for making future-oriented clinical and programmatic decisions. Using the individual case as the primary unit of analysis . . . not only guides future program decisions, but also helps direct service workers manage their cases. It provides a method for assessing client change across different stages of agency involvement and, as a result, helps workers focus their interventions more precisely on specific client needs.[19]

## Summary

*Administration and research are essential to the profession of social work. Social work education is placing more and more emphasis in these areas.*

*Administration is one of the major social work methods; it involves the transformation of social policies into social services. It is a process receiving greater recognition in the totality of social work practice. This process involves many basic principles and skills, which are important for adequate agency functioning.*

*Essentially, supervision is a staff development process but it also carries administrative responsibility. Supervision has been the logical outgrowth of the complexity of the job workers have been asked to do. It is a response to workers' needs to receive help on matters that often are of a difficult nature, and the solution of which have long-range consequences for the client.*

*Principles of casework and supervision are used in consultation. Consultation, however, does not include responsibility for administration. It offers a service to workers that will make them more effective in working with clients.*

*The services of an agency can be extended by consultation. They are expanded when the worker is helped to become more skillful and knowledgeable in role performance.*

*Collaboration is a social invention for combining skills and knowledge of several helping professions and various community resources in the service of clients. The clinic team composed of the social worker, psychiatrist, psychologist, and nurse is one of the best-known arrangements of collaboration among the professions.*

*Research is being recognized as a critical element in the preparation of social work practitioners. The future of the profession is dependent upon scientifically based research that adds to the social work knowledge base and answers practice questions.*

The central theme of all research is the scientific method. This method can be stated in a paradigm that guides logical thinking. On a general level, steps in the research process include problem selection; problem identification and formulation; development of a strategy or methodology; data collection; processing, organizing, and analyzing data; conclusions and interpretation of results; and report and application of the research.

Various research methods including the experimental, the historical, the social survey, the ecological, evaluation research, and the case study method are utilized to gain additional understanding about social functioning and the control and reduction of social problems.

Administrative and research knowledge and skills are essential for social workers. The two enabling processes strengthen the entire profession.

## Selected References

### Administration

GUMMER, BURTON, "Are Administrators Social Workers?: The Politics of Intraprofessional Rivalry," *Administration in Social Work,* II (Summer, 1987), 19–31.

GUTIÉRREZ, LORRAINE, LINNEA GLENMAYE, and KATE DELOIS, "The Organizational Context of Empowerment Practice: Implications for Social Work Administration," *Social Work,* 40 (March 1995), 249–258.

LEVY, CHARLES S., *Guide to Ethical Decisions and Actions for Social Service Administrators.* New York: The Haworth Press, 1982.

MIZRAHI, TERRY, and JOHN MORRISON, eds., *Community Organization and Social Administration.* New York: The Haworth Press, 1992.

PERLMUTTER, FELICE DAVIDSON, *Changing Hats: From Social Work Practice to Administration.* Silver Spring, MD: NASW Press, 1990.

SKIDMORE, REX A., "Administration Content for All Social Work Graduate Students," *Administration in Social Work,* 2 (Spring 1978), 59–73.

SKIDMORE, REX A., *Social Work Administration, Dynamic Management and Human Relationships,* 3rd ed. Boston: Allyn and Bacon, 1995.

SLAVIN, SIMON, ed., *Social Administration: The Management of the Social Sciences,* 2nd ed., 2 vols. New York: The Haworth Press, 1985.

### Research

BINGHAM, RICHARD D., and CLAIRE L. FELBINGER, *Evaluation in Practice.* White Plains, NY: Longman, 1989.

BLOOM, MARTIN, and JACK FISCHER, *Evaluation in Practice: Guidelines for the Accountable Professional.* Englewood Cliffs, NJ: Prentice Hall, 1982.

EWALT, PATRICIA, "Research Questions," *Social Work,* 40 (January 1995), 5–6.

GIBBS, LEONARD E., *Scientific Reasoning for Social Workers.* New York: Macmillan, 1991.

GILGUN, JANE F., "A Case for Case Studies in Social Work Research," *Social Work,* 39 (July 1994), 371–380.

GILLESPIE, DAVID, and CHARLES GLISSON, eds., *Quantitative Methods in Social Work.* New York: The Haworth Press, 1993.

KETTNER, PETER M., and LAWRENCE L. MARTIN, "Performance, Accountability, and Purchase of Service Contracting," *Administration in Social Work,* 17, No. 1 (1993), 61–79.

MARLOW, CHRISTINE, *Research Methods for Generalist Social Work.* Pacific Grove, CA: Brooks/Cole, 1993.

RUBIN, ALLEN, and EARL, BABBIE, *Research Methods for Social Workers.* Belmont, CA: Wadsworth Publishing Co., 1989.

SCOTT, DOROTHY, "Practice Wisdom: The Neglected Source of Practice Research," *Social Work,* 35 (November 1990), 564–568.

VIDEKA-SHERMAN, LYNN, and WILLIAM J. REID, eds. *Advances in Clinical Social Work Research.* Silver Spring, MD: National Association of Social Workers, 1990.

WAGNER, DAVID, "Reviving the Action Research Model: Combining Case and Cause with Dislocated Workers," *Social Work,* 36 (November 1991), 477–482.

WITKIN, STANLEY L., "Whither Social Work Research? An Essay Review," *Social Work,* 40 (May 1995), 424–428.

## *Notes*

1. Council on Social Work Education, *Statistics on Social Work Education in the United States:* 1994 (Alexandria, VA: Council on Social Work Education, 1995), p. 34.

2. Wayne A. Chess, Julia M. Norlin, and Srinika D. Jayaratne, "Social Work Administration, 1981–1985: Alive, Happy and Prospering," *Administration in Social Work,* 11 (Summer 1987), 68.

3. Ibid., p. 76.

4. John C. Kidneigh, "Social Work Administration, An Area of Social Work Practice?" *Social Work Journal,* 31 (April 1950), 58.

5. Herman Stein, "Social Work Administration," in *Social Work Administration: A Resource Book,* Harry A. Schatz, ed. (New York: Council on Social Work Education, 1970), p. 7.

6. Robert L. Barker, *The Social Work Dictionary,* 3rd ed. (Washington, DC: NASW Press, 1995), p. 8.

7. Rex A. Skidmore, *Social Work Administration,* 3rd ed. (Boston: Allyn and Bacon, 1995), p. 3.

8. Council on Social Work Education, Inc., *Curriculum Policy for the Master's Degree and Baccalaureate Degree Programs in Social Work Education* (New York: Council on Social Work Education, 1982), pp. 11–12.

9. Sue Spencer, *The Administration Method in Social Work Education, Curriculum Study,* III (New York: Council on Social Work Education, 1959), pp. 26–32.

10. Edward Newman and Jerry Turem, "The Crisis of Accountability," *Social Work,* 19 (January 1974), 12.

11. Charles A. Rapp and John Poertner, "Moving Clients Center Stage Through the Use of Client Outcomes," *Administration in Social Work* 11 (Fall/Winter 1987), 35.

12. Howard J. Doueck and Ann Bondanza, "Training Social Work Staff To Evaluate Practice: A Pre/Post/Then Comparison," *Administration in Social Work* 14, No. 1 (1990), 119.

13. Rex A. Skidmore, *Social Work Administration,* 3rd ed. (Boston: Allyn and Bacon, 1995), pp. 168–69.

14. Scott Briar, Foreword in Richard M. Grinnell, Jr., *Social Work Research and Evaluation,* 2nd ed. (Itasca, IL: F. E. Peacock Publishers, Inc., 1985), pp. ix–x.

15. Richard M. Grinnell, Jr., *Social Work Research and Evaluation,* 2nd ed. (Itasca, IL: F. E. Peacock Publishers, Inc., 1985), pp. 3–5.

16. Patricia L. Ewalt, "Research Questions," *Social Work,* 40 (January 1995), 6.

17. Norman A. Polansky, ed., *Social Work Research* (Chicago: University of Chicago Press, 1975), p. 15.

18. Carol H. Weiss, *Evaluation Research* (Englewood Cliffs, NJ: Prentice Hall, 1972), pp. 1–2.

19. Anthony J. Grasso and Irwin Eptstein, "Toward a Developmental Approach to Program Evaluation," *Administration in Social Work,* 16, Nos. 3/4 (1992), 199–200.

# Chapter 9

# *Mental Health Services*

*"Call the police. I've got to call the police now." That thought kept beating out a rhythm in my mind as I watched helplessly as my father made a shambles of my living room—throwing books on the floor, tipping over chairs and tables, smashing a lamp against the fireplace.*

*I knew I had to have help to subdue him—again. The officers came at my call, put him in restraints, and carried him screaming out the door. I committed him to the psychiatric ward of the hospital once again. Then I came back home to comfort my sons. How do you explain to 5- and 7-year-old boys that they are really not at fault, even though it was their noisy playing that made grandfather fly into a rage?*

*As usual, in three days he was back home, under the influence of tranquilizing drugs, quiet*

*and apologetic. Although he is very ill, the hospital cannot keep him because he refuses to commit himself. He is back because the issue has not been resolved about whether the mentally ill who are capable of harming themselves and/or others can be involuntarily restrained while receiving treatment.*

*My father is back with me, presumably because his constitutional right to freedom is the standard, not how desperately ill he is or how much he needs long-term hospital care. It appears to me that he is given the freedom to destroy himself, to destroy me and my own little family, as well as my home.*

*Are resources and social work services available to help?*

Mental health services have expanded and today Americans generally are able to talk about mental health problems. They are so important that three presidents and one First Lady, over a span of less than 25 years, have focused the nation's attention on this problem. In 1963 John F. Kennedy, in the first presidential message on mental health, highlighted three tasks that have come to be an imperative:

1. Seek out the causes of mental illness and mental retardation and eradicate them.
2. Strengthen the underlying resources of knowledge and above all of skilled manpower, which are necessary to mount and sustain our attack on mental disability for many years to come.
3. Strengthen and improve the programs and facilities serving the mentally ill and the mentally retarded.

By Executive Order, Jimmy Carter established the President's Commission on Mental Health on February 17, 1977. The commission was charged to "conduct such public hearings, inquiries, and studies as may be necessary to identify the mental health needs of the nation and to submit a report to the President recommending how these needs can be met, and identifying the relative priority of those needs."[1]

In 1987 President Ronald Reagan signed legislation (P.L. 99-660) mandating states to develop a three-year statewide comprehensive plan of services for the severely mentally ill in order to receive their share of federal funding for mental health services.

Nancy Reagan, during the presidency of Ronald Reagan, raised the consciousness of people everywhere to the growing need to attack the problems of drug abuse and alcoholism, stimulating interest among all levels of society. Public schools offer classes and workshops on drugs, and structure peer counseling for students, teachers, and parents. Many services have been set up and people everywhere have been made aware of the growing menace and threat of drugs to scores of basic social institutions.

Ever since President Kennedy first mandated his three tasks many billions of taxpayers' money have been spent in the struggle to "seek out the causes . . . and eradicate" mental illness. Almost every level of government has become involved; and the private sector, as well, is no less concerned. Private psychiatric hospitals have been built. Insurance companies have written into their health policies payment provisions for the treatment of claimants. Many thousands of people seek private help and often exhaust their savings to pay for services for themselves and families.

## Beginnings in Mental Health

Important changes were made in public opinion concerning the mentally ill that prepared the way for social work in the modern era. Exorcising, a barbaric and medieval method of treatment, made sense to those who believed that the mentally ill were possessed by demons, as did some means of cleansing and propitiation to those who saw sin as the cause of the malady. Such treatment methods seem absurd now in the light of physical, psychological, and social theories of causation.

Early attempts at care were crude and inhumane. The mentally ill were housed in overcrowded insane asylums, in almshouses with criminals and degenerates, and, not infrequently, in jails and prisons. Bloodletting was one of the regular treatments along with starvation, blistering, purging, surprise baths, and whippings. For a small fee, curious visitors to the asylums were entertained by "baiting" the madman.

Dorothea Lynde Dix, an outstanding crusader, worked to awaken public opinion to the suffering and the needs of the mentally ill; and many others have pioneered in the mental health movement. Study, diagnosis, and more humane treatment approaches began to be substituted for procedures based on superstition and ignorance of the needs of the mentally ill.

In the United States the first social workers in the mental health field worked in hospitals. Social work became a service in the Manhattan State Hospital in New York in 1906 and in the Boston Psychopathic Hospital in 1910. In 1919, after the end of World War I, the Surgeon General asked the American Red Cross (ARC) to establish social work in federal hospitals. The Red Cross assumed this responsibility and by January 1920, social service departments had been organized in forty-two hospitals. The ARC was still in army hospitals until after World War II when social workers were first commissioned in the armed forces of the United States.

The Child Guidance Movement, and its work with juvenile delinquents by William Healy, included social work. This movement made its greatest advance when, under the support of the Commonwealth Fund, demonstration clinics were established in Norfolk and St. Louis in the 1920s. In the next twenty years social work expanded rapidly in mental health activities, and although the mental hospitals were the first to make use of social work, the practice in clinics expanded more fully.

World War II dramatically brought to the nation's attention the need for some program of treatment for veterans who were disabled because of mental illness. The Mental Health Act of 1946 supported personnel development and training for the disciplines of psychiatry, social work, psychology, and nursing and later for an expanded team of mental health specialists.

Today mental illness and emotional disturbances are recognized as major health problems. As a result of an extensive door-to-door survey in 1984, it was concluded that 18.7 percent of Americans suffer from at least one psychiatric disorder.[2] Thus, mental illness affects nearly twenty people in every hundred.

Where do people get help when in need of mental health services? A wide assortment of services has evolved. An estimated four to five thousand mental health facilities have been established, including such agencies as community mental health centers, state and county hospitals, private hospitals, V.A. psychiatric services, residential treatment centers for children, free-standing hospitals and clinics, and others.

## Elements of the Mental Health Network

How a person or family gets into the mental health service network is illustrated graphically in Figure 9.l. Those who need counseling may be identified by workers in the major systems of our society, such as education, religion, corrections, welfare, health, or employment systems, or they may be self-referred. In Figure 9.1 the arrows of the referral process lead only to the periphery of the six-sided mental health network because there are so many possible referral points within the network that it is impossible to diagram them all. The large arrows on the side indicate the two basic services provided. The arrow on the left that moves from the clients to the network represents the mental health counseling service component, and the arrow on the right, moving from the network to its publics, represents the prevention component.

One of the most important elements of the mental health service network is the community mental health center (CMHC).

## Community Mental Health Centers

The center, a public support enterprise, provides comprehensive mental health services to citizens in every state of the country, including underserved minorities, elderly, some children, and to many living in sparsely populated, remote rural sectors of the country.

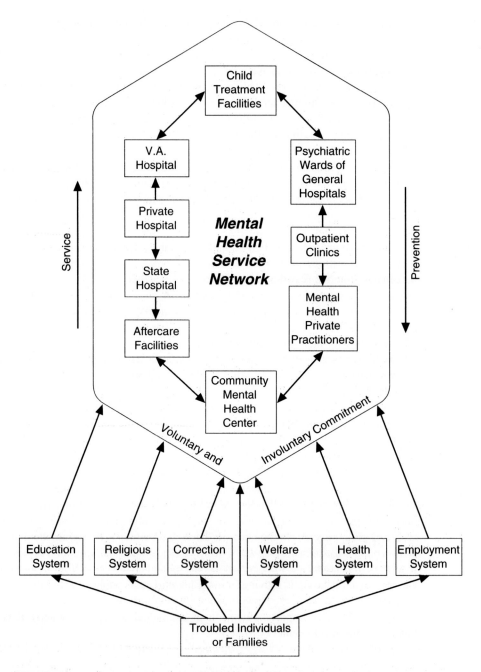

**FIGURE 9.1    How the Troubled Individual or Family Gets Help from the Mental Health Service Network.**

*Source:* Milton G. Thackeray, Rex A. Skidmore, and O. William Farley, *Introduction to Mental Health: Field and Practice* (Englewood Cliffs, NJ: Prentice Hall, 1979), p. 53.

Centers, funded by federal grants to states, are mandated to provide:

1. Inpatient, outpatient, day care and other partial hospitalization services and emergency services.
2. Programs of specialized services for the mental health of children and the elderly....
3. Consultation and education services for individuals and entities involved with mental health services (including health professions, schools, courts, law enforcement and correctional agencies, clergy, welfare agencies and health service agencies)....
4. Screening services of individuals being considered for referral to a state mental health facility, and provision, where appropriate, of treatment for such individuals.
5. Follow-up care for residents discharged from a mental health facility.
6. Transitional halfway house services for those discharged from a mental health facility....
7. Provision...of services for prevention and treatment of alcoholism, drug addiction and abuse and rehabilitation for alcoholics, drug addicts and abusers.

In addition, the services of the center:

1. Must be coordinated with the provision of services by other health and social service agencies....
2. Must be available and accessible promptly....
3. When medically necessary, must be available and accessible 24 hours a day, seven days a week.[3]

In the late fifties and early sixties community mental health centers were being planned. In the following thirty years more than 700 of the centers have been put into operation, but 2,000 are needed. Existing centers provide mental health care to millions of Americans.

## Essential Elements of Comprehensive Mental Health

A public system is patterned to provide help in all areas for those who are in crisis, those who need short-term care, and those who have serious mental problems requiring care in a restrictive facility over a long period of time. This care includes locating those who need the help, and providing it, either in a mental health center or in their homes.

The treatment services include twenty-four-hour-a-day crisis services. This makes it possible for anyone in need to receive immediate help and access to medical care and placement in either a residential facility or a hospital.

All patients receive a complete diagnostic evaluation by an interdisciplinary team, with input from the family if possible. From this comes a treatment plan that considers psychological, social, rehabilitation, and medical needs. A medical evaluation is made, and follow-up care is given as necessary.

Case management services by a person or team provide long-term, caring, supportive relationships, using whatever community resources are appropriate. The case manager provides direct assistance in obtaining needed services and coordinates and monitors services within and outside the mental health system with all agencies providing service. (For more information on case management see Chapter 19.)

Therapeutic day treatment is provided four or five days a week, including either Saturday or Sunday. Clinical day treatment services are provided for short-term stabilization, and these individuals are referred to less intensive services when feasible. Psychosocial rehabilitation services are designed to help severely mentally ill persons gain or regain skills needed to live, work, and socialize successfully in the community, so that hospitalization is not needed. Patients are taught to cope with life's situations, to develop skills that make it possible for them to live independently and to be successful in the workplace. This includes prevocational assessment, transitional and supported employment, and long-term support as necessary to maintain themselves in the job market.

Outpatient treatment, including individual therapy, group therapy, and supportive counseling, is available to all who can benefit from these services. An individual who needs twenty-four-hour supervision is provided for in a residential treatment center where the focus is on stabilization. They are helped to make the transition back to community living.

Two types of hospitalization are available. Short-term intensive care is provided in the local hospital to those who need constant supervision. No severely mentally ill person is discharged from a hospital without an agreed-upon place to go. For those who need longer care or a more secure setting, the state hospital is available to them. This option is selected only when less restrictive sources have been deemed to be inappropriate to the individual's needs.

The mentally ill need a complete support system, and the public mental health facility provides this. As patients are able to move from residential settings to independent living, they may need to move through group homes with staff supervision to affordable, normal housing. Follow-up case management is needed to assure that the skills they have practiced in day care or in the group home concerning hygiene and nutrition are being practiced. Support also comes from their peer groups and socialization groups, which may provide help with transportation, a meeting place, and activity planning.

Whenever possible, family support is encouraged so that family members can learn to handle crisis situations and behavioral problems. Mental health center staff see that the patient and the family learn about the nature of the illness and provide support in handling the problems arising from it. An important function of the center is to provide a period of respite services to the family members who care for severely mentally ill patients.

It is recognized that some of these elements are not now available in all centers. However, they are realistic, attainable, and very much in the planning and action stages for the 1990s. The description that follows illustrates the struggle over a period of many years of one mentally ill person.

---

Diane, who first heard voices and saw hallucinations as a young teenager, moved into a two-room apartment in a quiet neighborhood. She had just been released from a mental hospital. Diagnosed as chronic paranoid schizophrenic, she had lived at the hospital most of the time during the last 10 years.

Nearby her apartment was a neighborhood grocery store run by a couple who took a parental interest in Diane, and it was here that she got acquainted with other neighbors. Stabilized on medication and supervised by psychiatrists, social workers, and nurses at a nearby mental health center, Diane functioned adequately most of the time.

Although she was never employed, she got by on her Supplemental Security Income (SSI) payments and the generosity of her grocery store "parents" who also took over the daily dispensing of her medications because she so often couldn't remember whether or not she had taken her pills. This couple also provided daily conversation and in time a genuine caring for her.

When her fragile stability gave way to paranoia she feared for her own safety, and she was sure someone wanted to steal her meager possessions. Even with four locks on her door, she would call a neighbor at 3:00 A.M. to come to see if someone was prowling around her house.

Although she seldom attended church meetings, she had a high regard for the clergy and frequently sought their help when the "voices" became too insistent. Members of her church congregation became responsible for taking her shopping and to the laundromat, and for calls on the phone to check on her and to chat. Some of the male members responded to her need for household repairs and periodically to put a new lock on her door. She often remarked that what kept her able to live alone and kept her out of the hospital was her friends and her religious faith.

Diane was one of the fortunate mentally ill because she had an extended network of support, mostly voluntary. She lived in a neighborhood where the people were able to reach out to her. In her good times she was friendly and during the bad times her neighbors were understanding. With this help, she lived alone for almost 15 years.

Then her support system began to break down. Her little dog, a constant companion, had to be put to sleep because of old age. The grocery store went out of business and the proprietors both took full-time jobs. Her nurse at the mental health center transferred. Her landlord raised the rent beyond what she could pay. Her strongest support and best friends from her church moved away.

She was unable to cope with the changes in her life, and with her feelings about these changes. As she deteriorated, she spent a few weeks in a psychiatric ward of a general hospital, and was counseled not to try to continue to live alone. She moved into a nursing home.

## *Mental Hospitals*

Mental hospitals are an important part of the mental health service network and generally fall into three categories: (1) state and county hospitals, (2) Veterans Administration hospitals, and (3) private hospitals. Some hospitals are designated mental hospitals and all of their beds are used for psychiatric care, whereas other hospitals are a combination of both general and mental health care. Usually the V. A. hospitals and private hospitals have designated psychiatric wards.

Deinstitutionalization has had an impact on mental health hospitals. "In 1969 there were 468,831 inpatients in all facilities. By 1988, that figure had been cut to less than half, despite a growing population. The impact on state and county mental hospitals was even greater; their populations dropped from 387,629 to less than 100,000."[4]

The concept of the state mental hospital fell into disrepute in the later 1940s and early 1950s. The hope held out by people like Dorothea Lynde Dix had not been fulfilled. Rather than being a place of refuge with a healthy treatment atmosphere, the hospitals were too large, overcrowded, and understaffed. For example, one state hospital, built to house 250 patients, had a population of 1,400 patients in 1955. Many studies emphasize the fact that large institutions have negative effects on patients. The final report of the Joint Commission on Mental Illness and Health published in 1961 underscored this feeling about large state or county mental hospitals:

No further state hospitals of more than 1000 beds should be built, and not one patient should be added to any existing mental hospital already housing 1000 or more patients. It is further recommended that all existing state hospitals of more than 1000 beds be gradually and progressively converted into centers for the long-term and combined care of chronic diseases, including mental illness.[5]

The Joint Commission report also recommended that smaller state hospitals of a thousand beds or less be converted into "intensive treatment centers for patients with major mental illness in the acute stages or, in the case of a more prolonged illness, those with a good prospect for improvement or recovery."[6]

During the 1960s the trend was to "keep the patient out of the hospital at all costs." The CMHC was seen as a vehicle to "get rid" of the state hospital. In the 1990s, however, specialists recognized that small, well-staffed, regional state hospitals are an important link in community mental health services. These hospitals provide the environment for skilled observation that aids diagnostic clarification, as well as special medical, nursing, and rehabilitative efforts. In addition to the patient-centered tasks, the hospital can protect society from the effects of suicidal or homicidal behavior.

## Social Work in the Mental Hospital

The patient who is admitted to the hospital for the first time invariably possesses attitudes regarding the institution and the program of care that are inimical to his or her best interest. Furthermore, members of the family bring with them preconceived and distorted notions that seriously interfere with their efforts to assist in treatment plans. To many, the mental hospital is still the "end of the line." The idea persists that to hospitalize is to "put away" and that "once insane, always insane." For some, hospitalization means a loss of freedom. The denial to the patient of normal, simple pleasures is real. One patient said she disliked the hospital, not because she was mistreated or because the food was bad, but because she couldn't water her flowers or walk along the country lane. Many patients, hospitalized for the first time, fear other patients; they are apprehensive of attack, seduction, or lack of identity. The lonely and deprived patient feels rejection and a depth of loneliness deepened by the isolation of hospitalization. At admission, the social worker allays fears, helps the patient to become oriented to the hospital and eases the pain of separation. In similar ways, the social worker helps the family to accept hospitalization and the patient's treatment program. Families thus assisted support treatment efforts and hasten the day when the patient can be discharged.

Families sometimes mistakenly use hospitalization as a solution to their family problems. They have been living with the problem, frequently for long periods of time, and their tolerance may have broken down particularly when mental illness is accompanied by death, loss of employment, economic reversals, or other serious stress. The increase in hospitalized adolescents has revealed that frequently they are the victims of basic family conflicts. The social worker can help with these family-centered problems.

The ill individual is able to respond to treatment best when he or she has the assurance that the family continues to be involved. As the family is helped to mobilize its strengths, it can look ahead to reunion and the return to health of the ill member. The interaction within the family must be understood clearly before the problem can be resolved.

The importance of the family in rehabilitation is emphasized and families are increasingly involved in the treatment program. Treatment involving a family has many ramifications. Initially some families cannot bring themselves to think about the sick member's return home. For example, a wife who has been severely traumatized by her spouse may be reluctant to have him rejoin the family. A patient who hallucinates may not be welcomed by the family because she "hears voices" and talks to unseen audiences. A family and a neighborhood may need help to understand, accept, and live with hallucinatory behavior.

In one metropolitan community, citizens angrily protested when they learned that patients from a state hospital were to be placed in nursing homes in their area. They wrote letters to the local newspaper, circulated protest petitions among neighbors, held meetings with city officials, and forced reconsideration of the hospital's plan. Citizens need help to understand patients, their illnesses, and their capacity to lead normal lives in the community. In recent years nursing and foster home care of mental patients have become an important part of treatment, These programs are defeated, however, when patients are not given the freedom of the community or when the prevailing attitude of the neighborhood is one of mistrust, fear, and even hostility.

The social worker is concerned with all aspects of the patient's relationships within the hospital, as well as to his or her family and community. Patients respond to treatment best when they understand and cooperate with it, and can trust the staff responsible for its administration. Rehabilitation can be achieved best when the patient's interest in family, employment, and the community is sustained while he or she is undergoing treatment. The social worker is often the key person to assist the patient in maintaining sound interpersonal relationships. It is also the social worker who assists the patient in using the family and community resources for protection and restoration to normal activities.

## After-care Facilities

The mental health network provides after-care services to assist in the resocialization of patients. Many of these facilities are operated as part of the hospital, community mental health center, or free-standing outpatient clinic.

One specialized after-care facility is the halfway house providing living arrangements for people who have been hospitalized for mental illness and are trying to return to the community. It provides a transitional step for those who are not quite ready to participate in independent living. A nonmedical residential facility, the halfway house provides for recovering patients to be a part of the community and to participate in regular activities. It provides opportunities for reestablishing work, family and social relationships on a gradual basis under sheltered conditions. Many who leave institutions need a compassionate, warm, and empathic environment while they acquire skills and confidence to live in the community. Halfway houses that meet the highest standards provide for these needs.

While the halfway house provides a viable link in the care of some mentally ill people, caution has to be exercised in the control of these facilities. Many have become no more than holding tanks—understaffed and under-programmed. Care needs to be taken to ensure that these facilities do provide the means for a recovering mentally ill person to reenter the community.

## Therapeutic Clubs

Therapeutic clubs are one of the newer developments in aiding those who have been mentally ill. Fountain House, perhaps the first such facility, has been used as one model for others throughout the United States.

The Fountain House concept evolved from a group of former psychiatric patients who wanted to improve their chances of staying out of institutions. With the help of two community volunteers they sought other mental patients as *members* to join a *club*.

From this small beginning in the 1940s in New York City this one group has grown to more than a thousand members who attend club functions each month. The group has maintained these basic beliefs:

1. People with emotional disabilities, even severe ones, have productive potential. Every member has the ability to do something that is needed and will be valued by other club members.
2. Work is important for everyone. The club guarantees that each one will have the opportunity to work in the real world at regular, nonsubsidized jobs.
3. Everyone needs social relationships and the club provides opportunities for relaxing, social support on evenings every day of the year including weekends and holidays.
4. People need adequate housing. By leasing low-cost apartments, the club provides housing that is pleasant and affordable with congenial companions. Members pay their fair share of the cost.

From these basic concepts naturally evolved the work program that has members gaining skills by their working at needed tasks around the club—maintenance, cooking, clerical jobs, help with publishing a newsletter, answering telephones, etc., which provide social effectiveness and preparation for outside jobs. As they are able to handle other work, they are put into the transitional employment program, which helps them to find meaningful employment—often the biggest hurdle for mental patients. Jobs are secured in normal places of business where they are placed according to their skills, and are paid the prevailing wage rate. These jobs are temporary, and a member may have several jobs before finding a permanent work place.

Transitional employment is a part of almost all psychosocial rehabilitation programs. With the support of staff in easing members into the workplace, employers are guaranteed that the job will be done.

Viewed by both members and staff as one of the most important aspects of the program is the "reach out" feature. Members who do not come in for a time are sought out by staff and other members to let them know that they are missed, that they are cared about, and that the club wants to be of help. No one is forgotten just because he or she is absent. Regardless of how long it takes, each one is followed until the person is able to be completely independent.

Because Fountain House seems to be successful for many, similar programs have been set up based on this model. In 1980 there were 123 such programs, and by 1982 there were 456 employers in twenty-seven states involved in the transitional employment program.

By appealing to the basic human needs, this model emphasizes the cooperation between members and staff more as co-workers than client and superior, dignifies members' contributions, elevates their sense of self-worth, and improves their quality of life.

## *Outpatient Psychiatric Clinics*

Outpatient clinics in many places have become a part of the community's comprehensive mental health program for children and adults. With the spread of the community centers, their function is changing as they become an integral part of the expanded health care system.

Outpatient clinics are widely used for the care of emotionally disturbed children, which illustrates this mode of mental health service. These clinics are often sponsored by voluntary contributions through such funding sources as the United Way, but they also may be a part of university medical centers, mental hospitals, or community mental health centers.

Through interviews and testing, a diagnosis is made. Treatment is planned that will alleviate the problems by modifying the child's unacceptable behavior. Treatment is usually given by psychiatrists, psychologists, and social workers, whose roles have become increasingly flexible in the recent past.

Difficulty in disciplining, temper tantrums, poor relationships with peers and siblings, and poor adaptation to school are the most frequently encountered problems in the children's clinics. Clinic staff members have been increasingly more willing to accept problems connected with severe childhood disorders as well as minor difficulties, such as behavior problems.

In conjunction with working with the child, the workers involve the parents in the treatment process, helping them to understand the child's behavior and ways of dealing with it. Also, family conflicts are discussed in relation to their contributing to the situations causing the child to misbehave.

Social worker conducting behavioral therapy.

### *Residential Treatment Centers for Children (RTC)*

Residential treatment centers for children are another important element in the mental health service network. The RTC grew out of the child guidance movement, initiated in the early 1900s. The guidance clinics recognized that children needed to have special help with emotional problems and that early intervention could prevent more serious problems.

It is estimated that there are as many as 2 million children under the age of eighteen who have emotional problems severe enough to warrant urgent attention, and that there are 10 million to 15 million more who would benefit from psychiatric help of some kind.

The bulk of services to children are provided on an outpatient basis through private clinics and mental health professionals, but the residential treatment center is an allied resource. In addition to the residential centers, state, county and private hospitals care for emotionally disturbed children.

While the importance of working with children has been recognized, the services have not been developed in a coordinated, effective fashion. As a society we need to move more aggressively toward establishing a total mental health system for children that will be preventive in nature and will help them develop their full potential.

Although we have an extensive mental health network, the needs of many go unmet. Mental disorders are pervasive in our society and are of concern to lay people and professionals alike. What are a few of the areas of special concern?

## *Special Problems and Issues in Mental Health*

The plans in the 1960s were to create community mental health centers in 2,000 geographical areas. Today we have approximately 700 centers. Hospital beds have been emptied, but nothing was provided to take their place. When patients were discharged, the money did not follow them. Most of mental health funding still goes to mental institutions that house only a fraction of patients formerly housed there. More than 60 percent of the chronically mentally ill are at large in the community.

Many of the "comprehensive" services are less than comprehensive. For instance, there are too few beds; hardly more than lip service is given to prevention; transitional housing is almost nonexistent, and specialized services for children, the elderly, and other underserved populations are in short supply where they exist at all.

### *Mentally Ill Homeless*

A problem currently being addressed is what to do with the homeless mentally ill. It is estimated that as many as one-third of all homeless Americans (350,000 to 3,000,000) are mentally ill. Their only asylum or place of refuge is the streets. An increasing number of these are children and women. Children are subjected to child abuse; many women are raped. Homeless men, women, and children are more often the victims of crime rather than the perpetrators. Some end up in overcrowded jails. Many are suicidal and take their own lives. Some are homicidal. Hunger, cold, and disease take a heavy toll.

Earl Ruth dramatically illustrates the plight of tens of thousands of mentally ill homeless.

Earl Ruth is 47, partly deaf and schizophrenic. He heard voices for the first time at the age of six, spent most of his childhood in a foster home and an orphanage, and has lived much of his adult life in mental hospitals—sometimes voluntarily, sometimes not. Normally a gentle, apologetic man, Ruth is capable of violence: he once told a psychiatrist he was "fighting something evil, something powerful." He is both homeless and rootless. Although he spends most winters at church shelters in New York City, he usually heads across country each spring in a solitary and always fruitless search for a better life. This year, he says, he may take a trip to Houston.[7]

For the homeless there is a critical shortage of any kind of housing and employment opportunities. Income support channeled through a maze of bureaucratic organizations has decreased and is almost impossible to come by for those whose capacities are not impaired, much less for those who are mentally ill. Agencies tend to despair. They lack resources and find little reward in work that so much of the time is downside. In despair, some resort to the "Greyhound" therapy—one-way tickets to other parts of the country—for those expecting help. In winter "sunbirds" migrate to the sun belt.

Fortunately, chief executives and legislators are addressing the alarming and shocking problems of the homeless mentally ill. Many states are working to provide desperately needed housing. A Wisconsin project offers close supervision to those who have been deinstitutionalized. Maryland's Department of Mental Health has been mandated to supply appropriate services to women. In New Jersey, the Prevention and Homeless Act of 1984 affirms that "it is more socially desirable to place homeless people in suitable apartments, or to enable people to retain possession of their houses or apartments . . . than to house them in hotel rooms or other facilities intended for short-term occupancy." In Ohio, a concerted effort is being made to provide interest-free loans for low or moderate housing developments.

New York is taking on the herculean task of finding shelters for the homeless mentally ill. During the winter police are encouraged to pick up off the streets those individuals who appear mentally ill. If they refuse to go into a shelter, they are taken to a hospital for observation if the temperature is below freezing. California has embarked on an ambitious program to help those in ghetto areas, on the streets, and in the barrios. All across America, states and communities are reaching out to solve this problem, but the numbers are so overwhelming that it takes a lot of effort to make even a small impression.

It is a sad commentary that many skid-row chronically mentally ill prefer the risk of abuse from marauding gangs and hoodlums, even skid-row filth, rape, violence, and death, to being institutionalized even in the finest institutions. In skid row they find acceptance, human contact, and companionship. There they have freedom.

## *Voluntary and Involuntary Commitment*

In most states long-term commitment for the mentally ill has been abolished. Constitutional rights and liberty are deemed more important than the health of the patient, or the protection of society. Unless a person has demonstrated that he or she is a threat to himself or herself or society, no one—not even family members—can take away the right to freedom. The fact that because of the nature of their illness many are unable to make rational decisions about their care is not considered by the courts.

Because of the uniqueness of emotional problems, there is a need to retain, in some form, the concept of involuntary commitment. While some are aware of their needs and voluntarily ask for help, there are many who require involuntary commitment. All states have laws that govern commitment procedures. Because civil liberties have been reemphasized, states have acted to ensure the procedure of involuntary commitment and to protect the rights of individuals.

In one state an effort is being made to get a commitment law that will take the history of the patient into account. Performance or current behavior, taken in perspective, may be as important, or more important than the current mental status examination.

## The Chronically Mentally Ill

With the discovery and widespread use of psychoactive drugs and other therapies, hospital personnel found that fewer restraints were needed, bars and padded cells were removed, amenities were added. Hospitals were becoming therapeutic communities and patients were beginning to participate in governing. They responded to the drugs and personal attention.

Moving patients out of state hospitals into communities was a logical next step. Professionals made plans that would provide: (1) follow-up to make sure patients continued their medication, (2) professional help in communities through mental health centers, (3) support systems, (4) residential care as needed, (5) income for the patients' needs, and (6) help in getting and maintaining employment. The mentally ill would be able to function in the community because the *community* would be therapeutic.

What happened? It was found that the "community" is not always therapeutic. Life on the outside is not protected or stress-free. Smaller hospitals were never built. The panacea of drugs collapsed when patients didn't have the supervision and care of those who monitored their medication.

Consequently, millions of the mentally ill were released to the streets. It is estimated by the National Institute of Mental Health (NIMH) that 2.4 million are chronically mentally ill. It will take a national commitment to address their needs.

It has been widely assumed that the community would learn to accept and live with the mentally ill. This hasn't happened. Angry citizens protest halfway houses and other mental health facilities planned for their neighborhoods. They write angry letters to local newspapers, circulate petitions, threaten lawsuits, hold meetings with officials. They are willing for a hospital or nursing home to be built as long as it is located somewhere else. "Not in my back yard" (NIMBY) is their plaint. In the 1990s, society still lives with the luxury of thinking that the responsibility for the care and treatment of the mentally ill belongs to someone else. This attitude continues to be a major deterrent to effective community-based programs.

## Teenage Suicide

Suicide among teenagers has reached epidemic proportions. In the past twenty-five years suicide has increased 300 percent in the United States, and is the leading cause of death in the fifteen to twenty-four age group. The rate for this age group almost tripled from 4.5 per

100,000 in 1950 to 13.2 per 100,000 in 1990.[8] Many more suicides occur, but they are reported as "accidental deaths." Thousands of young people attempt suicide, but fortunately not all attempts are fatal.

Suicide in adolescence is correlated with sociological, psychological, and economic forces very much at the heart of the coping-social functioning dyad addressed by social workers. For example, there seems to be a correlation between suicide and high rates of youth unemployment. Unemployment, in turn, is associated with competition for jobs, and a sense of failure and loss of self-esteem to the unacceptably high number who don't find work. Feelings of helplessness and the inability to cope with problems or improve various life situations have been typically reported by depressed teenagers who are seriously suicidal.

Suicidal histories have been reported for teenagers who experience repeated school failures and who have long-standing behavioral problems. Youth who lack various kinds of social skills and handle stress situations poorly, if at all, are vulnerable.

Not having family support—no warmth, no security, families where the message seems to be that the youth are expendable or unwanted—correlates with high numbers of suicides and suicide attempt rates. Hepworth and colleagues report that:

> Cohesiveness between parents and children is typically low in families of suicidal adolescents. . . .
>
> Communication between adolescent suicide attempters and their parents is generally poor and conflict is high. In a study of adolescent drug overdosers, researchers found that about one-half of the group reported they felt unable to discuss problems with their mothers, and 89 percent felt similarly about communication with their fathers.[9]

The message of youth suicide is increasingly clear:

1. Employment opportunities for youth are imperative.
2. Success experiences will almost certainly reduce the risk of suicides.
3. All teaching-learning encounters need to emphasize the importance of good coping skills for youth.
4. Learning to deal with stress situations needs to be a high priority educational objective for all youth.
5. Finally, as a nation we need to reaffirm the value and worth of good family support systems, and the use of the nation's resources to strengthen the family.

## *Prevention*

In the public health sector, prevention includes health promotion and protection. At the "primary" level, it is centered on health education and concerns the general health and well-being of the population and is not directed at any particular disease or disorder. Examples include immunization, sanitation, and sound nutrition. At the "secondary" level, prevention means early diagnosis and prompt treatment; the aim is to relieve distress and shorten duration. "Tertiary" prevention is focused on chronic and serious illness and includes attempts to reduce pain and suffering.

Two potentially fertile fields for prevention in mental illness are the public schools and the workplace. We know much about human behavior and the causation of mental disorders. There is much unused knowledge of human behavior that could be used to help youngsters before they drop out of school, take their own lives, abuse drugs, or turn to premature sex to relieve boredom.

One group that needs the help offered by the schools are the recent immigrants who come from Asia, Central America, Mexico, and many other countries. Our way of life to them is foreign, our culture strange, and often they are poor and without means of support. In order to adapt and develop their potential, the children as well as the parents need help. Schools can help and social workers can play a decisive role by helping these people relate to the human service system, and providing services both direct and system-oriented.

The workplace in America is another area rich with opportunity for a truly preventive approach. Here, employees under stress and about to be lost can be helped with counseling for themselves and families, and to use the service network society has for them. Rehabilitation, once work is lost and the skills of the workplace atrophy from lack of use, is an example of secondary or even tertiary prevention.

## Work as Therapy

A strong case has been made for the therapeutic value of work for the mentally ill. Centers where work as therapy has been tried report that the days of care needed are greatly reduced. As with other workers, the mentally ill find daily meaning as well as daily bread in their employment, and they thrive on the recognition that comes from their fellow employees. Many of the nation's community centers and clubs have made finding nonsubsidized jobs for their people a top priority. Many become financially independent and are able to maintain themselves with minimal psychiatric supervision.

Because of the great gains made by those who have employment, NIMH has developed an approach to reduce discrimination by helping to stimulate employment opportunities for them. Of the more than two million chronic and acute mental patients living in the community, between 70 to 85 percent are estimated to be unemployed. It is impossible to generalize on how many of these are potentially employable because of individual differences and capabilities.

The President's Committee on Employment of the Handicapped has set up affirmative action and nondiscrimination programs for disabled people that apply to mentally restored persons as well as to the physically handicapped. Affirmative action tries to assure opportunities for work. However, applicants have to be "qualified"—capable of doing the work with reasonable accommodation. For mentally restored persons this may mean adjusting work schedules, restructuring jobs, and giving flexible leave. Many employers are making the necessary adjustments.

## Research

Continuing research is needed. Even with all the scientific and technological achievements of our society, mysteries of the human mind abound. We have difficulty understanding why people behave as they do, and we are baffled with such diagnosed mental problems as manic depressive illness or schizophrenia. Those with these illnesses are the vast majority of the seriously mentally ill. We need to know more about the genetics of human behavior and such biological factors as anatomy, physiology, morphology, and endocrinology. Little is known about the long-term effect of medical treatment. Many therapists report good results from planned, daily exercise including cycling, aerobics, jogging, hiking, and other physical exercise for depressed patients. Gene research offers hope in determining who may have mental health problems, and it may play a part in prevention and treatment.

Delegates to the White House Conference on Aging in 1995 passed a resolution on meeting basic mental health needs. In addition to support for providing affordable and quality mental health care, they asked for public and private long-term insurance plans to include mental disabilities. They supported expanded education and training programs for family and caregivers by faculty with clinical research expertise in mental health and aging.

## Integration of Resources—Values

In this chapter significant developments have been outlined in the mental health field, particularly as these pertain to social work. Though modest compared to the challenges that lie ahead, they are nevertheless impressive. A network of services is clearly identified. In the main these are generally well known by consumers. Remaining are problems and issues relating to the interplay of mental health, other human services, and the corporate and professional community. Perhaps this is some of what Alice Mu-jung P. Lin had in mind when she wrote the following: "The challenges for the mental health system are to integrate mental health services with the housing, social, and economic needs of the population."[10]

Finally, the future may well need to focus more on values. Viktor Frankl postulates the survival values of meaning in life. Patients recover when they have a purpose. Neuroses are not only conflicted, instinctual forces, but also result from failure to connect with important values and action guided by a value system.

In the course of time the social work treatment approach has been subjected to a plethora of emphases, including environmental manipulation, external sociological forces, depth psychology, a combination of psychological social determinants, role theory, and cultural identifications. Cornett, along with others, believes "The time has come for social work to again broaden its perspective, this time to include the spiritual aspects of the physical, phenomenological individual in her or his environment."[11]

Clients often express concern about issues and problems that have spiritual and religious connotations. The meaning of life, purpose, and belief systems encompass the idea that help for everyday problems can come from forces outside themselves. Metaphysical factors figure prominently in the lives of many, if not most, of our clients who struggle to cope with the problems confronting them. Social workers, though somewhat silent about their observances of these behavioral determinants, have known clients who seem to get help from these sources. When we fail to consider this content, we miss an important opportunity to assist our clients and even impoverish our thinking and our practice.

Professionals need to look at what is good and right. Perhaps no example serves better to illustrate this assumption than the one coming from the addiction model, where the best results are reported from the invoking of prayer, faith, and religious experience. Spiritual forces help to provide balance and fill dependency needs essential to self-sufficiency and independence.

## The DSM in Mental Health

For thousands of years attempts have been made to classify mental disorders. Resulting from these attempts various diagnostic systems have evolved and been discarded. Since 1952 the American Psychiatric Association has made serious attempts to develop guidelines, which have evolved in what today is known as the Association's Diagnostic and Statistical Manual IV (DSM-IV). This publication includes the names of disorders, various essential and associated features of disorders, and differential and diagnostic categories of mental illness. This classification is widely used in the practice of psychiatry; likewise by many social workers, particularly those in the mental health field and in private practice.

There are differences of opinion among social workers regarding the use of DSM. Some say that labels, names, or categories are unhelpful, and also potentially harmful to some clients. They maintain it is harmful when labels are used to silence political dissidents, force sterilization, justify brain surgery, or as a device for getting clients on welfare rolls because, for example, they lack reading or writing skills.

A positive point of view is that categorization of mental disorders facilitates communication among social workers and between other mental health professionals—psychiatrists, psychologists, and nurses—and social workers. They suggest that the system can be used reliably by clinicians and research workers. Social workers in private practice often use the system for third-party payments for services.

## Summary

National attention has been focused on the mentally ill by three presidents and one first lady, indicating the scope and magnitude of the problem of mental illness in the United States.

Roots of the mental health movement are identified with such luminaries as Dorothea Lynde Dix, William White, Sigmund Freud, G. Stanley Hall, and Adolph Meyer. Resulting from great resolve and determination over decades of time, mental health networks and related systems can now be identified and are impressively serving tens of thousands of children and adults.

Efforts addressing the problems of the mentally ill clearly recognize the complexity and seriousness of the problem. Hospital services have been dramatically recast to take into account the use of psychedelic drugs, greater community awareness and effort, and the not always welcomed deinstitutionalization of the mentally ill.

Aftercare facilities help to cushion the need for help when the patient is released from the hospital. Voluntary efforts such as Fountain House that engage patients in meaningful and productive work and other activities prove helpful in rehabilitation.

Problems of the mentally ill homeless are receiving greater understanding and help of state legislators and others in addressing this growing problem and blight.

More study, research, and a national commitment are required to solve the problems of the chronically ill and the growing incidence of teen suicide.

Becoming more prominent is the emphasis on values and the role and place of religion and spiritual components to the understanding and treatment of the mentally ill.

DSM-IV is found to be useful to social workers in the mental health field and in private practice. However, different views exist and continue to surface about the usefulness of this major diagnostic tool for social workers.

# Selected References

BENDER, KENNETH J., *Psychiatric Medications: A Guide for Mental Health Professionals.* Newbury Park, CA: Sage Publications, 1990.

BURGESS, ANN WOLBERT, and AARON LAZARE, *Community Mental Health: Target Populations.* Englewood Cliffs, NJ: Prentice Hall, 1976.

DAWSON, DAVID, HEATHER MUNROE BLUM, and GIAMIERO BARTOLUCCI, *Schizophrenia in Focus: Guidelines for Treatment and Rehabilitation.* New York: Human Sciences Press, 1983.

FINGARETTE, BERKELEY, *Heavy Drinking: The Myth of Alcoholism as a Disease.* Berkeley, CA: University of California Press, 1988.

MACIAS, CATHALEENE, RONALD KINNEY, O. WILLIAM FARLEY, ROBERT JACKSON, and BETTY VOS, "The Role of Case Management within a Community Support System: Partnership with Psychosocial Rehabilitation," *Community Mental Health Journal* 30 (August 1994), 323–339.

MAGUIRE, LAMBERT, *Understanding Social Networks.* Beverly Hills, CA: Sage Publications, 1983.

MECHANIC, DAVID, ed., *Improving Mental Health Services: What the Social Sciences Can Tell Us.* San Francisco: Jossey-Bass, 1987.

*Report to the President from the President's Commission on Mental Health,* Vol. 1. Washington, DC: The President's Commission on Mental Health, 1978.

DE SHAZER, STEVE, *Investigating Solutions in Brief Therapy.* New York: W. W. Norton & Co., Inc., 1988.

THACKERAY, MILTON G., REX A. SKIDMORE, and O. WILLIAM FARLEY, *Introduction to Mental Health: Field and Practice.* Englewood Cliffs, NJ: Prentice Hall, 1979.

WEISSMAN, HAROLD H., ed., *Serious Play: Creativity and Innovation in Social Work.* Silver Springs, MD: NASW Press, 1990.

WETZEL, JANICE WOOD, *Clinical Handbook of Depression.* New York: Gardner Press, 1984.

ZASTROW, CHARLES, and KAREN K. KIRST-ASHMAN, *Understanding Human Behavior and the Social Environment,* 3rd ed. Chicago: Nelson-Hall, 1994.

# Notes

1. Presidential Executive Order 11973, signed February 17, 1977.
2. Adapted from materials compiled by the Social Research Institute, University of Utah.
3. Milton G. Thackeray, Rex A. Skidmore, and O. William Farley, *Introduction to Mental Health* (Englewood Cliffs, NJ: Prentice Hall, 1979), pp. 63–64.
4. Leon Ginsberg, *Social Work Almanac,* 2nd ed. Vol. 1 (Washington, DC: NASW Press, 1995), 258.
5. *Action for Mental Health, The Final Report of the Joint Commission on Mental Illness and Health* (New York: Basic Books, 1961), pp. xv-xvi.
6. Ibid.

7. *Newsweek,* January 6, 1986, p. 16.
8. Ginsberg, op cit., 81.
9. Dean H. Hepworth, O. William Farley, and J. Kent Griffiths, "Suicidal Adolescents Correlates and Clinical Implications." Unpublished paper (January 1986).
10. Alice Mu-jung P. Lin, "Mental Health Overview," in *Encyclopedia of Social Work.* 10th ed., Vol. 11 (Washington, DC: NASW Press, 1995), 1710.
11. Carlton Cornett, "Toward a More Comprehensive Personology: Integrating a Spiritual Perspective into Social Work Practice," *Social Work,* 37 (March 1992).

$$C\ h\ a\ p\ t\ e\ r\quad 10$$

# Social Work
# in Health Care

*Mrs. M. was referred to the social worker because of her refusal to agree to an operation that would improve her hearing. She had been very hard-of-hearing since her birth. Mrs. M. had been hospitalized following an automobile accident. Doctors in the university hospital became confident that they could help her gain almost normal hearing.*

*Exploring Mrs. M.'s refusal of surgery, the social worker discovered a number of reasons for her reluctance. She was terrified of anesthesia and "being cut on"; she knew of persons who had not recovered from surgery. She had never been in a hospital until her accident—even her children*

*had been born at home. She found the procedures confusing, painful, and frightening, and wanted to go home as soon as possible. She was not sure just which one of the doctors who came to see her was really her doctor. To this medically unsophisticated woman, the pressure for a quick decision was too much, and she felt that it would be better to say "no" than to take a chance.*

*What needs to be done so that Mrs. M. can understand the risks of surgery as weighed against the possible benefits? How would a greater understanding on the part of the doctors and nurses concerning Mrs. M.'s fear aid in her decision?[1]*

In an era of tight money, the new intern, probing for ways to cut soaring costs for medical care, asked: "Why do we need social services in this hospital?" The administrator replied: "In the interest of quality health care, the hospital provides food, shelter and medication; why shouldn't it concern itself with the social and psychological needs of the patients? They, too, are important."

She further explained that social problems are basic to the understanding and total care and treatment of a patient; and if they are not considered, many times medical treatment fails.

What is social work in health care settings? What special knowledge and skill are required for practice in health services? Answers to these and related questions appear in this chapter.

Medicine and social work joined hands in 1905 with the establishment of medical social work at the Massachusetts General Hospital in Boston under the enthusiastic, able encouragement of Dr. Richard Cabot. He and others recognized the need to understand more about social factors related to illness and its treatment and to utilize social and community resources in comprehensive patient care.

The introduction of social workers into hospital and other medical settings has been slow but steady, so today many hospitals have professional social workers on their staffs. Of the 5,000 hospitals reporting to the American Hospital Association in 1995, 75 percent indicated having social work services.

There is hardly any aspect of health care in which social and emotional factors can be ruled out for purposes of diagnosis, treatment, and in the work of prevention of illness. As the practice of medicine has grown more psychosocial the role of social workers, with their social functioning orientation, has increased in importance in the broad spectrum of health care delivery. Bracht, affirming his own known views, and those of colleagues, attests to an overview of nationwide practice:

> There have been instances of the development of social work programs in virtually every type of primary health care setting—in prepaid group practices and health maintenance organizations; in fee-for-service practices and clinics, both solo and group; and in neighborhood and community health centers with outside funding. Some programs have provided social work practicum experiences. Many programs have enhanced physicians' residency experiences, especially in family medicine settings.[2]

A new development that will affect social workers is the growth of corporate health care. Forty-five corporations in the United States with revenues greater than $10 million reported in 1984 that they provide health care services. In addition, it was expected that by 1990 the top thirty nursing home corporations would control all of the nursing home beds.[3] This meant that social workers in the health care field would be increasingly employed by the private sector.

The total number of social workers in the health field continues to increase. In 1960 there were 11,700 health care social workers, and it was estimated that for 1986 there were 50,000. The majority of social workers were practicing in long-term care hospitals—16,500 administer various aspects of the Medicare program in hospitals; 2,700 work in extended care facilities; and 2,600 work in the Veterans Administration Hospital System.[4] Even with the large budget cuts in the health care funds, the role of social work in medicine is expected to expand.[5]

## Definition of Social Work in Health Care

Social work in health care settings is practiced in collaboration with medicine and also with public health programs. It is the application of social work knowledge, skills, attitudes, and values to health care. Social work addresses itself to illness brought about by or related to social and environmental stresses that result in failures in social functioning and social relationships. It intervenes with medicine and related professions in the study, diagnosis, and treatment of illness at the point where social, psychological, and environmental forces impinge on role effectiveness.

Social work relates itself to the goals set by official health agencies, voluntary health agencies, rehabilitation centers, and medical care divisions of public welfare agencies.

Social workers practice in public health at the local, state, federal, and international levels; general medical hospitals; county and state health departments; crippled children's hospitals; outpatient clinics; university teaching hospitals; nursing homes; neighborhood health centers; and private disease centers supported by such funding sources as March of Dimes, and the heart and cancer associations. In addition, social workers are employed in the offices of private physicians and are meeting the challenge of showing that their skills can be cost-effective for private practice.

In the past, because of the nature of the practice of medicine, social work in health services emphasized understanding illness. Practice was focused on work with sick people and members of their families. Because of newer emphases in medical care, the scope of social work has been broadened and now encompasses the preservation and promotion of health and the prevention as well as cure of disease. Consideration is given to psychological factors in prevention of disability as well as in diagnosis and treatment. Using the team approach, medical social workers collaborate with physicians, nurses, and other health professionals for reciprocal sharing of ideas so that the skills of each are employed in the total care of the patients.

One of the most important developments for social workers in health care was the Health Maintenance Organization (HMO) Act of 1973. This act opened the door for an entirely new medical care delivery system. Keigher has defined managed care as an alternative to fee-for-service health care whereby the financing and delivery of medical care are integrated through contracts with selected physicians and hospitals furnishing a comprehensive set of services to enrolled members, usually for a predetermined monthly premium. Managed care includes financial incentives for patients to use the services, and providers assume some financial risk as they try to balance the patient's health needs with the organization's cost-control efforts. Keigher further states:

> Powerful commercial forces are quietly transforming the U.S. health care system with far more effect than policy discourse. Although policy agendas in 1993 and 1994 were focused on managed competition, regulations, and employer mandates, profound restrictions were already being placed on the health prospects of the employees, retirees, and public-aid recipients fortunate enough to have insurance. "Managed Care," a health care delivery enterprise that barely existed a few years ago, has been enjoying phenomenal growth facilitated by businesses' benefits offices, state Medicaid offices, the federal Health Care Financing Administration (HCFA), and insurance companies.
>
> The majority of citizens have been gradually and "voluntarily" relinquishing their right to choose their doctors in return for a promise of lower premiums. Their affiliations with health maintenance organizations (HMOs), preferred provider organizations (PPOs), and other capitated reimbursement plans have moved us light years toward total capitalistic corporatization of health care, delimiting the parameters of potential policy reform.[6]

Originally the HMO Act required the provision of social services in HMOs. Several consequent congressional actions blunted the effects of the original act and the mandates for social workers were eliminated. There has been a positive social work thrust in new home health care and rehabilitation laws that allow Medicaid funds to enhance the ability of handicapped persons to live independently as family and community members. In 1983 Congress enacted one of the most radical changes in the history of Medicare. Until 1983 hospitals were reimbursed retroactively by Medicare, but as a result of the Social Security Amendments of 1983, hospitals are now paid prospectively by Medicare, based on prices determined by national averages of costs per diagnosis. This prospective pricing system (PPS) is the model for future health care reimbursement, both at the state and federal levels. Eventually the Department of Health and Human Service Health Care Financing Administration (HCFA) will include the PPS system to cover such problems as alcohol and drug abuse.[7] In nonprofit hospitals, social workers have been asked to do more work in the areas of preadmission and admission screening, but some proprietary hospitals have been cutting social workers in an attempt to maintain their profitability.

Health care costs are continuing to rise. In 1994 it was estimated that the United States spent more than $800 billion, or 12 percent of its gross national product, on health care. It was also estimated that there were 37 million Americans at or below the poverty level who experienced health risks associated with an inability to afford needed health care.[8] Health care reform was one of the major issues in the 1992 presidential campaign. The National Association of Social Workers played a key role in a major health care reform bill introduced in Congress on June 9,1992, by Senator Daniel K. Inouye. Senator Inouye stated: "The National Health Care Act of 1992 would significantly change the way our nation finances and delivers health care." The main elements of the bill included provisions to create a "single payer" health insurance plan that would be administered by the federal and state governments. Benefits would include primary, preventive hospital, dental and vision care, mental health and substance abuse treatment, rehabilitation services, prescription drugs, and long-term care for the elderly and for chronically ill people of all ages. The bill recommended that individuals would retain the freedom to choose their own physicians and other health care providers. Taxes would pay for the plan, but the bill sponsors hoped that savings would occur by eliminating the duplicative costs and paperwork of thousands of insurance companies as well as utilizing negotiated fee structures for all care providers.[9]

The National Health Care Act of 1992 proposed by President Clinton was never really considered by the Congress. Health care reform was absent from the Capitol Hill agenda of the 1995 Congress. Instead of health care reform, the Republican "Contract with America" seemed to be moving to reduce many public programs that served as a safety net for millions of Americans. In 1995 NASW published a brief analyzing the direction Congress was moving. The brief included the following points:

*Medicare.* The $160 billion Medicare program's size and its 10 percent per year growth rate make it vulnerable to budget cuts. . . .

*Medicaid.* The $125.2 billion Medicaid program will also be subjected to intense pressure as budget cuts are debated. . . .

*Supplemental Security Income (SSI).* A provision in the House welfare reform bill would deny SSI benefits and Medicaid to all people with drug and alcohol addictions who cannot qualify for SSI on the basis of other disabling conditions. . . .[10]

The results of the congressional debates will not be known for some time, but the large number of American citizens without health care insurance is a national tragedy and probably, in the long term, will prove to be more expensive for our society. The country will have to solve the health care crisis in the next few years. Regardless of the ebb and flow of federal legislation, social workers will continue to be considered an important health care member because of their special knowledge and skill in the psychosocial aspects of illness.

Social work in the health services accepts the World Health Organization's (WHO) definition of health as "a state of complete physical, mental, and social well-being and not merely the absence of disease or infirmity."

Social workers in health care services use the problem-solving method in assisting individuals, groups, and communities in solving personal and family health problems. Social work is involved at various levels of prevention:

*Primary*—health education, encouraging immunizations, good mental health practice in families, prenatal and postnatal care.

*Secondary*—early screening programs for detection of disease, checkups, encouraging treatment.

*Tertiary or rehabilitation*—preventing further deterioration of a disease or problem.

Social workers engage in research and add to a professional body of scientific knowledge. Through supervision and teaching, they assist paraprofessionals to develop scholarship and skill. They teach in schools of social work and serve in student-training units as field instructors.

What are the distinguishing knowledge and skill characteristics of medical social work practice? It is practice in responsible relation to medicine. Its concern is with the welfare of patients and the causal, contributing interrelationships of illness, family failures and breakdown, social stresses, and environmental pressures and influences.

Medical social work is shaped and guided by the attitudes, beliefs, knowledge, and acceptable ways of doing things by professionals serving in health care institutions and by the philosophy and practice of modern medicine. It requires a knowledge of illness and of the psychological and social impact of disease on the individual, the family, and the family interrelationships; it calls for the application and adaptation of social work concepts, principles, and ideas to the special needs of hospital and clinic clientele.

In the hospital social workers collaborate with medicine and a broad range of specialists, including nurses, dieticians, physical therapists, speech and hearing specialists, recreationists, and pharmacists. Outside the hospital they work with public health nurses and health educators.

As medicine has become highly technical and specialized, especially as practiced in the university hospital or complex rehabilitation setting, the social worker sometimes holds the process together, explaining the personnel and their functions to patients. If the patient moves from medicine to surgery, and back again, and changes in physicians occur, the social worker is the constant person.

Social work has a coordinate, rather than subordinate or ancillary, role to medicine and is responsible to the institution and the supporting public. The doctor is the clinical and medical authority and is held responsible under the law for medical practice. However, the doctor is only one member of the team in modern medical practice to whom the social worker relates.

## The Meaning of Illness

Illness encompasses medical, social, economic, and even spiritual components. Illness affects people in many ways, directly and indirectly, and is of particular consequence to individuals, families, and communities. The social worker plays a major role in interpreting illness to people and in helping them to muster their personal and social resources toward physical and mental well-being.

Webster's *International Dictionary* defines illness as a state of being ill or sick, bodily indisposition, disease. An ill person is one of "inferior quality, bad in condition, wretched, impolite, improper, incorrect, bad morally, evil in nature or character, malevolent, wicked, vicious, wrong." The word *disease* literally means want of ease, uneasiness. *Dis,* from the Latin prefix, means apart or asunder, and *ease* is a state of comfort or rest. The diseased person is a person wanting in ease. An invalid, on the other hand, is someone who is not valid, someone no longer able to bear the burdens of life, or who, for temporary or prolonged periods of time, simply cannot function.

As defined by doctors, disease is objective. Causation relates to agents that can be stained, tested for chemical qualities, measured, and described. The laboratory procedures used by medical personnel in hospitals, clinics, and in doctors' offices are objective devices used to determine the degree of seriousness of disability or pathology resulting from disease processes. Determinations are made of organic states such as result from bacteria, viruses, trauma, cellular dysfunction, and various circulatory disturbances.

Broadly speaking, illness—impaired role function—may result from factors not wholly organic, but social, psychological, cultural, and economic. Anything affecting the total well-being of the patient may support the illness and render the patient incapable of normal role performance. It forces dependency and reduces usefulness to the family and other significant people. It cuts off the individual's access to normal enjoyment and satisfaction. Social workers, in addressing themselves to other than organic factors, study and define illness in its cultural and environmental matrix and assist with the removal of barriers to health from these sources.

The increase in chronic disease among Americans has literally changed the meaning of illness for a great many people. In the 1940s infections such as tuberculosis, meningitis, and influenza were still major life threats. Polio was still maiming and killing people into the 1950s. Now, however, chronic diseases—heart disease, diabetes, emphysema, and stroke—are major threats.

The AIDS epidemic sweeping the world and the United States has strained health and psychosocial resources. Lloyd states:

> Because of the long asymptomatic period, the number of AIDS cases at any given time reflects the level of HIV infection from 3 to 5 years ago or from an even earlier date. The World Health Organization Global Program on AIDS (WHO/GPA) reported on December 31, 1989, that a cumulative global total of 203,599 cases of

AIDS had been reported from 152 countries. Of that number, 103,211 cumulative cases had been reported from the United States (WHO/GPA, 1989a). Because of significant underrecognition of the disease (especially in past years in many developing countries), underreporting, delays in reporting, and misdiagnosis, it is estimated that the actual cumulative global total of AIDS cases is nearly 500,000. This total is expected to double to more than 1.1 million cases by 1991.

Reports to WHO/GPA in mid-1988 were the basis for estimates that at least 5 million to 10 million persons worldwide probably were infected with HIV. In mid-1989, WHO/GPA projected that new infections could double or triple during the 1990s. The near-term prospects for a vaccine or cure are slight, and the numbers of infected men, women, and children are increasing worldwide. Seroprevalance in children and transmission through drug injection are increasing.

Given the epidemiology and demography of HIV and AIDS, it is doubtful that social workers can practice anywhere without being directly or indirectly involved with people affected by HIV infection and AIDS. Therefore, all social workers should be knowledgeable about HIV transmission and prevention, capable of adapting practice methods to needs of those affected by HIV or AIDS, and committed to applying social work values to ensure that people are not discriminated against in the workplace, social service agencies, or health care facilities because of their HIV status.[11]

People have to live with chronic disease, adjust to pain, change habits—diet, quit smoking, exercise, and change employment. With chronic conditions—arthritis, heart disease, AIDS, some cancers—the patient must be a partner in the care of the disease, in its prevention, and in its deterioration. Social work comes into the picture in helping the patient to adjust, to accept medical regimens, and to relate to the health complex involved in the broadened care aspects of chronic disease.

In addition social workers work with dying patients, allowing them to express fears, and help other hospital and medical care specialists deal with their own feelings in working with those who are dying.

Illness is always highly individual. For many, illness damages the self-image. Illness forces dependency upon relatives and society, which may be difficult for the ill person to accept. The Essei Japanese man, for instance, whose rearing emphasizes the interdependence of family members, may develop symptoms, become immobilized, or resort to self-destruction when he can no longer count on a comfortable place of eminence within the family and is forced to accept relief or nursing home care.

Illness often minimizes the usefulness of the individual to his or her family and loved ones. When it interferes with the breadwinning function of the wage earner, illness can result in disorganization of the entire family, and for the wage earner in a loss of self-respect, feelings of helplessness, and despondency. The enjoyment of the normal functions of the individual is denied to the ill person, whose responses are often distorted and detrimental to normal social relationships.

The small child who is ill and who has to be hospitalized for extended periods of time may lose the feeling of closeness to parents and experience separation trauma. Some children who are separated even for short periods of time, particularly under unfavorable circumstances for which no preparation is made, carry a scar for many years, if not for a lifetime. Infants and young children who have been hospitalized and separated from their families for long durations, who lack the closeness of a vital tie to a parent or other significant person, may suffer irreversible physical and emotional damage, become autistic, distrustful of others, and encounter difficulties in relationships all their lives.

The adolescent who suffers from a prolonged illness, who is confined and obliged to curtail activities, may lose peer group support at a time when it is greatly needed in his or her struggle for autonomy and independence. A wage earner suffering from a "nervous breakdown" clung desperately to symptoms for fear that he would be asked to return to work and a job he could not manage. He recovered only with skilled medical and social work help when he was assured that he would recover and be able to work again and support his family.

The aging may use sickness as a method of forcing their children to give them care and attention. A mother, for example, who during her childbearing period was preoccupied with the task of rearing and educating her children, in middle age and retirement found her usefulness often questioned, if not by others, by herself. Her children, long since established in their own homes, were independent and did not have the same need for her as when they were younger. She sensed that her role in the family had changed. She chose illness as an escape from the feeling that she was no longer useful, to force her children to live with and care for her. Unconscious regression to earlier states of dependency, helplessness, and illness are common reactions to stress. The ill person may be dependent, helpless, and under the care of others; nevertheless, the sick are also expected to cooperate with the hospital and other individuals who are responsible for assisting in their care and treatment.

## The Role of Social Work in Health Care

Social workers in the health care field work in hospitals, with families, and in public health.

### Social Work in Hospitals

Practice in hospitals is a major component of social work in health care. The functions of social work in the hospital include:

1. Assess the patient's psychological and environmental strengths and weaknesses.
2. Collaborate with the team in the delivery of services to assure the maximum utilization of the skill and knowledge of each team member.
3. Assist the family to cooperate with treatment and to support the patient's utilization of medical services.
4. Identify with a cadre of other professionals to improve the services of the hospital by an interdisciplinary sharing of knowledge.
5. Serve as a broker of community services, thus providing linkage of patient need with appropriate resources.
6. Participate in the policy-making process.
7. Engage in research to assure a broadening of the knowledge base for successful practice.

Social work is illustrated by the following case of a patient admitted to the hospital for a renal (kidney) transplant.

At intake the social worker was responsible for obtaining the history of Paul's illness. She learned that he had an acute renal disorder at age 14. In the years following, he had lived with a fear of death, as well as anxiety over the problems of daily living. During a long period of remission, he married, became the father of a son, was employed in a small family-owned printing business, and lived a "normal" life.

When he was 26 his kidneys failed again and he was hospitalized. After lengthy examinations and consultations, he was scheduled for a renal transplant. The medical team, including the social worker, shared the responsibility for preparing Paul and his family for this operation. The social worker discussed the many ramifications of the operation with Paul's father, who was the donor. It was apparent that although the father was motivated to help, he was also frightened by the prospect of giving up one of his kidneys. He needed the reassurance and support offered by the worker to become comfortable in his lifesaving role, and to dispel his feelings of guilt at his reluctance.

The social worker also was called upon to be the broker for handling the costs of hospitalization, surgery, and medication. These costs are often more than a family can handle, and if outside help is not available, can lead to bankruptcy, loss of self-esteem, a lowered standard of living, and serious deprivation. In planning for money to pay for the transplant, Paul and his family decided to sell the printing business to meet part of the medical costs. Arrangements also were made with governmental and private agencies to pay the remaining expenses.

In addition to practical problems, Paul and his family had to be prepared for possible rejection of the transplant. The social worker supported and amplified the physician's explanation of rejection.

Two days before the scheduled operation, Paul became ill with a serious respiratory infection, necessitating a postponement. This was disappointing and frustrating.

Several weeks after he first entered the hospital the transplant finally was made, but it was not successful. Even though there had been lengthy discussions about the possible rejection, there was much for the social worker to do in helping Paul and his wife handle their extreme disappointment and fear for the future. Paul's father, too, needed reassurance that he had done all he could, that it was not his "fault" that the transplant had not been successful, and that he could live a normal life with just one kidney.

The social work effort concentrated on all members of the family in helping them to sustain each other in this crisis and in introducing them to dialysis, the only means available for cleansing Paul's blood. Since the family lived some distance from a hospital with the necessary equipment for this treatment, it meant a 100-mile trip every other day, plus six hours for the dialysis. In addition, there were the constraints of living imposed by this necessity. All these problems necessitated constant support and help by the social worker.

A breakthrough came when a portable machine weighing 45 pounds became available to Paul. This gave him mobility and greater independence.

As his health improved, and after he had resolved his hostile feelings about his dependency and had adjusted to his dialysis schedule, he decided to further his education. From the warm association and concrete assistance given by the social worker during his long illness, he decided to become a social worker. Encouraged and sustained by his family, the social work school, and the community, he completed his work to become a practicing social worker, feeling that his experience with disease and disability would give him insight into the feelings and problems of others facing death or other medical problems. He stated, "If people can't talk about their disabilities, they'll have a hard time living with them."

Individuals who are qualified to help with social factors are important members of the comprehensive treatment team. Their services are related to (1) direct help to the patient, and (2) indirect aid through assistance to the family and/or others. Help to the patient is related to (a) intake, (b) hospitalization, (c) release, and (d) aftercare. The social worker can be most valuable at the time a patient is admitted to a medical setting. Through use of skills and knowledge, he or she can assist the patient to adjust better to the medical environment and treatment as well as offer help with financial arrangements when necessary. While the patient is in the hospital, the social worker can be of considerable assistance in providing an opportunity for the patient to talk to someone who will listen and who cares. This is usually therapeutically sound and helps in the total treatment plan. If a patient is worried about some problem, he or she is likely to feel better if the anxieties can be verbalized.

The following two cases illustrate other medical-social problems.

---

A 24-year-old woman was admitted to the emergency ward of a hospital after she attempted suicide for the third time. Because this was a hospital where there was no social service department, the administrator transferred her to another hospital where this service was provided. The main problem for this woman was familial, involving an alcoholic, mentally disturbed husband. It was only after the social worker gave help to the husband and family as a whole that the young woman could live with her situation.

---

A 15-year-old girl was hospitalized in the psychiatric ward of a general hospital. Part of her problem concerned her relationships with her mother and father. The psychiatrist worked with the girl in the hospital, and the social worker helped the mother and father to understand their daughter better—her needs, their relationships, and what could be done to open the door for communication among them. Through joint guidance of the psychiatrist and social worker, the girl was able to leave the hospital and return to an emotional climate at home that was more conducive to satisfactory daily living than it had ever been before.

## *Social Work and Illness within the Family*

A family is often controlled by its "sickest" member, with household activities revolving around the unhealthy individual. Small children are asked to curtail their natural exuberance when a parent or an elderly grandparent is ill, and older children are required to perform certain household tasks that previously may have been undertaken by the adults in the family. The family's entire way of life may be reorganized or drastically altered by the sickness of one of its members, and not infrequently, considerable family dysfunctioning results from the illness.

---

Mrs. Jones, an elderly mother, became an invalid when she broke her hip. Following a short period of hospitalization a plan was made by her and her children for her to live in succession with several of her daughters. This plan was intended to provide variety for Mrs. Jones and to relieve the nursing care responsibility of any one of the daughters. A soft spot appeared in the arrangement when Mrs. Jones decided that she did not wish to be shunted from one home to another, that she wanted more permanency in her old age than this plan provided, and that her preference was to remain in one place. The children agreed, which meant that as Mrs. Jones became increasingly dependent and bedridden the full burden of nursing care had to be carried by one daughter. It was no longer a shared family experience.

Despite her illness and dependency, Mrs. Jones, nevertheless, continued to exercise the authority of a parent over the daughter, ordered her about, made demands on her, and made the other members of the household uncomfortable, creating an impasse with the grandchildren. The family was weakened and threatened with disorganization. Finally, with social work help, a plan was made for Mrs. Jones to move into a nursing home.

---

Frequently, with the help of services within the community, it is possible for a family to mobilize its resources to care for a sick or handicapped child or adult. Although it is true that illness can foster family disorganization, it can also result in a constructive use of the family to achieve family unity and goals. Social agencies are available for help. Many handicapped or retarded children can be cared for by their families, either by arranging the family's own resources, by using services within the community, or by a combination of family and community resources. Such resources as community mental health centers, visiting nurses associations, homemaker services, and family service agencies can be called upon to strengthen and support the efforts of families. In his or her role, the social worker performs a function that supports the medical care given to a sick person and in so doing realistically appraises the needs of the family and the "assets and liabilities" within the family and community for meeting these needs.

One purpose of social work is to support and strengthen family life. In doing this the social worker makes use of existing services through referrals or assists in mobilizing the untapped potential of the community to prevent illness or to restore the sick and disabled to health and usefulness.

The case of Peter Simpson illustrates the social and psychological components of illness and the function of the social worker in working with a young adolescent and his family.

---

Peter Simpson, a 13-year-old boy, was treated for stress at the outpatient clinic of a general hospital. His response to the usual medical regimen for ulcer patients was unsatisfactory. The medication and diet did not bring his ulcers under control, and when he began bleeding internally, a full investigation of his circumstances was ordered. The social worker determined in an interview with his mother that Peter was the only remaining child living at home and that his father had died three years previously. Left alone following the death of her husband and the move of the older children from her home, Mrs. Simpson turned to Peter for comfort and advice. She assuaged her loneliness by talking to him and consulted him about living expenses, budget, and the family income. She often referred to him as the "man of the house," and expected him to shoulder the responsibilities of husband and father. Her affectional demands on the boy were heavy and unusual. She had him sleep with her because alone she was "nervous and uneasy."

Medical care brought no relief of Peter's symptoms because of a totally unrealistic home situation. Catapulted into the head-of-a-family position and made the object of impossible affectional demands at age 13, Peter collapsed. The social worker arranged for Peter to live with an older married brother and sister-in-law and referred him to the child guidance clinic for treatment. His symptoms were relieved.

Mrs. Simpson was able to accept the plan for Peter as she was helped to form new affectional interests and secure her economic position. Her relationship with the social worker served as an introduction to an everwidening circle of friends and to financial independence. She surmounted an extremely difficult hurdle when, at age 53, with the help of social service, she decided to go to work. She had not been on the labor market at any time in her life and her decision was filled with apprehension and doubt. However, she was healthy and intelligent and able to complete training needed to qualify for work in a sportswear manufacturing plant. Her beginning salary was double her AFDC check and the gains to her from employment of financial independence, association with others, and a growing self-actualization opened an entirely new life for her.

---

The medical care for Peter in this instance was aided by social services: first, through study and diagnosis, which focused on the social and emotional components of his illness; second, by a radical shift in living arrangements for Peter, which his mother was helped to support; third, by referral to and use of child guidance; fourth, by job training and employment for Mrs. Simpson resulting in financial independence and greater personal satisfaction.

## Social Work in Public Health

A community is a society of individuals that plans for the welfare of its members for mutual advantage. No community can afford to disregard the needs of people who are ill or who might require medical care even if the family cannot bear the burden without help. Recog-

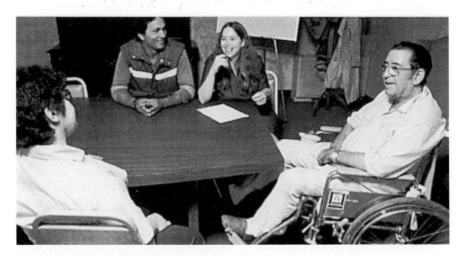

Social workers talking with a client.

nizing various motives, the community must take steps to protect the health of its members. The sick person, the handicapped one, and the disabled one who cannot get the care he or she needs cannot be a healthy, contributing force within the community. Therefore, in its own self-interest, the community provides hospitals, clinics, and other health services. Public health services have been developed in most communities.

The following case illustrates the role of the social worker in public health services.

---

A social worker in the public health department was asked to accompany the public health nurse on a home visit to a young mother whose 6-month-old infant was failing to gain weight. Several times in the past month, the baby had been brought to the hospital's emergency room in a severely dehydrated condition.

The public health nurse was trying to help the mother, a 19-year-old woman of borderline intelligence, with the tasks of child rearing. The baby's 50-year-old father, formerly a truck driver, was homebound because of a back injury.

On her visit, the social worker noted that the mother seemed depressed and lethargic and, although fond of her child, seemed uncertain about how to care for him. When the baby cried, she became panicky. Her husband was demanding a great deal of her attention. In addition, the young mother was on bad terms with her own parents, who had disapproved of her marriage, and she did not want to involve them in her problems now.

The social worker found herself working with a family where multiple health problems were interacting. Consequently she referred the father to vocational rehabilitation for retraining in a skill compatible with his physical limitations, and arranged for a homemaker to help the mother for several weeks so she could observe the details of child care and feeding from a competent model. The social worker also helped the mother reestablish a relationship with her own parents, who proved very interested in the progress of their new grandchild and helpful to their daughter.

---

## *The Future of Social Work in the Health Care Services*

The health care system of the United States is chaotic and costly. In 1989, health care spending averaged 40 percent more per person than health care in Canada, 90 percent more than in Germany, and twice as much as in Japan. One in five American children has no public or private health insurance coverage. One in four black children and one in three Hispanic children have no coverage.[12]

NASW, in preparing for the submission of the "single payer" bill (mentioned earlier in this chapter), developed a health care cost analysis. It states that the current cost of U.S. health care services is estimated to be $738 billion for 1991 and approximately $800 billion for 1992. Even more startling is the NASW projection that by the year 2002, if the current health care system remains unchanged, it is expected to cost $1.959 trillion, or 15.5 percent of the gross national product.[13]

It is reasonable to predict that social work will continue to have a function in the health services in the decades ahead. Care for the individual already is a widely recognized and accepted function of social work in acute care facilities. Numerous examples have been reported of social work's effectiveness in one-to-one arrangements in general hospitals, medical schools, clinics, and in mental health.

In addressing the future role of social work in health care, Rehr has developed the list of concerns, shown in Figure 10.1.

The personal and social health problems represented in Figure 10.1 will require the services of social work. Physicians are not trained to develop social-health solutions. For instance, one study[14] reports that elderly patients account for 38 percent of all days in short-stay hospitals. The elderly are often faced with multiple readmissions, and the elderly person is especially vulnerable to the complex interaction of medical, psychological, and social factors. Social workers can play an important role in helping the elderly and their family members to obtain appropriate medical services by preventing unnecessary hospitalizations, coordinating health planning, and doing discharge planning.

Community work is gaining prominence, particularly in the practice of community medicine and in comprehensive mental health centers. Social workers in medical centers, for example, serve on state medical care advisory committees for Medicaid and Medicare. They also serve on boards on alcoholism and planned parenthood. Increasingly, they are taking leadership on the health team, especially as health care is moving out of the hospital and into the community. Social workers also have been involved in research and evaluation, especially in patient satisfaction measures, which is likely to increase in the years ahead. In various ways social workers are relating themselves increasingly to the community aspects of care.

1. Chronic illnesses and their sequela in:
    the elderly
    infants and children
    the retarded and developmentally disabled;

2. Social-psychological-emotional disorders, including family disequilibrium and interrelationship problems;

3. Social diseases resulting from lifestyle and environmental factors such as: sclerosis, emphysema, hypertension, coronary disorders, and more recently, herpes and AIDS;

4. Social disorders:
    violence, substance abuse, accidents, suicides, person abuse, promiscuity, and excesses;

5. Stress anxiety, fear in the:
    worried well
    stabilized sick;

6. Minor ailments, self-limiting

**FIGURE 10.1   Major Personal and Social Health Problems in the Eighties.**

*Source:* Helen Rehr, "Health Care and Social Work Services: Present Concerns and Future Direction," *Social Work in Health Care,* 10 (Fall 1984), 71–83.

## *Prevention and Social Work*

The social worker is in a unique and enviable position to contribute to prevention. Social work is health oriented, conceptually and philosophically. It addresses the strengths of the individual or family in a given situation.

As a go-between of services, the social worker is the linkage between the person and a system of support that maintains health, or that may be the means of detecting illness early, or of preventing deterioration of the problem.

Social work organizes and develops the community, or mobilizes the resources for doing this. It is often the first to pinpoint needs and to engage in those activities designed to prevent breakdown for the person, the group, or for society. Social work has a resource and service focus and takes the position that no one can be healthy in a sick society.

## *Summary*

*Medical social work is social work in responsible collaboration with medicine. It is practiced in hospitals and clinics and in other settings that commonly are identified with the practice of medicine. The clientele of medical social work are those whose needs are social and psychological and whose functioning has been or is in danger of becoming impaired because of illness, disease, or disability.*

*The ill person, to the social worker, is one who is not performing adequately in the various social roles appropriate for him or her. There are many factors to illness and, in work with the ill person, social workers address themselves to those bearing directly on the person's perfor-mance in various roles—employee, employer, husband, wife, or child.*

*Illness has various and different meanings for the individual, family, and the community. The family's activities often are centered around the sick person, who is in a position to control the activities of the household.*

*Medical and health agencies within the community are established to assist the family in the performance of its role. The meaning of illness to the community lies largely in the need of the community to promote the health of its citizens. Social workers, particularly those in health care settings, are in strategic positions to give direction to the development of services in communities.*

## *Selected References*

BARTLETT, HARRIETT M., *Fifty Years of Social Work in a Medical Setting.* New York: National Association of Social Workers, 1957.

BINSTOCK, ROBERT H., and STEPHEN G. PAST, eds. *Too Old for Health Care? Controversies in Medicine Law, Economics and Ethics.* Baltimore, MD: John Hopkins University Press, 1991.

BRACHT, NEIL, F., *Social Work in Health Care: A Guide to Professional Practice.* New York: The Haworth Press, 1978.

EISENBERG, MYRON G., LA FAYE C. SUTKIN, and MARY A. JANSEN, eds., *Chronic Illness and Disability Through the Life Span: Effects on Self and Family.* New York: Springer, 1984.

KAVANAGH, KATHRYN H., and PATRICIA H. KENNEDY, *Promoting Cultural Diversity: Strategies for Health Care Professionals.* Newberry Park, CA: Sage Publications, 1992.

LINDENBERG, STEVEN PHILLIP, *Group Psychotherapy with People Who Are Dying.* Springfield, IL: Charles C. Thomas, 1983.

LINSK, NATHAN L., and REGGI E. MARDER, "Medical Social Work Long-Term Care Referral with HIV Infection," *Health and Social Work,* 17 (May 1992), 105–127.

MECHANIC, DAVID, ed., *Handbook of Health, Health Care, and the Health Professions.* New York: The Free Press, 1983.

MCNEIL, JOHN S., and STANLEY E. WEINSTEIN, eds., *Innovations in Health Care Practice.* Washington, DC: National Association of Social Workers, 1988.

REAMER, FREDERIC G., ed. *AIDS and Ethics.* New York: Columbia University Press, 1993.

ROSENBURG, GARY, and HELEN REHR, eds., *Advancing Social Work Practice in the Health Care Field.* New York: The Haworth Press, 1983.

## *Notes*

1. Adapted from the work of Rosalie A. Kane, former Associate Professor of Social Work, University of Utah, Graduate School of Social Work.

2. Neil F. Bracht, *Social Work in Health Care: A Guide to Professional Practice* (New York: The Haworth Press, 1978), p. 212.

3. David Stoesz, "Corporate Health Care and Social Welfare," *Health and Social Work,* 11, no. 3 (Summer 1986), 165–171.

4. Doman Lum, "Health Service System," *Encyclopedia of Social Work,* 18th ed., 1 (Silver Spring, MD: National Association of Social Workers, 1987), pp. 720–731.

5. Thomas Owen Carlton, "Highlights of a Decade," *Health and Social Work,* 10 (Fall 1985), 308–312.

6. Sharon M. Keigher, "Managed Care's Silent Seduction of America and the New Politics of Choice," *Health and Social Work,* 20, no. 2 (May 1995), 146–47.

7. Terry Mizrahi, "Prospective Payments and Social Work: Obstacles and Opportunities," in *Innovations in Health Care Practice,* John S. McNeil and Stanley E. Weinstein, eds. (Silver Spring, MD: National Association of Social Workers, 1988), pp. 1–13.

8. William J. Spitzer and Rachel Kuykendall, "Social Work Delivery of Hospital-Based Financial Assistance Services," *Health and Social Work,* 19, 4 (November 1994), 295–297.

9. National Association of Social Workers, "NASW Health-Reform Bill Is Introduced," *NASW News,* 37 (July 1992), 7.

10. National Association of Social Workers, "Health Reformers Skirmish with 'Deformers'," *NASW News,* 40 (June 1995), 9.

11. Gary A. Lloyd, "AIDS and HIV: The Syndrome," *Encyclopedia of Social Work,* 18 ed. supplement (Silver Spring, MD: National Association of Social Workers, 1990), p. 13.

12. Youth Policy Institute, "National Health Care Reform: an Overview," *Youth Policy,* 14 (June/July 1992), p. 15.

13. Terry Mizrahi, "Toward a National Health Care System: Progress and Problems," *Health and Social Work,* 17 (August 1992), 169.

14. Barbara Berkman and Ruth D. Abrams, "Factors Related to Hospital Readmission of Elderly Cardiac Patients," *Social Work,* 31 (March/April 1986), 99–103.

$$Chapter \quad 11$$

# Social Work in the Schools

It's a long road to the White House from Marshall, a mountain hamlet in the Appalachians of western North Carolina. Few people make the trip. Fewer still are asked to hold forth once they get there.

But Regina Lynn, 23-year-old single mother of four, a former dropout, addressed the luncheon crowd in a firm, steady voice. Her smile was infectious.

"I can't believe I'm here," she told the gathering of foundation officers, convened in January 1990 by the Barbara Bush Foundation for Family Literacy. "Two years ago, I wouldn't even talk to the grocery store clerk when he gave me the wrong change."

But humor soon gave way to earnest talk.

The outlines of Ms. Lynn's story were familiar to many in the crowd. They knew her as Natalie, author of the poem "A Place to Start," popularized in a booklet of that name released by the National Center for Family Literacy in September, 1989.

Ms. Lynn retold her story to the White House crowd—her past as a dropout, a single mother with no prospects for the future . . . her present as a GED diploma holder, a straight-A student at Mara Hill College, a mother aware and active in the education and the psycho-social development of her children . . . her future, yet to be discovered, but filled with promise beyond anything she dared to imagine before a social worker appeared at her door two years earlier.

The social worker, Regina explained, convinced her to enroll with her four-year-old son B.J. in a demonstration program of the Kenan Trust Family Literacy Project. There, she and B.J. found their place to start.

"I used to drive by the college as a kid, but I knew I'd never get there," she said. "The Kenan program gave me my dream."

Regina explained how the program inspired the change in her life—and the lives of her children.

"At first I wouldn't talk to the people in the class because I didn't think what I had to say was important," she said. "But they began to make me feel different about myself, and I started to ask questions." She also began to learn about building an atmosphere in her home that supports education: Evenings now, her older children line up for help with their homework, the younger ones look forward to sitting by as she reads a nighttime story.

The luncheon was a triumph for Regina. It was also a triumph for the expanding family literacy movement, a sign that finally, after years of obscurity, family literacy is taking its proper place at the top of the national agenda.

At the heart of this movement—its chief catalyst, advisor, and training and research center—is the National Center for Family Literacy in Louisville, Kentucky.

With the Center's support and guidance, model family literacy programs have been launched to serve:

*—migrant workers in Oregon...*
*—welfare dependent families in*
   *West Philadelphia...*
*—mining and farm families in*
   *Eastern Kentucky...*
*—Eskimos in Alaska...*

*—and hundreds more throughout*
   *the nation.*

*The full harvest of family literacy is still some time off. But the National Center for Family Literacy is planting and nourishing the seeds.*[1]

> All, regardless of race or class or economic status, are entitled to a fair chance and to the tools for developing their individual powers of mind and spirit to the utmost. This promise means that all children by virtue of their own efforts, competently guided, can hope to attain the mature and informed judgment needed to secure gainful employment, and to manage their own lives, thereby serving not only their own interests, but also the progress of society itself.[2]

The American public school system always has been looked upon as something everyone owned. Americans agree that all citizens are entitled to a fair chance to develop mind and spirit. All children guided by competent teachers can hope to become mature enough to secure employment and manage their own lives so that they can serve both themselves and society.

That is a lofty goal, but even as it was being written there were storm clouds over the education system, and T. H. Bell, Secretary of Education in 1983, called upon the National Commission on Excellence in Education to assess American education and to make recommendations for creating excellence in our public schools.

After more than a decade of reform, our nation's schools are still at risk, and some are deteriorating further. All states have adopted some reforms, and several have made drastic changes in their systems; students are required to pass tests to graduate, teachers' salaries have increased, and competency tests are required of teachers in almost all states.

Yet high school dropout rates range from about 30 percent overall to as high as 50 percent in some urban areas, with minorities failing to graduate in even higher percentages in some cities. More than 25 million American adults are functionally illiterate. American students consistently score low in mathematics and science among industrialized nations, and American businesses spend billions of dollars annually in remedial training programs for new employees.

Perhaps the greatest good that has come is that the level of public consciousness concerning the tragic conditions of the schools has been raised. People have become aroused, angry, and determined to do something to make education more effective. The vocal proponents of change are being heard. There is much churning. Experiments on a wide scale are being tried.

Some of the programs that show promise are discussed in the sections that follow.

## The Education Delivery System: New Approaches

The National Center for Family Literacy, which was started in Kentucky by Sharon Darling, seeks to end the intergenerational cycle of poverty and undereducation resulting in economic failure, hopelessness, and despair by fostering education where disadvantaged parents and children attend school together as partners in learning, partners in success. Funded largely by private industry, this concept has spread to many cities throughout the United States and has met with success in helping parents to gain more self-confidence, to get better jobs, to create a better home life for the entire family. They are able to change their lifestyle and learn to socialize. The children get a better start in their education; they expect and get help from their parents with their schoolwork, and they learn to communicate within the family and elsewhere.

Where there has been a high incidence of adult illiteracy it was found that 70 percent of the children did not graduate from high school. This created a never-ending cycle of dead-end jobs and welfare for parents, then for the children. Thus, parental involvement is crucial to student success.

Working within the public school system, the Alternative High School program has shown some promise. During the past decade 25 percent of all eighteen-year-olds have failed to graduate from high school. The alternative school program, designed to reach dropouts and potential dropouts, has been a solution for many. Creating an environment of learning involving all personnel, staff and faculty in a caring and helpful atmosphere, teachers in small classes (usually five to ten students) are free to teach. Counselors, usually social workers, are available full time to provide in-depth discussion of personal and emotional problems, often involving the student's family, or the community if the student is in trouble with the legal system.

Specific rules are made by each school district. Some allow a degree of freedom for habits the students may have—for instance, some may permit smoking, but not drinking alcohol or using drugs. Many admit older students who have been dropouts, teenage mothers, and those who are recovering alcoholics or drug abusers. Most encourage the student's taking responsibility for attendance, and completion of schoolwork without involving the parents. Students, teachers, counselors, and staff become friends. Graduates receive a regular high school diploma.

One program gaining momentum is the Freedom to Choose plan, which allows parents to select their children's schools. Since this involves expenditure of public funds, it has become a hot political issue with sharply divided opinion. The basic plan is that public funds will be provided to pay part or all of the tuition for a student to attend a private school, including religious schools. Nearly five million school-age children were enrolled in private schools in 1991, with more than half in Roman Catholic schools, and the rest enrolled in other religious schools or in private nonsectarian private schools.

Those favoring this plan point out that private schools educate students for about half the cost of public schools, saving taxpayers about $2,000 per year per student. Private schools, according to proponents, do a better job of teaching than do public schools. Competition would force public schools to become better.

Opponents say freedom to choose will destroy the public school systems. They argue that schools always have been "free" and compulsory, and should remain that way.

As an example of how troubled the public school system really is, many parents are opting to teach their children at home. While this was a rarity in all but very isolated areas a few years back, large numbers of youngsters are now being taught by their parents, usually the mother. With the high rate of educated young parents, they are capable of teaching their children, and they can also teach religious and moral values as they choose. Parents find that life revolves around the family, not the school; they see their children excel scholastically and socially, and develop good communication skills and discipline.

States have set up guidelines for home teaching, the number of days of instruction per year, and number of hours each day the student is to be taught. Parents are required to teach the same subjects as in the public schools and to give standardized tests.

## Problems Plaguing the Public Schools

What are the problems in the schools that have turned the public against the system? Some of the most glaring will be discussed here.

### Discipline

There is great emphasis today on an individual's "rights," from the unborn to the dying, and students don't want to be left out on this important issue. No longer does the teacher have authority over students, with the result that some teachers spend a lot of time trying to bring order to the classroom. This, of course, varies from school to school and among teachers; but one thing is certain: It is difficult to teach when students are disruptive. Students need structure and guidance, with clear, specific communication if they are to develop acceptable behavior and achieve academic success. An adult must be in charge to have a successful classroom.

### Violence

With the relaxed discipline in many classrooms, the next step leads to violence. Students who are unable to control their emotions find themselves frustrated, angry, and combative, and they respond to the tension by attacking students or teachers. In the past we have said, "That only happens in the ghettos," but we are now faced with the reality that violence erupts on school playgrounds and in classrooms in all neighborhoods. While it is true that these acts often identify students who need social workers to help them work through their problems, violent behavior creates an atmosphere that makes it difficult for others to learn, or for teachers to teach.

### Drugs

"Drugs" are defined as anything that interferes with the healthy functioning of the user. In addition to narcotics and other illegal substances, nicotine, alcohol, and anabolic steroids are also included. Unfortunately, these are all found in the public schools, particularly in high schools, but also in the lower grades. They not only interfere with a student's health but also are detrimental to the student's capacity to learn, and to the student's emotional and mental health. Students who are using these substances make classroom teaching difficult. Social workers know that just saying "no" will not keep youngsters off drugs. It takes more than a warning to teach young people to cope with the pressures of adolescence.

The Supreme Court ruled in 1995 that public schools may randomly test their student athletes for drugs. While this ruling (*Veronia School District* v. *Acton*) concerned testing for marijuana, cocaine, and amphetamines in a sports program, lawyers predict that it may be used as a first step toward testing entire student bodies if there is reason to suspect illegal drug use.

## Cheating

With students from other industrialized nations excelling in science and math, along with other academic subjects, schools in America have sought ways to keep students competitive. To urge them to greater achievement, standardized tests were devised and required of students at various grade levels in virtually all public school systems. Teachers may feel threatened if their scholars don't meet certain standards; principals feel they have to have top performances from their schools; district officials get salary boosts and public recognition if their schools excel. Schools may receive financial bonuses if their students are in the top percentile; others are punished if their students score low. These may be some of the reasons for the rampant cheating that is found in many schools, but they are not excuses.

Why is widespread cheating common in many public schools? Students cheat so they can be the top in their class; teachers ignore the dishonesty, or in some cases encourage it by focusing on the specific questions found on standardized tests, using the same tests year after year, or changing answers on tests for some students. Some principals have admitted altering test scores after being pressured by parents who want their children to be the best regardless of how they get there.

Many critics maintain that it is the entire educational system that fosters dishonesty. Until schools stress learning over grades, until universities and colleges look more to the whole individual rather than GPAs, and until parents are willing to send their children to good schools that may not be Ivy League, academic deceit is likely to continue.

In those schools where the cheating problem has been openly confronted, school personnel have been able to tighten testing and grading procedures and to create a better learning environment. However, until there is a wholesale change in the entire philosophy of learning there will continue to be problems in the schools.

Social work is one of the disciplines that can help deal with the myriad problems that plague the public schools. Many students, particularly adolescents, find it difficult to adjust to the changes that come into their lives. Regardless of the setting where they attend school, some students require the careful guidance of concerned counselors who meet their needs through individual sessions, group therapy, or community channels.

## Teaching Values

There has been growing controversy about teaching values in the schools, with the big question: whose values will be taught? Lawsuits and threats by parents and organizations have left teachers feeling it is easier to avoid the problems by ignoring values in their teaching. In practice, schools depend on value systems—they punish students who cheat on examinations, who steal textbooks, who assault other students and teachers. But most schools no longer give instruction in self-discipline, honesty, courage, good work habits, and being responsible.

William J. Bennett, Secretary of Education under President Reagan, advocates the teaching of moral education.

> Moral education—the training of heart and mind toward the good—*must* provide training in good habits.
>
> ...If we want our children to possess the traits of character we most admire, we need to teach them what those traits are and why they deserve both admiration and allegiance. Children must learn to identify the forms and content of those traits. They must achieve at least a minimal level of moral literacy that will enable them to make sense of what they see in life, and, we may hope, help them live it well.[3]

## Beginnings in School Social Work

Social work services have been a part of the public schools since 1906 when Boston, Hartford, and New York incorporated this help in their districts. It has evolved steadily with support from school boards, schools of social work, and publications until today many schools have social service workers available for their students. The authors recommend this service to all schools.

Through the years the place of the social worker in the schools has been one of child advocacy based on individual considerations. It has moved away from a "child problem" approach to one that recognizes that children learn in a milieu that supports learning.

## Social Work Practice in the Schools

The Improving America's Schools Act of 1994 signed into law by President Clinton ensures a greater role for school social workers in improving educational opportunities for students. While the goal of the act is to help all children succeed in school, it makes provisions for help in specific areas with vulnerable groups—minorities, limited-English students, those with disabilities, and the economically disadvantaged. It also provides for social workers to receive interdisciplinary training with others on the professional helping team.

As the environment of schools changes, social workers may change their approach to specific problems, but the basic premises that have guided them over the years are still valid.

Social workers—brokers of services—facilitate the application of need and resource. Social workers help by working with the individual student, in group activities, and, in a larger sense, by working with the community to make it possible for learning to occur.

Along with school administrators, they may identify problem areas and possible solutions, as well as help formulate school policy that would address these concerns.

With parents, social workers help to bring about better lines of communication, helping both child and parent gain understanding and acceptance of each other. Through groups of other parents and students, problems often are solved. Community groups help to identify the larger issues that may affect many in the school, and social workers act as agents of change in relation to the school and community.

Social workers need to maintain a liaison between social agencies and the legal practice and to become a catalyst in the evolving patterns of social structure.

The following examples involving social work with individuals and groups can be found in many schools.

## *Work with Individuals*

A national problem impacting our schools is the high number of teenage pregnancies. Studies show that 70 percent of teenagers who become pregnant do not finish high school. Although a greater number than ever before are now opting to keep their babies, seldom is a teen ready for the responsibility of parenthood. The experience for her has negative emotional, social, and financial consequences. In some schools social work helps with the prevention of teen pregnancies. Sensitive to the pressures felt by some students, social workers can help them handle the pressures and not be pushed into relationships for which they are not yet ready.

Knowing that it is not the "norm" for teenagers to talk through feelings, or to think about consequences, the social worker helps them to look to themselves for answers. Good results have followed in reducing the number of pregnancies where school districts have a planned effort including groups, social workers, and teachers. While much can be accomplished in the classroom or in small-group discussions, each pregnant teen presents an individual problem and needs one-on-one counseling. It is only through confidential discussions that all the options can be weighed and the choice that is right for her can be made.

In endeavoring to modify behavior in a child—either to accelerate, decelerate, or extinguish—cooperation and understanding of teachers and parents are very important. Through the help of the child's associates, positive reinforcement can be given during the treatment process and after the modification has taken place.

This treatment method can be effective and achieve the desired results in a short time, as illustrated in the following case.

---

Jan cried. She cried with tears, sobs, drippy nose, and red eyes. Sometimes she cried for 45 minutes at a time, sometimes for all evening.

In school she cried when she could not answer a question, or when someone called her "crybaby," or for no reason at all. At home she cried when asked to clean her room, or wash the dishes, or for no reason at all.

Her junior high teachers constantly complained to Jan and the school counselor about the problem the crying caused in their classrooms. Her parents complained, too. The other students, even her old friends, avoided her because they were annoyed or embarrassed by her crying, so she spent most of her time alone.

In conference with Jan's parents, the counselor explained that he thought Jan cried because of the reinforcement (the increased attention) she received for this behavior. Jan's mother said, "There have been times when Jan was working and crying at the same time, and I told her to leave the work if she couldn't do it without crying." The counselor explained that this was placing more emphasis on negative behavior than on positive behavior.

He asked for permission to have Jan come to his office for two consecutive class periods a day (90 minutes) until she modified this behavior. The parents agreed, and Jan was released from the classes for treatment.

When Jan came to the office the following Monday, the counselor assigned her a place to sit and then, looking at her with good eye to eye contact, said, "Now, Jan, I want you to cry, and don't stop until I tell you to." Jan gave a puzzled look and started crying. This continued every day for a week. At that time her crying started to weaken and she had to be reminded to cry.

The second Monday Jan knocked on the door and asked to talk. She said, "I haven't entered your office so I don't have to cry. Right?" The counselor said, "That's right, Jan." Then she said, "I don't want to cry any more. Will you let me stop?" He responded, "As soon as you enter my office, I want you to cry."

That day Jan cried for 80 minutes. Each day thereafter she cried less and less. On Friday of that week, the counselor told Jan she would not have to come to his office if she would stop crying at home and in her classes, even when she was asked to do something she did not want to do. She said she had not cried either at home or at school for several days. A check with the parents and teachers confirmed this.

Jan did not cry again for the rest of the 30-day experimental period. Checks with teachers showed that she had made fantastic changes. Her parents, too, rejoiced at her improvement at home.

The parents and teachers were helped to see the need for positive reinforcement once the negative behavior had stopped and they learned how to provide this encouragement.

As the other students gradually accepted the new Jan, she became just another member of the group.[4]

## Social Work Using a Group Approach

At a time when resources are at a minimum, social workers in some districts have mobilized an untapped resource in the schools—peer helpers. These individuals become assistants, facilitators, special friends to help others deal with adjustment problems. In groups, they are taught the important skills regarding the nature of helping, confidentiality, acceptance, understanding, trustworthiness, and caring.

Peer groups have proved particularly effective in preventing drug abuse among high-risk students. In one such group the social worker taught a group of students the basics of helping others. Then they identified high-risk students: new in school, racial minorities, underachievers scholastically, and so forth. The first group actively sought out the second group and included them in one-on-one activities and in larger group activities; they provided tutoring if needed with class assignments and became their friends.

Results of this activity were rated very good as a preventive measure, and it had some value when used with students who had previously acquired drug or alcohol problems.

A social worker and children painting.

## *Practice Related to the School System*

Problems may arise because of certain dysfunctional influences within the school system itself. Such influences are suspect when a disproportionate number of students from a particular system are involved. When such factors as teacher perspectives or record systems are involved, a systems approach to solving the problem is suggested. For example, if the dropout rate is excessive, this says something about the school's failure to provide experiences that keep children in school and the failure of school experiences to compete with other influences in the child's life.

With a dropout rate of 28 percent (3 percent higher than the state average) in each of the grades 10 through 12, the school superintendent in a rural district was alarmed. With a declining enrollment and state funds based on average daily attendance, important programs were being curtailed. In addition to the dropouts, much student unrest and dissatisfaction were extant. The social worker was asked to monitor the program, to find out what was wrong, and to suggest what might be done.

An example of what was done in this school follows:

A group consisting of two teachers, four students (two leaders, two nonachievers), their mothers, a counselor, and a social worker met weekly. Key administrators attended a few sessions.

Focusing on the dropout rate and student dissatisfaction, the group discussed other problems they were aware of. In a climate of trust, nonachievers and their mothers learned they could express their frustration and anger over their failure, and the failure of the school to meet their needs. It became apparent that those who were not being served needed to be included in the planning if problems were to be solved.

The group recommended that students with poor attendance and low GPAs, who were excluded from participating in sports and other extracurricular activities, be actively recruited for the "fun" things with the expectation that school would be more appealing to them.

Students and parents who previously felt powerless in reaching school administration with their ideas and suggestions for changing policy were encouraged by the opportunity this group afforded them.

Teachers supported the students, who wanted to change some school policies, and concurred that the school should be a place of fulfillment for all students. They supported the final report recommending that the committee continue to discuss problems as they arose.

In still another school system the social worker became one of the decision-makers in a small rural community.

The dropout rate over a period of three years had risen to 25 percent. Students were pushing and abusing drugs, and there was virtually no social life for them. Teacher morale had dropped to a low ebb. The principal of the high school was charged with misappropriating funds.

The director of mental health in the county, an MSW social worker, repeatedly unsuccessful in his efforts to help individual students, turned his attention to the school system. He discovered that some teachers were lacking in ability to handle pupils and were misassigned. One principal consistently blocked efforts to improve the climate of the school by punitive action against both pupils and teachers. The social worker was unsuccessful in gaining support from the district office. A recalcitrant school board did nothing to improve the operation of the schools except to hire and fire three superintendents in three years.

The social worker concluded he needed to be in a position of influence on the five-member school board. He ran for office. Getting elected was not difficult for the community was disillusioned and ripe for change. Within a year he was named chairman of the board. In a position to influence board decisions, he functioned as a community organizer. He influenced the system.

## School Social Work and the Community

With the community as the target, one social work educator became involved in local government, ran for public office, and was elected city commissioner. She became involved in setting priorities for orderly development and in supporting government officials and the members of the community seeking to develop resources. She worked at planning, budgeting, financing, and engaged in formal and informal lobbying efforts at the local and state levels. Her role on boards, councils, and social service committees was a model for students in training. Observing her, students were able to understand the broadened concept of social work practice.

What were some of the gains of this community-centered effort? Giant strides were made in providing recreational facilities—municipal swimming pool, roller- and ice-skating rinks, tennis courts, and a golf course. Service organizations accepted responsibility for equipment for the recreational center, and for scholarships, awards, and special recognition for school achievement. They also raised funds for medical and dental care for those in need.

Social workers on local boards, such as the community services council, mental health board, and planning boards, opened the door to the community by providing important linkage to the power structure of the community.[5]

## Working with Minorities

Asians, Cubans, Koreans, Haitians, Mexicans, and countless children and adults from a great many countries are arriving in America, and our schools are being pressured by unprecedented numbers of people who are seeking to make a home here. It has been estimated that by the turn of the century the population of the United States will increase to more than 300 million—attributable not to a high birth rate, but to immigrants and refugees. The monumental effort it will take to acculturate and train these new arrivals has only begun. Excellence in our schools as called for by the National Commission on Excellence will make unimagined demands on us all. If new arrivals are to have a "fair chance" at developing their abilities and a chance to attain the mature and informed judgment needed to secure gainful employment, they will have to be trained.

Social work, concerned with the social functioning of individuals and youths in various group arrangements, will have a role in this effort. It has the expertise to help people adapt to their environment and to develop their potential. It is particularly suited to help people cope with change. In instances where social work skills and methods have been applied in the schools to help minorities, satisfactory results have been reported. Certainly more is needed. We need more personnel and clearly defined roles for social work in schools for the benefit of administrators, teachers, and other school staff. There needs to be a broadening of social work practice beyond traditional methods to include a spectrum of direct and indirect practice. This is the challenge for social work in the schools for the remainder of this century and into the next.

## When the System Fails

The dramatic, real-life story "Cipher in the Snow,"[6] written by a schoolteacher and counselor (see Chapter 1 for an explanation of the role of the school counselor as opposed to the social worker), was awarded first place in the National Education Association's teachers' writing contest in 1964. According to the author, the story is true except for such minor changes as were needed to protect the privacy and confidentiality of the characters in the story.

The story is a grim reminder of disturbing conditions in public schools. It suggests a role for social work when a lonely, insecure child who cannot ask for help falls prey to destructive social influences. This story applies to teachers, but it has been used by social work educators to teach systems theory.

## *Cipher in the Snow*

It started with tragedy on a biting cold February morning. I was driving behind the Milford Corners bus as I did most snowy mornings on my way to school. It veered and stopped short at the hotel, which it had no business doing, and I was annoyed as I had to come to an unexpected stop. A boy lurched out of the bus, reeled, stumbled, and collapsed on the snowbank at the curb. The bus driver and I reached him at the same moment. His thin, hollow face was white even against the snow.

"He's dead," the driver whispered.

I didn't register for a minute. I glanced quickly at the scared young faces staring down at us from the school bus. "A doctor! Quick! I'll phone from the hotel. . . ."

"No use. I tell you he's dead." The driver looked down at the boy's still form. "He never even said he felt bad," he muttered, "just tapped me on the shoulder and said, real quiet, 'I'm sorry. I have to get off at the hotel.' That's all. Polite and apologizing like."

At school, the giggling, shuffling morning noise quieted as the news went down the halls. I passed a huddle of girls. "Who was it? Who dropped dead on the way to school?" I heard one of them half-whisper.

"Don't know his name; some kid from Milford Corners," was the reply.

It was like that in the faculty room and the principal's office. "I'd appreciate your going out to tell the parents," the principal told me. "They haven't a phone and, anyway, somebody from school should go there in person. I'll cover your classes."

"Why me?" I asked. "Wouldn't it be better if you did it?"

"I didn't know the boy," the principal admitted levelly. "And in last year's sophomore personalities column I note that you were listed as his favorite teacher."

I drove through the snow and cold down the bad canyon road to the Evans place and thought about the boy, Cliff Evans. His favorite teacher! I thought. He hasn't spoken two words to me in two years! I could see him in my mind's eye all right, sitting back there in the last seat in my afternoon literature class. He came in the room by himself and left by himself. "Cliff Evans," I muttered to myself, "a boy who never talked." I thought a minute. "A boy who never smiled. I never saw him smile once."

The big ranch kitchen was clean and warm. I blurted out my news somehow. Mrs. Evans reached blindly toward a chair. "He never said anything about bein' ailing."

His stepfather snorted. "He ain't said nothin' about anything since I moved in here."

Mrs. Evans pushed a pan to the back of the stove and began to untie her apron. "Now hold on," her husband snapped. "I got to have breakfast before I go to town. Nothin' we can do now anyway. If Cliff hadn't been so dumb, he'd have told us he didn't feel good."

After school I sat in the office and stared bleakly at the records spread out before me. I was to close the file and write the obituary for the school paper. The almost bare sheets mocked the effort. Cliff Evans, white, never legally adopted by stepfather, five young half brothers and sisters. These meager strands of information and the list of D grades were all the records had to offer.

Cliff Evans had silently come in the school door in the mornings and gone out the school door in the evenings, and that was all. He had never belonged to a club. He had never played on a team. He had never held an office. As far as I could tell, he had never done one happy, noisy kid thing. He had never been anybody at all.

How do you go about making a boy into a zero? The grade school records showed me. The first and second grade teachers' annotations read "sweet, shy child"; "timid but eager." Then the third grade note had opened the attack. Some teacher had written in a good, firm hand, "Cliff won't talk. Uncooperative. Slow learner." The other academic sheep had followed with "dull"; "slow-witted"; "low I.Q." They became correct. The boy's I.Q. score in the ninth grade was listed at 83. But his I.Q. in the third grade had been 106. The score didn't go under 100 until the seventh grade. Even shy, timid, sweet children have resilience. It takes time to break them.

I stomped to the typewriter and wrote a savage report pointing out what education had done to Cliff Evans. I slapped a copy on the principal's desk and another in the sad, dog-eared file. I banged the typewriter and slammed the file and crashed the door shut, but I didn't feel much better. A little boy kept walking after me, a little boy with a peaked, pale face; a skinny body in faded jeans; and big eyes that had looked and searched for a long time and then had become veiled.

I could guess how many times he'd been chosen last to play sides in a game, how many whispered child conversations had excluded him, how many times he hadn't been asked. I could see and hear the faces and voices that said over and over, "You're dumb. You're dumb. You're a nothing, Cliff Evans."

A child is a believing creature. Cliff undoubtedly believed them. Suddenly it seemed clear to me: When finally there was nothing left at all for Cliff Evans, he collapsed on a snowbank and went away. The doctor might list "heart failure" as the cause of death, but that wouldn't change my mind.

We couldn't find ten students in the school who had known Cliff well enough to attend the funeral as his friends. So the student body officers and a committee from the junior class went as a group to the church, being politely sad. I attended the services with them, and sat through it with a lump of cold lead in my chest and a big resolve growing through me.

I've never forgotten Cliff Evans nor that resolve. He has been my challenge year after year, class after class. I look up and down the rows carefully each September at the unfamiliar faces. I look for veiled eyes or bodies scrouged into a seat in an alien world. "Look, kids," I say silently, "I may not do anything else for you this year, but not one of you is going to come out of here a nobody. I'll work or fight to the bitter end doing battle with society and the school board, but I won't have one of you coming out of here thinking himself into a zero."

Most of the time—not always, but most of the time—I've succeeded.

---

The isolation felt by Cliff Evans was extreme but suggests problems not uncommon in public schools. Students commit suicide, "cop out" on drugs or alcohol, or vanish from school.

This story suggests the need for social study, individualizing needs, and the broker-mobilizer-coordinator role of social work. Community or school provisions obviously were not favorably impacting Cliff Evans or his family. A further implication for social work lies in the disturbing anonymity in the account, suggesting the need for a study of the system itself and, possibly, for the initiation of change.

There is not enough known about what causes school failures. Research is needed to provide answers on the prevention and treatment of school-related problems, and research is one of the functions of social work in the schools.

Thus, in the schools, the role of social work is one of individualizing, bringing services to bear on problems, coordinating those services to get the best results, intervening directly for counseling and group treatment, and addressing the elements of the system that produce the problem or contribute to it.

# Summary

*School social work is embedded deeply in the roots of society's mandate to the schools to educate and train "all the children of all the people" to the maximum of their potentials and capacities. It is a corollary to compulsory school attendance, since not all children, unaided, are able to make profitable use of their formal learning experiences.*

*Specialists have been attached to the school for the purpose of helping the child achieve his or her potential in the academic setting. These specialists include social workers who relate themselves to the role performance of the child and his or her social and intellectual opportunities.*

*Social workers focus on social functioning and on the needs of the child to make the best possible use of the learning experience. They are concerned with the fact that forces within and outside the child, and often outside the school itself, may block the pupil's use of the school experience. They intervene to remove barriers to learning. In so doing,*

*they may work with individuals, groups, the school itself and ally themselves with the community in support of the school's purposes and objectives.*

*Social workers work with teachers, principals, pupils, or parents. Frequently they work with the teacher and the principal striving for greater understanding of the difficulty that confronts the pupil. One-to-one arrangements with students may be a treatment mode used by the workers or provided in their role of broker.*

*They may relate to families in helping them to accept the purpose of school, the needs of the pupil, and in bringing the two together. Parents frequently function inadequately, simply because of their own needs and unsolved problems. School social workers help in solving problems that interfere directly or indirectly with the pupil's schooling. They work with the team—teachers and other specialists—to bring about the maximum educational benefits.*

## Selected References

ANDERSON, RICHARD J., ed., *School Social Work and PL 94–142: The Education for all Handicapped Children Act.* Washington, DC: N.A.S.W. Continuing Education Series 7, 1977.

CAMPBELL, JEAN, "Individualized Educational Programs as a Tool in Evaluation," *Social Work Education,* 2 (April 1980), 19–24.

COSTIN, LELA B., *Social Work Services in Schools: Historical Perspectives and Current Directions.* Washington, DC: N.A.S.W. Continuing Education Series 8, 1978.

EHRENKRANZ, SHIRLEY M., EDA G. GOLDSTEIN, LAWRENCE GOODMAN, and JEFFREY SEINFIELD, eds., *Clinical Social Work with Maltreated Chil-*

dren and their Families: Introduction to Practice. New York: New York University Press, 1989.

LOMBANA, JUDY H., *Home-School Partnerships: Guidelines and Strategies for Educators.* New York: Grune & Stratton, 1983.

MORGAN, SHARON R., *Children in Crises: A Team Approach in the Schools.* San Diego, CA: College-Hill Press, 1985.

ROBINSON, BRYAN, *Teenage Fathers.* Lexington, MA: D.C. Heath, 1988.

VALENTINE, MICHAEL R., *How to Deal With Discipline Problems in the Schools: A Practical Guide for Educators.* Dubuque, IA: Kendall/Hunt, 1987.

## Notes

1. National Center for Family Literacy, "Spreading the Word, Planting the Seed" (Louisville, KY, 1991), p. 5.

2. United States Department of Education, *A Nation at Risk: The Imperative for Educational Reform:*

*A Report to the Nation and the Secretary of Education* (Washington, DC: April 1983), p. 4.

3. William J. Bennett, ed. *Book of Virtues, A Treasury of Great Moral Stories* (New York: Simon & Schuster, 1993), p. 11.

4. Case material adapted from a presentation by Richard Johansen, behaviorist, Weber County Schools, Utah.

5. The leadership of Professor Phyllis C. Southwick, Graduate School of Social Work, University of Utah, is acknowledged in the development of this model.

6. Jean E. Mizer Todhunter, "Cipher in the Snow," *National Education Association Journal* (November 1964), 8–10. Reprinted by permission.

$Chapter$ $12$

# Social Security and Public Welfare

The 26-year-old mother of two little children was alone in the world as she arrived in a new city. She had left her husband of nine years because of abuse. He had been on drugs for a long time and when he started using cocaine she knew his attitude toward her would not improve, and that there would never be enough money to support her, the children, and his drug habit.

With her two boys, ages 7 and 3, she settled in another state where she looked for a job. She had never had a paying job; she had married upon graduation from high school. When she could not find work she applied for welfare assistance and was put on AFDC.

Although it was not mandatory that she begin a program to become independent of welfare, she opted for "self-sufficiency" training. By placing her youngest child in day care (both children when there was no school) she was able to begin an educational program.

The "self-sufficiency" worker at the agency steered her into a program where she could learn a skill and become employable. She attended the state technical college to learn computer operation and office work.

Her AFDC allowance and food stamps met her basic needs. The welfare worker approved her application for subsidized housing, paid for child care and school expenses. She also was given "heat assistance" and paid a reduced amount for electricity. She was eligible for Medicaid. When she first arrived her youngest child was anemic and she received help from WIC, a program for women and children which gave basic instruction in nutrition and aid in providing a balanced diet.

At the end of her two-year course, she had excellent skills in office work and was placed with a large company. As her financial condition became stable, she was allowed to remain in her subsidized housing, but her rent increased with her ability to pay, and she continued to receive limited assistance until she became totally self-sufficient.

The two years had been lonely for her as she had no family support system near her. With her school classes, studying, and time with the children she had little time to make new friends. By turning again to the coordinator, who had been her advocate in school and during the early weeks on the job, she found the help needed to develop social skills and find new friends. Informal support systems also helped sustain her until the time when she could normalize her relationships and find the security of really belonging. Only by the linkage of many resources—workplace, welfare, new support systems—does it become possible to help women in poverty. Nothing short of total community effort can be expected to relieve this serious malaise. AFDC as provided under public welfare helped.[1]

**189**

What is public welfare? Public welfare means different things to many people, and what it means depends somewhat on who these people are and through what lens they view the picture.

To some, public welfare is the "garbage heap" for human wreckage—the idle, the shiftless, the unemployable, the sick and decrepit, the transient, loafers, malingerers, beggars, and certain ne'er-do-wells. In the minds of many, public welfare is income, medical and dental care, and commodities—public support for widows, the blind, the disabled, the disabled dependent children, and sick people unable to cope without help in a complex, ever-changing society.

Individuals see public welfare in different ways. "Some, for example, see it as an aggregation of quite distinct programs, grouped together by most states and localities for administrative convenience in a public welfare department but quite independent from each other in purpose, origin, criteria of performance, and logic of development. Others by contrast . . . see public welfare evolving toward organic unity of function and purpose, a single whole in which the parts, however specialized in their functioning, derive their vitality and character from the parent body."[2]

Public welfare includes income and health maintenance programs for the aged, the blind, the disabled; aid to families for care of dependent children; medical care to the indigent and aging; and various social-rehabilitation services to eligible children, families, and single adults.

## Government's Responsibility for Welfare

Basic responsibility of government for welfare was established in England with the Elizabethan Poor Laws, and relief under the provisions of those laws was a local matter, limited to specialized kinds of need and extending only to those whose claims of settlement could not be disputed legally.

Residual elements of relief in kind, means test approaches, public responsibility for only certain kinds of need, work and residence requirements, and characteristics of colonial relief still are found in various services and assistance provisions, particularly at the state and local levels of government. Although many of these measures are repressive and intended to discourage their use, it is well to remember that they do, nevertheless, affirm the principle of governmental responsibility.

The *federal* government's responsibility for welfare started in the earliest days of the republic when in 1785 Congress made grants of public lands to states for schools. Other responsibilities were extended when the people, through their elected representatives, added other agencies such as the Federal Office of Education, the Children's Bureau, and the Vocational Rehabilitation Administration; but a comprehensive plan for the protection of citizens against income risks did not become an *enduring* principle of federal responsibility for welfare until 1935 with the passage of the Social Security Act. Reinforcement of this principle has been a clear result of the many amendments to the act legislated by Congress.

The Department of Health, Education, and Welfare (HEW), created in 1953, with cabinet status, is an outgrowth of a widely held view that the federal government has a responsibility for the *general welfare.* In 1980, HEW was divided into two cabinet-level departments: The Department of Education and the Department of Health and Human Services.

The federal government now assumes responsibility to insure virtually all American workers and their families against the loss of income from retirement and disability. Survivors of insured workers also are protected. Risks to employed workers from unemployment for a specified period of time are assumed as a federal-state responsibility. A system is yet to be developed to protect workers for long periods of unemployment and various work stoppages.

An expanded health care system, the "largest human service system" in the history of the United States, further affirms the role of government as an instrument of social policy. Medical care under Social Security protects retired workers, their families, and certain disabled persons. A comprehensive national health plan has not been adopted but has been widely debated in congressional committees and the Clinton administration has promised to provide universal health care to all Americans.

The federal government assumes financial responsibility for the aged, blind, and disabled under the Supplemental Security Income (SSI) program, and in cooperation with the states extends protection to families covered under the Aid to Families with Dependent Children program, and other citizens who qualify for assistance under other provisions of the Social Security Act as a statutory right, including medical care to indigent recipients of public assistance (Medicaid) and to the aged whose income is too low to provide this care.

With the presidency of Ronald Reagan there was a shift in the thinking about government's responsibility for welfare. It is sometimes asked, will the thinking of former President Reagan become a trend, implemented in policy and a new approach to welfare, or will the people and Congress resist more than cosmetic changes?

## President Ronald Reagan's Ideology

Ronald Reagan "redrew the ideological landscape." His political and fiscal philosophy and his views on the role of government were in sharp contrast to Franklin Roosevelt's *New Deal* and Lyndon Johnson's *Great Society.*

As governor of California and as President, Reagan preached a limited role for government—it should do only what people could not do for themselves. He argued for fewer, not more, government regulations and for citizens to have greater freedom in the management of their lives and their money. He slashed taxes and urged the paring back of government programs, including those for the poor and disadvantaged, insisting that these should remain at the state and local levels. Reagan believed that people should get help when needed from families, neighborhoods, and local charitable, religious, and governmental entities; that power concentrated in Washington made serious inroads on individual freedom.

Reagan's philosophy impacted social legislation and continues to be debated in the halls of Congress. The jury, however, is still out and what to do about health and welfare is hotly debated. That these issues and problems are at the front of national concern where policy decisions are made is very much in the country's interest. It is hoped that the poor, the disadvantaged, the homeless, and those who are ill will be served by governmental and nongovernmental agencies seeking solutions to these most difficult social problems.

## The Social Security Act

The cornerstone of public welfare in the United States is the Social Security Act, passed August 14, 1935. In general, this act, with its many amendments, is the chief means by which government at the local, state, and national levels provides income security to citizens.

Discussion in this chapter centers on provisions under old age, survivors, disability, and health insurance; unemployment compensation; old-age assistance; aid to families with dependent children; aid to the blind; aid to the disabled; and social services.

### Old Age, Survivors, Disability, and Health Insurance (OASDHI)

The national old age, survivors, disability, and health insurance, popularly referred to as Social Security and administered by the federal government, is the largest and most important of the income and health insurance programs in the United States. Cash benefits from this program are designed to partially replace income lost when a worker retires or becomes disabled. Cash benefits also are paid to survivors of "insured" workers.

The program also provides partial health-care benefits for old age and disability under Medicare. Amendments to the Social Security Act in 1965 set up a contributory health insurance plan for nearly all people aged sixty-five and over: a compulsory program of hospital insurance (HI) and a voluntary supplementary insurance (SMI) to pay for health services. Other amendments also extended coverage to certain severely disabled persons under age sixty-five, including disabled workers, disabled widows and widowers, and childhood disability beneficiaries.

Since its inception, Social Security has extended its benefits so old age, survivors, disability, and health insurance coverage approaches universal dimensions.

OASDHI is a contributory system. It is not to be confused with insurance in the private sector; it is *social* insurance. Payments to beneficiaries are based on previous earnings; equity can be claimed for the system. Beneficiaries of OASDHI are not subject to investigation or a test of means to establish eligibility. They do not have to prove they are poor to receive benefits. Records are maintained accurately and "claims" are processed and paid with technological efficiency. The system's administration is handled efficiently and non-judgmentally. Other retirement income and that derived from interest on savings, stocks, and bonds, rental property, and annuities—regardless of the amount—do not limit payments. On the other hand, limits *are* placed on the amount of income retired workers can earn from employment while receiving Social Security payments.[3] To understand this constraint it may be helpful to recall that the Social Security Act was passed in 1935 when the country was experiencing the Great Depression. Many workers were unemployed. Retirement was written into the law to encourage workers aged sixty-five and older to retire to make way on the labor market for younger, unemployed men and women. In times of high employment or labor shortage, the act might well have to be changed to induce workers not to retire but to continue in the labor force. Incentives for workers to continue employment now exist in the form of earning levels workers may attain without losing payment benefits.

Taxes, under the provision of the Federal Insurance Contribution Act (FICA), are collected from the employee and employer during the productive working life of the worker to pay for OASDHI. Self-employed workers pay the full amount of the tax. In 1935 the tax was one percent each for the employee and the employer on an income base of $3,000 per year. In 1995 the tax base had been raised to $61,200.

In adopting OASDHI, the United States radically departed from reliance on the family, the church, private philanthropy, local government, and unending emergency measures, to provide a bulwark against want and income need. Many believe that such a departure was warranted and that for the retired, disabled, and survivors of insured workers, OASDHI offers greater security and financial independence than they previously knew. Five and one-half million persons were receiving Social Security in 1953.

At the end of August 1991, a total of $22 billion in monthly cash benefits was paid to 40,307,337 beneficiaries. Sixty-two percent of all OASDI beneficiaries were retired workers. Disabled worker beneficiaries numbered 3,124,129.

The concern raised about financing Social Security has to do with Medicare, not retirement and survivors' insurance. Authorities appear to be somewhat agreed that we can count on OASDHI being paid until 2020. To provide this assurance the tax on earnings has been increased on an income base of $61,200 in 1995 with provisions for further increases in the years ahead.

The spiralling costs of medical care pose a threat to the solvency of the system. This problem is being addressed, and we can be assured that steps will be taken such as caps on what the system will pay for medical procedures, limits the system will pay hospitals, higher costs to consumers in premiums, or some universal system of health care for everyone. Beginning in 1992 the base income taxed for Medicare had risen to $130,000. This is 1.45 percent for employers and employees each, and 2.9 percent for self-employed people.

When Social Security was enacted only workers in commerce and industry were covered. Since then major changes have been legislated, and today about 95 percent of the jobs in this country are covered. Medicare was expanded in 1972. The Medicare Catastrophic Coverage Act of 1988 is an example of government wanting to further reduce the financial risk on the elderly for prolonged health care and costly medical procedures; however, the major provisions of the act were repealed in 1989. The elderly themselves objected to the increase in their income taxes and lobbied Congress to repeal the legislation.

Under the provisions of this act, taxes on income of the nation's elderly would have paid for medical care. Some argued that the tax was fair, and that those receiving the benefits should pay for them. Others argued against it, using the logic that the elderly, who don't go to school, are nevertheless taxed to help pay the cost of educating youth. There seems to be a growing consensus that the costs of common human needs should be equitably shared and socially-distributed. Additional expansion covering the health care field can be reasonably predicted in the years ahead.

In times of recession and high unemployment, the number of workers paying into Social Security is decreased, thus reducing the money available to pay beneficiaries. Also, inflation forces upward adjustments of payments, making heavier demands on the Social Security tax. The decline in the birth rate, not a major concern in the 1980s, may become so in the years ahead, when the retired population will be disproportionately large to the younger working population.

An alternative to government management would be to privatize the system in part or in full. Many believe that this would provide more generous retirement and cut back on the burden to the taxpayer. One objection to this approach is that those most likely to benefit would be the younger, more affluent, who also would not be contributing to the less affluent.

What is likely is that changes mentioned above and possibly others will need to be made. The stakes are too high for the country to do nothing. Changes will have to be made and, as more Americans come to this realization, changes can be expected.

Basically, the system is a pay-as-you-go arrangement. Wage earners are taxed to pay benefits to retired and disabled workers and their dependents. Resistance to the system might be expected as taxes increase causing pay checks to shrink. Also, an increasing number of workers believe that the private sector can offer greater benefits than Social Security. While this is undoubtedly true for many workers, for the vast majority of the population Social Security offers more income security for retired workers, the disabled, and their survivors. Social Security is a form of *social* insurance and a reasonably well accepted mechanism for sharing costs and transferring income.

Congress appears unwilling to make the changes in Social Security that many believe necessary for the system to continue to be viable well into the next century. Scholars and analysts agree that the demographics of today are different from when the system was enacted and that the world for which it was designed no longer exists. For example, in 1950 there were 16 workers paying taxes for every retiree. In 1995 only three taxpayers support each retiree. By 2030 two workers will support each person receiving benefits. Taxes on workers have increased from 3% on $3,000 in 1950 to 12.4% for workers and employers on $61,200 in 1995. It is estimated that for the system to remain solvent, taxes will have to be raised to 17%, a figure that appears to be unacceptable to the economy.

Most scholars and economists agree that changes can and should be made. For example:

1. An increase in the age of retirees to reflect the changes in demographics; men and women are living years longer.
2. The formula used today to increase benefits based on cost-of-living index should be more in line with private pensions.
3. Retirees independently wealthy and those with large incomes would receive less Social Security, if any.
4. Raise taxes.
5. A combination of the above, and possibly other changes as well.

Social work basically supports Social Security as a method of income transfer. It approaches universality in application. It is nondeterrent. It is a contributory system that makes it more acceptable to recipients as it is compatible with the ethic of "working for what you get." It is *social* as distinguished from regular insurance, suggesting a role of government in the welfare domain. Some central system of income maintenance for the retired and disabled workers and their survivors is essential.

## Unemployment Insurance

OASDHI and unemployment insurance are the two insurance provisions of the Social Security Act. Unemployment insurance serves to cushion workers whose income is interrupted by work stoppages and layoffs. Most states will pay unemployment compensation for a maximum of twenty-six weeks. In 1970 extended benefits became a "temporary" measure of a federal-state program for workers who had exhausted their entitlements in periods of high unemployment. The extended benefit provided for a 50 percent increase in benefit duration up to a maximum of thirteen weeks or a total of thirty-nine weeks of regular and extended benefits. Extensions of benefit periods were approved by Congress in 1974 and again in 1975. Extended benefits, in times of recession or periods of high rates of unemployment, may be "triggered" by the states or by the federal government up to an additional thirteen weeks, or for as many as two extended periods of thirteen weeks each. The maximum for which any insured worker has been covered is sixty-five weeks.

Unemployment insurance is no protection of income against strikes or long periods of unemployment resulting from economic recession and depression. The American system makes no income provisions for prolonged unemployment except to a few workers who can qualify for Aid to Families with Dependent Children or residual general assistance.

Unemployment compensation is a *nondeterrent*[4] *insurance* rather than a public assistance program. To be eligible to receive this compensation, in most states a person must:

1. Demonstrate attachment to the labor force by a specified amount of recent work in covered employment.
2. Be ready, able, and willing to work.
3. Be registered for work in a public employment office and file a claim for benefits.
4. Not be disqualified for benefits by some act that would indicate he or she was responsible for his or her unemployment.
5. Demonstrate that unemployment is due to a lack of work for which the employee is qualified.
6. Not be unemployed because of a labor dispute or refusal to accept suitable employment.

Unemployment insurance is financed almost completely by a tax on employers. The employer pays the tax but to show a profit may pass this tax on to the consumer in higher costs of goods and services, or on to the employee in lower wages, or both. Workers, as consumers, also pay for unemployment insurance in higher costs of consumer goods and services. Extended benefits, those paid to workers beyond the period provided in their state plans, are financed equally by federal and state funds.

## Public Assistance

Public assistance is an income-maintenance system that should not be confused with the insurance provisions of the Social Security Act. Four main categories of clients are classified under this system: the aged, the blind, the disabled, and the families of dependent children.

### Supplemental Security Income

Under the Supplemental Security Income program (SSI), the federal government pays monthly checks to people in need sixty-five years of age and older and to those in need at any age who are blind or disabled. People qualify for these payments who have little or no

**TABLE 12.1   SSI—Number of Persons Receiving SSI and Payment Amounts**

| Category | Federally-Administered Payments (May 1992) | | State-Administered Payments (January 1992) |
| | Number | Average Payment | Number |
| --- | --- | --- | --- |
| All recipients | 5.3 million | $357 | 308 thousand |
| Aged | 1.5 million | $229 | 120 thousand |
| Blind | 85.0 thousand | $374 | 4 thousand |
| Disabled | 3.8 million | $406 | 183 thousand |
| Age 65 or older | 2.1 million | … | … |

Federal payment, 1992 (for persons in their own household, no other countable income)

| | |
| --- | --- |
| Individual | $422 |
| Couple (both eligible) | $633 |

*Source: Social Security Bulletin* (Summer 1992).

regular cash income, who own little, if any, property, or who have little cash or few assets that can be turned into cash, such as stocks and bonds, jewelry, or other valuables.

Payments under SSI, managed by the Social Security Administration, are based on the recipient's assets and income. States have the option of supplementing the payments. Financed from general revenues, not from Social Security contributions, SSI is not a contributory system; that is, no payments have been previously made by recipient or recipient's employer. Benefits are not presumed to have been "earned."

Table 12.1 shows the number of individuals receiving SSI and the payment amounts in January 1992.

## Aid to Families with Dependent Children

Income through Aid to Families with Dependent Children (AFDC) is available to those who qualify under provisions of the Social Security Act.

For example, AFDC families must satisfy such requirements as:

1. The child must be under 18 years of age (21 if attending school or training full time).
2. The family must reside in the United States and be citizens or otherwise permanently residing here under legal provisions.
3. No limits are placed on ownership of a home occupied by the family. Other personal and real property is limited to a net value of some specified amount.

AFDC is the most controversial of the welfare programs, and is the concern of economists as well as politicians. It is a program that needs strong advocates, for the children involved are unable to speak for themselves. But at the rate it is growing, it is clear that some changes need to be made.

In January 1992, some 13.5 million Americans were on AFDC, up 2.2 million from two years earlier. Sixty percent of poor families with children are headed by women. The amount of money the recipients receive varies by states. In addition to AFDC grants, recipients also receive food stamps and Medicaid, which may bring their total income higher than those who are working in low-paying jobs.

A major overhaul of the AFDC system was made in 1988 with the Family Support Act, which sought to modify the handling of grants. These new options are a step in the right direction. However, changes do not come quickly, and some of these need more time and study.

Highlights of the reform are:

1. Beginning in January 1994, states are required to withhold court-ordered child-support payments.
2. States are required to meet federal standards in establishing paternity.
3. States are mandated to establish a Job Opportunities and Basic Skills (JOBS) program to provide education, training, and employment, with the objective of helping people leave the welfare rolls.
4. Most adult clients will be enrolled in JOBS, with exemptions for parents with children under the age of 3.
5. Child care, transportation, and work expenses will be provided, and wage rates will be not less than minimum rates.
6. Beginning in 1994 an unemployed parent will be required to work a minimum of 16 hours per week.

Although these work incentives sound good, there has not been a rush to enroll in JOBS. This program depends upon state funds, and some states have not fully implemented the plan because of budget problems. Also, the definition for "exemptions," "participation," and "able-bodied" are so imprecise that those who do not want to be a part of the program can easily find a way to circumvent it.

With the enormous financial drain on federal and state budgets, and the wasting of the young men and women in our country, there is clearly a need to replace or reform the welfare system. Politicians, economists, and other leaders suggest solutions to this problem. Some of their suggestions are:

1. All able-bodied recipients are to be off the AFDC rolls after two years. They will be provided with child care, medical care, and job training while on the rolls.
2. To able-bodied recipients, 25 percent of the aid will be cut after six months.
3. No additional money will be given for any babies born while the mother is receiving AFDC.
4. Recipients are required to work toward self-sufficiency while receiving benefits.
5. Stricter discipline will be set for those receiving aid: parents must be in training, children in school.
6. Public-works-type jobs will be available for those able to work.

President Clinton has promised change. Among the changes proposed for AFDC are several of the above and others: work requirements for the able-bodied, training and education for high-tech jobs, and public works for the homeless and those who may not be trainable.

In their "Contract with America" the House Republicans state that their goal by 2003 is to have half the adults on AFDC—91% of whom are women—in the workforce, working a minimum of 35 hours per week.

While all the suggested solutions sound feasible, they do not take into account the reality of the situation of welfare clients. The reason that many AFDC parents cannot be put to work and taken off welfare rolls is that they are not employable. They lack education and aptitude. Two-thirds of recipients on the rolls for two years or more have not graduated from high school; their reading and math skills are so low that they cannot solve even basic problems. The majority have no work experience and no work ethic. Because of low self-esteem many become depressed. One-third of AFDC mothers are disabled or have a disabled child. A large number of welfare mothers are in an abusive relationship with a spouse or boyfriend. Many of them refuse to leave their children in day care because they fear the children will be abused.

A Health and Human Services study in 1994 found that 16 percent of welfare mothers have substance abuse problems that require treatment before they can succeed in the job market.

With more unwed teenage mothers keeping their babies, the welfare rolls continue to rise. The Contract with America would not provide money or housing for mothers under age eighteen if they had children out of wedlock. Yet often the parental home of the mother is unsuitable for the teenager and the baby. Teens, often without schooling or marketable skills and without family support, develop welfare dependency as a way of life. Special programs for them are indicated if the cycle of pregnancy and dependency on AFDC is to be broken.

The Family Support Act sets up the Job Opportunities and Basic Skills (JOBS) program, which provides training for a place in the workforce. This, with various state-operated Job Club opportunities, is producing some results. It is possible to make some improvements. Some governors are asking for more leeway in administering the funds, stressing that at the state and local levels social workers can deal with their particular problems. They can work with individuals in job training and education to make the clients become employable. Programs in some states and communities show progress, but it is slow.

It is a challenge to planners to find ways for single mothers to climb out of poverty so that they and their children have sufficient means to live a decent life.[5]

The perfect solution has not yet been found, and there is not just one answer to this overwhelming problem. However, pilot programs in small areas both in inner-city ghettos and in middle-class communities have provided new insights into what works and what does not. People become dependent upon welfare for many reasons, and they resist giving up the security of a regular paycheck to an unknown job where performance is a determining factor as to whether the money will continue to arrive.

## *Poverty*

Poverty continues to be a reality for many Americans. It has been reported that poverty rates in this country reached a 17-year high in the recession year of 1982. The Census Bureau reports increasing numbers of people below the poverty line. Income maintenance systems and such programs as work relief, food stamps, school lunches, and Medicaid haven't done the job. The rolls of poverty have not been reduced and there is no end in sight.

Many taxpayers are convinced that the system is ineffective and should be dismantled. Some say it provides too many disincentives, and that it favors those who don't work over those who can't. It is criticized because it is fragmented into a patchwork of overlapping out-of-control programs. While recognizing the cost to the country in a loss of productivity (people have little or no incentive to work because of the alternative—unemployment compensation, food stamps, etc.), some still believe the gains of the "welfare state" offset its losses.

Americans who address themselves seriously to the problems of poverty seem to agree on one thing: there are no easy victories where poverty and need are concerned. Perhaps offering as much hope as anything are those efforts that (1) recognize the existence of a problem of major proportions, (2) attempt to mobilize the talents of interested, capable men and women to work at the problem, and (3) recognize that a concerted, consistent, and independent pressure must be maintained to deal with the problems of poverty and material deprivation. Social work is one of the professions that, because of its value system, knowledge base, and methodology, helps find solutions to these serious problems. Increasingly, social work expects to provide some of the answers—both ameliorative and preventive—to problems resulting from poverty and economic deprivation.

The efforts and resources of the total community will have to be mobilized to make inroads on this problem. If the Great Society of the Lyndon Johnson administration proved anything, it was that resources alone will not do the job. Leadership is needed. Commitment and dedication are needed. Teamwork involving the sustained and united efforts of society's major institutions—political, educational, industrial, professional, governmental, religious—is the best hope for the prevention and "cure" of poverty.

## Women in Poverty

In 1982 the number of persons living in poverty reached the highest level in this country since 1965. Although the economic recession of the early 1980s has pushed more working adults in general into poverty, the number of poor female-headed families has risen more rapidly than other segments of the poor. Since the late 1960s as the number of births to unmarried women and the divorce and separation rates have increased, the number of female-headed families has grown tremendously, and the rate of increase is greater for blacks than it is for whites. The number of female-headed families has more than doubled since 1970, and their proportion within the poverty population has also increased. Although more single mothers are entering the labor force, their earnings are far lower than those of single males. The substantial income gap between female-headed families and husband-wife families is greater than it was in 1960. The plight of female-headed families among the working poor, therefore, must be a major focus of national concern.[6]

Women who find themselves single after marriage—whether through death of a husband or through divorce—learn that being the "head of a household" brings with it a set of special problems. If there are children still living at home problems are compounded. In addition to the distress, loneliness, sense of loss, and often a loss of self-esteem, there are other problems such as facing financial obligations.

A woman who has been emotionally and financially dependent upon a husband may be unable to cope with the heavy load of responsibility. Widows in their forties or fifties are

Welfare reform—a national problem.

too young for Social Security and may be left with mortgages, medical bills, and limited savings. Divorcees face similar circumstances and are often displaced from their homes, and find that the courts have awarded inadequate child support payments, and limited, often temporary, alimony. Divorce almost always has the greatest impact on women for it causes a bigger change in their lives than in the lives of the men involved. Women most often are given custody of the children, and while this attachment is satisfying, it also adds problems. These women must get jobs. Many do not have marketable skills or requisite knowledge.

As more and more women work in business, industry, and the professions and early in life become career-oriented, this will be less of a problem. But for the millions of women who face this problem now, it can be overwhelming. They need time to deal with their loss because until they come to grips with personal problems, they cannot cope with a job. Usually an employer will recognize the applicant who is not in control, and will not trust her to perform. Mothers have to deal not only with their own personal problems, but also with the doubts of the children. Time, patience, and understanding are required.

Responding to the needs of these women, displaced homemaker centers are in operation in virtually every city. Here women, often with the help of social workers, are able to become independent. Through individual and group counseling they work through their grief and sense of loss to find their true identity and to define their values. Through guidance, women learn to assess their potential and find self-confidence and self-worth.

Displaced homemaker services, operating under a variety of names, are sometimes associated with colleges and universities. Others are independently operated or are under city, county, or state support. They offer help in becoming independent, and give women an opportunity to discuss their problems, vent their anger and feelings of hopelessness. They also act as referral agencies to those who need immediate psychological, financial, or legal advice. Often they are staffed with single women who have faced the problems their clients face and who have successfully made the transition from dependence to independence.

Usually the next big problem is to become employable. Wives and mothers who have efficiently cared for their homes and families and who have been involved in community activities may find that they have skills that lead them into employment without further training. Others need varying amounts of education or training. Counselors help them focus their energy toward a job, and at the same time provide information where they can get the education they need.

Single women find that they can climb from the bottom to find a new life with its security and independence, and on the way find new friends, new interests, skills, and self-confidence in learning to cope with their individual problems.

## General Assistance

General Assistance (GA), residual to OASDHI, is intended to aid those who cannot qualify under the federally financed SSI program for the aged, the blind, or the disabled, or AFDC, or who are not covered by social insurance. There were 1,221,625 recipients of General Assistance reported in the United States in September 1990.

General Assistance is not a popular program, from the standpoint of both the administration and the beneficiary. Since taxes for it must be raised at the state and local levels, the program usually is poorly funded because local taxes may not yield enough revenue. Payments tend to be minimal and grudgingly made to discourage people from applying or becoming dependent on welfare. Subject to such unpopular practices as voucher payments and giving assistance in kind, this form of aid carries with it the presumption that those who receive it are incapable of managing their own affairs. Other rules some states insist upon require the recipient to work for low wages at menial jobs, be re-evaluated often, have payments so low it discourages applicants, and other requirements that are unacceptable to those who are in need. The GA program in some parts of the country is demoralizing, a disgrace to the community, and has much in common with the poor relief of the Elizabethan period.

Able-bodied employable men and women are sometimes found in the ranks of General Assistance, and there exists a strong aversion to their receiving public "handouts." Also on GA are those whom Gladwin has labeled the "undeserving poor."

> It is not that these people are dirty, or dishonest, or unfaithful in marriage. We have no trouble in respecting the natives of other lands who never bathe, and at least some crooks, and the majority of movie stars. The real reason, in my opinion, is that they are unwilling to undertake responsibility on their own behalf. We like to help people who are trying to help themselves. However pitiful the individual, or

unsavory his circumstances, if he is really trying to improve his lot we will help him, and we will respect him for trying.

The people with whom we are here concerned do not try. Some of us, certainly most social workers, may be able rationally to understand that in their unhappy environment these people have never learned to try; or, perhaps, even learned that it is better *not* to try. Nevertheless, our objective judgment that their apathy is not their fault seems to help even us professionals very little to persuade our subjective selves that we should accord them real respect. These are, in the immortal phrase of Alfred P. Doolittle in George Bernard Shaw's *Pygmalion,* the undeserving poor.[7]

Social work as a profession identifies with those in society who favor more constructive measures and interpretations, which include:

1. Providing an income floor for all citizens and the elimination of hunger and destitution, or their threat, as an instrument of social policy.
2. Extending relief to applicants who can qualify under eligibility requirements; that is, remove it from subjective, biased, and capricious considerations. Relief should be based on need as it is determined to exist by objective, rather than subjective, criteria and as a legally determined right.
3. It is assumed that workers, generally, prefer income from employment to public welfare and that motivations to work are built into the economy in the form of social, cultural, and economic advantages to the employed man or woman.
4. Psychological and social barriers sometimes stand in the way of rehabilitation and employment. Counseling and other services may be needed to restore certain individuals to economic and social self-sufficiency.
5. Preservation of the independence and self-respect of the applicant for assistance is a prime consideration in the administration of programs of relief.
6. A punitive approach defeats the purpose for which assistance is used, namely, the restoration of the individual to normal functioning; it deepens feelings of inadequacy and dependency, causes embarrassment and humiliation, and brings destructive psychological defenses into play.
7. There are many pulls in society that tend to make work more appealing than public welfare—a higher standard of living, the prestige and sense of importance one receives from work, tenure, the emoluments of society, and others.

## Homelessness

*Home!* The word conjures up images of warmth, comfort, food, a bed, love—the American dream. But for a growing number of men, women, and children it is *only* a dream, for they are the homeless. Although experts argue over the number, estimates range from a low of 600,000 to a high of three million Americans who are without shelter in a place of their own.

Caring for these people takes more than just providing a house or apartment, for their problems are many and varied. Some are homeless because housing costs increased up to three times faster than income. Even though many of them have jobs, they are unable to find housing that they can pay for on their minimum wages. Each year as many as two and a half million people are displaced by rent inflation, economic development plans, condominium development, abandonment, and arson. Although the waiting lists for new federally funded housing units are growing, the number of units available has decreased by nearly 90 percent since 1981.

Besides housing, many need much more help to solve their problems. Large numbers of homeless parents are minorities with few job skills and little experience in the work place. Many subsist on welfare.

A growing number of single parents, often in their teens or early twenties, with small children, are joining the ranks of the homeless. They, too, are without job training. Estimates place this group at about one-fourth of those in shelters or on the streets. Often they are driven from their homes by violence—which presents yet another special need.

School-age children (perhaps as many as 700,000) who move from shelter to shelter change schools frequently. They not only have a difficult time academically, they also have more chronic illnesses and need the services of mental health specialists more often than children who live in their own homes.

Homeless individuals often have serious personal problems. Approximately one-third of the adults are alcoholics, one-fourth are drug abusers, another one-fourth have had a felony conviction or have served time in a state or federal prison. A smaller number are mentally ill. (Many fit more than one category.)

In 1989 the NASW launched a campaign "There's No Place Like Home" designed to show how homelessness affects families and children. Their goal was to bring greater understanding to the American public of the magnitude of the problem and to suggest solutions through cooperation between the public and private sectors in providing better employment, better distribution of funds, and adequate housing. Through the efforts of social workers in their communities, services for the homeless, legislative reforms, and more involvement by volunteers have taken place.

## *Medicare*

In 1965 Congress legislated health insurance for the aged and disabled under the provision of the Social Security Act, thus establishing the principle of a nonmeans test approach to health care.

Medicare is a compulsory hospital insurance (HI) plan and a voluntary supplementary medical insurance (SMI). HI, without the payment of monthly premiums, is for everyone aged sixty-five or over entitled to Social Security or railroad retirement. Others over age sixty-five may enroll for HI by paying monthly premiums. HI *helps* pay such costs as inpatient hospital care, nursing home care, and various services. SMI *helps* pay for physicians' services, outpatient hospital services, home "health" visits under certain conditions, outpatient physical therapy, and certain other prescribed services.

Title XVIII, an amendment to the Social Security Act, is the authority for Medicare. The action by Congress to provide Medicare hailed the beginning of what many leaders predict eventually will become a national health insurance program providing "coverage" for virtually all Americans. It can be assumed that some plan to underwrite some, if not most, of the cost of medical care and hospitalization will be legislated. Under Title XVIII the federal government has accepted in principle the centralized mechanism of support for medical care, by borrowing a funding arrangement—namely, the tax on payroll—from social security income maintenance.

Social Security as a "universal" income-maintenance program has been maturing as an enduring principle for workers and their families for more than fifty years. Social insurance appeals to Americans' sense of independence and justice. Provisions for health care should benefit from the nation's experience with social insurance. Nevertheless, it can be predicted that proponents and opponents will hotly debate the issues, with emerging patterns clearly showing the results of compromise.

Medicare was expanded by the 1972 amendments to extend the coverage to certain disabled workers, disabled widows and widowers, and childhood disability beneficiaries. Workers and their employers, including the self-employed, are taxed to pay for health insurance. As coverage is extended, the tax increases and results in the transfer of income from one group to another. How much and whose income will be transferred is a political issue. How much of the total cost will be paid from a payroll tax is also a political decision. Some leaders argue for general taxation and universal coverage, suggesting that eligibility should not be subjected to the payroll tax, which in the opinion of many fails to meet tests of equity or universality. Others argue that the payroll tax is more acceptable to vast numbers of Americans who want to "pay their own way." However, as benefits are extended and costs climb, a growing resistance to the payroll tax can be expected.

Congress is planning a rate of growth that is not to exceed the current rate of inflation. Proponents argue that it will not be possible to balance the budget by 2002 unless proposed cuts are made in both Medicare and Medicaid. Opponents to cuts in these programs argue that proposals now being offered will be too painful, particularly to the elderly in case of Medicare and to the poor in case of Medicaid.

## Medicaid

Medical care for low-income people (Medicaid) is administered by the states. Direct payments are made to providers of services. Those persons who qualify for assistance under the federally financed income-maintenance program, SSI, are eligible for Medicaid. In addition, states have the option to include persons who are able to provide for their own daily living but whose income and resources are not sufficient to meet all of their medical costs.

Families who have larger incomes may be eligible for Medicaid provided their income, after they deduct for medical expenses, is within the limits set by the state for meeting maintenance expenses.

Under the 1972 amendments states are required to make family planning available on a confidential and voluntary basis to recipients of Medicaid.

Under provisions of both Medicare and Medicaid, hospital and nursing homes are required to use review committees and procedures (Peer Review Organization) established to provide assurance of appropriateness, necessity, and quality of medical and nursing care.

The main advantages of Medicaid are: it may be used to provide hospital and medical care for poverty-stricken people who have no regular income from employment, and it may be used for others whose income is so low that they are unable to pay the high cost of medical and health care for themselves and their families. The limitations are those of a means test system—namely, poverty has to be proved, the system lacks uniformity of application, availability to people in need depends on a wide range of interpretations of the law and its intent, and applicants for health care who have not "earned the right" to medical care may be made to feel they are objects of charity.

## *Social Services and Social Work*

Public services, as distinguished from assistance payments, under the broad provisions of the Social Security Act, are available to certain categories of the population. These services provide for children, families, and certain adults.

Social workers play a major role in the administering of services and as providers. Service programs are financed under state-federal financial arrangements and are administered by the states and local communities. The particular service modality varies widely.

Until 1972 service and assistance were combined under one administration. Generally, it was assumed that services were needed for purposes of rehabilitation. In the minds of many, rehabilitation meant becoming independent of assistance. What has not been generally accepted is that assistance payments are made mainly for the benefit of dependent children, their parents (usually an unemployed mother), to the aged, the disabled and the blind, and to a few employable males and to mothers needed in the home to provide for their children.

Administered at the local level, service patterns are widely diverse. Nevertheless, services have received acceptance in many places as their need has been demonstrated, and although there is much criticism of service programs, studies in some places show that the public generally supports these services.

Under Title XX each state develops its own Comprehensive Annual Services Program Plan (CASP). The services to be provided are spelled out in each state plan. Fifty states and the District of Columbia listed 1,313 services reported in Social Services U.S.A.[8] Table 12.2 summarizes the kinds of services offered to children and adults for the quarter ending June 1978.

**TABLE 12.2   Services to Children and Adults**

| | | |
|---|---|---|
| Adoption Services | Foster Care—Children | Unmarried Parent Services |
| Case Management Services | Foster Care—Various | Socialization Services |
| Chore Services | Health-Related Services | Special Services—Alcohol and |
| Counseling Services | Home Delivery Congregate Meals | Drug |
| Day Care—Adults | Homemaker Services | Special Services—Blind |
| Day Care—Children | Home Management | Special Services—Child and Youth |
| Day Care—Various | Housing Improvement | Special Services—Disabled |
| Diagnostic and Evaluative Services | Information and Referral | Special Services—Juvenile |
| Education and Training Services | Legal Services | Delinquents |
| Emergency Services | Placement Services | Transitional Services |
| Employment-Related Medical | Protective Services—Adults | Transportation |
| Services | Protective Services—Children | Vocational Rehabilitation |
| Employment Services | Protective Services—Various | Work Incentive (WIN) Medical |
| Family Planning | Recreational Services | Examinations |
| Foster Care—Adults | Residential, Care and Treatment | Other |

## Government and Public Welfare

There is a growing realization that government cannot solve all problems. Failures of the Great Society (President Lyndon Johnson's war on poverty) did not result entirely from a lack of resources. In some ways these failures resulted from a lack of leadership. Community action programs and the Model Cities program failed because power was given to some groups not ready to use it and because it was not recognized that great social changes cannot be mandated or brought about overnight. Change must be an extension of the past, and the war on poverty appeared to lack the impulse necessary for its survival.

The largest nondefense program, Social Security, expanded rapidly after 1965 into a set of programs. The question is raised: Has it promised too much to too many? It is a fallacy to assume (1) the nation has unlimited resources and (2) *only* money is needed to solve personal and family problems. The fact is that resources do not exist to provide all things for all people. Choices from alternatives will have to be made. A nation that invests in general health care may be unable to provide good pensions, and the assumption of resources that do not exist can lead to colossal failure in national policy.

With their vast experience in working with troubled families and individuals, social workers know that some problems defy complete solution and that money is needed, but so are understanding and compassionate regard. Money cannot provide these, nor is mere desire to help enough. Someone has described social work education as a "pasteurization process for taking the bugs out of the milk of human kindness." Robert Frost, speaking to the Israelis, justified education because it "raised human pain and suffering to a higher plane of regard." The solution to many human problems calls for widespread regard for the worth of the individual, and this cherished value cannot be legislated or purchased. Social work can help.

It is true that the voluntary field is experiencing some extremely difficult periods and that some national agencies are in trouble. However, voluntary agencies most likely will continue to play an important role in "public" welfare in the future. Some people have observed that centralized, computerized federal programs, including Social Security, often are not responsive to the special needs of individuals and localities. A tenet of social work is that the smaller private agencies have the edge on larger computerized governmental systems in regard to unmet, unplanned for, and unanticipated needs. Volunteerism in general is needed today as never before, particularly in the human service area.

Since 1935 and the passage of the Social Security Act the federal government has increasingly assumed responsibility for the protection of citizens against want as an *enduring* principle.

Fifty years later Ronald Reagan strongly argued for less government, greater local control of welfare, and a *market* economy.

## Summary

Government responsibility for welfare has become an enduring *principle with passage of the* Social Security Act of 1935.

A shift in thinking about welfare marked the administration of Ronald Reagan. It has been asked, will the Reagan views about welfare shape policy in the future and become a trend? Are the costs of state-funded welfare programs becoming greater than the country can bear or is willing to afford, and will Congress make the hard choices and reduce spending on such programs as income for the elderly, Medicare, and Medicaid?

*Supplemental Security Income (SSI) and AFDC programs are the main public assistance programs. AFDC is criticized for the increasing numbers of young women who seem to rely on it as a way of life. Teenagers, becoming pregnant out-of-wedlock and unable to provide for themselves, are at the heart of the debate in Congress over what to do with our welfare system.*

*Poverty and the feminization of poverty continue to be major social problems, notwithstanding the gains that have been made toward the equalization of opportunities for women in industry and in the professions.*

*General Assistance is a public response to those in need who don't qualify for federally* financed help. This assistance is paid for from taxes by local entities and is often barely adequate to provide for the needs of these recipients.

*Medicare and Medicaid provide for the health care of the aged and others in need of doctor's care and hospitalization. Hospitals and doctors are available to covered workers under the provision of OASDHI. Medicaid provides care for low-income families who are not covered by the insurance provisions of Social Security.*

*Social services to children and adults, provided to certain categories of recipients, are generally seen as needed for purposes of rehabilitation.*

*Income needs are but a part of the problems people face. Values and ethics provide guidelines for practice, and a concerted effort of many elements of society is needed to solve complex social welfare problems.*

## Selected References

AXINN, JUNE, and HERMAN LEVIN, *Social Welfare: A History of the American Response to Need.* New York: Dodd, Mead & Company, 1975.

BRIAR, KATHARINE HOOPER, *Social Work and the Unemployed.* Silver Spring, MD: National Association of Social Workers, 1988.

BURNS, EVELINE, *Social Security and Public Policy.* New York: McGraw-Hill, 1956.

CATES, JERRY R., *Insuring Inequality: Administrative Leadership in Social Security.* Ann Arbor: University of Michigan Press, 1983.

ELL, KATHLEEN, and HELEN NORTHERN, *Families and Health Care: Psychosocial Practice.* New York: Aldine de Gruyter, 1990.

FUNICIELLO, THERESA, *Tyranny of Kindness: Dismantling the Welfare System to End Poverty in America.* New York: Atlantic Monthly Press, 1993.

KINGSON, ERIC, R., and EDWARD D. BERKOWITZ, *Social Security and Medicare: A Policy Primer.* Westport, CT: Auburn House, 1993.

MAGILL, ROBERT S., *Community Decision-Making for Social Welfare: Federalism, City Government, and the Poor.* New York: Human Sciences Press, 1979.

MURRAY, CHARLES, *Losing Ground: American Social Policy 1950–1980.* New York: Basic Books, 1984.

PARDECK, JOHN T., and JOHN W. MURPHY, eds., *Computers in Human Services: An Overview for Clinical and Welfare Services.* Chur, Switzerland: Harwood Academic, 1990.

PILCHER, DONALD M., *Data Analysis for the Helping Professions: A Practical Guide.* Newbury Park, CA: Sage Publications, 1990.

RODGERS, HARREL, JR., *Beyond Welfare: New Approaches to the Problem of Poverty in America.* Armonk, NY: M. E. Sharpe, 1988.

TRATTNER, WALTER I., *From Poor Law to Welfare State.* New York: The Free Press, 1974.

# *Notes*

1. Case material provided by Phyllis N. Johnson, MSW, self-sufficiency coordinator at Utah Issues, a nonprofit referral system advocacy for low-income people of Utah.

2. Elizabeth Wickenden and Winifred Bell, *Public Welfare, Time for Change,* a report of the Project on Public Services for Families and Children (New York: The New York School of Social Work, Columbia University, 1961), p. 13.

3. No limits are placed on the income a person can earn after he or she turns 70.

4. Nondeterrent systems, as opposed to deterrent *means test* programs, eliminate tests of need. Beneficiaries are not "investigated," they do not have to be indigent to be eligible, and it is presumed that benefits are earned by the worker. Not only are repressive measures not employed, the OASDHI actively tries to locate workers eligible for benefits who have not filed claims.

5. Whitman et al., "Welfare the Myth of Reform," *U.S. News and World Report* 118 (January 16, 1995), 30–39.

6. John S. Wodarski, T. M. Jim Parharm, Elizabeth W. Lindsey, and Barry W. Blackburn, "Reagan's AFDC Policy Changes: The Georgia Experience," *Social Work,* 31 (July/August 1986), 273.

7. Thomas Gladwin, "The Anthropologist's View of Poverty," *The Social Welfare Forum, 1961* (New York: National Conference on Social Welfare, 1961), pp. 76–77.

8. *Social Services U.S.A.: Third Quarter Report, FY1978* (Washington, DC: U.S. Department of Health and Human Services, 1978), p. 38.

Chapter *13*

# Family and Child Welfare Services

*Sybil was a distraught young mother when her plane touched down in Denver. She had been fearful that when her fiance learned she had a child he would not marry her. So, she had decided to leave her home in the east to place her one-year-old son, Tony, for adoption; once in Denver, she was advised by Traveler's Aid to seek help from a local child placing and adoption agency. After signing legal papers, she tearfully left on the next flight east. Tony was placed in foster care.*

*Two weeks later the agency received a telephone call from Sybil frantically seeking to have Tony returned to her. She had married, and when she could no longer bear the thought of living without her son, she confessed to her husband. Wanting to be helpful to make a home for young Tony, he supported her in getting the child back. In a few days, arrangements were completed for Sybil to fly west and pick up her son. For her, the children's agency was a temporary measure; it provided a home and protection for the child while she got her act together.*

*In times of crises when forces assail the very foundation of society—the family—social agencies stand ready to give assistance; they serve as substitute families, if need be, but preferably shore up families who need their support.*

The family is recognized as humanity's basic institution. Sociologists, social workers, psychiatrists, anthropologists, lay leaders, and average citizens agree that the family is fundamental to society. No other established pattern has been found more effective in molding the personality of children and adults. Social, personal, and emotional ties inhere more intimately in this relationship than in any other social dimension.

The family is the cradle for children, not only physically but psychologically. So powerful is its influence that many experts indicate that a child's basic personality traits have been developed by the time he or she is two years of age, with the family playing the major role in their formation.

This book is family-focused, and much of it describes and illustrates the influence of the family on personal and group behavior. This chapter highlights some specifics in regard to family and children—especially those related to marriage and family counseling services and child welfare services available to strengthen families or to substitute for them.

## *Marriage and Family Counseling*

If today is an average day in court in the United States, a judge's gavel will rise and fall and the words "divorce granted" will echo from the courtroom walls more than 4,000 times—adding up to more than a million divorces by the end of the year.

Before 1850, divorce statistics were practically unknown. In 1867 there were only about 10,000 divorces in the entire United States. However, since then there has been a steady increase—that has jumped at times—amounting to 613,000 in 1946 at the end of World War II and reaching an all-time high of 1,213,000 in 1981. The trend was downward during the recession of the early eighties. In 1991 there were 1,172,000 divorces and 2,421,000 marriages in the United States. There are more than 100,000 desertions each year, in which the husband walks out the door, never to return. In addition, desertions by wives are increasing at a startling rate. There are also thousands of separations in which husbands and wives agree to live apart. There are other thousands of "psychologically shattered" homes, in which husband, wife, and children walk on the same carpets, eat at the same tables, but socially and emotionally live miles apart. They remain together only because of religious, economic, psychological, or other pressures. Such homes provide barren or meager emotional climates for children as well as adults.

In other words, the family is in trouble! What can be done about it? What is being done about it? Social work provides one answer. It is not the only answer, but it is an effective attempt that aids many marriages, families, mates, and children.

If an automobile breaks down, there is a service station available for repairs on nearly every corner. If a marriage or a family falls apart, where can its members go for help? Marriage counseling resources are developing rapidly and social work is playing a major role.

Historically, marriage counseling of a sort has taken place as long as families have existed. Early Hindu writings reflect a concern about the family and the usefulness of marriage counseling. In Old Testament days, the importance of counseling was illustrated by the statement from Proverbs (11:14): "Where no counsel is, the people fall: but in the multitude of counselors there is safety." St. Paul, in the early Christian era, attempted to safeguard the family in assuming the role of an authoritative counselor.

In modern times marriage counseling was instituted with the development of clinics, particularly premarital clinics, in Germany and Austria. In 1919 the Berlin Institute for the Study of Sex, a private agency directed by Magnus Hirshfeld, was established as a consultation center for advice and guidance regarding sex and marital problems. In 1922 in Vienna the first matrimonial health consultation center for marriage candidates was opened, sponsored by the Municipal Board of Health. Centers later were opened in other cities in Germany and Austria and in other European countries. Clients of these European marriage bureaus were essentially of three types: (1) those seeking premarital guidance, (2) spouses wanting advice on problems in their existing marriages, and (3) people in and out of marriage seeking guidance and help on sex and other personal problems.

In the United States the roots of professional marriage counseling are many and varied. Attempts to provide marital and family help came from the private welfare agencies, developed as a part of the charity organization movement more than a century ago. Particularly after the depression of 1873, an aftermath of the Civil War, there was a need for financial assistance to individuals and families. Within a few years, welfare agencies were organized in many cities throughout the East and Midwest. Although the main emphasis was on economic assistance, many families were helped to face other family problems and work through them.

Numerous agencies that have provided services directly or indirectly to strengthen families have emerged. The most significant one was the Family Welfare Association of America, established in 1911 to promote family agencies and services. In 1946, its name was changed to the Family Service Association of America to denote its changing role. It now has member agencies in the larger communities throughout the country. In 1983 the name was changed to Family Service America (FSA).

The first private "marriage consultation center" in the United States organized specifically for marriage counseling was the Marriage Counseling Center of the Community Church of New York. It was established originally in 1929 at the Labor Temple by Dr. Abraham Stone and his wife, Dr. Hannah Stone. The American Institute of Family Relations, initiated in 1930 by Dr. Paul Popenoe in Los Angeles, and the Marriage Counsel of Philadelphia, begun in 1932, were additional pioneer counseling agencies. In 1914 the Court of Domestic Relations operating in Cincinnati started to help reduce family problems and breakdown through counseling. Gradually, other private and public family counseling agencies have been developed.

On the professional level, the establishment of the National Council on Family Relations in 1938—with an emphasis on family values and their enhancement—was a significant development. In 1942 the American Association of Marriage Counselors was established. It has become an important professional body and changed its name to The American Association for Marriage and Family Therapy. Its membership includes social workers, psychiatrists, psychologists, lawyers, ministers, and others qualified to do marriage and family counseling.

In 1972, under the leadership of James J. Rue, the National Alliance for Family Life was founded to "promote and strengthen family life." One of its aims was to strengthen marriage and family life in America by improving the quantity and quality of marriage and family education and counseling.

## Kinds of Services

Counseling in this service area may be divided into three kinds or levels: premarital, marriage, and family.

Premarital counseling is the assistance of a person or couple in regard to courtship and marital plans and problems. Couples preparing for marriage utilize it in making plans and in solving personal and courtship problems. In increased numbers, social workers participate in premarital counseling in family service associations, university and college settings, and numerous other private and public agencies. Their aim is to assist people in preparing for marriage, and in assisting them to move toward or away from marriage depending on the individual situation in a mature manner.

In California premarital counseling has been required since 1970 before a marriage license will be issued to anyone under eighteen years of age.

Marriage counseling is concerned with husband-wife relationships, plans, and problems. Each year thousands of couples talk with social workers and seek help with their marriages. Most get the assistance they need; some do not. Most are helped to strengthen their marriages; some are assisted to separate and move toward other meaningful relationships.

Family counseling includes the husband-wife-children constellation. Problems relating to child discipline, money, education, communication, and so on may require assistance to a family by a trained counselor.

In addition to counseling with traditional nuclear family units, counselors today work with many new kinds of marital and family patterns, for example: step families, that by the year 2000 may outnumber all other types of families in the United States; the homosexual parent caring for children and having different affectional relationships; serial mating; one parent households; and unmarried couples living together (2.9 million in 1990—up 80 percent from 1980).

Social workers use a variety of helping methods and approaches that include: role theory, exchange theory, transactional analysis, Gestalt therapy, systems theory, family therapy, behavior modification, psychoanalytical approach, reality therapy, and bioenergetics. Although most marriage counseling is done on an individual basis, group process also is used extensively. Five or six couples meet regularly with a social worker to work on their problems. Single parent families discuss their difficulties in groups where many methods of helping are used, including marathons, conjoint family therapy, and other new techniques.

## Kinds of Agencies

Social workers participate in marriage and family counseling in a variety of agencies and arrangements, both public and private. Much counseling is done by social workers in county welfare departments including work with AFDC single parent families. Many courts have social workers attached to their organizations. Others play important roles in university and college counseling centers in providing marriage counseling, and such services are beginning to appear at the secondary school level.

Social workers play important roles in private family counseling agencies, illustrated by the services of local affiliates of Family Service America. Social work practitioners in such agencies—nonprofit and voluntary—throughout North America help to provide counseling services and to strengthen families through education and other endeavors. Examples of the needs and problems of people with whom they work include the following: a marriage breaking up, premarital concerns, broken and single parent families, unwed parents, drug use, alcoholism, need for information about resources, help to neglected children, training, consultation, foster home placement, adoption, and numerous related community problems.

Many social workers are in private practice in marriage and family counseling.

## Battered Women

In recent years a whole new segment of the population needing help has surfaced: battered women. A statement by the American Medical Association affirms that as many as a third of women's injuries coming into emergency rooms are not from accidents. "Most are the result of deliberate, premeditated acts of violence. And frequently they occur over and over until the woman is killed. Family violence is one of America's most critical health issues. . . ."[1] Whether this is an actual increase in the number of abused women or whether they are only recently becoming more visible is not entirely known. But they have captured the attention and sympathy of not only the helping professions but also of the general public.

As a result of the need and the visibility, social agencies in almost all cities have set up facilities to protect and care for those who are forced to leave their homes because of physical and/or emotional abuse. Funding for these projects is often shared by Family Services, United Way, Social Service departments, and philanthropic grants.

Victims, who come to the shelters after being beaten or stabbed, with broken bones and bruises, or who show no signs of physical abuse but have been put down so much that they cannot even tell their last names, receive a variety of services to meet their individual needs. Many agencies provide temporary housing where they may stay for anywhere from a few hours to several weeks until permanent facilities can be found. Counseling is provided in individual or group sessions, and support groups are available for continuing help. Often there is counseling for the abusers. Most of the agencies that have housing facilities for the women also care for young children of the family. U.S. Catholic bishops have declared that parishioners are not required by their religion "to submit to abusive husbands." Further, it is reported that violence is sinful in any form and parish priests should provide a "safe place" for women seeking help.

Who are the abusers? They are men from all walks of life, of every economic background. Often they are respected men in their communities, well educated, who hold high positions in business and professional circles. Most of them are unable to accept help when it is offered. However, if there has been some contact with the court system, and the judge has mandated that they receive counseling as a condition of the court action, they are then more likely to participate in a program. In an attempt to protect themselves and their children, women often have a difficult time filing complaints against their husbands, so frequently there is no court involvement.

Regardless of whether the husband gets help, agencies respond to the needs of the women and children. Women are helped to find housing, to get jobs, and to find adequate child care, and they are supported in their decisions. It is a needed service and a welcome one for those who are suffering.

## *Rape Crisis*

Rape—a terrifying crime against women—has been brought into the open. More victims are seeking medical and legal help, and more are reporting the crime to police. Support and help are increasingly available to them by social workers.

Victims of rape are more often women who are vulnerable—hitchhikers, the homeless, aged women, young girls, and women in significant crisis situations. However, almost any woman is a potential target.

Because of the need and demand, rape crisis centers offering 24-hour help have been organized in almost all cities. These centers provide immediate crisis intervention, including information regarding availability of medical help and support in contacting the police. Later the centers sustain victims through the lengthy adjustment period that is usually needed to restore feelings of safety, self-worth, and freedom.

Women have complained that the police and courts have not been sympathetic to them when they report rape, and in the past many women refused to involve the police. It is true that the police have been most concerned with finding the criminal; the courts have sought to prosecute the rapist. The medical profession has served the victim's medical needs. Through an ongoing program, all who serve rape victims are being made aware of their deep emotional needs. The result is that doctors, police, and the courts now have a greater understanding of their problems and are able to care for them with more sensitivity.

It is the rape crisis centers, however, that primarily deal with the emotional problems women face after such an encounter. Workers help the victims rebuild their lives by sustaining and strengthening them with counseling and support groups. The women's movement is a strong supporter of rape crisis intervention and has helped in the education of the public. The result is that women are more aware of the help available, and more are asking for help when the need arises. Most come for immediate help at the time of the attack, but greater numbers of women who were molested years before but have not worked through their feelings and needs are coming to the centers to talk.

The majority of rape victims are attacked only once; however, those who continue in vulnerable situations may continue to be assaulted.

## Family Disorganization and Child Neglect

A great many children live in homes with only one parent. A substantial number of children living in two-parent homes have a stepparent. By the year 2000 more than half of all families may be stepparent families. Invariably, the children in these homes will have two sets of parents and will be shunted back and forth between them. A current trend in divorce cases is for the court to award joint custody, with the rearing of children being shared by both parents.

Whatever arrangement is worked out by the lawyers and the parents, divorce is never easy for anyone. Children often blame themselves for the divorce. When they are pawns in the struggle between the parents and are forced into alliances, their security is undermined and they are torn in their loyalties. The resulting problems and issues may be too difficult for them to handle without help.

A disproportionate number of children of divorced parents are dependent upon public assistance. For these, the community's network of public services is often the first line of defense and its only organized support system.

Day-care centers have mushroomed, and problems related to caring for babies and small children of working mothers are an important policy issue debated today at the highest levels of government.

Single parents shouldering the responsibility of two parents are often unable to provide the role models, parenting, or needed income found in households with both parents.

Many changes affecting the family have occurred in social roles and role expectations of individual members. In a relatively stable society, where social change is gradual, children learn the requirements of the group by imitation and observation. Their tasks tend to be simple and concrete rather than abstract. In America in 1850, when 85 percent of the total population lived in rural areas and only 5 percent in cities of 100,000 or more, children were valued for their work and productive effort. There was a radical change in the picture a century later, when about 60 percent of the total population was living in 168 metropolitan areas.

Few children today have the opportunity to learn vocational skills by working with their parents, and fewer children augment the family income by their employment. The variety of activities, roles, and the models from which youth may choose is infinite. But variety of choices and the rapidity of social change have resulted in bewilderment, loss of identity, and role confusion.

Roles have changed also for women who compete in industry and the professions and who often find themselves simultaneously in the dual major roles of housewife and employee. At the turn of the century, only one-sixth of all workers gainfully employed were females. Today more than half of all employed workers in the labor market are women. Six of ten mothers with school-age children work, and nearly half of women with children under six years of age are employed outside the home.

Family problems resulting in child abuse and neglect have become so vast as to result in new legislation in a nationwide attempt to do something. Child abuse—physical or mental injury, sexual abuse, negligent treatment, or maltreatment of a child under the age of eighteen by a person who is responsible for the child's welfare—was the focus of the 1974 Child Abuse Prevention and Treatment Act. Research showed that 60,000 children were being abused each year, but that little was being done for them or for their troubled families. This law was the outcome of investigation into the incidence, nature, and cause of child abuse, and was aimed at prevention, identification, and treatment of this problem.

Prior to this act, no one at the federal government level was assigned to work on this problem full-time. The limited funding of the existing child welfare programs through Social Security resulted in negligible work being accomplished on the state and local levels. The act provided funds to persons and agencies willing and able to take action, but who previously had been hampered in their efforts by lack of money.

The number of children who are harmed or threatened with harm by the acts or omissions of their parents, or by other persons responsible for their welfare and care, is estimated to exceed one million each year.

Because of family problems, society has created services to help them. An example of a family problem with mental health overtones follows.

---

There sits a boy, eight or nine years old, in a chair that's too big for him. He's small for his age and thoroughly intimidated by the situation.

His mother and father sit to one side. They're obviously troubled. They speak earnestly and smile nervously at times.

A mental health worker, a specialist in family problems, sits on the edge of the desk. He has an open sort of posture, a friendly, now-what-seems-to-be-the-problem attitude.

In bits and pieces, hesitant at first and then more confident, the parents spill out their story:

Jon (the boy) has been suspended from school—for the third time. He beats up on smaller children. The principal won't let him come back to school until his behavior improves. They don't know what to do. He's always been a problem.

Jon's parents are fed up, but they're trying not to show it. Jon doesn't say much.

At this point, half an hour into an initial interview, our family specialist knows that there's something wrong. That's clear. Whatever it is, it may be inside the child or outside, perhaps both in greater or lesser amounts.

He also knows that Jon has failed to live up to the expectations of those around him, notably his parents. Jon may or may not be emotionally disturbed. There's no way to be sure of that just yet.

And he knows one thing more. Whatever is wrong, it's wrong with his *family,* not just with Jon. That's not to say that anyone is to blame. Our specialist isn't in the business of blaming; it's just not a very useful concept when you're trying to help people.

The business at hand is to get this family unit back to the point where it can function reasonably well again. The odds? Pretty good, but with some big *ifs:*

IF they can discover together the dynamics of the family structure: who does what to whom; who gets what from whom; what are the rules, the roles, the games; who is sabotaging what . . . and why?

IF the family can realize that it's not just Jon's problem;

IF they can work out ways to meet each other's needs more constructively, in a fashion that's less damaging to the whole family;

IF they can, in short, open up communication. . . .

Suppose we do begin to work with Jon in the mental health center's day care unit for children. There, specialists in behavior modification, people with an abiding love for children and a deep understanding of them, will tailor a program for Jon. They'll systematically encourage his more socially acceptable behavior and, just as systematically, they'll discourage his attacking behavior. They'll try to rechannel his energies. They'll be firm, but genuinely kind and concerned. They'll guide him and teach him. They'll accept him as a real person in his own right, a person with special, individual needs. They'll love him, in a way, no less than his parents do. And, in a few weeks, they'll work the minor miracle. . . . They can do it for nine Jons out of ten.[2]

## Child Welfare Services

The comprehensive program of child welfare services consists of efforts to promote the physical, mental, and social well-being of all children and youth. Child welfare is: (1) a field of service, (2) a social work practice area that encompasses a variety of child welfare activities, (3) a practice field that focuses attention on issues, problems, and policies related to the welfare of children, (4) the application of knowledge and skill to problems of children, and (5) the enhancement of social functioning of children.

Services to children are developed by various governmental agencies, religious institutions, and philanthropic organizations.

Child welfare services include provisions for children in their own homes, in substitute family homes, and in many institutions. Group living arrangements exist for unmarried mothers awaiting confinement, for abused and neglected children needing refuge and protection at a time of stress within a family, for children in detention waiting disposition or relocation into more permanent arrangements, and for children who have birth defects or who suffer from debilitating handicaps and illnesses. Short-term services exist for meeting

Children enjoying day care.

emergencies within families resulting from illness or death. However, for many children such services as foster care or mental health may be needed throughout their childhood.

Statutory provisions in most states stipulate that except for the most compelling reasons, a child should not be deprived of a home or of the opportunity to be nurtured by his or her own parents.

Regardless of the kind of substitute care made for children, the entire arena of child welfare practice requires great sensitivity, maturity of judgment, extensive knowledge, and the finest skills of professional social work. They are needed to provide services for the children and their parents to maintain and strengthen their ties, and if separation takes place, to develop provisions for reuniting the family. When this is not possible, more permanent arrangements for the child must be made to have an acceptable substitute family. This could mean permanent foster care or adoption. Only in the event of major, irreparable breakdown in family life is it desirable to separate children permanently from their natural parents.

The program of Aid to Families with Dependent Children, which in September 1990 provided financial aid to 4,092,876 families—11,794,968 children and their parents—was designed to make it possible for children to remain at home with their own parent or parents. The guiding philosophy of AFDC is that children should not be separated from their parents for reasons of poverty. Chapter 12 of this text discusses more fully the AFDC program and the changes resulting from the Family Support Act of 1988.

Specifically in this chapter reference is made to such services as care of children in their own homes, foster care, group living, adoption, services for unmarried parents, and protective services.

## Home Care of Children

Child welfare workers have long known that children are best nurtured in the care of loving parents who can offer food, clothing, shelter and the health care growing bodies and minds require. Permanency and stability are key policy objectives.

The Federal Adoption Assistance and Child Welfare Act of 1980 (Public Law 96-272) makes reasonable efforts to keep children in their own homes. This act has resulted in a shift of focus from child-centered care to family care, and a further shift to a multisystems approach in the care of children. This approach can best be described as one that addresses several levels of care aimed at preserving the family entity. Cimmarusti identifies four important elements to be considered in preserving the family.

> The following four levels are generally important in each family preservation case: (1) *the family* includes all entities such as the members of the nuclear family (mother, father, and children).... (2) *the extended family* includes any significant relatives, grandparents, aunts, "play" parents, and partners.... (3) *the community* includes significant people from the neighborhood, peers, church, or school and.... (4) *the family preservation intervention group* includes the family preservation worker, supervisor, agency, public welfare agency, legal system, and other service providers....[3]

It is clearly recognized that parts of the surroundings include not only the child and mother (often the only parent in a home) but also the father and the extended family. Grandparents, aunts, uncles, and other relatives are pivotal to the kind of nurturing a child needs. With the rapid increase in one-parent families, the milieu includes a complex of babysitter, day-care center, the playground, recreation and health care provisions, and other services. These all impact the growing child and must be addressed (see Figure 13.1).

The aim of care is to strengthen the family, to empower, and to build upon existing resources. All families and the systems that may be arrayed to serve them have strengths. The preservation worker's task is to identify these and communicate them. People need to be pointed toward achievement and to experience success. We tend to be what we experience and what is expected of us and our known capacities. Eliza Doolittle in *My Fair Lady* was a lady because she had success in what she did, because Colonel Pickering treated her like a lady, and because she *was,* inherently, a lady.

Are we getting results in the practice of preserving the family? The verdict, in the main, is still out. However, some rather gratifying results have been reported in research findings by Pecora and co-workers. Therapists using a "variety of clinical methods, including parenting training, active listening, contracting, values clarification, cognitive-behavioral strategies, and problem management techniques" reported that Intensive Family Preservation Services (IFPS) "indicate that family-based programs, and IFPS programs in particular, are successful in preventing placement in 40% to 95% of the cases referred to them."

In studies in two states, Washington and Utah, Pecora and colleagues stated:

> Across all 581 children from 446 eligible families, the placement prevention rate at *case termination*—an outcome measure used by Nelson et al. (1988), Yuan et al. (1990), and others—was 92.9%. For Utah (n = 172), the rate was 90.7%, and for Washington (n = 409), it was 93.9%.[4]

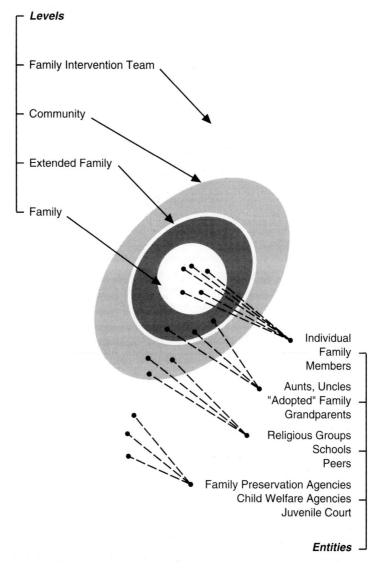

**Levels**

Family Intervention Team

Community

Extended Family

Family

Individual
Family
Members

Aunts, Uncles
"Adopted" Family
Grandparents

Religious Groups
Schools
Peers

Family Preservation Agencies
Child Welfare Agencies
Juvenile Court

*Entities*

**FIGURE 13.1    Multilevel Family Preservation System with
Select Entities.**

*Source:* Rocco A. Cimmarusti, "Family Preservation Practice Based Upon a
Multisystems Approach," *Child Welfare,* 71 (May–June 1992), 249.

More research is needed. However, the family preservation models are a promising
trend toward keeping families together. We know that substitute family care is not the
answer for many children. It is an option, usually for short periods of time when family
weaknesses and problems are so overwhelming that intensive family preservation efforts
simply don't suffice.

## *Foster Care of Children*

Foster care is a residential arrangement for children outside their own homes. It includes care in foster homes or in a variety of institutions. For many it is of short duration, ending in adoption or return to the natural parents; for others it is a way of life, extending for long periods, perhaps ending only when the child establishes himself or herself by becoming financially independent.

It was hoped with the passage of P.L. 96-272 that temporary care would be virtually eliminated. The law has helped, but living with the natural parent or parents may not be desirable or even possible for some youngsters who are severely handicapped or emotionally disturbed and who require specialized care, or for those who are abused and neglected and whose parents are incapable of parenting. For these and for other children, substitute care provides the optimum of nurturing. Foster parents provide good family care, and the foster parent movement is one of the finest examples of volunteerism deserving public support and acclaim.

Foster care brings radical changes in a child's life; he or she must become a part of a new home group, may be enrolled in a new school, and must adapt to different living conditions. This whole process may recur for those whose home conditions do not improve. Often children are shunted from one home to another over a period of years.

The social worker and the agency may be the only link to permanency for these children. The social worker studies the foster home and family, assesses strengths and limitations for a particular child, and makes and supervises the placement when it is made. The social worker is supportive of both the foster family and the child. Relating to the network of community services, and trained to know their organization and purposes, the social worker selectively brings need and resource together, and often over an extended period of time the social worker becomes the constant in the life of a child confronted with change.

There were 274,000 children in foster care in 1982, in 1995 more than 400,000 youngsters were in foster care on a single day.

Foster home care, usually preferable for babies and young children, is also the choice for older children able to benefit from individualized relationships with foster parents. To be successful in a home, the child must be able to adjust to the family and his or her behavior be such that the child is not dangerous to him- or herself or others. Helping the child and the foster family make this adjustment may be the most important contribution the social worker will make. This is a continuous process and invariably is needed as long as the child requires a substitute family.

Group living arrangements, substitutes for family care, are frequently recommended as a treatment mode for some children. They include agency-owned foster homes where the parent or parents are employees of the agency, residence clubs for older children, boys and girls "ranches," and congregate type institutions for larger numbers of children. Children who act out excessively, who have serious conduct and behavior disorders, who steal, set fires, or who sexually "act-out" ordinarily are not candidates for care in private homes. Furthermore, some children who have experienced prolonged emotional deprivations resulting in emotional stunting and who are unable to form close and satisfying relationships may not accept a family as a substitute for their own parents.

Some children benefit from the professional services that can be provided only in a group setting. Those who find it impossible to tolerate the demands of making attachments to new sets of parents are relieved in the group where such demands are minimized. For these and other children, group living experiences can, and often do, provide a healing experience.

A child living in a group home or institution can direct aggressive feelings against many more people safely. He or she is not under the same necessity to form close emotional ties and attachments. The child can move into the group at his or her own pace and is not traumatized by pressures to give or accept affection. The routine of the institution provides tangible security—meals at regular intervals, a place to sleep, medical care. With planning on the part of administration it can offer privacy and a place for the child's personal belongings. Child-centered group living is a treatment resource for the emotionally disturbed and socially disorganized child.

---

Gary, age 11, had lived in nine foster homes in three years. The only constant in his life was the Children's Service Society, which supervised the homes. Foster parents had complained that Gary was disobedient, cruel to animals and small children, and lacking in manners and appreciation. For short periods of time they could "stand" him, but as his behavior lowered their level of tolerance they would demand that he be taken from their homes.

Gary was placed in a cottage-type institution where houseparents, aided by social workers, provided continuity of care, a chance to relate to peers as he was ready for this experience, and professional help.

---

## Reasons for Placement in Foster Care

Studies show many reasons for the placement of children in foster care. The following list is illustrative only and not comprehensive:

Mental and/or emotional incapacity of caretaking parent
Parent unwilling to care for the child
Family problems, including family disorganization
Environmental problems (inadequate housing, financial need)
Specialized care the natural family cannot provide
Death of the caretaking parent
The child's behavioral or emotional problems
Neglect and abuse

Children may be placed in foster care by court commitments if they are dependent, neglected, or delinquent. The natural parents may make voluntary application for foster care.

When faced with a problem of seriously disturbed home situations, alternatives to foster care are considered to assist parents to keep their children at home. With help, parents are often able to improve the quality of care for their children and maintain an intact family.

If placement is inevitable, the question may arise about the type of foster care that will best meet the needs of the children. Regardless of whether they are placed in a home or group setting, children usually need counseling and other help to counteract physical and emotional deprivation.

If a foster home setting is chosen, care must be taken to match the children with parents who will be able to respond to their particular needs, to continue their support during periods of stress, and to be satisfied with the children's progress.

## Social Work with a Foster Child

The case of Betty, placed in foster care, shows what was done for an adolescent and her family by foster home placement.

---

Following a violent quarrel with her father, Betty, aged 16, went to a friend's home and hysterically declared she would kill herself if anyone attempted to send her home.

The oldest of five children in a middle-class family, Betty was an intelligent high school junior, but she could no longer cope with the beatings and abuse of her father. A psychiatrist on the staff of the social service agency that was called for help detected some psychotic tendencies such as mild delusions, unreasonable guilt, severe depression, and a definite suicidal tendency. Betty related poorly to adults and her peers, but got along well with children. His recommendation was parental-substitute care and one-to-one counseling.

Foster home care was selected as the treatment of choice, and Betty was placed in a home of a couple with two young sons. The mother worked with a teenage organization of her church and felt she could get Betty involved with other young people. The father was easygoing, likable, and relaxed. They felt that they would be able to work out any problem with the help of the social worker. They lived near the high school Betty had been attending so there would be no interruption of her schoolwork.

Betty accepted the foster parents and was glad they had young children. She felt some ambivalence about seeing her own family; she wanted to see her mother and younger sisters, but was afraid of her father. Her parents accepted the placement, but refused to give financial aid, although they did send her personal belongings.

Problems apparent in the early relationship were Betty's lack of attention to personal care—bathing, changing into clean clothes, washing her hair—and her intense fear, amounting almost to panic, if she were in the room alone with the foster father.

Household chores assigned to her were carried out if she clearly understood what was wanted. However, she was unable to volunteer to help in any way, and was withdrawn, often spending long periods alone in her room.

Betty was conscientious in completing her schoolwork, and showed a talent for creative writing. She had one friend, a girl from her old neighborhood, and they spent hours talking on the phone. She seldom went any place except to school, church, and an occasional outing with the foster family.

In counseling, she and her social worker identified her pressing problems. They included her extreme hostility and fear of her father, her need for his approval, her pity for her mother, her concern and guilt for "deserting" her sisters and her role in her family's dynamics, her poor self-image, and her role identity.

After two months Betty had not communicated with her parents, and they had not initiated any inquiry about her. During this time they had sought counseling to help them resolve the difficulties that had been plaguing the family. They made some progress toward building a better relationship between husband and wife and with the children at home.

Gradually Betty became active in a group of girls in the neighborhood, but she could not express appreciation, and did not take any initiative in doing tasks around the home. She learned to trust the foster father, and he became important to her.

Betty had many strengths. She was intelligent, and worked hard at her studies. She felt responsible for her actions and wanted to help her mother and sisters. She was honest and had a high sense of personal morality.

As she gained understanding of herself, she became more attractive physically, being more careful of her dress and personal habits. Socially she made new friends, and occasionally had a date. She learned to express her feelings and became more independent. She occasionally spent an afternoon with her mother.

Despite relapses of acute depression and withdrawal, Betty made steady progress. When her parents asked her to go to Disney World with them she spent a week of indecision before she decided to go. The trip was relatively successful and she came home with a more objective view of her parents.

With the support of the social worker's counseling, the parents and Betty decided she could return home. Her counseling continued and her family met with a mental health group. Her problems were many, and did not disappear easily, but her strengths were able to compensate for them, and over time Betty was able to make a good adjustment.

For Betty, foster home placement was a good choice because of the intimacy and personal attention that was possible and the opportunity it provided for her to learn to trust those she shared a home with.[5]

## *The Foster Parent Movement*

With the expansion of foster home care, increasing attention is given to this mode of providing for children. Much attention in the past focused on the foster child, the natural parents, and the social worker and their *use* of the foster family. Increasingly, attention is being paid to the foster parent as a *member of the team* with coordinate rights and responsibilities.

The foster parent movement is one of the newer developments in child welfare, with the first National Conference of Foster Parents being held in March 1971, with annual meetings since then. More than 150,000 foster families work with 2,000 social agencies.

Organizations of foster parents have a threefold purpose: (1) to strengthen and improve the quality of life for children in foster homes by sharing experiences, (2) to raise foster care to a higher plane of regard, and (3) to have an effect on legislation that concerns children and their natural parents. The movement recognizes the importance of foster parents in a triad of roles: parent surrogate, agency employee, and child advocate for all foster children. The organization has defined the substitute parent role and spelled out the elements of team relationships necessary for the effective nurturance of children whose biological natural parents for whatever reason do not, or cannot, function in the parental role. The organization addresses such questions as status for foster parents, salary and benefits, upgrading the quality of foster home care, permanency in arrangements for children, and participation in the decision-making processes affecting its own and the child's interest.

The movement seeks to remove the barriers to the sense of fulfillment that foster parents seek. In a special report reflecting views and attitudes of foster parents from the Greater Victoria Foster Parent Association, Tinney[6] makes a case for the reexamination of foster parent roles, responsibilities, and rights. Believing that traditional roles are too limited and inadequate, foster parents seek greater recognition and status. (See Figure 13.2.) It is apparent from this study that foster parents in Victoria, British Columbia, perceive aspects of what they do as being professional. Although their role as substitute parents is frequently noted, high numbers list the role of teamworker, child advocate, consultant, child care counselor and professional with a high degree of frequency. Assuming this trend continues, as foster parents gain in knowledge and become even better organized, they might well aspire to be candidates for training in colleges and universities offering work in child welfare. Some elements of the work of foster parents is professional, and services to children in foster homes would benefit by formal community recognition and encouragement for foster parents to become better educated and trained.

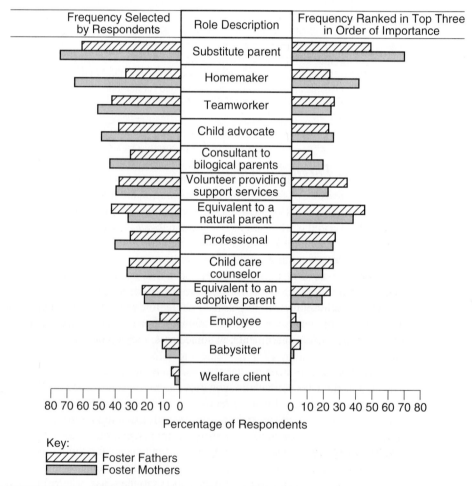

**FIGURE 13.2    Respondents' Perceptions of their Roles as Foster Parents.**

*Source:* Mary-Anne Tinney, "Role Perceptions in Foster Parent Associations in British Columbia," *Child Welfare,* 64 (January–February 1985), 76. A publication of the Child Welfare League of America.

## Adoption Services

Adoption of children appears in the earliest recorded histories. The Babylonian Code of Hammurabi established adoption practices more than 4,000 years ago. The Bible refers to adoption; the ancient Romans practiced it as part of their civil law; adoption law was found among the remains of the early Spaniards; and the practice was known among Anglo-Saxon tribes.

The first legislation on adoption in the United States was enacted in 1851 in Massachusetts. Other states followed, and by 1867 Pennsylvania, Wisconsin, and Illinois had statutes on adoption. Today all states have legislation regarding adoption.

The number of children placed for adoption in the United States increased from 17,000 in 1937 to approximately 169,000 in 1971. This number was down from 175,000 in 1970, marking the first time since 1957 that there was no increase in adoption. In 1982 the total number of adoptions had dropped to 141,861, with 50,720 of these being unrelated; that is, neither of the adopting parents was related to the child adopted.[7] Since 1982 there appears to have been a further decline in the number of adoptions. In 1990 approximately 119,000 children were adopted.[8]

The number of infants available for adoption through agencies has decreased in the last decade because of: (1) family planning, (2) legalization of abortions, (3) acceptance by society of the single parent status, (4) an increase in the number of independent placements, (5) changes in values of society, (6) the Supreme Court's ruling that natural fathers in out-of-wedlock births have legal rights to their offspring, (7) income maintenance programs, food stamps, and subsidized housing for single parent families, (8) the mandating of education for pregnant teenagers, and (9) the reduction in the number of maternity homes.

Children are placed in adoptive homes by one of two methods, either by social agencies licensed to place children or by interested, independent parties. *Independent placement* ranges from "selling" infants to other transactions involving intermediaries making placements independent of state-regulated agencies.

Independent placements lack protection and safeguards to all parties. Unwed mothers seen in social agencies years following the placement for adoption of their babies are still "suffering" because they didn't get the services they needed. With independent placements these services are not provided. Putative fathers often are completely ignored by the lawyers handling independent placements; in some cases, they do not even bother to ask who the father is.

Adoptive parents need preparation for adoption. Life for adopted children isn't the same as life for other children. Those parents not prepared for the differences in rearing adopted children are ill equipped to handle the demands adoptions will make on them which are greater and different from the demands made on the biological natural parents. This preparation isn't provided with independent placements; moreover, too many families adopting children independently of agencies would not be accepted by agencies because they would not qualify under the standards of the licensed agency.

In spite of the disadvantages of independent placement, as of 1993 only six states outlawed independent adoptions.[9] These placements are on the increase and likely will continue to increase. Independent placements have such attractions as: the biological mother can more easily avoid the putative father or her own parents; she may be offered money to pay boarding, medical and confinement expenses; she can usually elect to have a physician of her choice.

The attraction to adoptive parents is that they can have more control over the selection of a child, a child might be more readily available to them and they can sometimes avoid long waiting periods, and they might be able to get a child they could not qualify to get through an agency.

Research is needed in almost all aspects of adoption: to determine the advantages of agency placements compared with independent placements, to test many of the current assumptions regarding the needs of adopted children, and to determine the preparation needed by adopting parents. The value and importance of newer methods of preparing adoptive parents for parenting can hardly fail to benefit from critical review and evaluation of these efforts.

Social work supports agency placements because children, the adopting parents, and the natural parents are provided safeguards in agency arrangements not available in independent placements. It is a deeply held conviction that adoption is an appropriate concern of society and needs all the protection that legal, social, and other instrumentalities can provide.

As the number of babies available for adoption decreases, an increase can be expected in the number of "black market" (selling babies for profit) arrangements. Childless couples, even though they may agree with the idea that social agency placements are preferable, often frantically seek a baby from any source when agencies are unable to provide them. In some cities newborn babies reportedly have sold for more than $1,000 an inch or for as much as $20,000 to $25,000.

It is estimated that fewer than half of all adoptions are nonrelative adoptions. More than half of the children are adopted by stepparents or other relatives.

Social agencies arrange for more than three-fourths of all nonrelative adoptions. However, as fewer babies become available for adoption, childless couples who cannot satisfy their desires for children through the licensed agency may turn to the "black market" and "gray market" for adoptions, and thus reverse the trend for adoptions to be arranged through socially sanctioned governmental and nongovernmental licensed agencies.

Black market adoptions are made "independent" of agencies and do not have social sanction; they are made for a financial consideration—literally sold for a price. Gray market placements are made by intermediaries (usually attorneys or physicians) for and on behalf of friends or acquaintances of people wanting to adopt, or of a mother trying to find a suitable and permanent home for her child. Gray market placements are not made for financial gain. Babies are not sold in the marketplace, and the placement is usually viewed by the parties concerned as a favor or service, not a commercial transaction.

The first state laws on adoption required only a simple petition to the court of local jurisdiction by those wishing to adopt. If the parents were living, their consent was required. If the court was satisfied, the adoption was granted. Legislation has met with only indifferent success to require an investigation of the suitability of the proposed adoption home, provisions for a probationary period in the home of the applicants, safeguards of confidentiality of records, and other such measures as will best protect the welfare of the child.

In no particular is the adoptive applicant protected more than by what is done on behalf of the natural mother, who will be able to accept the decision to give up her child provided the following conditions are met:

1. The agency takes the release when she is ready to give it.
2. Her views and wishes (including religious beliefs) are respected.
3. Her doubts, uncertainties, and guilt are discussed and dealt with.
4. She has reason to believe that the best possible arrangement will be made for her child.

On the other hand, when the natural mother is not part of the process of relinquishment, when her release is taken under pressure, when practices are followed that do not recognize her rights and wishes, she may be unhappy, in doubt, and guilt-ridden, and later may attempt to have the adoption set aside and regain parental control.

Many couples unable to find children to adopt from their own race, turn to babies of other races or of mixed racial backgrounds as an alternative. In the past few decades children in countries ravaged by war have become increasingly available for adoption in the United States. These adoptions fill a twofold need. The parents want children to nurture, and the children need homes where love and affection are freely given. For many the alternative would be severe emotional and physical deprivation in their native lands.

Controversy continues among professionals and others toward interracial or biracial adoptions. Among whites there doesn't appear to be as much controversy possibly because of their insensitivity to the meaning of loss of cultural identity and because of their insensitivity to ethnic minorities not being prepared by white families to compete in a society that practices racial discrimination.

Legislation prohibits biracial adoptions among Native Americans, and the National Association of Afro-American Social Workers opposes biracial adoptions. International placements continue to be a source of infants and small children for a large number of American families; however, here again the problem of ethnic and cultural identity is still to be resolved. Agencies are only beginning to move toward policies on adoption that are truly biracial, recognizing fully the rights and responsibilities alike of all ethnic groups.

## Applicants for Adoption

Adoption is one answer to the problem of (1) finding suitable homes for many children who might otherwise not know what it means to have parents, and (2) childless couples who long for children and to become parents. The following real-life situation, narrated with permission of the adopting parents, illustrates this point.

---

"She is so beautiful, so perfect, it is so wonderful to have her in our arms." These were our thoughts when we held little Dawn that first time in the agency room. As we examined her through our tears of joy, she really smiled at us.

Since the social worker called just a few hours earlier saying, "I have a beautiful six-week-old daughter for you. Can you come get her today?" my mind had been in such turmoil with questions and doubts, and feelings of unreality. Although our social worker had assured us that we would sometime get a baby, we had not expected one so soon. Our one-year waiting period had just elapsed, and he had repeatedly told us it would be several months before we could expect to have a child. To get one so soon seemed unreal. I asked myself if she were six-weeks old, why had they not placed her, was something wrong with her, had others rejected her, if she were handicapped would we be able to accept her? Then, too, I had not told anyone at work that we were adopting. What would my boss say? How could I just not go to work anymore? All in all, it had been a long ride, those 70 miles from our home to the agency. But when we saw her, the questions vanished and we knew that she was meant for us.

It had been a long road from our happy wedding day to this joyful union nine years later. Both Don and I came from big families, and as we had just finished college we decided that having a family right away was what we wanted. But after 18 months and I still wasn't pregnant we started looking for help at a fertility clinic. At that time we were in the Philippines where Don was in the Air Force, but as we moved seven times in three years we had little opportunity to complete the tests. When we returned to civilian life and Don was in law school, we were settled for three years and went through a lot of roller coaster rides of excitement, hope, then crashing each month. Don had surgery for a minor difficulty they thought would raise his sperm count, then doctors discovered I had endometriosis and I had surgery. I kept temperature charts, our life became methodical, and we both did a lot of crying inside.

Our families were difficult and we began avoiding family gatherings with all the nieces and nephews playing about. My family blamed Don, and his family blamed me; they all offered lots of advice, but little understanding.

Our road eventually led us to Houston, Texas, where we found an excellent fertility clinic and the tests started all over again. Although we never gave up hope of having our own baby, we were advised to begin adoption proceedings. We had a social worker who knew how we felt, and it was a relief finally to talk with someone who understood. After the compatibility tests and all the paper work were completed, he told us that it would be a year before we would be eligible to receive a baby, and that in reality it would probably be 18 and possibly 24 months before we would get a child. We continued with the fertility clinic and I had surgery again.

So it was a shock when we got the call just one month after we became eligible. I had not prepared myself psychologically for this event, and I had made no preparation at my work to terminate. We had bought a crib and had it set up, and we had a few essentials, but not nearly enough. We were extremely busy during the next week getting organized into being parents, but it was such a happy time that nothing was too much for us to do. Six months later we went before a smiling judge who finalized the adoption.

Many people ask if there was any effort by the agency to match a baby to us. All I can think of is that the birth mother was very tall, as I am, and the worker may have thought that this physical characteristic could possibly play a part in the adjustment of our little girl as she grows up, if she, too, is tall.

One of the thoughtful things our social worker did was to write a detailed description of both the mother and father. This couple was married, but had decided to divorce, and neither felt they could care for a child. The agency had worked with them toward a reconciliation, and had placed the baby in a foster home for six weeks. Because the social worker knew both parents, he was able to give us details about them that we will be able to share with Dawn when she becomes interested in her birth parents.

As we watched her grow and we knew the joy she brought us, we realized that we wanted another child to grow up with her. We had moved again, and worked with a different agency, but when Dawn was not quite three years old we got another exciting call—"Come get a baby boy at 3:00 o'clock today." We were there and welcomed a biracial baby boy as a part of our family. Don has very dark hair and eyes and our newest addition seems to fit right in.

With greater insight the second time, I wrote a letter to the birth mother which was delivered by the agency, expressing my love for her child, and my deep respect for her, recognizing that she had made the supreme sacrifice in giving up her child for adoption. This letter which was good therapy for me, gave me the opportunity to recognize her for bringing life into the world, and having the courage to give him to us. I feel that women who give up their babies need to be recognized for their part in bringing great happiness to others although they feel a great sense of loss.

This couple's experience with adoption is somewhat typical of licensed agency placements. True, they were among the more fortunate few. Many couples desirous of adopting infants find it extremely difficult since there are far fewer babies than there are eligible couples who want them.

Older children and developmentally disabled youngsters may be the answer for some of these couples. However, adopting older children often presents the problem of dealing with the effects of long periods of neglect and abuse, the child care difficulties in the wake of prolonged trauma. Adopting the physically or mentally handicapped, depending on the disability, may result in extra expenses—medical and/or surgical care, long periods of hospitalization, special education—that many families are unable to pay. Public and private agencies, eager to find homes for these children, sometimes are able to assist with these expenses; but the costs to the family still may be heavy.

The provisions made for the mother who legally surrenders her infant for adoption is a most vital part of sound placement. Adoption services can be no better than what is done for the natural parent.

Any parent faced with giving up a child most likely needs help. Although values are changing and society in general is now more accepting of the unmarried mother, she still may encounter public condemnation. Whatever the situation, the mother and to a lesser extent, the father, must make the important decision of whether or not to keep the child. The social worker can help.

It is almost axiomatic in child welfare that unless the natural mother, and increasingly the father as well, has accepted relinquishment (and acceptance in this sense is more than signing papers), adoptive parents cannot have the assurance that at some future date, when ties have been formed, the natural parent will not try to regain her or his parental rights. Lawsuits have been filed—some successful, others not—to recover a child, based on parental rights following questionable procedures of relinquishment.

## Protective Services

In one sense, all child welfare work is protective work. Children are placed in day care centers while their parents work to protect them from neglect. Children who go into foster homes receive care they are unable to find in their own homes. Physical and emotional abuses are often the stark alternative.

Courts and law enforcement agencies give protection to children and to the community. Modern juvenile court philosophy stresses protection, treatment, and restoration.

Protective services are aimed at preventing abuse, neglect, and exploitation of children. Their aim is to preserve the family unit by assisting parents to develop the capacity for rearing children. Teenagers who become pregnant may not be ready for parenthood and frequently will need help with child care. The focus in protective care is on the family where unsolved problems have led to neglect and/or abuse, and have become a hazard to the physical and emotional well-being of children.

Few services offered by social workers are demanding of greater skill and competence than those involved in seeking out neglect and abuse and in helping resistive parents to accept the services of an agency in providing stability, nurturance, and love.

This service is usually initiated by the agency upon a complaint being filed by a physician, school teacher, neighbor or relative who is aware of the circumstances. The agency explores, studies, and evaluates the effect of neglect and abuse on the children. It may involve the court to constructively use its authority to secure protection for children, if parents are unable or unwilling to work in a voluntary relationship with the agency.

Protective services have been greatly expanded and improved to ensure the prevention of abuse and neglect and to provide services to children who are victims of serious and continued mistreatment. A few of the practices and issues of concern follow.

Demographics of children needing protective services and the type of mistreatment to which they have been exposed are capsulized by Ginsberg.[10] See Figure 13.3. A few of the practices and issues of concern follow.

### *Issues and Practices in Protective Services*

1. The *reporting* of abuse and neglect has been greatly improved and many states have strong reporting legislation. This is making it possible for children and for families to get

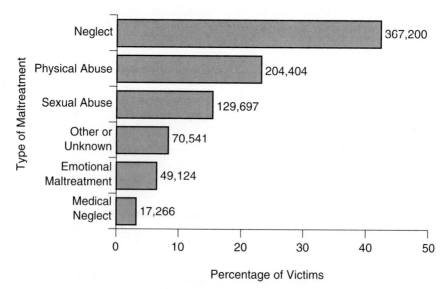

**FIGURE 13.3    Number and Percentages of Child Abuse Reports, by Type of Maltreatment: 1991**

*Note:* Total number of maltreatment types (45 states reporting) = 838,232.

*Source:* Adapted from U.S. Department of Health and Human Services, National Center on Child Abuse and Neglect. (1993). *National child abuse and neglect data system working paper 2: 1991 summary data component* (p. 29). Gaithersburg, MD.

help. Neighbors, relatives, the police, schools, juvenile courts, nurses, doctors, and many others are now reporting abuse and neglect practices that in the past went unnoticed.

2. The creation in the states of *child protective services* (CPS) has made it possible for people who need help to get it. Responsible citizens report abuse and neglect when they know that something can and will be done about it.

3. A *total service system* is at the disposal of the CPS worker who may initiate a process that will tie the family into the system. This includes an array of such services as: assistance payments, testing services, child rearing and development classes, counseling services, homemaking services. Big Brother and Big Sister services, and Share a Parent Services. Parents and other family members can be "pulled" into these services and often receive the help they need to handle their personal and family problems to aid in preventing abuse and neglect, or to contain it.

4. The *needs of parents* are addressed by these services as well as the needs of the mistreated children. Blaming or punishing parents is rapidly being discarded by the knowledge that their neglect and abuse is often symptomatic of a need for help. As help is made available they can often provide the parenting their children need. If it should be determined that for some reason parents cannot be rehabilitated or effectively trained as parents even with help, and that they cannot nurture and care for their children, substitute parental care may be arranged for the child or children.

5. The *courts are shifting* in their position and increasingly recognize that both parents and children have rights and should be protected alike under the law. Courts often work collaboratively with child protective agency workers and provide helpful and constructive use of authority.

6. *Medical care* is available as needed for children and parents and available to the CPS agency for help of its clients.

7. Personnel are *trained* to provide the services needed. The training social workers receive in schools of social work has been expanded greatly with the training and licensing of BSW social workers. In addition ongoing training on the job is provided by agencies as new knowledge is developed and new skills required.

8. The issue of the CPS role in the public agency continues to be explored with resulting refinement of practice.

9. Study of ways to make the CPS agency *increasingly functional* continues. Such study addresses such issues as work load standards, making creative use of personnel and resources, kinds of training needed for CPS workers, and how to coordinate services and to cooperate with other professional disciplines.

10. There is a growing concern that *national standards* for CPS agencies and workers be formulated and adopted.

11. Other critical issues include: legal aspects of CPS services and the training needed by the CPS worker to handle legal questions; the reciprocal responsibility of the courts and the CPS worker; training CPS personnel; what to do with "neglect of neglect" cases; enlisting community support for protective services.

## Physical Neglect and Abuse

Physical neglect is defined by all state laws, but standards vary from one community to another so that it is difficult to evaluate the actual neglect.

Physical abuse is illustrated by a teacher and his wife, who were reported when neighbors observed that the man beat his two adopted daughters.

Examinations by the school nurse disclosed open sores on the scalps of the two girls and bruises on their bodies. The father, a teacher in the public schools, held status in the community that shielded his sadistic treatment of the girls. When the beatings were brought to the attention of the school nurse, she determined that no medical care had been provided, although the scalp wounds were deep and infected. The nurse brought the matter to the attention of the protective service center, whose investigation disclosed gross neglect and abuse. The father was referred for treatment and determined unfit to have the children, who were placed by the court temporarily in a foster home while the father received counseling.

A dramatic increase in the number of teenage pregnancies is reported with most young women keeping their babies. The tenfold increase in child abuse is assumed to be referable in a large measure to teenage mothers who are not prepared for parenthood. In one state[11] a constructive "protective" and preventive approach to abuse and neglect is used to achieve such objectives as to: (1) provide a home environment for mothers and infants, (2) help mothers develop skills they need to be parents, (3) provide modeling of parenting skills, (4) schedule and transport mothers for therapy appointments, (5) have teen mothers participate in agency training sessions, (6) set up treatment plans, (7) assist mothers to make educational and vocational plans, and (8) introduce mothers to community resources.

This program recognizes that teen pregnancies can be a national disaster when as many as 8 out of 10 young women who give birth are between the ages of 15 and 17, never finish school, 90 percent unemployed and 70 percent are on welfare.

## Child Sexual Abuse

Child sexual abuse is a horror story—a national disgrace. Tens of thousands of children—infants through adolescence—are the victims. The perpetrators—neighbors, acquaintances, "friends" of the family, extended family members, fathers—are mostly adult males.

Is this a crime of the age—an aberration—or a sudden outcropping hidden from the public in the past, and only now uncovered and recognized? We can't say, but we suspect that child sexual abuse has been around for a long time, possibly exacerbated by recent cataclysmic changes in a fast-changing social system. What we do know is that people are outraged and that the trauma for victims goes unchecked.

The issue needs to be seriously addressed and social workers—protective service workers, mental health workers, and many others—may be the first in the network to learn about abuse and to see its ugly consequences. They have a responsibility. However, if the tide of abuse is to be stemmed the entire community needs to join forces in an unrelenting drive to stamp out the problem.

We know that convicting and imprisoning perpetrators, often leading to breakup of families, depriving them of the major source of support, disrupting neighborhoods, is not the answer. Protracted court procedures with charges, countercharges, confessions followed by denials and the gamut of feelings and behaviors surrounding abuse are not enough.

A modern civilized community can do better. We must find ways to check abuse without destroying people in the process. Victims who are invariably traumatized must be protected and offered the best possible treatment. Perpetrators who themselves may have been victims are invariably sick, and sick people need help. We need to know more about what causes this type of behavior. We need to determine the kind of help these people can use and address ourselves to treatment and rehabilitation appropriate to their diagnosed illnesses. More education is required. Research is needed, as is treatment. And community recognition of the ramifications of the problem is needed. Social work can help in a coordinate role with other helping professions and an educated and aroused public.

## Summary

*Humanity's basic institution, the family, is effective in shaping the lives of children and adults. But when the family is in trouble, social workers may provide help through marriage and family counseling.*

*Husband-wife relationships and husband-wife-children constellations are the concern of various services established to assist families with problems, and to strengthen the family unit. A variety of agencies have been established to provide these services.*

*Child welfare is a widely diversified program of services for children and their families when the help of the community is required. These programs have the underpinning of community interest, concern, and substantial financial support. Professionally staffed, they are the means of preventing social breakdown or restoring the functioning of families when breakdown threatens or has occurred.*

*Services to children in their own homes has the highest priority. Empowering families is an objective of preservation systems, addressed to strengths, that make use of a variety of resources.*

*Strengthening the quality of life for children, raising foster care to a higher plane of regard, and favorably affecting legislation are purposes of the foster care movement.*

*For children who are unable to live with their natural parents, foster care, a residential living arrangement, is often recommended. Group-living is also provided as a treatment of choice for certain children. Both of these may be temporary arrangements.*

*Adoptions provide a permanent arrangement for children whose natural parents relinquish their parental rights. Agencies offer a needed service to those who wish to adopt.*

*Protective services provide support so that family strength is maintained and children helped to adjust in their own homes. Physical abuse, neglect, sexual abuse, medical neglect, and emotional maltreatment are a few of the concerns of protective services. These services, established in state divisions of family services, take action to prevent abuse when it is reported.*

## Selected References

ADAMS, PAUL L., JUDITH R. MILNER, and NANCY A. SCHREPF, *Fatherless Children.* New York: John Wiley & Sons, 1984.

AINSLIE, RICARDO C., ed., *The Child and the Day Care Setting.* New York: Praeger Publishers, 1984.

ALSTON, FRANCES KEMPER, *Caring for Other People's Children: A Complete Guide to Family Day Care.* Baltimore: University Park Press, 1984.

BARTH, RICHARD P., JILL DUERR BERRICK, MARK COURTNEY, and VICKY ALBERT, *From Child Abuse to Permanency Planning: Child Welfare Services Pathways and Placements.* New York: Aldine de Gruyter, 1994.

BERRY, MARIANNE, *Keeping Families Together.* New York: Garland, 1994.

COSTIN, LELA B., *Child Welfare: Policies and Practice,* 2nd ed. New York: McGraw-Hill, 1979.

EKELING, NANCY B. and DEBORAH A. HILL, *Child Abuse and Neglect: A Guide with Case Studies for Treating the Child and Family.* Boston: John Wright, PSG, 1983.

EWALT, PATRICIA L., "Who Cares for the Children?" *Social Work,* 40 (March 1995), 149–150.

FILIP, JUDEE, PATRICIA SCHENE, and NANCY MCDANIEL, *Helping in Child Protective Services: A Casework Handbook.* East Englewood, CO: The American Humane Association, 1991.

FOLBERG, JAY, and ANN MILNE, *Divorce Mediation: Theory and Practice.* Brooklyn, NY: Guilford Publications, Inc., 1988.

FRASER, MARK W., PETER J. PECORA, and DAVID A. HAAPALA, *Families in Crisis: The Impact of Intensive Family Preservation Services.* New York: Aldine de Gruyter, 1991.

GILL, OWEN, and BARBARA JACKSON, *Adoption and Race.* New York: St. Martin's Press, 1983.

HUMPHREY, FREDERICK G., *Marital Therapy.* Englewood Cliffs, NJ: Prentice Hall, 1983.

LEVANT, RONALD F., *Family Therapy: A Comprehensive Overview.* Englewood Cliffs, NJ: Prentice Hall, 1983.

MAUGANS, JOY GARLAND, *America's Forsaken Children: The Foster Care Dilemma,* 2nd ed. Charlotte, NC: John Russell Publishing Co., 1990.

ROSENFELD, ALVIN, and SAUL WASSERMAN, *Healing the Heart: A Therapeutic Approach to Disturbed Children in Group Care.* Washington DC: Child Welfare League of America, 1990.

SCHULZ, DAVID A., *The Changing Family,* 3rd ed. Englewood Cliffs, NJ: Prentice Hall, 1982.

WOLD, MICHAEL S., J. M. CARLSMITH, and V. H. LEIDERMAN, *Protecting Abused and Neglected Children.* Stanford, CA: Stanford University Press, 1988.

## *Notes*

1. Kevin Fullin, "Battered Women Are Caught in a Cycle of Violence," *U.S. News and World Report,* October 12, 1992, p. 11.

2. Nevada Division of Mental Hygiene and Mental Retardation, "Troubled Families," *People* (Spring 1973), pp. 8–9.

3. Rocco A. Cimmarusti, "Family Preservation Practice Based upon a Multisystems Approach," *Child Welfare,* 71 (May–June 1992), 248.

4. Peter J. Pecora, Mark W. Fraser, and David A. Haapala, "Intensive Home-Based Family Preservation Services: An Update from the FIT Project," *Child Welfare,* 71 (March/April 1992), 178.

5. Case material provided by Marah Grist, former Associate Professor of Social Work, University of Utah.

6. Mary-Anne Tinney, "Role Perceptions in Foster Parent Associations in British Columbia," *Child Welfare,* 64 (January–February 1985), 73–79.

7. *Adoption Factbook,* 1985, *United States Data, Issues, Regulations and Resources.* Prepared by the National Committee for Adoptions, 2025 M Street, Suite 512, Washington DC 20036.

8. Richard P. Barth, "Adoption," in *Encyclopedia of Social Work,* 19th ed., Vol. I. Washington, DC: NASW Press, 1993), pp. 48–49.

9. Ibid., p. 49.

10. Leon Ginsberg, *Social Work Almanac,* 2nd ed. (Washington, DC: NASW Press, 1995), p. 73.

11. Grace W. Sisto, "Therapeutic Foster Homes for Teenage Mothers and Their Babies," *Child Welfare,* 64 (March–April 1985), 157–163.

# Correctional Services

*An 18-year-old senior stole a Cadillac from a wealthy family and was sentenced to 30 days in jail. During his first three years in high school he had worked well and had received excellent grades; then he began to fail his classes. His father had given him a car, money, everything he wanted—in fact, too much—and he had finally been arrested by the police for theft. A social worker attached to the Youth Bureau talked with the judge, who agreed to have the boy spend each*

*night in jail, but have his father pick him up and take him to and from school each day. Prior to completion of the sentence, the social worker checked with the boy's teachers and found that he was doing very well.*

*What would be the possible influence of the following on the boy's behavior: the boy himself, the father, social worker, jail sentence, and peer pressures?*

## The Social Problems of Delinquency and Crime

Delinquency and crime are major social problems of modern society (see Figure 14.1). They are of concern not only to those who are involved directly as victims and otherwise but also to those who consider present and future implications of the increasing amount of antisocial behavior. In 1993, serious offenses amounted to 14,141,000 in the United States. Violent crimes—the kind that terrify people—had included 24,530 murders and nonnegligent manslaughters and 104,810 forcible rapes. In addition, there were 2,834,800 burglaries and 1,561,000 thefts of motor vehicles.[1]

Economically it is estimated that delinquency and crime cost the people of the United States today more than $300 billion annually.

On January 1, 1984, there were 419,820 prisoners under the jurisdiction of federal and state correctional institutions in the United States, 402,391 male and 17,429 female, more than double the number in 1970. At the same time the average daily population in the 3,500 jails in the United States exceeded 150,000 with more than 6 million commitments each year.[2] By 1993 there were more than 900,000 men and women incarcerated in state and federal prisons.

The National Center for Juvenile Justice[3] estimated that in 1977 there were 1,355,490 cases processed by courts with juvenile jurisdiction in the United States, of which 76.5 per-

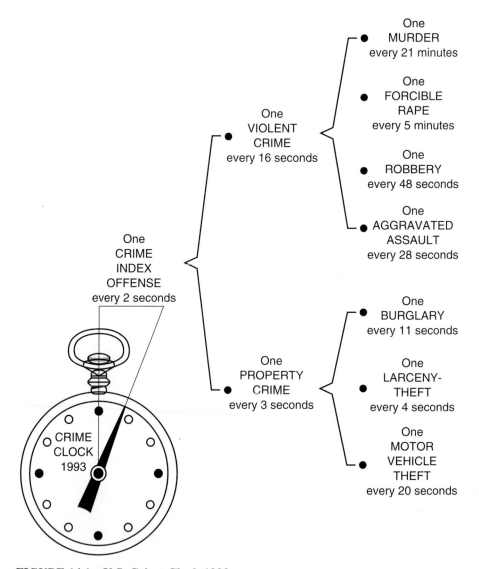

**FIGURE 14.1   U.S. Crime Clock 1993.**

*Source: Crime in the United States*—1993, p. 4.

cent were male and 23.3 percent were female. At this rate it meant that in an average 24-hour period about 11,000 boys and girls were handled by law enforcement officers, about 3,500 appeared before a juvenile court, and more than 300 spent the night in one of our jails or lockups, most of which are unfit places for keeping children or youth. By 1993 the FBI indicated that arrests for serious crimes for those under eighteen reached 1,904,763, based on agency reports representing an estimated population of 200,200,000.

*Gang violence* has become a major problem in the last two decades in cities of all sizes, especially in the larger urban areas. It involves youth and young adults of different ages, and their offenses include vandalism, fighting, violating of many laws, drug crimes, bodily injuries and many homicides. In numerous neighborhoods many families are moving elsewhere because of concerns and fears related to these antisocial behaviors.

Social workers are employed by a variety of agencies including police departments, juvenile courts, prisons, schools, churches, and community service programs to help prevent and reduce the number of violations. It is clearly evident that we need more knowledge and improved skills to face these difficult situations. Regulus suggests that for effective gang intervention and violence reduction there must "be the inclusion of effective interpersonal engagement of gangs and gang memberships in the intervention process."[4]

The President's Commission on Law Enforcement and Administration of Justice, in its monumental report of 1967, summarized the challenging problems related to crime and delinquency as follows:

> Many Americans take comfort in the view that crime is the vice of a handful of people. This view is inaccurate. In the United States today, one boy in six is referred to the juvenile court.... Another Commission study suggests that about 40 percent of all male children now living in the United States will be arrested for

Reaching for gang peace.

a nontraffic offense during their lives. An independent survey of 1,700 persons found that 91 percent of the sample admitted they had committed acts for which they might have received jail or prison sentences.

In addition to the dollars and statistics, antisocial behavior rends the heartstrings of thousands of parents and loved ones. A single act of delinquency or crime may change the whole existence of a particular family; and as families are weakened and filled with tension, society is injured and threatened.

Social workers are playing prominent roles in administrative and practice positions in federal, state, and local correctional programs. Through the years social work also has provided a variety of services to help reduce and prevent delinquency and crime; today it is one answer to help with these perplexing and frightening social problems. Social workers are active in providing services in most correctional agencies and programs.

## Social Work and Corrections

Throughout human history, punishments, especially corporal and capital, have often been offered in answer to antisocial behavior. Public hangings, floggings, mutilation, branding, banishment, the stocks and pillory, and many other physical penalties have been utilized to "punish the culprit and be a lesson to others." It was only toward the end of the eighteenth century, at the Walnut Street Prison in Philadelphia, in the shadows of Independence Hall, that the beginning of a new method—the use of time sentence in an institution—came into general usage. Enlightened humanitarians claimed that it was inhumane and unwise to torture offenders or put them to death. Instead the *penitentiary system* was developed, devised to give the offender a chance to think, have a "change of heart," and "mend his ways" through meditation in solitary confinement. Subsequently various kinds of penal institutions evolved to allow for incarceration. Eventually the use of probation came into being as a substitute for imprisonment through the efforts of John Augustus, a Boston shoemaker, and other benevolent reformers.

As offenders were sentenced to institutions and were placed on probation and parole, various professional groups became interested in making these efforts as effective as possible. Social work was one of these.

During the nineteenth century the roots of the emerging profession of social work were growing rapidly and a major area of focus involved the offender. For example, the *Proceedings of the National Conference of Charities and Correction* indicate that at the conference convened in 1885 a portion of the program was devoted to consideration of employment in reformatories, prison reforms, jails and police, and even to discussion of prevention of related social problems. During recent years there has been a revived interest in the field of corrections by social workers. This is epitomized in the Curriculum Study of the Council on Social Work Education.

The modification of the penalty system did more than require a different kind of administrative structure and personnel. It made possible the idea of treatment. . . . With the increasing knowledge about the dynamics of human behavior and how it is modified, which has become available in the 20th century, it has become possible to give attention to the rehabilitation of the offender.[5]

*Corrections* is one of four social processes utilized in the administration of criminal justice. They include "(1) law enforcement, which is concerned with the collection of evidence about reported offenses and with the detection and arrest of suspected offenders; (2) prosecution and defense, or the preparation and presentation of criminal cases before the court; (3) judicial process, which is concerned with the legal determination of guilt and the assignment of penalties; (4) corrections, which is responsible for administering the assigned penalties."[6] The *Social Work Dictionary,* 1995 edition, defines corrections as "the legal specialty that seeks to change and improve the behaviors of convicted law offenders through *incarceration, parole, probation,* and ideally educational programs and *social services.*"[7]

Corrections, in one sense at least, is the total process of helping persons who have violated the law to be rehabilitated. The social worker plays a very important role in the total process. His or her basic goal is summarized as follows: "The correctional process has come to mean the administration of the penalty in such a way that the offender is 'corrected,' i.e., his current behavior is kept within acceptable limits at the same time that his general life adjustment is modified."[8]

The aim of the social worker in assisting boys and girls who are in trouble with the law is basically to rehabilitate rather than to punish them. The goal is to help them to understand themselves, their relationships with others, and what is expected of them as members of the society in which they live. Corporal and physical punishment have been pushed aside, in the main relegated to history, and the emphasis is upon trying to bring about positive change in behavior patterns. Reformation and rehabilitation are the key words today. These are all important in working with persons in trouble, and, in particular, in attempting to help them adjust better to society.

The social worker's aim is to help the offender, not to retaliate or to punish. The goal is to utilize the knowledge and skills of the profession in a corrective manner, to rehabilitate individuals, to help them to help themselves so that they can return to and become part of society, and to guide them toward becoming comfortable with themselves and their associates. "More than in any other social service, the correctional social worker's task is defined in terms of changing the values of the client so that they become congruent in action with the values of the community."[9]

The social worker often works as a member of a team, including probation and parole officers, psychologists, psychiatrists, vocational counselors, educators, and others in providing services and in assisting the offender to change his or her behavior.

The social worker aims to help the offender change patterns of behavior so that the offender can relate constructively to others and become socially acceptable. This is done through two avenues: (1) working with the individual to help him or her change through better understanding of self and by tapping the person's own strengths and resources, and (2) modification of environment to bring about a more healthy social climate in which to live.

Examples of individual problems of offenders with which the social worker helps are: serious feelings of inferiority and inadequacy, inability to socialize, lack of status, negative feelings toward relatives, sibling rivalries, and family disorganization. The worker encourages the offender to talk about problems, feel about them, and come to an insightful understanding of self, accompanied by socially constructive behavior.

In regard to environmental problems, the worker may help the offender to bolster his or her abilities to accept and withstand the pressures and/or assist in bringing about changes that alleviate such conditions as inadequate housing or diet, a family where no one cares, inadequate vocational training or job placement, and economic stresses.

In working with both individual and environmental situations, the social worker keeps close to the family unit; in fact, social work is family-centered.

## Social Work Practice in Corrections

"Social Work practice," according to the 1967 Code of Ethics, National Association of Social Workers, "is a public trust that requires of its practitioners integrity, compassion, belief in the dignity and worth of human beings, respect for individual differences, a commitment to service, and a dedication to truth."

In working with offenders the social worker attempts to achieve socially desirable objectives within two kinds of settings: institutional and noninstitutional—probation or parole. Time is an influencing factor. For example, most juvenile delinquents who are placed on probation by the juvenile courts are given a sentence of three to nine months depending on their individual situations. During this time the social worker endeavors to establish a meaningful relationship with the individual and to help him or her alter behavior patterns in keeping with the values of society. Although inmates of reformatories and prisons receive longer sentences, most offenders return to society sooner than is generally supposed. Even murderers spend only a portion of their sentences in prisons. According to the U.S. Bureau of Justice Statistics the median time convicted murderers spend behind bars is only seven years, and one of every seven persons sentenced for "life" serves three years or less.

For inmates in prisons the social worker, where available, attempts to establish a relationship that, over a period of time, frees the individual to express feelings in a cathartic manner, muster ego strengths, change some personal values, and become a law-abiding citizen. This relationship is the essence of the social worker's contribution—along with the use of community resources. It means that the worker accepts the client, understands, and respects him or her and that the client develops feelings toward the worker, and shares ideas, emotions, and problems. Then through a bond of warmth and support, changes may be effected. The social worker is nonjudgmental, sensitive to needs, and conveys a feeling of respect for the integrity and individuality of the client regardless of questionable conduct.

In institutions with social work staff, the worker may meet weekly with the client for about an hour, and, through interviewing, help him or her to achieve goals. The pattern outside institutions is fundamentally the same and includes the periodic interviews that give support and assistance to the offender, focusing on treatment rather than punishment, reform rather than punitiveness.

The social work process consists of four parts: *social study* (finding the facts), *assessment* (defining and evaluating the problems), *treatment* (solving the problems), and *termi-*

*nation.* The first three ordinarily proceed simultaneously from the beginning, although in emphasis there is usually sequential order. Often the first interview, or two or three, is utilized for social study and assessment; then treatment entails varying numbers of interviews, depending upon individual problems and environmental situations.

The number of interviews is significant. Many social workers leave the number open to the worker and client to ascertain as they move along together; others stipulate a specific number of interviews, so that termination goals and dynamics may be anticipated. Although a common pattern is for interviews to take place weekly, the number can be increased or decreased depending on the needs of the client in the rehabilitative process. During emergencies the social worker may be needed at once.

The social worker acts as a catalytic agent who makes it possible for an offender to gain self-understanding, to feel better, and in particular, to interact with others more constructively. The worker helps the offender to tap his or her own strengths, bringing about better harmony within the person and in associations with others. Studies show that offenders often need help in learning to function adequately in interaction with others, particularly in close, personal relationships.

Although some problems may be eased by the social worker in an interview or two, most persons who are in legal trouble need assistance over a period of time and require guidance in making effective use of community services and resources.[10]

Timing is also important in the social worker's role. There are certain periods when he or she can be particularly effective, such as: during intake, when emergencies occur, in preparing for release, and in aftercare treatment. A meaningful relationship between worker and client can make easier these time-bound experiences, resulting in desired change.

Eskridge raised some questions about training needed for probation officers—even though the American Bar Association in 1970 had reaffirmed a standard previously suggested that attainment of a master's degree be the preferred norm—and suggested that probation as a profession "should proceed cautiously before adopting any firm educational standards or inservice training programs."[11]

Since the mid-1960s, considerable efforts have been extended to develop training and hiring of paraprofessionals and those who have completed undergraduate training in social work or social welfare. Indigenous workers among paraprofessionals have been sought, particularly among some of the minority groups.

The President's Commission in 1967 stressed the need for more and better qualified staff when they stated: "The system of criminal justice must attract more people and better people—police, prosecutors, judges, defense attorneys, probation and parole officers, and corrections officials with more knowledge, expertise, initiative, and integrity." Social workers can fulfill significant roles in several of these positions.

## Processes and Principles

What are the methods utilized by the social worker in assisting with antisocial behavior? Traditionally there have been three in particular: *casework, group work,* and *community organization.* Research and administration also bolster social work services both directly and indirectly.

A few of the key principles social workers keep in mind as they work with offenders and their families are: (1) to utilize a *relationship* to help clients to help themselves; (2) to not condemn or moralize, accepting clients as they are, and also their behavior, regardless of what has been in the past; (3) to respect their right of self-determination, that is, to assist them to think and feel through their problems and situations, but not to make basic decisions for them, helping to provide an emotional climate in which they can face their problems and work out appropriate solutions; (4) to recognize that one has to study and understand normal behavior as well as antisocial behavior in order to comprehend the *why* of delinquency and criminality and what should be done about them; (5) to provide a security-giving firmness, not physical punishment, but not "coddling," as some maintain, recognizing that in many ways a child is like a coil spring, and that the harder one pushes the farther he or she will be likely to spring back when an opportunity arises; and (6) to use authority in a positive manner to help offenders to help themselves face their problems and readjust their thinking and behavior.

What are the specific functions of a social worker in relation to juvenile delinquency and crime? Some of the main functions are:

*Helping to strengthen motivation* is a primary function of the social worker. Many boys and girls, or adults, do not care much about what they do in life or what they do not do. The social worker, through talking with them sympathetically and understandingly, can usually be of aid. For a person to know that someone is interested, and will accept him or her as is, is a tremendously motivating factor. One delinquent, for example, who talked to a probation officer over a period of many weeks, said: "He was just like a hypnotist. I couldn't say no to him. To know that someone cared enough about me to spend time with me, to try to understand and help me, led me to where I am today." His desire to become a law-abiding citizen had been increased and supported.

*Allowing for ventilation of feelings* is a second service of the social worker. Most youths and adults who come to a probation officer need to share with someone, in confidence, their inner feelings, their fears and frustrations, as well as their hopes and aspirations. The importance of this is illustrated by the man who talked to a worker for more than sixty minutes, giving the listener only an opportunity to nod his head and acquiesce. At the end he stood up, greatly relieved, and said, "I feel much better. Thanks for all your wonderful advice!" Youths and adults have feelings well up within, and social workers provide a safe emotional climate in which they can express and verbalize them.

*The giving of information* is another important function of the social worker. Many youths and adults need help in understanding who they are, where they are going, and where they might go. Many times they do not comprehend the society to which they belong, and the social worker can help them to develop such an understanding and to acquire insights into their proper roles.

The probation officer *helps offenders to make decisions.* They do not make decisions for them, but help them to consider, rationally, their problems and the alternatives that face them. Should they obtain employment? Should they stay with their own family or move out? Should they continue to associate with their old friends? Should they return to school? How can they alter their behavioral patterns? These are some of the typical questions that arise.

The social worker helps the client to *define the situation.* He or she assists the individual not only in *thinking* about a problem or a situation, but also in *feeling* about the situation.

A positive illustration is the young boy who has serious feelings of inferiority and, as a result, is in legal trouble on a compensatory, acting-out basis. The social worker helps him to think and feel about himself and his behavior, and thereby to realize that his feelings of inferiority are not based on facts. This new understanding and insight can alter his whole pattern of living.

*Assisting in modification of the environment* is another major function. With knowledge of community resources, the social worker is able to help persons and families tap various financial and social resources to meet their individual needs. The social worker may help a boy who is on probation to get a part-time job. He or she may assist the individual in finding a place to live; may help him or her become enrolled in a vocational training program to prepare for worthwhile citizenship for the rest of his or her life.

*Helping offenders reorganize behavior patterns* is one of the most difficult functions of the social worker. This includes help for the chronic alcoholic, the drug abuser, and those with other personality problems. The social worker may refer such a person to another expert or talk to the individual personally, depending on his or her background, training and experience. These kinds of cases usually require long periods of treatment, and many never "make it."

Another major function is in *facilitating referral.* Sometimes the job is "helping Susie to get to the clinic." Often it is difficult for a person to take personal problems to another, and he or she needs support in so doing. Referral may be made to a psychiatrist, minister, internist, geneticist, or other person who may help with a particular situation. The social worker's comprehensive knowledge of community resources is used to advantage in making referrals.

## Social Services and Case Examples

### Police Departments and Youth Bureaus

Social workers are sometimes utilized in working with the police, particularly in their youth bureaus. In many larger cities professionally trained social workers are integral parts of police departments. They act as consultants to help the law enforcement officers to better understand the boys and girls whom they apprehend. They help the total department to develop a rehabilitative attitude rather than a punitive one, and, in particular, to facilitate the rehabilitative processes. A new role for social workers is going on patrol with police officers on night duty, answering emergency calls, and assisting with serious family quarrels and other personal or family difficulties. In addition, they play an important role in trying to prevent antisocial behavior among children, youths, and adults. The social worker is in a strategic position to utilize existing community resources and to draw upon whatever may be most needed to assist a particular offender to change hostile attitudes and behavior to those within societal standards.

To illustrate, young Rebecca, who was picked up on the street at 2 A.M., was interviewed by a social worker, who found that her family was "psychologically broken" and disorganized. The social worker, in cooperation with the police, accompanied the girl to her home. In the next several days, the worker interviewed the mother, father, and some of the neighbors. After several weeks, the mother and father, through the help of the social worker, were enabled to become more effective parents. Within a few months, the family constellation changed from one of constant bickering, trouble, and hostility to one on the pathway to becoming a solid, functioning family. The daughter, who had been in trouble with the police several times prior to her escapade, settled down and began to do well in school and otherwise.

## *Courts*

Social workers are attached to juvenile courts, district courts, federal courts, and to some municipal courts, performing the role of probation officer. In this connection, they have several functions. The first is conducting investigations to find out the facts and the feelings involved in a particular violation of law. Because of their training, social workers can usually be objective yet sympathetic and can secure a picture of the total situation that is most helpful to the court. Judges are making decisions regarding disposition of cases based on facts and understandings supplied through the investigation of the social worker. Investigations are primarily related to the offender but nearly always involve the family, close relatives, and other key persons in the lives of the accused.

An example of this function is the case of a young man brought before a California judge on a charge of "stealing state property." The young man was handsome and appeared to be intelligent, but was a person who had been "kicked around from place to place." He had been born into a family where he was not wanted. He had run away from home many times, had been placed in foster care on several occasions, and for years had been "on the road." The judge took a personal interest in him and asked his social worker to make a careful investigation. The social worker reported the significant facts with his professional interpretations. On the basis of this investigation, the judge befriended the boy as no one had ever done before. The boy felt the sincere interest of this judge and social worker. The disposition was that the boy would be allowed to go into the service to perform his military obligation, which was mandatory at the time. When he filled in his papers, he asked the judge if he could put the judge's name down as the person "closest to him, who would always know his whereabouts." The judge said he would be complimented to be so designated. The boy was accepted into military service and adopted a mature pattern of living. His changed behavior was clear evidence of the need of one young man for understanding and interest from judges, social workers, and others who might supply these when they have not come through a regular channel.

A major function of the social worker is to represent the court after the judge has made a decision. Probation involves regular interviews and contacts between the probation officer and the offender. Again, the social worker attempts to use his or her best knowledge and skills to help bring about desired changes in the thinking, feeling, and behavior of those with whom he or she works. Many offenders for the first time in their lives have someone, the social worker, who really cares about them and is trying to help them to understand themselves and their relationships with others. The essence of this service is illustrated by the statement of Joe, age seventeen, who said, "For the first time in my life I was important to someone, and was wanted."

Another service, recent in appearance, is provided by the social worker as an expert witness in the courts. Gothard reports that before 1980 social workers rarely qualified as expert witnesses in legal proceedings.[12] Since the mid-1980s the profession has gained status, and individual social workers have been recognized as having sufficient expertise in several areas to qualify as experts in courts of law. This has placed social workers on a par with other professionals, who have long been qualified as experts in the courts. Social workers are now invited to state their opinions and thereby influence the judgment or verdict. A recent development is the use of social workers as expert witnesses in child abuse cases.

## Social Work in Institutions

Although many youth development centers, detention homes, and prisons do not have trained social workers on their staffs, it is encouraging to note that the number that do is growing. Within such institutions, the social worker can play an extremely important role. He or she is usually assigned several inmates with whom to work on a face-to-face, individualized basis. The social worker ordinarily meets with them weekly, giving them an opportunity to talk over their problems in relation to society and life, especially in relation to their families. All kinds of cases exist indicating that thousands of boys and girls, youths, and adults are being helped by social workers who open the door for rehabilitation. Not only is social work with individuals used advantageously within these institutions, but the group approach is also more common.

That youths and adults need help in institutions is illustrated by the example of two seventeen-year-old boys who had been placed in a state prison for robbery. They were "ideal" prisoners. When they had served their time and were about to leave, the warden cautioned them to be truthful and law-abiding. They walked out of the prison gates with about $15 in their pockets. They located some stores, bought a few things they had not had for some time, and then began to look for jobs. When the applications were handed to them, they were faced with the question, "Have you ever been in prison?" They answered truthfully. No one would give them a job. Three nights later, about midnight, the two boys returned to the prison, rang the bell at the gate, and asked if the warden would give them a place to sleep. He, of course, granted their request. The next morning the guards passed a hat around, making a collection for the boys. More important, a social worker called employers and arranged for a job for each of them. Several years later, it was ascertained that these two young men had followed the warden's instructions, had lived law-abiding lives, and were respected citizens in their communities.

The 1973 Delegate Assembly of the National Association of Social Workers evidenced deep concern about delinquency and crime in this country and what social workers might do to combat and prevent them. They adopted a platform of fourteen objectives to help alleviate these devastating problems. Three of the salient ones were:

1. NASW should work for greatly increased use of alternatives to incarceration to replace present excessive reliance on institutional commitment in the treatment of convicted offenders.
2. NASW should advocate that no new major large-scale institutions for either adults or juveniles be countenanced and that present large-scale juvenile institutions be phased out within a five-year period.

**3.** NASW should encourage greater emphasis on sound treatment programs within the community for most offenders.

With increased numbers of social workers being hired in correctional institutions comes the challenge to provide more effective services, a genuine challenge. Severson suggests that "providing social work services to the inmate and the institution concurrently requires that the social worker perform a balancing act. On one hand, incarcerated clients are entitled to the same protections that clients in mental health agencies or private practices are afforded. On the other hand, the institution has the need to know the forces that are affecting the population."[13]

In recent years there has been a movement toward closing institutions for juveniles and/or decentralizing them, establishing smaller units in more communities. Massachusetts has closed down its correctional facilities for juveniles altogether and other states are looking carefully at this alternative. The basic premise is that too many juveniles are needlessly channeled through courts and institutions with scant regard for their offenses, civil liberties, and treatment. Additional emphasis is being given to the goals of diversion and rehabilitation rather than punishment.

Although "hard-core" violators of the law are maintained in most states in institutions, various "alternative programs" are also available, for example, residential care, proctor advocate programs, and residential treatment centers. Social workers may play significant roles in all of these.

In recent years there have been tough new laws passed to increase the punishment of offenders, particularly adults. New prisons and longer sentences are being introduced to try to combat increases in crime. Consequently, the number of inmates in U.S. prisons jumped by a record 7.3 percent during the first six months of 1989 to a total of 673,565, the highest rate of increase recorded during the sixty-four years the government has counted prisoners. As already stated, by 1993, over 900,000 men and women were being held in federal and state prisons in the United States. Most penologists and social workers have questions about these developments; they maintain that the certainty of punishment and rehabilitation are usually more effective than the severity of punishment.

Stiffening of penalties and punishments is illustrated by the move to shift more juvenile delinquency violations from juvenile courts to regular adult courts for processing. Another example of "getting tougher in places where a crime-weary public seems bent on vengeance" is the "return of the chain gang"[14] in some penal institutions. In Alabama, for example, the state is buying leg shackles for 300 inmates who will pick up roadside litter.

## *Parole Activities*

Most youths and adults who spend time in correctional institutions leave on parole. This means that they are released to a person who meets with them periodically and endeavors to help them. Social workers are used in this challenging position. Again, a social worker in such a position can be a most valuable anchor to a person who has an inadequate place to go or a family that really does not want him or her. A parole officer can not only support and sustain a person but can work with the family, helping to bring about changes in the total constellation that are helpful to all concerned.

## Citizenry Involvement

Illustrative of the interest of leaders and responsible citizens in relation to the problems of crime and delinquency has been the effort extended by the Chamber of Commerce of the United States. In 1972 they issued a booklet entitled *Marshaling Citizen Power to Modernize Corrections,* which made a strong plea for new programs "making use of community approaches to corrections as alternatives to incarceration, and also as a means of facilitating reintegration of the offender back into the community following a release from an institution."

They stressed that community corrections can be "cheaper and more humane." They described several types of community and traditional release programs that have demonstrated value in rehabilitating offenders and reducing social costs of recidivism, among which are pretrial intervention, probation, halfway houses, work release programs, prerelease centers, and parole.

## Youth Services Systems

One of the 200 recommendations of the President's Commission on Law Enforcement and Administration of Justice related to the establishment of community correctional services. The Commission recommended that every community should consider establishing a Youth Service Bureau, "a community-based center to which juveniles could be referred by the police, the courts, parents, schools, and social agencies for counseling, education, work, or recreation programs and job placement" that would be "an agency to handle many troubled and troublesome young people outside the criminal system."

Gemignani discusses a national strategy for the prevention and reduction of juvenile delinquency. The broad plans of the strategy were developed at a meeting called by the Youth Development Delinquency Prevention Administration in early 1970. Within the first two years twenty-three pilot programs were launched throughout the nation. The thrust was described as follows:

> The strategy calls for the establishment, nationwide, of youth services systems which will divert youth, insofar as possible, from the juvenile justice system by providing comprehensive, integrated, community-based programs designed to meet the needs of all youth, regardless of who they are or what their individual problems may be.[15]

A current example of an agency under this youth services system is a Youth Service Center in a metropolitan area. It is an agency planned to be an advocate for youth and the family and is located in the city proper. It aims "to divert or offer alternative programs so the young people do not become involved with the juvenile justice system." The Youth Services Center (YSC) provides coordination and cooperation with all social agencies in the county in an effort to offer opportunities for each young person or family to overcome their problems. The service is open to any young person or family upon their request or from referral from law enforcement or other agencies; it is especially helpful for youth involved in status offenses. The agency does everything it can to help the child or the family in an informal, friendly manner. Social workers are on the staff. Action may result in any of the following: release with no follow-up, release with YSC counseling, referral to "cluster management," placement in a YSC receiving home, or detention placement. The service is open to youths and families twenty-four hours a day, seven days a week. YSC often helps young people to gain employment.

Gemignani describes a typical example of how a youth services system may actually work in practice:

> In this case the mayor's office is the grantee agency. The boy is a school dropout with no job skills, and he is estranged from his family, and experiencing the effects of an overdose of LSD. He refuses traditional professional help. However, he comes in contact with the project when he calls its youth-manned Hotline, reporting that he is on LSD and wants to talk to someone about his problem. A sympathetic youth talks him into visiting the Hotline's adjunct drug crisis center. The center finds the youth to be under heavy influence of LSD. An ex-addict counselor is brought in to help the youth accept hospitalization. Within a few days of intensive contact with the ex-addict, the young man decides to accept some professional help.
>
> A plan is developed with him by the social worker at the center. It includes counseling for both him and his family; tutoring to prepare him for a GED (tests for general educational development); prevocational training; and the removal of now-unwanted tattoos from his hands. The counseling is rendered by the social worker at the center. The system's central information retrieval bank shows that the parents are already being seen by a local private agency and communication on the case is established with that agency. Tutorial services for the GED are supplied by a teacher from the local school assigned to work at the center. The prevocational training is rendered in the facilities of the local department of employment. The tattoo removal takes place in the plastic surgery clinic of a local private hospital, improving the youth's appearance and self-confidence.
>
> As a result of the counseling program, the young man is able to understand his problems and begin to do something about them. Although a reconciliation with his family is unsuccessful, a suitable independent living arrangement is made in a local boarding house. He is eventually awarded a GED. He gains some vocational skills and through the cooperation of the local chapter of the Junior Chamber of Commerce is placed on a job. In this case, the young man continues his relationship with the program following his rehabilitation. He donates two nights a week to answering the Hotline telephone—a service to others that returns great satisfaction to him.[16]

## The Halfway House

Since the 1960s a major surge has developed in providing halfway houses in the field of corrections for adults and youths, particularly for children and youths. A place "halfway" between the institution and the community, developed historically in the area of mental health, is being used in many communities, particularly in populated centers.

A halfway house in corrections, which often utilizes social workers as administrators or as staff workers, may be used in two ways: to help those about "halfway out" of an institution or to help those about "halfway in." A halfway house may be utilized for a youth or an adult who has been in a detention home, youth development center, or a prison as a major step toward the community and total freedom. It is also being used as a place, particularly for children, to be housed in lieu of going to a formalized institution. It is a valid attempt to rehabilitate and prevent difficulties rather than to punish.

The philosophy of the halfway house is reflected by Rachin in the following:

> The Halfway House is intended to meet a need for client services between highly supervised, well structured, institutional programs and relatively free community living. In its popular function the halfway house has been a kind of decompression chamber through which institutional releases are helped to avoid the social-psychological bends of a too rapid reinvolvement in the real world.
>
> . . . The need for short-circuiting unnecessary institutional commitment has led to the development of the "halfway-in" house. Utilized primarily at this time for youth, treatment considerations and responsibility-oriented, reality-bound programming have been the hallmarks of these facilities. In addition to its traditional function, then, the halfway house can provide a means for diverting people from the institutional mill, which, as so many have pointed out, has more often harmed than helped.[17]

## *Prevention*

Social workers are becoming more and more interested in preventive aspects of delinquency and crime. Philosophically, they believe that if more time and talent can be put into preventing antisocial behavior in the first place, society, as well as individuals and families, will be much better off. Prevention has many sides to it and involves all of the helping disciplines. Education is particularly important. Several studies show that there are many boys and girls in school who are near-delinquent and who will get into trouble if something is not done to help them solve their problems and adjust better to school, their families, and life in general. Marriage and family counseling, particularly premarital counseling, is another avenue that seems to be promising in preventing social ills.

Classes on parenting are becoming popular in public and private educational programs as well as in community-sponsored offerings. Social workers are being employed as key teachers in many of these programs. These classes aim to strengthen parent-child relationships and to reduce and prevent anti-social behavior.

Recreational activities and clubs can be utilized for prevention where there is proper leadership. An example was in the city of Battle Creek, Michigan, where in one dilapidated area the police arrested each year an average of 135 of the 450 boys and girls who called it home. Through the efforts of an energetic, enthusiastic police chief and other community and professional leaders, a clubhouse was built in this area. During the next twenty-two months not a single boy or girl from this poor neighborhood landed behind bars. There are many other kinds of challenging activities open to those who would like to work toward reducing and preventing antisocial behavior.

The President's Commission stressed the importance of prevention. In fact, it listed the following as the first objectives that need to be vigorously pursued:

First, society must seek to prevent crime before it happens by assuring all Americans a stake in the benefits and responsibilities of American life, by strengthening law enforcement, and by reducing criminal opportunities.[18]

The President's Commission explained its position further:

The prevention of crime covers a wide range of activities: eliminating social conditions closely associated with crime; improving the ability of the criminal justice system to detect, apprehend, judge, and reintegrate into their communities those who commit crimes; and reducing the situations in which crimes are most likely to be committed.

Every effort must be made to strengthen the family, now often shattered by the grinding pressures of urban slums.

Slum schools must be given enough resources to make them as good as schools elsewhere and to enable them to compensate for the various handicaps suffered by the slum child—to rescue him or her from his or her environment. . . .

Employment opportunities must be enlarged and young people provided with more effective vocational training and individual job counseling.[19]

An encouraging example along the prevention path was the National Symposium on Addressing Violent Crime Through Community Involvement, which was sponsored by the FBI and held at the FBI Academy in Quantico, Virginia, October 16–17, 1991. This was the first such gathering of civic leaders and law enforcement officials by the FBI on a national level. It helped establish many important lines of communication essential to cooperative prevention and reduction of violent crime. Such statements as the following surfaced: "Using the combined resources of the police department and social agencies can go a long way in addressing crime" and "in order to get a handle on violence—the police must form working partnerships within the community.[20]

## *Summary*

*Juvenile delinquency and crime are major problems in modern society. Four social processes utilized in modern administration of criminal justice are law enforcement, prosecution and defense, judicial process, and corrections.*

*Social work has a major contribution to make in the control and prevention of juvenile delinquency and crime. Social work attempts to help the individual, family, and the community to face*

*and solve delinquency and crime problems through utilization of individual, family, and community resources. The social worker in corrections works with individuals, groups, and communities. The social worker helps particularly with police departments, courts, probation, institutions, parole, youth service systems, halfway houses, and prevention. The social worker is really just beginning to tap individual and com-*

munity resources in the control and prevention of delinquency and crime. As alternatives to incarceration are developed and sound community treatment programs become common practice, more professional social workers will be asked to share the responsibility of providing improved professional service.

## Selected References

"A Symposium on the Causes and Correlates of Juvenile Delinquency," *The Journal of Criminal Law and Criminology,* 82 (Spring 1991), 1–118.

BERGSMANN, ILENE R., "The Forgotten Few: Juvenile Female Offenders," *Federal Probation,* 53 (March 1989), 73–78.

BRENNAN, THOMAS, P., AMY E. GEDRICH, SUSAN E. JACOBY, MICHAEL J. TARDY, and KATHERINE B. TYSON, "A Vision for Probation and Court Services, Forensic Social Work: Practice and Vision," *Federal Probation,* 51 (March 1987), 63–70.

CARTER, DIANNE, "The Status of Education and Training in Corrections," *Federal Probation,* 55 (June 1991), 17–23.

CUMMINGS, SCOTT, and DANIEL J. MONTI, *Gangs: The Origins and Impacts of Contemporary Youth Gangs in the United States.* Albany: State University of New York Press, 1993.

EISENBERG, MICHAEL, and GREGORY MARKLEY, "Something Works in Community Supervision," *Federal Probation,* 51 (December 1987), 28–32.

LYNCH, RUFUS SYLVESTER, and JACQUELYN MITCHELL, "Justice System Advocacy: A Must for NASW and the Social Work Community," *Social Work,* 40 (January 1995), 9–12.

MASON, MARY ANN, "Social Workers as Expert Witnesses in Child Sexual Abuse Cases," *Social Work,* 37 (January 1992), 30–34.

MASON, MARY ANN, "The McMartin Case Revisited: The Conflict between Social Work and Criminal Justice," *Social Work,* 36 (September 1991), 391–395.

MILLS, DARRELL K., "Career Issues for Probation Officers," *Federal Probation,* 54 (September 1990), 3–7.

SCHWARTZ, SANFORD, and HERMAN V. WOOD, "Clinical Assessment and Intervention with Shoplifters," *Social Work,* 36 (May 1991), 234–238.

SEVERSON, MARGARET M., "Adapting Social Work Values to the Corrections Environment," *Social Work,* 39 (July 1994), 451–456.

SOLOMON, PHYLLIS, and JEFFREY DRAINE, "Issues in Serving the Forensic Client," *Social Work,* 40 (January 1995), 25–33.

TREGER, HARVEY, "Police Social Work," in *Encyclopedia of Social Work,* 19th ed., Vol. III. Washington, DC: NASW Press, 1995, pp. 1843–1848.

UMBREIT, MARK S., "Crime Victims and Offenders in Mediation: An Emerging Area of Social Work Practice," *Social Work,* 38 (January 1993), 69–73.

## Notes

1. *Crime in the United States—1993* (Washington, DC: FBI, U.S. Department of Justice, 1994), p. 58.

2. Dennis W. Nielsen, "U.S. Probation Officers as Jail Monitors: A New Responsibility on the Horizon," *Federal Probation,* 48 (September 1984), 29.

3. Daniel D. Smith, Terrence Finnegan, and Howard H. Snyder, *Delinquency 1977, United States Estimates of Cases Processed by Courts with Juvenile Jurisdiction* (Pittsburgh, PA: National Center for Juvenile Justice, 1980), p. 7.

4. Thomas A. Regulus, "Gang Violence," in *Encyclopedia of Social Work,* 19th ed., Vol. II (Washington, DC: NASW Press, 1995), p. 1050.

5. Elliot Studt, *Education for Social Workers in the Correctional Field,* Curriculum Study V (New York: Council on Social Work Education, 1959), p. 7.

6. Ibid., p. 6.

7. Robert L. Barker, *The Social Work Dictionary,* 3rd ed. (Washington, DC: NASW Press, 1995), pp. 81–82.

8. Studt, op cit., p. 7.

9. Ibid., p. 47.

10. For interesting analyses regarding short-term contacts, see Joseph R. Silver, "Social Case-work in Jail," *The Prison Journal,* 39 (October 1959), 51–55; also Harvey Treger, Doug Thomson, and Gordon Sloan Jaeck, "A Police-Social Work Team Model," *Crime and Delinquency,* 20 (July 1974), 281–290.

11. Chris W. Eskridge, "Education and Training of Probation Officers: A Critical Assessment," *Federal Probation,* 43 (September 1979), 48.

12. Sol Gothard, "Power in the Court: The Social Worker as an Expert Witness," *Social Work,* 34 (January 1989), 65.

13. Margaret M. Severson, "Adapting Social Work Values to the Corrections Environment," *Social Work,* 39 (July 1994), 453.

14. *U.S. News & World Report,* March 13, 1995.

15. Robert J. Gemignani, "Youth Services System," *Federal Probation,* 36 (December 1972), 48.

16. Ibid., p. 51.

17. Richard L. Rachin, "So You Want to Open a Halfway House," *Federal Probation,* 36 (March 1972), 30.

18. *The Challenge of Crime in a Free Society* (Washington, DC; U.S. Government Printing Office, 1967), p. vi.

19. Ibid.

20. Lee P. Brown, "Violent Crime and Community Involvement," *FBI Law Enforcement Bulletin,* 61 (May 1992), 2–5; and "Focus on Community Partnerships," *FBI Law Enforcement Bulletin,* 61 (May 1992), 12–13.

# *Occupational Social Work*

*Because of chronic absenteeism, Mr. A. was threatened with being fired from his job. Fortunately for him, he was employed by Kennecott Corporation, which maintained an INSIGHT (social work) program for its employees.*

*In the initial interview Mr. A., who was 52 years old, revealed that while he had been drinking for 30 years he had never accepted the fact that he had an alcohol problem. On several occasions during his 28 years of employment, his supervisors had suggested he become involved in an alcoholism recovery program, but it was not until his job was in jeopardy that he was willing to accept this suggestion.*

*Since Mr. A. had had no previous involvement with treatment he was sent to the Alcohol and Drug Abuse Clinic at the University of Utah for professional evaluation and recommendations for treatment.*

*Like many alcoholics, Mr. A. found that his quest for sobriety was long and difficult. Through the INSIGHT program he and his wife and children became involved in therapy both individually and in groups. Through this involvement he was able to view his alcoholism realistically and bring it under control. The family benefitted also through the help they received with marital, financial, and legal problems.[1]*

Social work in the work place is on the cutting edge of practice. Several businesses and industries, large and small, have introduced social workers into their personnel systems to help employees and their families with personal, family, and community problems. There has been a duality of purpose in mind: humanitarianism and more efficient and effective production. It has been recognized that employees who are bogged down with personal and family problems will likely not produce optimally on the job. One answer is for social workers to help workers and their families understand their problems, face them, and solve them.

## *Definition*

Akabas offers a general, current definition of occupational social work as "policies and services, delivered through the auspices of employers and trade unions, to workers and to those who seek entry into the workplace."[2]

Occupational social work, according to Barker, is the:

provision of professional *human services* in the *workplace* through such employer-funded programs as *employee assistance programs* (EAPs) and occupational *alcoholism* programs. The goal is to help employees meet their human and social work needs by providing services . . . and dealing with emotional problems, social relationship conflicts, and other personal problems. Occupational social work can be involved in *Macro Practice* (such as organizational interventions on behalf of employee groups) as well as individual clinical activities. Many social workers use the term synonymously with *industrial social work.*[3]

Akabas observes that:

Two organizational auspices—employers and labor unions—sponsor workplace programs. These institutional arrangements and the programs they finance are exquisite in their diversity. Employing organizations number more than 4 million in the United States. . . . More than 100 labor unions, representing approximately 14 percent of the labor force, cover workers in the for-profit, nonprofit, and government sectors.[4]

## Background

The roots for social work in the workplace reach into the past. Jorgensen suggests that "social work in industry seems to have forgotten its industrial ancestry. The profession apparently owes its name to industry. The first American usages of the term 'social work' in 1892 and 1893 seem to be direct translations of the German 'arbeiten sozial.' This referred to housing, canteens, health care and other amenities provided to workers by Krupp munitions plants (among others) for the purposes of supporting and stabilizing the industrial work force. Hence, social work complemented industrial work. Industry served as society's means of goal attainment while social work served as a means of integration."[5]

Jorgensen indicates that "industrial social work has existed as a licensed occupation in France and Germany since World War I even in wartime. Peru, India, and the Netherlands, among other nations, also possess large numbers of industrial social workers. . . . By contrast, industrial social work developed between 1890 and 1920 in the United States and England and, after that, was largely dormant until a decade ago."[6]

During World War II, there were federally sponsored social work programs for the National Maritime Union and United Seaman's Service. By the spring of 1943, more than 5,000 of the union's members had been killed at sea by planes and submarines. Their families frequently needed help in making claims for death, injuries, or losses, procuring ration books, locating sailors who were stranded in foreign ports, and in assisting bereaved families. A director and seven caseworkers with master's degrees in social work were employed, acceptable by the union because they were members of the Social Services Employees' Union. The project was highly successful but was terminated in 1947 when war mobilization ended.

Schools of social work in recent years have been instrumental in developing a field of practice in industry and the workplace. An innovative effort was begun in 1964 when a joint grant from the National Institute of Mental Health and the Rehabilitation Services Administration launched a project which was operated by the Columbia University School of Social Work and the Sidney Hillman Health Center, a union-operated facility. Dr. Hyman Weiner initiated this project and developed the Industrial Social Welfare Center at Columbia University. This center offered courses and student placements and conducted research and demonstration projects.

Another prominent example of industrial social work is at Boston College School of Social Work, where Professors Fidelia A. Masi and Bradley Googins in 1975 developed courses and field placements. Industries involved in the placement program have included Northeastern Bell Telephone, Hanscom Air Force Base, Boston College, J. F. Kennedy Federal Center, and the Taukton Consortium (which consisted of ten small industries).

Since 1965, the Graduate School of Social Work at the University of Utah has placed students in industrial settings for field practice and has utilized such firms as Kennecott Copper Company, U.S. Steel, Mountain Bell Telephone, and the First Security Bank. A recent innovation provided for student training with the Federal Aviation Administration, offering services for employees and families related to the Salt Lake International Airport and other western flying facilities.

Alcoholism has been one of the major problems of concern in business and industry and social work has been invited on various occasions to use its skills and resources to help treat and prevent this problem. Heyman reported that several nationally known firms have been pioneers in the employee-sponsored programs for helping with alcoholism in employ-

**FIGURE 15.1**

ees.[7] The companies include duPont, Allis-Chalmers, Eastman Kodak, and Consolidated Edison of New York. Throughout the nation management and labor have slowly become aware that alcoholic employees could be aided through constructive action. Heyman indicated "there may be one thousand companies with some kind of program for their alcoholic employees."[8] Social workers are just beginning to participate in such programs yet their role is an important one, particularly in the development and use of a wide range of community resources that can be tapped for assistance in resolving such problems.

Jorgensen suggests there have been three predominant means through which social work has appeared in industry: graduate schools' field placements, family service agencies' contracting with business and industry, and private practitioners' making contracts with industry.[9] The first, begun in 1964 in the Industrial Social Welfare Center at Columbia University, has provided placements in a variety of businesses and industries. The second means developed through family service agencies making individual contracts with business and industry. Examples of this were Xerox Corporation in Rochester and Maywood Corporation in Amarillo, in which organizations made specific contracts to have counseling services provided for their employees. Eimco and Sperry Rand in Salt Lake City have contracted with the Family Counseling Service, a United Way Agency, to provide services for their employees.

In 1980 Xerox Corporation and the Family Service Association of America (FSAA) announced they had joined forces to design and implement a nationwide program, the first of its kind, to help Xerox employees and family members deal with individual and family problems.[10] A unique feature of the arrangement was the involvement of FSAA's affiliates throughout the United States as the designated centers for assessment of problems of Xerox employees and/or family members. Xerox Corporation and FSAA have contracted that FSAA will develop agreements with member agencies situated in localities near the more than 140 Xerox offices and facilities in the United States. Under the agreement, member agencies will "tender assessment/diagnostic service to employees and/or family members who are referred by Xerox or seek help on their own."

A third means has been a route illustrated by Otto F. Jones, formerly of Kennecott Copper, who created Human Affairs, Inc., a private counseling corporation. This organization has made contracts with U.S. Steel plants in South Chicago and in Provo, Utah, with the Valley Bank in Phoenix, and many other firms, to provide counseling for their employees.

Philosophically, there are many reasons for introducing social work practice in the workplace. Weiner, Akabas, and Sommer share some of these as follows:

> The new professional stance is based on the concept that treatment is as much a contribution of the industrial institution as it is a function of clinical input. Modesty is the hallmark of the professional who can enlist industrial representatives as genuine partners, not as "mother's little helpers." This new professional stance requires an individual who can mobilize resources and connect people up with institutions and still feel satisfaction from his work; who can offer concrete services and still feel pride in his professional identity; who can function as a consultant and still feel he is a practitioner.
>
> A new professional technology is necessary at the same time. As the new professional stance requires a modesty of person, the new professional technology requires a modesty of goals. Changes in the intrapsychic makeup of the individual

are sought only in relation to those dimensions which impinge on his functional ability. The clinician, therefore, must be extremely competent and flexible and able to tune in quickly to the patient's problem, how it interlocks with the work world, and what parties can play a significant role in resolution. An important element of the new technology is the diagnostic process itself."[11]

Jorgensen suggests that the social worker in the workplace has been tried and is being tried in a variety of settings. She points out that many large companies have social workers providing direct services or helping in advising in training and management, either as full-time employees or as outside consultants.[12] She gives numerous examples, illustrated by the following brief descriptions of social work programs in large companies:

1. A New York City transit company has provided services for the alcoholic worker for nearly 20 years.
2. U.S. Steel's program in Chicago has 11,000 employees and includes preventive treatment, direct services, consultation, and training.
3. A large bank in Tucson, Arizona, with 6,000 employees and an electronics manufacturer in Phoenix with 5,000 employees have included social services under their standard benefits.
4. Polaroid Corporation in Boston has been offering social work services to its employees for nearly 20 years. Its counseling department, started in 1958 with a part-time social work consultant, presently includes four full-time social workers with MSW degrees who serve nearly 12,000 employees, including managers and line workers.
5. More than 7,300 employees of Utah Copper Division, Kennecott Copper Corporation, are served by a social work program called INSIGHT. This program assists both employees and dependents. In ten years of operation the program has been used by more than 5,500 people, about half employees and half dependents. Problems have included family, alcohol, legal matters, marriage, financial, and drug abuse.

## *Educational Developments*

The Council on Social Work Education (CSWE) in May 1976 sponsored a meeting with practitioners, educators, representatives of organized labor and industry along with an NASW staff member to discuss social work practice in business and industry.[13] Participants in this meeting recognized the need for many programs of social work education to consider curriculum implications for future developments in social work employment in industry. CSWE and NASW joined together in a cooperative effort to develop further education and practice in industrial social work.

Through the initial project studies, four schools of social work were identified as having established specializations in industrial social work: Boston College, Columbia University, Hunter College, and the University of Utah. Several other schools were also offering some classes or other experiences in this relatively new field.

On June 7, 1978, a hundred industrial social work practitioners from across the United States and Canada met in New York City to discuss, debate, explore, and examine the nature of industrial social work practice and the settings in which it currently takes place. "The conference was an historic first—practitioners in this evolving professional arena had not previously come together—and conferees experienced the stimulation and exhilaration of celebrants at a rite of passage."[14] Highlights from the conference summary reflect current interests and potential functions for social work in industry in the years ahead:

> The conferees concluded that the future is promising for the growth and explanation of industrial social work practice. Indeed, it was noted that social work is uniquely suited to the labor and industrial setting, given the profession's commitment to a "social functioning" perspective, as opposed to a health versus illness approach common to other helping professions. Moreover, the social worker's comfort with a psychosocial framework for assessing situations is particularly compatible in these settings, since it gives respect to the central role of environment in influencing human behavior. The strong emphasis on values in social work complements such a person-in-situation frame of reference and provides a professional benchmark in assessment that honors both client and organizational need.
>
> Above all, it was noted that social work as a profession holds a dual commitment to social service and social change, which best meets the multifaceted interests of trade union or employer sponsorship....
>
> The Conference established the goodness of fit between social work practice and the service needs of workplace populations, settings, and auspices. The possibilities for the future seem unlimited—bounded only by the availability of appropriately trained professional personnel and the openness of the workplace to incorporate these professional services.[15]

The joint project of the Council on Social Work Education and the National Association of Social Workers on social work in industrial settings (March 1977–October 1979) represented a major commitment by the profession to further the development of industrial social work education and practice. The final report, issued in March 1980, included the following selected recommendations:

To CSWE:

1. The curriculum policy statement for graduate education should include a requirement that content on the significance of work and work institutions be included in the *core* graduate curriculum.
2. Industrial social work should be considered a subject of the specialization area—economics/world of work.
3. *Training for practice in industrial social work should be at the Masters level and beyond.*
4. Continuing education for industrial social work practice should be a primary component of a total industrial social work education program.

To NASW:

1. The Board of Directors of NASW is asked to appoint an ad hoc task force as a first step in the development of a practice specialty group.
2. NASW should develop a national clearing house on industrial social work as part of an ongoing full time staff role.[16]

## *Need for Social Work in the Workplace*

Social workers and others differ considerably on the need for social workers in the workplace. Many affirmatively maintain that this emerging field is one of the most important for the profession. They emphasize the U.S. Department of Labor statistics that 64 percent of the population sixteen years of age and over, nearly 114 million people (1984) were in the civilian labor force—121,000,000 in 1993—and that if social workers are really going to serve humanity, this is one arena that provides golden opportunities for social work services. A few visionary social workers even suggest that by the turn of the century there may be more social workers employed in business and industry than in all other areas of service put together.

### *Basic Services Provided*

Social work traditionally has worked with disadvantaged persons. Counseling and therapy with individuals and families have been the bulwark of this service. Such services are much needed in the workplace. Actually, most of these social services in business and industry are offered to individuals or their families—a direct service approach. An effort is made to help individuals, employers—and often, their families—to understand their problems in social relationships, face the problems, consider alternatives, and move ahead with action that seems best for their solution.

In recent years two additional services have come to the fore: prevention and enrichment. In 1959, the classic curriculum study of the Council on Social Work Education mentioned that prevention was one of three basic functions of social work practice. Attempts are being made in most social work settings and agencies today to push ahead on this front. The basic premise is that if efforts can prevent problems from happening there will be significant savings in the lives of people, as well as financially. Many social workers in business and industry are actively using their skills to prevent or reduce such problems as alcoholism, drug abuse, and family or marital conflicts.

An even more recent development has been the introduction into the workplace settings of a focus on enrichment in living. This action is based on the premise that nearly all persons and families can taste of life and enjoy life more than they are at present, even though most are proceeding at a meaningful pace. It is possible with increased knowledge and abilities for individuals and families to expand and deepen relationships and their meanings.

Enrichment may be provided in individual counseling, family counseling, or on a broader level. For example, one large corporation sponsored a series of noonday lectures for employees who wished to attend with topics such as the following presented by specialists: Conflicts in Marriage, Parenting, Human Sexuality, Handling Crises, and Understanding Your Emotions. Fifty to seventy-five employees attended each of these sessions and evaluations were positive.

Another contribution of social work in the workplace is with older adults who are healthy and are interested in continuing working. Mor-Barak and Tynan[17] suggest several areas for aiding elderly workers, including: advocacy, linking older job seekers with interested employers, advising companies on work arrangements and training programs, and counseling older workers and their families.

# Social Work Methods

All of the traditional social work methods are utilized in workplace settings including case-work, group work, community organization, research, and administration. Much of social work practice, so far, has been in clinical or direct practice, but utilization of the other methods is on the increase.

## Casework

Most social work services in workplace settings are based on clinical or direct practice, working mainly with individuals and/or families. Individual problems include a wide variety such as alcohol, drug abuse, depression, anxiety, inferiority feelings, and marital and family difficulties including child or spouse abuse. The social workers often work directly with employees or members of their families. At other times they make referrals to appropriate agencies in the community. The basic philosophy for industrial clinical practice is that if a person is upset individually or family-wise, he or she may not be an effective employee. Numerous examples reflect that employees who have received casework help from social workers have been able to perform better on the job. This approach usually involves a series of interviews, often weekly, for about an hour. Often the client and the therapist make a tentative agreement about the number of interviews that will take place between them.

## Group Work

Group work, the method or process of working with problems in social relationships, utilizes the group as the therapeutic tool. In industrial settings, groups are meeting more often than previously under the direction of qualified social work practitioners. Groups of eight to twelve persons with a problem in common meet weekly for an hour or two to consider problems, share feelings and experiences, plan together, and help each other. Other groups may involve five or six couples who are having marital difficulty, who again use a similar approach to try to understand their problems, face them, and work them through. Group interaction can be a powerful tool in helping people to understand themselves and improve their human relationships.

## Community Organization

Community organization, a process which taps and ties together community resources, is being utilized by many businesses and industries. Social workers in these settings can and do make referrals to specific agencies in the community that are specialized and that can assist with particular kinds of individual or family problems. Social workers are also used as consultants to help businesses plan, coordinate, and integrate their total services in working with employees, particularly in relation to social services and humanitarian interests.

Again, social workers help businesses to understand the total community in which they live, utilize its resources, and benefit the community as well as their own organization. They are helpful in assisting executives to understand more about community social problems, legislation, and other actions that may strengthen the community. Community consciousness and community development are becoming well known and more meaningful to both management and labor as a result of the skills and services of professional social workers.

## Research

Research, the process of ascertaining facts and truth, is being utilized by social workers in industrial settings. Focus is on a variety of problems. The aim is to help businesses or industries understand realities in employer-employee relationships, their problems, and actions that may be taken to alleviate them including studying relationships between supervisors and employees with the goal to improve these for the benefit of all.

## Administration

Social work administration is the process of translating social policies into services. In business and industry it is an attempt to translate industrial social policies and goals into action. Some social workers are hired in regular administrative positions in business and industry as a result of the impressions they have made and the abilities they have demonstrated. Others are used as consultants and advisors for management, labor, or both. Some social workers are in the center of helping with management/labor problems and relationships and are effectively assisting in this relatively new role.

A new technique, "shadow consultation,"[18] is being used by social workers with casework, group work, and administrative skills to help managers change their leadership and management behaviors, to become more effective and humane in their work. Such a social work consultant observes the manager during a typical day of work with meetings, conferences, and telephone calls. At the end of the day, they discuss feedback related to the "manager's effectiveness in relating to and directing his or her associates and team."

## Results

Although most businesses and industries are interested in social work programs because of humanitarianism, they also are interested because of the cost-effectiveness factor. They expect to receive financial benefits. A few studies have been made to evaluate job effectiveness of social work and counseling programs in the workplace with some positive results.

Illustrative of results of counseling in industry is a report from Kennecott Copper Corporation, Utah Copper Division.[19] This company studied a sample of 150 men who had been assisted through its social work program, many with marriage and family problems. They were observed on a before/after basis. Their absenteeism, costs of weekly indemnity, and hospital, medical, and surgical costs were calculated over a six-month period prior to their involvement with INSIGHT, the counseling service, and compared with similar calculations made immediately after a six-month period of participation in the program. "Findings indicated that after an average of 12.7 months in INSIGHT, these 150 men improved their attendance by 52.0 percent; decreased their weekly indemnity costs by 74.6 percent; and decreased their hospital, medical, and surgical costs by 55.4 percent."

Rodney C. Brown, pastoral counselor for R. J. Reynolds Tobacco Company, Winston-Salem, North Carolina, indicates that across four years of providing counseling services for their employees, including marriage and family counseling services, it is estimated that about 55 percent of those with drinking problems have had noticeable improvement, based on satisfactory job performance and attendance, and that this figure has remained about constant during this time.

Although the results of counseling provided by the Valley National Bank of Phoenix, Arizona, are fragmentary, nevertheless preliminary surveys reflect some significant data.

A study of a twelve-month period from September 1972 to September 1973 of 700 Valley Bankers (350 users of CONTACT—counseling service—and 350 nonusers) reflected that the medical-surgical insurance cost was cut 74 percent from what it was before CONTACT usage.[20] The report indicated: "This obvious decrease in insurance claims enables CONTACT to more than justify its benefits to the employees' mental and physical well-being. It also enables CONTACT to financially justify its existence since it shows that its intervention has reduced the use of the insurance package."

The study further reflected that absenteeism for CONTACT users for sick leave was as follows:

|  | Hours | Cost |
|---|---|---|
| Before using CONTACT | 71.83 | $308.16 |
| After using CONTACT | 61.04 | 261.08 |
| Difference | 10.79 (15.0%) | 47.08 (15.3%) |

Gould describes several counseling programs in the industrial arena and includes the following data: General Motors calculates a return of almost $3 for each dollar provided in their counseling program, which resulted in an estimated savings of $37 million in 1980.[21] With 24,000 employees, Ohio Bell saved $4 million annually with a 60 percent recovery rate in its alcoholism treatment program. Of employees referred by their supervisors to AT&T's Employee Assistance Program for poor work performance, 85 percent were no longer considered poor performers after their treatment.

One of the pioneers in introducing social work into business and industry was Otto Jones,[22] a social worker who was the creator and president of Human Affairs International, Inc., a Salt Lake City–based company with offices in 50 states and 15 foreign countries, with annual revenues of more than $8.5 million.

Jones's staff of social workers and psychologists (800 full- and part-time counselors) provided services for such firms as IBM, Exxon, U.S. Steel, Procter & Gamble, and Kodak. The company operated overseas in Europe, Japan and the Pacific Islands, counseling with American-based companies with foreign offices. The total operation worked with about 3 million employees around the world.

Jones has suggested that he and his associates are in the "people maintenance" business and that they help with family problems, employment difficulties, drug abuse and many other personal problems.

When the stock market crash occurred in October 1987, many people consulted social workers to handle their feelings and fears. Stress-reduction workshops, for example, heavily staffed by social workers, were organized in Miami, Florida, for stockbrokers and other financial professionals.[23]

Ramanathan did a study of employee-assistance program (EAP) services in relation to personal stress and productivity, in a hospital in a moderate-sized midwestern city.[24] He found that although personal stress and employee productivity are related, employee-assistance program interventions improved employee productivity without reducing employee stress. He also emphasized the need for empirical research to learn more about occupational social work results.

## Women in the Workplace

Both men and women are employed in business and industry in social work positions; both are making innovative and substantive contributions, aiding individual workers and their families and benefiting firms in production and humanitarian efforts. At the same time, it is clearly evident that women social workers as a whole are discriminated against. Sexism does exist in many workplaces.

For example, salary information from a 1971–72 survey of members of the National Association of Social Workers (NASW) indicated that women received less compensation than men for their services. Although 39 percent of the men reported an income of $16,000 or more, only 20 percent of the single women were in the same salary range. More than 50 percent of the currently married women earned less than $12,000 a year, compared to 36 percent of the single women and 18 percent of the men.[25]

Women are discriminated against in other ways also. They do not receive their share of administrative appointments in business and industry or in most other social work settings. Differentials exist even in relation to sexual harassment on the job. Maypole reports that in a cross-sectional survey of 50 percent of the members of the Iowa chapter of the National Association of Social Workers, 27 percent of the women and men surveyed reported they had experienced sexual harassment at work.[26] A gender differential was reported that indicated that over one-third of the women and only one-seventh of the men surveyed experienced such victimization.

In regard to administrative leadership, Jayaratne and Chess reported data collected from members of the National Association of Social Workers as part of a national survey on work stress and strain. The members were working full time, possessed MSW degrees, and identified themselves as administrators or as caseworkers. Although males comprised only 35.6 percent of the total sample, 52.8 percent of the administrators were male. In contrast, 74.1 percent of the caseworkers were female.[27]

Ozawa explains the cultural dilemma that exists in regard to women and careers:

> ...there seems to be a cultural schizophrenia in the United States which places women in a no-win situation. In an achievement-oriented society like ours, women are encouraged to succeed in their work but not to the extent they lose their femininity. If they fail in their work, they are not meeting their own standards of performance; if they succeed in it, they may not be living up to societal expectations regarding the role of women.[28]

A survey of NASW members in North Carolina was conducted in 1983 with a questionnaire mailed to a random sample of two hundred people. The results indicated that gender was a better predictor of salary than either job position, experience, or education. "When these three variables were controlled, males were found to earn an average of $5,645 more per year than females."[29]

Hanlan observes that "social work administration is generally perceived as a male role within a female profession." She suggests that the stereotypic habits and thinking need to be altered, and the following may be helpful: (1) firmly and unequivocally reject the notion that male administrative enclaves ought to be protected; (2) there should be specific training of women for managerial positions; and (3) thought should be given to the possibilities of differing career patterns and their applicability to managerial and administrative positions, to allow for differing backgrounds and preparation of women.[30]

## Training Social Work Students

Several schools of social work offer specialized emphasis and training in industrial settings. Students in these programs take their first or second year of field work in an industrial setting or both.

Students in industrial settings provide an excellent opportunity for executives, labor leaders, and others to learn firsthand about social work services. Learning experiences are provided in working with individuals, families, community activities, research, and administration. Some students provide direct services to employees and their families, individually or in groups. Other students, under the supervision of competent social work educators, help as consultants in developing programs for prevention of social problems and enrichment in family living. Professional social work today is optimistic about the development of social work practice in industrial settings although a few traditional social workers question the advisability of this development.

Jorgensen sent questionnaires to 150 social work practitioners in business and industrial settings, to 221 business leaders, and to 87 schools of social work.[31] The study revealed that 85 percent of the businesses contacted did not employ social workers and 70 percent indicated they did not plan to do so. The business leaders appeared to have no negative attitudes about social workers, "just little knowledge of their professional qualifications or experience with the potential impact on worker's needs and ultimately company productivity." She concluded that "there is an obvious need for communicating the potential and viability of social work practice in business and industry, not only to people in the world of work, but to schools of social work and professionals themselves."

## Establishing Social Work Services in Workplace Settings

Experiences in establishing social work services in industry and other workplace settings have been limited. However, several steps and suggestions have been found to be helpful including the following:

1. A professional relationship is essential. The social worker conveys the impression that here is a person who cares about people—the employees—and who wants to help strengthen the business.
2. An open friendly attitude is important. No force or pressure should be exerted.
3. Explaining potential economic benefits along with humanitarian contributions is a helpful approach.
4. A focus on specific personal and social problems can be effective, i.e., absenteeism, alcoholism, drug abuse, child abuse, and psychosomatic illnesses.
5. Sharing results of established social work programs is beneficial.
6. Follow through is important. Continued contacts and interest can bring desired results.
7. The importance of maintaining confidentiality of records and interviews should be stressed.
8. Contacts need to be made with top-level executives who have the power to make decisions and instigate social services.

## Summary

*Social work practice in the workplace is on the cutting edge of change in the profession. It appears to be a promising development, opening new channels for helping individuals, families, and communities. It provides a way in which millions of people may benefit from skills of social workers.*

*Professionally trained social workers are providing social services to a client group, workers, who heretofore have not been reached in large numbers. The employment and support of social workers by business and industry creates a promising opportunity for jobs and provision of social services. Executives are recognizing the values of social work services, both from humanitarian and cost-benefit points of view. The cooperation of industrial and labor leaders, social workers, and community agencies indicates there will be increased community coordination in both the delivery and the effective utilization of service. Social work education needs to adapt to this new thrust in providing innovative classwork experiences and field work placements.*

## Selected References

AKABAS, SHEILA H., "Occupational Social Work," in *Encyclopedia of Social Work,* 19th ed., Vol. III. Washington, DC: NASW Press, 1995, pp. 1779–1786.

AKABAS, SHEILA H., PAUL A. KURZMAN, and NANCY S. KOLBEN, eds., *Labor and Industrial Settings, Sites for Social Work Practice.* New York: Columbia University School of Social Work, Hunter College School of Social Work, Council on Social Work Education, National Association of Social Workers, 1979.

FORTUNE, ANNE E., and LOU LOENTAL HANKS, "Gender Inequities in Early Social Worker Careers," *Social Work,* 33 (May–June 1988), 221–226.

GOOGINS, BRADLEY, *Occupational Social Work: A Bibliography.* Silver Spring, MD: National Association of Social Workers, 1987.

GOULD, GARY M., "Developing Industrial Social Work Field Placements," *Journal of Education for Social Work,* 20 (Spring 1984), 35–42.

GOULD, GARY M., and MICHAEL LANE SMITH, *Social Work in the Workplace.* New York: Springer, 1988.

HAYNES, KAREN S., *Women Managers in Human Services.* New York: Springer, 1989.

KURZMAN, PAUL A., and SHEILA H. AKABAS, eds. *Work and Well-being: The Occupational Social Work Advantage.* Washington, DC: National Association of Social Workers, 1993.

MOR-BARAK, MICHÀL E. and MARGARET TYNAN, "Older Workers and the Workplace: A New Challenge for Occupational Social Work," *Social Work,* 38 (January 1993), 45–55.

RAMANATHAN, CHATHAPURAM S., "EAP's Response to Personal Stress and Productivity: Implications for Occupational Social Work," *Social Work,* 37 (May 1992), 234–239.

SAFFORD, FLORENCE, "Value of Gerontology for Occupational Social Work," *Social Work,* 33 (January–February 1988), 42–45.

STRAUSSNER, SHULAMITH LALA ASHENBERG, ed., *Occupational Social Work Today.* New York: The Haworth Press, 1990.

TEARE, ROBERT J., *National Survey of Occupational Social Workers.* Silver Spring, MD: National Association of Social Workers, 1987.

## *Notes*

1. Rex A. Skidmore, Daniel Balsam, and Otto F. Jones, "Social Work Practice in Industry," *Social Work,* 19 (May 1974), 283.

2. Sheila H. Akabas, "Occupational Social Work," in *Encyclopedia of Social Work,* 19th ed., Vol. III (Washington, DC: NASW Press, 1995), p. 1779.

3. Robert L. Barker, *The Social Work Dictionary,* 3rd ed. (Washington, DC: NASW Press, 1995), p. 260.

4. Sheila H. Akabas, op cit., p. 1779.

5. Lou Ann Birkbeck Jorgensen, *Social Work in Business and Industry,* unpublished DSW dissertation, Graduate School of Social Work, University of Utah, June 1979, p. 2.

6. Ibid.

7. Margaret M. Heyman, "Employer-Sponsored Programs for Problem Drinkers," *Social Casework,* 52 (November 1971), 548.

8. Ibid., p. 549.

9. Jorgensen, *Social Work in Business and Industry,* pp. 26–28.

10. Family Service Association of America, *Highlights,* 6 (March–April 1980), 1.

11. Hyman J. Weiner, Sheila H. Akabas, and John J. Sommer, *Mental Health Care in the World of Work* (New York: Association Press, 1973), p. 150.

12. Jorgensen, *Social Work in Business and Industry,* pp. 50–52.

13. Ibid., p. 8.

14. Akabas, Kurzman, and Kolben, *Labor and Industrial Settings,* p. 3.

15. Ibid., pp. 34–35.

16. Nancy S. Kolben, *Final Report,* CSWE/NASW *Project on Social Work in Industrial Settings* (New York: Council on Social Work Education, 1980), pp. 3–4.

17. Michal E. Mor-Barak and Margaret Tynan, "Older Workers and the Workplace: A New Challenge for Occupational Social Work," *Social Work,* 38 (January 1993), 45–55.

18. Hy Resnick and Josephine King, "Shadow Consultation: Intervention in Industry," *Social Work,* 30 (September–October 1985), 447–450.

19. Rex A. Skidmore, Daniel Balsam, and Otto F. Jones, "Social Work Practice in Industry," *Social Work,* 19 (May 1974), 282.

20. Information supplied by Joyce H. Vesper, Director, CONTACT, Valley National Bank, Phoenix, AZ.

21. Gary M. Gould, "Developing Industrial Social Work Field Placements," *Journal of Education for Social Work,* 20 (Spring 1984), 36.

22. *Deseret News,* June 1, 1986, p. M-3.

23. "Social Workers Counsel Brokers, Investors," NASW *News,* 33 (January 1988), 3.

24. Chathapuram S. Ramanathan, "EAP's Response to Personal Stress and Productivity: Implications for Occupational Social Work," *Social Work,* 37 (May 1992), 234.

25. David Fanshel, "Status Differentials: Men and Women in Social Work," *Social Work,* 21 (November 1976), 448–454.

26. Donald E. Maypole, "Sexual Harassment of Social Workers at Work: Injustice Within?" *Social Work,* 31 (January–February 1986), 32.

27. Srinika Jayaratne and Wayne A. Chess, "Job Satisfaction: A Comparison of Caseworkers and Administrators," *Social Work,* 31 (March–April 1986), 144.

28. Martha N. Ozawa, "Women and Work," *Social Work,* 21 (November 1976), 458.

29. Reginald O. York, H. Carl Henley, and Dorothy N. Gamble, "Sexual Discrimination in Social Work: Is It Salary or Advancement?" *Social Work,* 32 (July–August 1987), 336.

30. Mary S. Hanlan, "Women in Social Work Administration: Current Role Strains," *Administration in Social Work,* 1 (Fall 1977), 259–265.

31. Jorgensen, *Social Work in Business and Industry,* pp. v–vi.

$C\ h\ a\ p\ t\ e\ r$ *16*

# Services for the Aged

*"What have you fed your immortal soul today?" was a question my father repeatedly asked me when I was young. I adored my father and wanted to please him, so I always tried to learn something worthwhile during the day. As I grew older I would think of that question as I got into bed each night and recall what I had read that day. If I had read nothing of value, I would get up and read from the Scriptures or passages from my literature books, often memorizing the lines. The values and standards I learned from my books have been a guide all my life, and have helped me understand myself and my associates.*

*Now that I am nearing my 90th year, the infirmities of age have overtaken me, and my eyes no*

*longer let me read books I love so much. My hearing is so poor that I cannot listen to them on records. I have to depend on what I learned earlier. I think of the characters in literature, and the ideas and concepts expressed in the Scriptures; they are part of me and sustain me as I live alone, giving me the support I need to live at peace with myself. Although I no longer can give to others I try to maintain a serene attitude, for I remember the teachings of Plato: "He who is of a calm and happy nature will hardly feel the pressure of age, but to him who is of an opposite disposition, youth and age are equally a burden."*

Governmental agencies, universities, and private organizations have been studying older citizens to learn everything about them. Who are these people? What are their sources of income? Where do they live? What occupies their time? What is their state of health? Who cares for them? What is the role of social work in the provision of services for the elderly?

These older Americans are mothers and fathers, brothers and sisters, grandparents and great-grandparents. The great majority of them do not fit the stereotype of rocking-chair sitters, slow and poor and sick elderly people. Today, those over 65 have better health because of an awareness of the benefits of a moderate lifestyle, better nutrition, increased physical activity, and better care from the medical profession. They are becoming better educated, with many attending universities and colleges to pursue degrees or just to learn. They are active in political parties, both as candidates for office and as workers. They have more money to spend as they follow the sun in the winter and seek the cool northern breezes in summer in their mobile homes. They are survivors. They have lived through the Great Depression of the 1930s, a world war, and a lifetime of sacrifice and struggle to become financially independent. A few are wealthy, and most are able to care for their financial needs.

While the majority function independently or with the aid of their families, the requirements of those who are in need of services are often so great that they cannot continue to live without help. Some need financial assistance. Approximately 12 percent live at or below the poverty level. Others need health and personal care. There are 25,000 centenarians in the United States today, and the Census Bureau estimates that by the year 2050 there will be one million people over the age of 100.

As people pass the age of 85, it becomes increasingly difficult for them to care for themselves. Although many are cared for by family, it is often 75-year-old "kids" caring for 95-year-old parents. As it becomes increasingly difficult to cope with the problems— whether they are physical, mental, emotional or financial—it may be necessary for the elderly person to be placed in a nursing home. Although only about 5 percent of the elderly are in institutions at any one time, those who are there need to be watched over and provided with constant care.

They live in all states and in all levels of society. Because the elderly make up a large percentage of our population, and because many have special needs and many others are potentially "needy," their problems become the problems of society. The solutions are a challenge to science, government, industry, education, and especially to the helping professions, including social work.

The "pyramids" in Figure 16.1 show the increase in the population of the United States projected to the year 2030 and the dramatic rise in the number of people over age 65.

In 1900 there were approximately 3 million people 65 and older in the United States. In 1950 there were approximately 12.4 million, and projections made by the Bureau of the Census place the number in the year 2000 at 35 million. By 2030 there will be 8 million Americans in the 85+ population, the ones most in need of health care and social programs.

The 1950 figure resembles a Christmas tree with a young population of 152 million people. Bars representing recent births are wider at the base, and bars representing older ages gradually narrow as mortality depletes the population.

The 1989 figure is larger because the population had grown to 249 million. Life expectancy was 75.2 years. Declining mortality rates cause bars at the top to widen.

By 2030 the shape is almost a rectangle with a projected population of 301 million. The number of deaths outnumber births, and life expectancy will be about 79 years.

## Older Americans Act of 1965

The first White House Conference on Aging, in January 1961, was a nationwide citizens' forum designed to focus public attention on the problems and potentials of older Americans. At this conference, delegates made recommendations on research, training, federal organization, and other aspects of aging that prepared the way for the passing of Public Law 89-73, known as the Older Americans Act of 1965.[1]

This legislation and subsequent amendments to the act provide assistance to older persons through grants to the states for community planning and services; training and research; and to establish within the Department of Health and Human Services an operating agency designated as the "Administration on Aging."

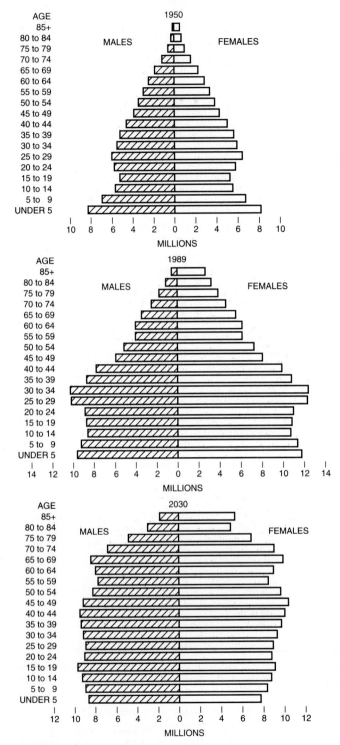

**FIGURE 16.1    The Graying of America.**

*Source:* Donald G. Fowles, "The Numbers Game: Pyramid Power," *Aging,* 362 (Washington, DC: Administration of Aging, 1991), pp. 58–59.

This law and its amendments are the basis for financial aid given by the federal government to assist older people. Ten objectives of the act are to secure:

1. An adequate income.
2. Best possible physical and mental health.
3. Suitable housing.
4. Restorative services for those who require institutional care.
5. Opportunity for employment.
6. Retirement in health, honor, dignity.
7. Pursuit of meaningful activity.
8. Efficient community services.
9. Immediate benefit from research knowledge to sustain and improve health and happiness.
10. Freedom, independence, and the free exercise of individual initiative in planning and managing their own lives.[2]

Appropriations are made to the states and communities for their programs on aging. Monies are allocated for (1) planning and coordination of programs, (2) activities valuable in reaching the goals, (3) training of personnel, and (4) establishment of new or expansion of existing programs.

Anyone working with the aging needs to be fully aware of the provisions of the Older Americans Act, including the current conditions attached to the appropriations and the many changes made and projected because of Gramm-Rudman, and shifts in funding patterns from federal to state and local structures.

## White House Conference on Aging, 1971

Delegates to the second White House Conference on Aging, held in 1971, were asked to formulate a comprehensive plan to meet the needs of older people.

In preconference meetings thousands of individuals who had contributed to the building of the country expressed their desire to continue to be a part of future plans. Representatives of all states and ethnic groups, all economic levels and social organizations, set four goals for making life more rewarding for the elderly:

1. An adequate income.
2. Appropriate living arrangements.
3. Institutional responsiveness and a new attitude toward aging.
4. Independence and dignity.

## Adequate Income

In 1980 about one-third of the older population were living at or below the poverty level. In 1990 the number is down to approximately 11.4 percent. Americans over 85—believed to be the fastest growing segment of the population—are far more likely to be poor than those 65 to 80 years old. Many live in apartments or hotels in the urban inner cities with inadequate living conditions. Their neighborhoods are frequently a threat to their peace of mind since drug addicts, thieves, and alcoholics surround them.

Inflation is unacceptably high for those on meager, fixed incomes. In the early 1990s there are still some people who were wage earners in the Great Depression years of the 1930s. Although wages for most did increase dramatically, there were many, because of lack of education or other reasons, who were unable to move upward with the economic times and were unable to save adequately for their old age.

Recognizing the need for additional income for retired workers, Congress passed the Social Security Act, which has been repeatedly changed to increase monthly payments, to give wider coverage to workers, and to make retired workers independent. The "automatic escalator" clause was included in 1974, providing an increase in payments when the Consumer Price Index increased.

Those who also have sufficient assets in savings, home ownership, life insurance, and pensions are able to care for themselves through their retirement years. Those who have only Social Security find this inadequate. A Supplemental Security Income program for those without social security provides eligible recipients cash payments each month. Important considerations of this program are that recipients are not required to give a lien on their homes, and children are not forced to contribute to their support. Also, the older person may own life insurance and property in a limited amount.

It is readily apparent that Congress cannot assure every person a monthly income equal to his or her preretirement level. Many people need help in planning during their productive years to prepare for the loss of income that comes at retirement.

The need problem of inadequate income could be alleviated by permitting those who wish to continue working to do so without restriction, instead of forcing them to retire with the threat of decreasing their social security payments if they continue to earn.

Congress has moved to eliminate forced retirement because of age, and raised the limit on earning for people 65 through 69 to $10,200 in 1992; $7,440 for people under 65. The exempt amount will automatically increase as wages go up. These limits are a modest gain at best, and workers under 70 still may not claim full Social Security benefits while continuing employment.

## Appropriate Living Arrangements

The goal for housing the elderly has been greatly broadened from the old concept of providing a quiet place in the country to providing a variety of choices from which older persons can select one suited to their needs. For most, the preferable way to live is to remain in their own homes or to live with their children or relatives. Public and private housing developments are being built in answer to the needs of the large number of elderly persons who are looking for a place to live. Some promote independent living facilities with recreational and activity programs; others provide such services as congregate meals and personal services; others have facilities providing limited medical care, food, and homemaker services.

The Department of Housing and Urban Development (HUD) is constantly reviewing and changing its program to provide better housing for the elderly. Crises often develop in inner-city areas when new industrial developments necessitate the removal of buildings used to house the elderly poor. Many times these facilities are inadequate living quarters, but to those being displaced, they are "home." Legislation has been passed to assure tenants that adequate housing will be available before they are displaced.

For those elderly who are well enough to stay at home, but need some help, a variety of social and health services have been started. As their value becomes more apparent, they probably will be more widely available. These include homemaker services, meals on wheels, visiting nurses, shopping, and counseling.

## *Institutional Responsiveness and a New Attitude Toward Aging*

No one ever dies of "old age"; there is no such disease, according to the American Medical Association. Yet, almost invariably, aging results in physical changes in the individual. About 75 percent of the elderly have suffered one or more chronic illnesses by age 75. Among the more common ailments are the same diseases that affect younger people: cardiac disease, hypertension, asthma, diabetes, arthritis, as well as the disabilities usually associated with old age—loss of hearing, impaired eyesight, mental disorders including senility, and disabilities resulting from accidents, particularly falling, which accounts for the hospitalization of 11 percent of the elderly.

Medicare pays some of the costs for hospitalization and various medical services. However, those who thought it would be the answer to all medical care needs have been disappointed. Some of the most frequently mentioned shortcomings are that it does not pay for long-term care in nursing homes, prescription drugs, eyeglasses, dental expense, or hearing aids. Prescribed medicines are often the largest medical expense for the chronically ill.

Medicaid, a federal state-administered welfare medical program, may pay medical bills not covered by Medicare for the elderly poor, those with a low income and few assets who cannot afford the cost of private health care insurance.

Some of the difficulty in securing proper medical care lies with older persons themselves. They often neglect to seek help until it is too late because they fear cancer or other terminal illnesses, or because they have lost their regular physicians. Many have not been educated to the need for regular checkups, the dangers of self-doctoring, or accident prevention. Some are afraid of hospitals, others resist seeking help because they cannot afford to pay. Furthermore, families dismiss early symptoms as a part of growing old.

Older people have nearly twice as many home accidents as the average adult, and three times as many fatal accidents. Their illnesses last longer and if hospitalization occurs, the stay is, on the average, twice as long as for younger people. Nearly half of the older citizens with arthritis, rheumatism, hernias, or who have trouble seeing or hearing are not now under care. One out of seven with a heart condition is not receiving medical attention.

While in the recent past there were only a few members of medical school faculties who were identified primarily with aging, this is changing. Older people are becoming organized and by their sheer numbers they are gaining political and economic clout. They are being recognized for their power, and gradually changes are taking place in medical schools to give more emphasis to the needs of this large segment of our population.

Defining "old" as anyone over the age of sixty-five, we find that approximately three-fourths of them function independently of their families or institutions. This is true because of the large numbers of the younger old people, those aged sixty-five to seventy-five.

While both husband and wife are alive they often continue to live on their own, caring for each other. Because most women have longer life expectancies and marry men who are older than themselves, they are much more likely than their husbands to assume the role of caregiver for a spouse. Research indicates that

> in old age men generally depend more on their wives than women depend on their husbands. Studies have shown that even when an aged wife becomes ill due to stress and the burden of caregiving and needs assistance, she will neglect her health and continue to care for her disabled husband. . . . Because of their nurturing skills and sensitivity to human interactions, women are considered more responsive to pain and suffering and more willing to take on arduous and often unrewarded personal duties. Performing stressful and often painful duties without pay is assumed to be a labor of love, an activity that is taken for granted for the female population. . . . Many elderly wives believe that, for better or for worse, they must respond to the needs of their disabled spouses without regard for their own unheralded personal and emotional sacrifices.[3]

A married couple may get along well especially if they live in close proximity to some of their children. While the population has become more mobile, most people still live close enough to some of their kin to be able to have some assistance when needed. In the beginning this assistance may be just for transportation, shopping, and emotional support, but as health deteriorates additional duties are added such as help in making social contacts, phoning, visiting, decision making, participation in family events, listening, having someone to rely on, someone who cares.

If a spouse dies and the survivor is unable to live alone, it may be necessary to take the second best option—to live with one's children.

Where it is feasible an elderly parent looks to the daughters for support. When sons are called upon to become the major caregiver to their parents, it is usually the daughter-in-law who provides the day-to-day personal care because this is perceived as women's work. Sons play a role in providing money management and are helpful in decision making, for these are perceived as men's work.

In her research, Elaine M. Brody, head of the Department of Human Services at the Philadelphia Geriatrics Center, found that

> families have reacted responsibly—even heroically—to the vastly increased demand for parent and parent-in-law care. It is the women in the family—wives, daughters, and daughters-in-law—who provide the vast majority of services needed by dependent older people, with daughters predominating in helping those elderly who are the most severely disabled. The needs of the disabled older people have exceeded the capacities of many caregiving women. In addition, societal val-

ues about women's roles have been changing so that the different values they hold may pull them in opposite directions. . . .

To put the matter in perspective, it is emphasized that the vast majority of women *want* to care for elderly parents and *do so willingly.* They derive many positive benefits from parent care such as satisfaction from fulfilling what they see as their responsibilities, adhering to religious and cultural values, expressing their feelings of affection, seeing to it that the parent is well cared for, reciprocating help the parent had given them in the past, and feeling that they are serving as a good model for their own children to follow.[4]

While social workers in the past have focused mainly on the elderly patient, more and more they are considering the younger caregiver as also being in need of support and help. With the added responsibility of caring for someone who is ill or disabled, a woman who may still have children of her own at home, who has a place in the working world, has hobbies and social commitments, and who may be slowing down herself may find that her energy level is too low for all that needs to be done.

It becomes increasingly difficult if the elderly parent has Alzheimer's disease or related mental disorders. If it is an inherited disease the caregiver may think, "Will this happen to me?" Where an older member of the family is depressed or has other mental disabilities, it is more damaging to the relationships of other family members than when the older person is physically impaired.

As greater numbers of people live to old age, caring for parents will become a universal experience and problem. Ways will be found to address this problem more adequately. We believe that such efforts as reported by the American Association of Retired Persons (AARP)[5] may be a milestone and one of the answers.

## Case Management Applied

"Aging in place" is a concept used to denote a program for elderly Americans. Iowa has tried this program. According to the 1990 Census, Iowa was the state with the most "old old" people (85+) in proportion to the population. Keeping old people in their own homes as long as possible, helping them remain independent, and reducing inappropriate use of long-term nursing home care are goals set by Iowa.

By the year 2010 the percentage of "old old" Americans in other states will catch up with Iowa. But Iowa, which did not have the luxury of waiting until then, has the problem now. What Iowa is now doing may well be a bellwether for the rest of the country.

A top priority is keeping the elderly in their own homes. In Cedar Rapids, Iowa, 110 old people live at home who would otherwise be living in long-term nursing homes, affording them more dignity and saving their own money and that of the taxpayer. This is achieved in large part by implementing a "case management" concept. Case management works by orchestration of a multiple number of services (32 in Cedar Rapids) used in the delivery of vitally needed assistance, tailored to fit individual needs. Iowa has pulled together disparate elements: family service professionals, public and private agencies, and volunteers.

Ninety-two-year-old Harold Mills is an example.

Nancy Hanson cleans his house, gives him a back rub (to alleviate a painful rash), takes him grocery shopping or runs errands. Other aides bring hot meals at noon and do yard work and snow shoveling. A social worker drives by to see how he is doing....[6]

Nancy Hanson, the home-health aide..., comes from the Linn County Department of Human Resources Management. The aide who cuts his grass is sent by Aging Services, Inc., a private non-profit firm that also provides a visiting social worker. His meals are delivered courtesy of Family Service Agency, a private nonprofit group. And he gets an emergency response hookup from Mercy Medical Center.[7]

---

Thirty-two agencies work in a consortium. The agency providing the greatest number of services is designated case manager and client advocate. Eighty thousand volunteers, mostly over age sixty, provide a wide range of services coordinated by the case manager. In addition to case management more than a dozen programs have sprung up since 1980. Despite all that is done by professionals, paraprofessionals, and organized services, the family, neighbors, and friends continue to provide the lion's share of elder care. After family resources have been exhausted, or when the elderly parent's life is so precarious that twenty-four-hour nursing care is needed, they then turn to the next option—nursing homes.

## *Nursing Homes*

More than any other group, except perhaps the very young, the elderly are in need of the helping services offered by the social work profession. This is particularly true of those in institutions who are infirm or have disabilities that make them incompetent—who are ill as well as old.

Fortunately, nursing homes billing Medicare and Medicaid are now mandated by law to provide psychological and social services; some networking of services is offered. Counseling and friendly visiting are increasingly made available to patients.

Prior to 1966 there were comparatively few nursing homes in America. As the need increased, and after Medicare and Medicaid were introduced, government and private money was channeled into the building of facilities for the care of the long-term ill. Because of the genuine need for nursing home care for those unable to be cared for in any other place, it is important that the quality of care be improved. About 5 percent of the 30 million Americans sixty-five and older live in nursing homes on a long-term basis. In addition about one of five older people will spend some time in a nursing home for short-term medical care or physical therapy.

In addition 1.3 million receive home health care. Another 1.1 million live in congregate living facilities where they receive some help. Many of these 2.4 million would be unable to maintain themselves outside a nursing home without these supportive services.

Old people look upon nursing homes with fear and hostility; they believe that going into a home is a prelude to death. Higher death rates are recorded among those in nursing homes, and some experts charge that the shock of uprooting is the cause. But many go to a nursing home only when their physical condition is so precarious that life cannot be sustained without constant medical supervision.

Volunteer-lead activities in a nursing home.

There is a popular belief that families use nursing homes to get rid of elderly relatives, but studies reveal that this is not true. Elaine Brody and others have reported that as many as 14 million elderly live with their spouses and 4 million with other relatives.

> Although the rest live on their own, about 80 percent have children, and about 55 percent of those who don't live with their adult children do live within 30 minutes distance from them. A recent survey showed that more than three quarters of those surveyed had seen at least one of their children within the previous week. More-over, as much as 50 percent of home-help services received by the elderly are pro-vided by family and friends. A great deal of care is provided by social workers and other health and mental health professionals outside the family.[8]

Nursing homes employing professionally trained social workers provide such essential services as: interpret the program to patient and family, explain the nature of the illness, dis-cuss ways of coping with the problem, provide the opportunity for the family to share their grief and to express guilt and concerns, and assist with the mobilization by the family of resources needed to sustain the family and the patient.

Educational programs have demonstrated that a group relationship is one therapeutic way of resolving feelings of anxiety, guilt, and hostility, as well as for sharing experiences and thereby gaining the reassurance to be able to move toward a positive resolution of one's problems. Adult children who participate feel relief of guilt when they understand the process of aging, feel the support of the social workers, and know that their experiences are shared by others whose problems parallel their own.

The depressing situation families found as they looked for nursing homes before the passage of the Older Americans Act is changing. The care and services in many homes have improved. Confronted with the frustration and dissatisfaction of families and the standards mandated by state and federal authorities, nursing home owners have moved ahead to upgrade services and meet the standards people are demanding. Society has also created the mechanism needed with Social Security, Medicare and Medicaid to pay for these improvements. Experimental programs, started to prove the feasibility of providing social work and other services in nursing homes, have proven their relevance.

## *Alternatives to Nursing Home Care*

Most older people would prefer to remain in their own homes or homes of relatives. When home health care, meal and homemaker services are available, such care may not only postpone, but possibly prevent, more costly institutional care.

Home health services include visiting nursing, laboratory services, physical therapy, drugs, and sick room equipment supplied by members of the medical profession.

Food service programs have been greatly expanded and are basically of two types; the delivery of meals to the home six days a week, or the serving of meals in a common dining room.

Homemaker services have been developed to provide for the needs of those who are not ill, but who are dependent upon someone to perform the tasks that they are no longer able to do for themselves. Thousands who would have to depend upon government money to maintain them in nursing homes have adequate income and savings to maintain themselves with these services. With imagination a community may hit upon the answer to a difficult social problem as reported in the following incident.

Fifty people who had been receiving homemaker services under the Division of Family Services were declared ineligible because they were receiving Social Security payments above the welfare-grant level. Some were receiving help only a few hours a week for such essential services as grocery shopping and being taken for medical care. The homemaker had helped them to remain in their own homes. For many the alternative seemed to be the much more expensive solution of going into a nursing home.

The director of the family service program sought help through the daily newspaper. An appealing feature story picturing one elderly woman told the plight of all. In one day offers to help came from 80 individuals as well as numerous church and civic groups.

Although the director had at first appealed for help on a temporary basis until other funds could be arranged, the overwhelming public response made him turn to the community's volunteer program as a permanent solution.

## Day Care Centers

Many individuals who live at home require some of the services offered by an institution. The high cost of nursing home care and the desire of the individuals and their families for them to remain in the community have brought about the development of day care centers.

They are designed primarily to provide a protective environment and emotional support during the daytime hours. Social workers are generally utilized to act as liaison between the families and the program, and between other agencies and the center. Because the program is new, there is a need to educate the public and, more particularly, the older people and their families to the opportunities provided by these facilities. The activities are determined by the needs of the group, and help those who participate to function adequately in their social groups.

This service gives the family some relief from twenty-four-hour-a-day care, prevents or postpones institutional care, and provides a program designed to maintain maximum functioning, both physical and emotional.

## Mental Health

Between 15 and 25 percent of the elderly living in the community are said to have moderate to severe psychiatric impairment. They are able to remain in the community because they are able to carry out the activities necessary to keep themselves functioning, even though it may be in a limited way, and they are cared for and protected by their families.

A growing number of severely ill who will not accept commitment to public hospitals are found among the homeless wanderers who live on the streets in our larger cities.

A cliche states that the old are set in their ways—"they are too old to change." Yet at no other time in life are so many drastic changes thrust upon one. Included in these changes are: loss of spouse; loss of a job with its accompanying role in the community; loss of accustomed income often necessitating changes in activities and sometimes changes in living accommodations; poorer health; and loss of friends and relatives through death or moving.

People who have adjusted to changes in earlier life usually are able to accept these losses and make the necessary changes in attitudes and activities. Others unable to cope with the new situations are unable to find suitable substitutes.

For those who cannot adjust, it is only a short step to becoming isolated, lonely, fearful, suspicious, hypochondriacal, and depressed. The depression is frequently expressed by somatic symptoms. When seen by their physicians, these people are treated for bodily aches and pains and not the underlying depression.

At the conclusion of an eleven-year study, the National Institute of Mental Health identified two major sociopsychological barriers to good mental health in the later years: (1) the inability to bounce back from psychosocial losses, and (2) failure to maintain "meaningful" life goals.

Because withdrawal symptoms are common among the aging population, many families feel it is just a part of "growing old." These conditions do not necessarily have to go uncorrected, for there are mental health organizations that offer services. Social workers, teaming with other professions, work with these individuals to keep them in touch with reality, compensating for their losses in acceptable ways, and providing emotional support.

Zoroaster, a Persian prophet of the sixth century B.C., wrote of good mental health:

> Nobody grows old merely by living a number of years; people grow old by deserting their ideals. Years wrinkle the skin, but giving up enthusiasm wrinkles the soul. Worry, doubt, self-distrust, fear, and despair—these are the long years that bow the head and turn the growing spirit back to dust. You are as young as your faith, and as old as your doubts, as young as your self-confidence, as old as your fears, as young as your hope, as old as your despair.

## Independence and Dignity

Senior citizens need to maintain a high degree of independence and self-mastery resulting in self-respect and dignity. As they grow older, people need the reward of a secure place in the world where they have a serene sense of belonging, and of adding significantly to society. Dignity and self-worth are qualities the majority of older people are able to maintain.

A retired person must remain an individual, not a statistic, or an anonymous member of the group called "aged." With the power of his or her judgment, knowledge, and skill acquired over the years, he or she has the opportunity to display dynamic maturity, to continue to contribute to society, and to live a satisfying life.

## Employment—Retirement

Some gerontologists feel that the changes in one's life at retirement constitute the most critical major adjustment an older person has to make. Even with pensions, individuals too often feel they are being eased out of a job that others think they are no longer capable of performing. Accompanying the loss of a job is the loss of social status that employment gives.

Common mistakes that many people make related to retirement are lack of planning on what to do with time, failure to consider alternative plans, and lack of planning in relation to reduced buying power.

Individuals in their sixties are not old. Many people are urged to retire at a time when they are most valuable to their company or organization. Wisdom that accompanies years of experience cannot be replaced by younger workers who possibly move a little faster.

For those who want to continue working, two factors must be considered: who wants to earn money and who wants to give of their time in public service.

With an increasing number of older people looking for ways to be gainfully employed, some employers are realizing that experienced workers bring skills, knowledge, good judgment, and dependability to their organizations. The Commerce Department estimates that 11 percent of people sixty-five or over are employed either full- or part-time.

Governmental agencies help older, low-income persons to find work. Foster Grandparents help children in institutions who need individual care and love. Green Thumb, Inc.

employees work to beautify highways, build parks, and work with conservation programs. Senior Aides provide home health services and homemaker services. Senior Community Service workers help in community action programs.

Two national organizations that offer opportunities for people of any age or financial status are the Peace Corps and Volunteers in Service to America (VISTA). Peace Corps members work overseas in education, agriculture, health, housing, public works, and community development programs, serving a minimum of two years. VISTA members serve in institutions and in impoverished urban and rural communities in the United States.

Bertrand Russell wrote: "It is the great reward of losing youth that one finds oneself able to be of use." For many, retirement brings the first opportunity to spend freely large blocks of time serving others. This can be an exciting adventure to the worker, and his or her contribution may be more valuable than money.

Volunteer work in veterans hospitals, Red Cross, welfare, and social agencies is largely under the direction of social workers, who maintain active recruiting and training programs for volunteers. Social agencies use volunteers for a wide variety of agency functions, including transportation for clients, entertainment of patients in hospitals and other institutions, shopping for the homebound, tutoring, maintenance work, and various professional and semiprofessional services. Social workers interpret the need for services, develop programs, and direct the activities.

Volunteers are concerned people who want to be busy. They make friends easily, have empathy and sympathy for others, and a religious conviction of love for their neighbors.

## George Black, A Peace Corps Volunteer

At retirement, George Black did not abandon his interests and activities, but changed the emphasis and reassessed his values. The sharing of his skills brought satisfaction to him and help to another country.

For more than 80 years, this man has been making bricks by hand in Winston-Salem, North Carolina, his own special way of doing it. He is a master craftsman.

When he came in to see me, he didn't look it but he told me he was 93 years old. But his productive years were not over. So our government, under one of the programs that we fortunately had, sent this remarkable man to a country that needed to learn about that almost forgotten skill of making bricks by hand. George Black went to Guyana, in South America, so that he could share his skills with the people of that less developed country.

When I asked him about his trip, this is what he said: "I have always asked the Lord to let my last days be my best days. I feel like He is answering my prayers."

George Black's prayer is the prayer of millions of Americans—"to let my last days be my best days." And for them, as for him, its answer depends not only on what they are given, but on what they continue to give.

Older Americans have much to give to this country. The best thing this country can give to them is the chance to be a part of it, a chance to play a continuing role in the great American adventure.[9]

Many older persons have discovered that education just for the sake of learning is rewarding. They accept the counsel of Seneca who wrote, "As long as you live, keep learning how to live." Men and women of all educational backgrounds enroll in classes in art, music, foreign languages, and other cultural subjects; or in crafts, or sewing or carpentry, or woodworking. Community schools, colleges, and universities beckon with a wide variety of subjects to those interested. Some offer free or reduced tuition to those over sixty-five.

## The White House Conference, 1995

Delegates to the White House Conference on Aging in 1995 gave approval for the reauthorization of the Older American's Act with its broad concern for the health and welfare of older citizens.

Reflecting the national debate, delegates focused on the financial and health needs, passing a resolution to preserve Social Security for now and into the future. They opposed arbitrary cuts in Medicare and voted for a resolution that opposes block granting of the Medicaid program. Universal health care and expanded development of home- and community-based long-term care services were high priorities; as also was medical research into diseases, both mental and physical, of the aging.

For the first time in White House Conference history, they adopted a resolution to provide assistance to grandparents who are primary caregivers for their grandchildren.

Affordable housing in safe neighborhoods was addressed. Resolutions were also passed concerning assuring the dignity and worth of individuals including the right of personal choice and right for education or training for employment if needed.[10]

## The Aging Are Individuals, Too

An increasing number of healthy, competent men and women are joining the ranks of the "aging" in the United States every day. In addition to the basic needs of good housing, adequate income, and medical care, they need to be independent to choose the kinds of activities they pursue. They need to make decisions concerning their lives. Social workers have the responsibility to see that older people are given these opportunities. The more responsibility they take for themselves and the direction of their lives, the longer they will remain interested and be competent to do productive work.

With emphasis on service to those who need it, the American Association of Retired Persons, the largest secular organization in America, has as its purpose "to enhance the quality of life and promote the independence and dignity of older persons." Through the lobbying efforts of this organization, changes have been made in programs involving health advocacy, tax aid, women's and minority initiatives, widowed persons services, mature driver's training, and other issues affecting older people.

Social workers help. They support the established trend among the elderly to organize and become strong consumer groups. They support their ongoing efforts to maintain and strengthen the income base that provides economic security and financial independence. Schools of social work ally themselves with interdisciplinary efforts to educate and train professionals to address the issues and problems of the elderly. They provide curriculum emphases that will sensitize and assist their graduates in overcoming myths and biases and acquire the expertise that will make it possible for them to shape social policy. The family is the basic institution for helping the elderly, and the social work role is ancillary to the family. We are helped with this perspective by the words of Elaine Brody.[11]

> Today's adult children provide more care and more difficult care to more elderly parents over longer periods of time than ever before....Most do so willingly. Some go beyond the limits of endurance....
>
> The vast majority of helping services to the aged are provided by the family, not by government, professionals, or agencies . . . only 4 percent of those receiving help with activities of daily living (an intense level of caregiving) received subsidized assistance from the formal system. In fact, all formal services together accounted for less than 15 percent of all "helper days of care. . . ."
>
> Services given by professionals, government, and agencies do not reduce family services; rather, they complement and supplement the family's helping activities. Moreover, when formal services are offered, families are extremely modest in their requests. . . .
>
> The family mobilizes, coordinates, and monitors informal and formal services—which professionals characterize as "case management" and like to think of as their own discovery . . .
>
> Adult daughters, the main filial caregivers, deal with the multiple demands on their time and energy. . . .
>
> Families do not dump older people into nursing homes. Most often, institutional placement is preceded by prolonged, strenuous, and exhausting efforts to keep the older person in the community.

### *Joy in Working with the Aging*

David Soyer, who had extensive experience working with older people, reports the joy and satisfaction received from meeting the needs of people in their declining years.

> There is a certain purity about working with the aged, especially those who are beyond the productive years. One does not justify this work on the basis of crime prevention or helping to develop untapped, potentially productive forces or freeing the oppressed so as to ward off summer insurrection or any other instrumental value. One justifies it only on the basis that each human being has value—intrinsic value, the meaning and dignity of being human. So many of our clients we serve for this reason alone. That is why social work is concerned about those in whom our society loses interest.
>
> I believe that working with the aged is one of those fields in social work that, by setting forth the issue so clearly, gives the worker a chance to test, temper, and affirm this core value of our profession. . . .
>
> When one works with younger people and the world is open and one is looking ahead, there can be a terrible striving to make one's client normal within whatever definition the worker has of that concept. In work with the aged the perspective is different. There is a look backward. No longer is there the dream of

what life may become, but there is a stark look at what it was. There is a search for the things that gave life meaning. Sometimes they have been big: the coming to America, the founding of a labor union or of a family. Sometimes they are smaller: memories of old baseball stars, of neighborhoods or countrysides as they were long ago, bittersweet thoughts of old business ventures with high hopes and small returns.[12]

## Summary

*Science, government, industry, education, and the helping professions focus their attention on the 30 million older Americans and their needs. What are their special needs?*

*1. An adequate income to ensure physical necessities.*

*2. The best possible physical and mental health.*

*3. Suitable housing, whether they live alone or with others.*

*4. Opportunity for employment if they wish to work.*

*5. Retirement in honor and dignity.*

*6. Restorative services for those in institutions.*

*7. Pursuit of meaningful activity.*

*8. Efficient community services for special needs.*

*9. Benefits from research to sustain and improve their health and happiness.*

*10. Freedom, independence, and the free exercise of individual initiative in planning and managing their own lives.*

*Social workers individualize problems and administer the services that preserve the respect and dignity of the aging who receive them.*

## Selected References

ANETZBERGER, GEORGIA, *The Etiology of Elder Abuse by Adult Offspring.* Springfield, IL: Charles C. Thomas, 1987.

BRODY, ELAINE M., *Long-Term Care of Older People.* New York: Human Sciences Press, 1977.

BRODY, ELAINE M., *Women in the Middle: Their Parent-Care Years.* New York: Springer, 1990.

BROWNE, COLETTE, V., "Empowerment in Social Work Practice with Older Women, *Social Work,* 40 (May 1995), 358–364.

BUMAGIN, VICTORIA E., and KATHRYN F. HIRN, *Helping the Aging Family: A Guide for Professionals.* Glenview IL: Scott, Foresman & Co., 1990.

COX, ENID O., and RUTH J. PERSONS, *Empowerment-Oriented Social Work Practice with the Elderly.* Pacific Grove, CA, 1993.

FONER, NANCY, *Ages in Conflict: A Cross-Cultural Perspective on Inequality Between Old and Young.* New York: Columbia University Press, 1984.

HARRINGTON, CHARLENE, ROBERT J. NEWCOMER, CARROLL L. ESTES and ASSOCIATES, *Long-Term Care of the Elderly: Public Policy Issues.* Beverly Hills, CA; Sage Publications, 1985.

MONK, ABRAHAM, LEONARD W. KAYE, and HOWARD LITWIN, *Resolving Grievances in the Nursing Home: A Study of the Ombudsman Program.* New York: Columbia University Press, 1984.

MOODY, HARRY R., *Abundance of Life: Human Development Polices for An Aging Society.* New York: Columbia University Press, 1988.

MOTENKO, ALUMA KOPITO, and SARAH GREENBERG, "Reframing Dependence in Old Age: A Positive Transition for Families," *Social Work,* 40 (May 1995), 382–390.

*Older Americans Act of 1965, as Amended, Text and History.* Washington, DC: U.S. Department of Health, Education, and Welfare, 1970.

QURESHI, HAZEL, and ALAN WALKER, *The Caring Relationship: Elderly People and Their Families.* Philadelphia: Temple University Press, 1989.

SMITH, ELIZABETH D., "Addressing the Psychospiritual Distress of Death as Reality: A Transpersonal Approach," *Social Work,* 40 (May 1995), 402–413.

STEINBERG, RAYMOND M., and GENEVIEVE W. CARTER, *Case Management and the Elderly: A Handbook for Planning and Administering Programs.* Lexington, MA: D.C. Heath, Lexington Books, 1983.

## *Notes*

1. *Older Americans Act of 1965, as Amended, Text and History* (Washington, DC: U.S. Department of Health, Education, and Welfare, 1970).

2. Ibid., p. 2.

3. Vanessa Wilson, "The Consequences of Elderly Wives Caring for Disabled Husbands: Implications for Practice," *Social Work,* 35 (September 1990), 85.

4. Elaine M. Brody, *Women in the Middle: Their Parent-Care Years* (New York: Springer, 1990), pp. 40–41.

5. Robert Lewis, "Iowa Back to the Future," *AARP Bulletin* (November 1992), pp. 1,16,17.

6. Ibid., p. 1.

7. Ibid., p. 16.

8. *NASW News,* 31 (January 1986), 3.

9. *Toward a National Policy on Aging, Proceedings of the 1971 White House Conference on Aging,* 1 (Washington, DC: Government Printing Office, 1971), 143.

10. *Official 1995 White House Conference on Aging, Adopted Resolutions* (Washington, DC: May 2–5, 1995), 1–3.

11. *NASW News,* 31 (March 1986), 9.

12. David Soyer, "Reverie on Working with the Aged," *Social Casework,* 50 (May 1969), 292–294.

# Chapter 17

# *Drug Abuse and Social Work*

*Bill was brought to the attention of school social workers when he was 10 years old and was sniffing glue. He was reprimanded, and he stopped for a time. He moved on to tobacco and occasionally drank beer in junior high. Social workers were again asked to help, but there was no in-depth effort to work through his problems.*

*During his junior year in high school, Bill discovered marijuana and alcohol, and he became engrossed in the use of amphetamines, which were easy to obtain from pushers at the school or by occasionally burglarizing a drugstore.*

*At the beginning of Bill's senior year the school social worker sought to rehabilitate him and several others in his group, involving the parents. With individual counseling sessions and regular group therapy meetings with the students alone, parents alone, and all together, they slowly worked their way through problems in communication and relationships. The parents, who were concerned about their children, were able to offer better home relationships, understanding, and support in the boys' efforts to get off the drugs.*

*There were relapses at test time and when disappointments came from school activities, but the group made progress. At the end of the school year, the group was disbanded, with the social worker expressing confidence that the boys would be able to remain drug free.*

*During the summer Bill worked and saved his money so that he could go to the local junior college the next year. He was often restless, and his leisure time posed problems for him. But he was determined that he was not going to slip back into his old habits.*

*As fall approached he showed some signs of anxiety over facing the new school situation, but his parents were not particularly concerned for it had been about five months since his last relapse.*

*The night before he was to begin classes at the college, he was restless and went out quite late for a walk to relax before going to bed. He never returned. A few blocks from his home was a small drugstore. He climbed the roof, removed a skylight, and was trying to enter the store through a narrow air vent.*

*His body was found the next day, his head hanging down, and his pant leg inextricably caught on a protruding plank.*

*Drugs!* No other word in the American language has caused more concern to the American people in recent times. All America watched as drugs spilled over the nation in the 1960s. Drugs had long been a problem for the ghettos in our large cities, but now they had spread to the suburbs, to high schools, and university campuses in epidemic proportions, affecting all ethnic groups and classes of society.

What was the cause of this "sudden" eruption? There are many hypotheses. The psychological shock caused by unprecedented technological advances and social upheaval had an impact on attitudes and lifestyle. Mobility and affluence took social activities out of the homes and neighborhoods into the community.

Television sold pills and potions for every body ailment, stressing that no one need to be uncomfortable even for a moment. Sponsors wanted one to believe that there was a ready solution to all problems in the home medicine cabinet or at the corner drugstore. No one suggested that there are other, lasting solutions to inner stress; pills were pushed for "instant happiness."

Doctors in mental hospitals began using mood-altering drugs in the 1950s to treat psychotic patients who were unable to control their emotions—tranquilizers to make the anxious peaceful, stimulants to help the depressed become active. Drugs became the panacea for coping with all of the stresses of life.

"Pep" pills were passed out freely to overweight adults and chubby teenagers, to the night truck driver, to the college student cramming for exams, to the depressed business person. Tranquilizers were prescribed for the anxious club president, the struggling executive, and the harried young mother. Many people sought a solution to all life's disappointments and anxieties in a pill bottle.

Disillusioned by the hypocrisy and deceit of some adult leaders, young people protested in the 1960s—the Vietnam War, political involvement in faraway places, their parents, the police, the "Establishment," and what they expressed as inequality in the laws. Many adopted drugs as a means of refocusing attention and to make themselves heard. The "hippie" culture developed with long hair, beards, dirty jeans, communal living, and "doing one's own thing" attitudes. Alienated, under stress, and struggling for identity, they took drugs to escape the reality they were unable or unwilling to face. Marijuana became the symbol of dissatisfied American youth, and its use quickly spread from communes to young people all across the country.

A leader for the drug culture arose. The articulate Timothy Leary wrote and preached the gospel of drugs. He not only advocated the unrestricted use of drugs, but actively recruited dealers. Blum quotes from an underground press article of 1969 written by Leary:

> I think that this is the noblest of all human professions and would certainly like to urge any creative young person sincerely interested in evolving himself and helping society to grow to consider this ancient and honorable profession. . . . The righteous dealer is . . . selling you the celestial dream . . . he is peddling . . . freedom and joy.[1]

A number of powerful forces continue to influence increasing numbers of youth toward the use and abuse of drugs. Many use drugs because their peers think it is "cool" and peer control among teens is often decisive. Growing up is difficult and painful and drugs seem to relieve confusion. The environment exposes youth to the drug culture. Commercial marketing techniques make the use of drugs appear deceptively innocuous.

In addition to the peer pressure and advertisement, the American society seems to be producing more stress for both youth and adults. One inappropriate answer to the stress is to increase the use of drugs. The three best-selling drugs in the country are the stress-related drugs of Tagamet (ulcer medication), Inderal (hypertension drug), and Valium (tranquilizer). The heavy use of stress-related drugs may very well add to an atmosphere or a culture that condones the use of drugs to solve life's problems.

Cocaine has received national attention because it has been linked to the deaths of young and promising athletes. In fact, the entire professional sports world is struggling with the problems of increased cocaine use. Steroids have also created problems for many athletes, as was evidenced by the disqualification of a gold-medal winner in the 1988 Olympics. The 1992 Olympics in Barcelona seemed to have less drug abuse, but commentators were always referring to more sophisticated methods of using steroids. Commentators even raised the issue of athletes using steroids in training and preparation, but stopping the practice just in time so that the drugs could not be detected at the Games.

Various musical groups also seem to condone the use of drugs through song lyrics and by presenting themselves as individuals who have achieved success while abusing drugs. Both athletes and musicians can provide young people with strong role models that subtly encourage drug abuse.

The problem of drug abuse is real. On Friday, September 29, 1989, federal drug agents seized 20 tons of cocaine with an estimated street value of $20 billion in the city of Los Angeles. In Miami, in the fiscal year of 1988, 31.7 tons of cocaine were confiscated.

President Bush tried to combat the problem of drugs by appointing a "drug czar" to coordinate all drug prevention programs as well as oversee the enforcement of drug laws. President Clinton is trying to prevent drug abuse by funding programs for children and youth. He believes that programs such as Headstart will assist children to have a better self esteem, which in turn will prevent drug abuse. The Clinton administration is also allocating money to create employment for teenagers all over the country which he hopes will ameliorate drug abuse. Several states have been trying to address the drug problem. Two Utah state legislators stated:

> Utah should have a drug czar that, like the federal government's William Bennett will coordinate the fight against the war that is killing our children....
>
> Legislators can run, but they can't hide from this fight. Parents know the problem. Many are fighting to save their children; no other generation has had this scourge. The parents have been fighting this war alone, and the state doesn't have a lot of solutions. If you haven't been touched by the drug problem, you're lucky.
>
> I'm serious when I say the drug war is more of a threat to our nation than nuclear war. It's here.[2]

There are indications that the many programs designed to eliminate drug abuse are having a positive effect. In December 1990, Louis W. Sullivan, Secretary of Health and Human Services, released results of the department's 1990 National Household Survey on Drug Abuse. He stated that the study showed declining use of most illicit drugs by Americans, including a dramatic 45 percent drop in "current" cocaine use (used at least once in the past month). The 1990 survey also found a 44 percent reduction in current use of any illicit drug in the past five years, down from 23 million users in 1985 to 12.9 million in 1990. Secretary Sullivan was pleased to report progress, but he also warned that many pockets of serious drug abuse remain.

In their 1993 National Survey Results on Drug Use, Johnston et al. recognize the fact that even though there have been appreciable declines in the use of a number of the illicit drugs among seniors in high school, college students, and young adults, worrying new data signal problems ahead. They state:

> While the general decline resumed in 1986 and, most importantly, was joined by the start of a decline in cocaine use in 1987 and crack use in 1988, in 1992 we heard a number of alarm bells sounding. While the seniors continued to show improvement on a number of measures in 1992, the college students and young adults did not. Further, the attitudes and beliefs of seniors regarding drug use began to soften. Perhaps of greatest importance, the eighth graders exhibited a significant increase in marijuana, cocaine, LSD, and hallucinogens other than LSD, as well as a not-quite significant increase in inhalant use. (In fact, all five populations showed some increase on LSD, continuing a longer term trend for college students and young adults.)
>
> In 1993 still more alarms went off. The eighth graders continued to show an increase in their use of a number of drugs and (as their prior shifts in attitudes and belief foretold) the tenth graders and twelfth graders joined them. Rises are seen in a number of the so-called "gateway drugs"—in this case marijuana, cigarettes, and inhalants—which may bode ill for the use of later drugs in the usual sequence of involvement. The softening of attitudes about crack and other forms of cocaine also is a basis for concern. . . .
>
> Of particular concern here is not only the possibility that there may be an increase in the use of particular drugs like LSD and inhalants, but that we may be seeing the beginning of a turnaround in the drug abuse situation more generally among our youngest cohorts—perhaps because they have not had the same opportunities for vicarious leaning from the adverse drug experiences of people around them and . . . through the media. Clearly there is a danger that, as the drug epidemic has subsided considerably, newer cohorts have far less opportunity to learn through informal means about the danger of drugs. This may mean that the nation must redouble its efforts to be sure that they learn these lessons through more formal means—from schools, parents, and focused messages in the media, for example—and that this more formalized prevention effort becomes institutionalized so that it will endure for the long term.[3]

## Misused Drugs and What They Do

By affecting the central nervous system, drugs produce a change in the behavior, emotional responses, or reactions of the abuser. The change may be harmless or a threat to the abuser and society.

The major classes of drugs that have the potential for abuse are narcotics, stimulants, depressants, hallucinogens, marijuana, inhalants, and alcohol.

## Narcotics

Narcotics are used medically to kill pain and induce sleep. In addition, they allay fear and anxiety, and offer an escape from boredom, loneliness, and even reality. Opium, heroin, morphine, codeine, synthetic opiates, and cocaine are classed as narcotics. Prolonged or incorrect use can lead to physical and psychological dependence. Tolerance—the necessity for increasingly larger doses to satisfy the craving—develops, and withdrawal can be painful and dangerous.

## Stimulants

Stimulants, principally the amphetamines, increase the activity of the central nervous system. Users become excited, their activity is increased, and they can go without sleep for long periods of time.

Abusers develop an emotional dependence, and tolerance develops. Methamphetamine, or speed, has been widely abused, and abusers lack the judgment and consideration to perform in a responsible manner. The drug culture slogan "Speed Kills" indicates that the users are aware of its potential dangers.

**FIGURE 17.1**

## *Depressants—Sedatives*

Depressants that act as a calming agent include the barbiturates, synthetic sedatives, and some tranquilizers. Excessive dosages result in loss of balance. Users may develop a quick temper and a quarrelsome disposition that can lead to violent behavior and psychotic episodes. Physical dependence occurs, tolerance develops, and withdrawal symptoms can be dangerous and even cause death. Overdoses, particularly when taken with alcohol or other drugs, can be fatal.

## *Hallucinogens*

Hallucinogens are mind-altering drugs that distort and intensify the user's sense of perception and alter judgment and objectivity. The effects are unpredictable and range from illusion and exhilaration, to panic and serious accidents, sometimes mistaken for suicide.

## *Marijuana*

The most controversial drug in use is marijuana, known to humans for nearly 5,000 years, but one of the least understood of all natural drugs. The dried flowers and leaves of the cannabis plant when smoked affect the user's mood and thinking. The smoker usually takes suggestions from others, and generally cannot do tasks that require effective reflexes.

The use of marijuana is legally restricted in almost every country, but the rapid rise of the use of marijuana in the United States has brought a growing acceptance of its use. Users have pushed for its legalization. As more research is completed it is anticipated that this drug will be better understood and competent judgments will be made.

The heated arguments advanced for the use of marijuana have spurred medical researchers to determine its effects upon users and upon the unborn children of users. In one effort to determine effects on the chromosomes of a group of healthy college students, forty-nine users and twenty control subjects were studied. From this study came the following conclusions:

> The data presented seem to indicate that the use of marijuana is a cause of chromosome breakage in lymphocytes of users:... In addition, the data seemed to show that the degree of use is not critical as light users (those using marihuana one time or less per week) had about as great a chance of having chromosome breakage as did heavy users. Thus, it appears that with respect to chromosome breakage the type of exposure afforded by the breaking agent even with occasional use is strong enough to do damage.
>
> ...Since marihuana is widely used, particularly in the young individuals of our society, this possibility takes on a spectrum of overwhelming significance.[4]

The Department of Health and Human Services reported findings that showed the potency of marijuana had greatly increased, that it was a complex drug and could be a detriment to learning, negatively affect motor coordination, and lead to serious health problems.

## *Inhalants*

Inhalants come in the form of aerosol products such as lighter fluids and paint thinners. These products are usually inhaled, creating loss of coordination, confusion, and hallucinations. An overdose can cause convulsions or death. Also, the use may develop permanent damage to lungs, brain, liver, or bone marrow.

## *Alcohol*

Alcohol in small quantities causes people to be relaxed and socially responsive. However, alcohol is a depressant. Certain behavior and attitudes usually repressed are exhibited by a person who has drunk alcohol. Typically, he or she becomes disoriented, confused, and drives a car or performs other physical activities erratically.

Alcohol is generally socially accepted, although alcoholism is one of the most prevalent addictions and a major health problem in this country. Some of the long-term effects of alcoholism include:

Liver damage, especially cirrhosis (scarring of the liver); alcoholic hepatitis, cancer of the liver.

Heart disease, including enlarged heart, congestive heart failure.

Ulcers and gastritis, due to irritation of the stomach lining by alcohol.

Malnutrition, because alcohol has no food value. Alcohol robs the body of some vitamins and minerals and interferes with digestion of food that is eaten.

"D.T.'s" (delirium tremens), resulting from alcohol withdrawal, characterized by disorientation, memory impairment and sometimes hallucinations, etc.

Cancer of the mouth, esophagus or stomach, due to irritation by alcohol.

Brain damage, possibly leading to psychosis.

Damage to developing fetus if mother drinks while she is pregnant.[5]

One of the findings resulting from research on the effects of alcohol has to do with "fetal alcohol syndrome." This condition is characterized by physical deformity and abnormality and mental retardation; it results when the mother drinks during pregnancy. Some authorities believe that the effects of drinking on the fetus are more damaging than thalidomide. Animal studies suggest that a pregnant woman clearly risks harm to her baby if she drinks three or more ounces of absolute alcohol per day. Three ounces of absolute alcohol are equivalent to six average sized drinks. Alcohol appears to be a major factor in the development of birth abnormalities.

## *Tobacco*

Tobacco is one of the most abused of all drugs. Nicotine, an active ingredient of tobacco, is a stimulant. When tobacco smoke is inhaled it causes the heart to beat faster and the blood pressure to elevate. Tar in smoke causes cancer and such respiratory disorders as shortness of breath, coughing, and cardiovascular difficulties. The agents in smoke are a cause of serious health problems such as arteriosclerosis, emphysema, chronic bronchitis, heart disease, lung cancer, and cancer to other parts of the body. Women who smoke during pregnancy run the risk of having babies who weigh less, and they more frequently lose their offspring through stillbirth or death soon after birth.

## *Extent and Cost of Drug Abuse*

It is extremely difficult to estimate the number of persons who are abusing drugs. Those who use marijuana, barbiturates, amphetamines, and hallucinogens are discovered only when they are involved in criminal action. Through controlled surveys it is estimated that there are as many as 20 million users of marijuana in this country. Marijuana is used much more than any other drug, except alcohol. Surveys in schools show that between 20 percent and 30 percent of the students have used marijuana at least once, and indicate varying rates of use of other drugs. Many reporting use in college started in high school, and an increasing number reported starting in junior high.

Estimates are that 10 percent of the 66 million children under 18 live in homes that abuse drugs. Two-thirds of child abuse and neglect deaths are related to substance abuse. A Boston hospital reported that 69 percent of babies born to mothers who were chronic drinkers are born with one or more mental or physical deformities. Fetal alcohol syndrome (deformities of infants born to drinking mothers) is a major and growing health problem.

Many people involved in drug abuse are lost as productive members of society. They often suffer poor health, and their families endure emotional conflicts and financial loss. In addition, drug abuse pours millions of dollars into organized crime, society loses hundreds of thousands of dollars worth of property, and the taxpayer pays to reclaim the abusers. The impact on the nation's economy will be over $200 billion because of crime, health-care costs, fires, and lost productivity due to alcoholism and drug abuse.[6]

More deaths and accidents occur as the result of alcohol than from other drugs. Half of all highway fatalities, nearly half of all arrests, half of all homicides, and one out of three suicides are alcohol-related. The suffering of families is not measurable.

Opium, marijuana, alcohol, and cocaine have been known since the earliest recorded times. More than 600 new drugs have been put on the market since 1940, many of them with abuse potential.

Research has found that a person abusing one drug is likely to abuse others, because he or she may be exposed to a variety through other abusers and sellers, and because of an "addictive personality."

As one reviews Table 17.1, there are some disconcerting trends. The '92–'93 change column indicates significant increases in the use of illicit drugs by high school seniors. The increased use of marijuana, LSD, and PCP indicates that some backsliding in drug use has begun. Perhaps the fact that drug abuse has received less national attention in the past few years has triggered this negative trend.

**TABLE 17.1  Long-Term Trends in *Lifetime* Prevalence of Various Types of Drugs for Twelfth Graders**

Percent ever used

| | Class of 1975 | Class of 1976 | Class of 1977 | Class of 1978 | Class of 1979 | Class of 1980 | Class of 1981 | Class of 1982 | Class of 1983 | Class of 1984 | Class of 1985 | Class of 1986 | Class of 1987 | Class of 1988 | Class of 1989 | Class of 1990 | Class of 1991 | Class of 1992 | Class of 1993 | '92–'93 change |
|---|---|---|---|---|---|---|---|---|---|---|---|---|---|---|---|---|---|---|---|---|
| Approx. *N* = | 9400 | 15400 | 17100 | 17800 | 15500 | 15900 | 17500 | 17700 | 16300 | 15900 | 16000 | 15200 | 16300 | 16300 | 16700 | 15200 | 15000 | 15800 | 16300 | |
| *Any Illicit Drug* | 55.2 | 58.3 | 61.6 | 64.1 | 65.1 | 65.4 | 65.6 | 64.4 | 62.9 | 61.6 | 60.6 | 57.6 | 56.6 | 53.9 | 50.9 | 47.9 | 44.1 | 40.7 | 42.9 | +2.2s |
| *Any Illicit Drug Other Than Marijuana* | 36.2 | 35.4 | 35.78 | 36.5 | 37.4 | 38.7 | 42.8 | 41.1 | 40.4 | 40.3 | 39.7 | 37.7 | 35.8 | 32.5 | 31.4 | 29.4 | 26.9 | 25.1 | 26.7 | +1.6 |
| Marijuana/Hashish | 47.3 | 52.8 | 56.4 | 59.2 | 60.4 | 60.3 | 59.5 | 58.7 | 57.0 | 54.9 | 54.2 | 50.9 | 50.2 | 47.2 | 43.7 | 40.7 | 36.7 | 32.6 | 35.3 | +2.7s |
| Inhalants | — | 10.3 | 11.1 | 12.0 | 12.7 | 11.9 | 12.3 | 12.8 | 13.6 | 14.4 | 15.4 | 15.9 | 17.0 | 16.7 | 17.6 | 18.0 | 17.6 | 16.6 | 17.4 | +0.8 |
| *Inhalants, Adjusted* | — | — | — | — | 18.2 | 17.3 | 17.2 | 17.7 | 18.2 | 18.0 | 18.1 | 20.1 | 18.6 | 17.5 | 18.6 | 18.5 | 18.0 | 17.0 | 17.7 | +0.7 |
| Amyl & Butyl Nitrites | — | — | — | — | 11.1 | 11.1 | 10.1 | 9.8 | 8.4 | 8.1 | 7.9 | 8.6 | 4.7 | 3.2 | 3.3 | 2.1 | 1.6 | 1.5 | 1.4 | -0.1 |
| Hallucinogens | 16.3 | 15.1 | 13.9 | 14.3 | 14.1 | 13.3 | 13.3 | 12.5 | 11.9 | 10.7 | 10.3 | 9.7 | 10.3 | 8.9 | 9.4 | 9.4 | 9.6 | 9.2 | 10.9 | +1.7ss |
| *Hallucinogens, Adjusted* | — | — | — | — | 17.7 | 15.6 | 15.3 | 14.3 | 13.6 | 12.3 | 12.1 | 11.9 | 10.6 | 9.2 | 9.9 | 9.7 | 10.0 | 9.4 | 11.3 | +1.9ss |
| LSD | 11.3 | 11.0 | 9.8 | 9.7 | 9.5 | 9.3 | 9.8 | 9.6 | 8.9 | 8.0 | 7.5 | 7.2 | 8.4 | 7.7 | 8.3 | 8.7 | 8.8 | 8.6 | 10.3 | +1.7ss |
| PCP | — | — | — | — | 12.8 | 9.6 | 7.8 | 6.0 | 5.6 | 5.0 | 4.9 | 4.8 | 3.0 | 2.9 | 3.9 | 2.8 | 2.9 | 2.4 | 2.9 | +0.5 |
| Cocaine | 9.0 | 9.7 | 10.8 | 12.9 | 15.4 | 15.7 | 16.5 | 16.0 | 16.2 | 16.1 | 17.3 | 16.9 | 15.2 | 12.1 | 10.3 | 9.4 | 7.8 | 6.1 | 6.1 | 0.0 |
| Crack | — | — | — | — | — | — | — | — | — | — | — | — | 5.4 | 4.8 | 4.7 | 3.5 | 3.1 | 2.6 | 2.6 | 0.0 |
| Other Cocaine | — | — | — | — | — | — | — | — | — | — | — | — | 14.0 | 12.1 | 8.5 | 8.6 | 7.0 | 5.3 | 5.4 | +0.1 |
| Heroin | 2.2 | 1.8 | 1.8 | 1.6 | 1.1 | 1.1 | 1.1 | 1.2 | 1.2 | 1.3 | 1.2 | 1.1 | 1.2 | 1.1 | 1.3 | 1.3 | 0.9 | 1.2 | 1.1 | -0.1 |
| Other Opiates | 9.0 | 9.6 | 10.3 | 9.9 | 10.1 | 9.8 | 10.1 | 9.6 | 9.4 | 9.7 | 10.2 | 9.0 | 9.2 | 8.6 | 8.3 | 8.3 | 6.6 | 6.1 | 6.4 | +0.3 |
| Stimulants | 22.3 | 22.6 | 23.0 | 22.9 | 24.2 | 26.4 | 32.2 | 27.9 | 26.9 | 27.9 | 26.2 | 23.4 | 21.6 | 19.8 | 19.1 | 17.5 | 15.4 | 13.9 | 15.1 | +1.2 |
| Crystal Meth. (Ice) | — | — | — | — | — | — | — | — | — | — | — | — | — | — | — | 2.7 | 3.3 | 2.9 | 3.1 | +0.2 |
| Sedatives | 18.2 | 17.7 | 17.4 | 16.0 | 14.6 | 14.9 | 16.0 | 15.2 | 14.4 | 13.3 | 11.8 | 10.4 | 8.7 | 7.8 | 7.4 | 7.5 | 6.7 | 6.1 | 6.4 | +0.3 |
| Barbiturates | 16.9 | 16.2 | 15.6 | 13.7 | 11.8 | 11.0 | 11.3 | 10.3 | 9.9 | 9.9 | 9.2 | 8.4 | 7.4 | 6.7 | 6.5 | 6.8 | 6.2 | 5.5 | 6.3 | +0.8 |
| Methaqualone | 8.1 | 7.8 | 8.5 | 7.9 | 8.3 | 9.5 | 10.6 | 10.7 | 10.1 | 8.3 | 6.7 | 5.2 | 4.0 | 3.3 | 2.7 | 2.3 | 1.3 | 1.6 | 0.8 | -0.8s |
| Tranquilizers | 17.0 | 16.8 | 18.0 | 17.0 | 16.3 | 15.2 | 14.7 | 14.0 | 13.3 | 12.4 | 11.9 | 10.9 | 10.9 | 9.4 | 7.6 | 7.2 | 7.2 | 6.0 | 6.4 | +0.4 |
| Alcohol | 90.4 | 91.9 | 92.5 | 93.1 | 93.0 | 93.2 | 92.6 | 92.8 | 92.6 | 92.6 | 92.2 | 91.3 | 92.2 | 92.0 | 90.7 | 89.5 | 88.0 | 87.5 | 87.0 | -0.5 |
| Been Drunk | — | — | — | — | — | — | — | — | — | — | — | — | — | — | — | — | 65.4 | 63.4 | 62.5 | -0.9 |
| Cigarettes | 73.6 | 75.4 | 75.7 | 75.3 | 74.0 | 71.0 | 71.0 | 70.1 | 70.6 | 69.7 | 68.8 | 67.6 | 67.2 | 66.4 | 65.7 | 64.4 | 63.1 | 61.8 | 61.9 | +0.1 |
| Smokeless Tobacco | — | — | — | — | — | — | — | — | — | — | — | 31.4 | 32.2 | 30.4 | 29.2 | — | — | 32.4 | 31.0 | -1.4 |
| Steroids | — | — | — | — | — | — | — | — | — | — | — | — | — | — | 3.0 | 2.9 | 2.1 | 2.1 | 2.0 | -0.1 |

*Notes:* Level of significance of difference between the two most recent classess: s = .05, ss = .01, sss = .001. '—' indicates data not available.

*Source:* U.S. Department of Health and Human Services, *Monitoring the Future: A Continuing Study of the Lifestyles and Values of Youth* (Rockville, MD: National Institute on Drug Abuse, 1994).

## Programs for Control, Prevention, Treatment

Before the 1960s the problems connected with drugs mainly concerned law enforcement officers. There was little effort to cure or rehabilitate addicts, for their numbers were few and it was believed that once a person was addicted there was little that could be done for him or her.

But when the problem assumed epidemic proportions, and especially when it reached the suburbs, a now concerned public began to look for ways of stopping the spread of drug use, of salvaging the victims, and of restoring the families. To accomplish this task takes the combined efforts of a concerned community—law enforcement, the medical profession, schools, legislators, and social agencies—all working toward a common goal.

### Government Agencies

The Bureau of Narcotics and Dangerous Drugs (BNDD) was established in 1968 to control the illicit use of narcotics and dangerous drugs through law enforcement, education, training, and research. It supports the efforts of state and local governments, gives aid to industry, universities, and others concerned with drug abuse. It is responsible for the enforcement of laws relating to narcotics, marijuana, depressants, stimulants, and hallucinogens. It also controls the legal trade in narcotics, insuring an adequate supply for medicinal purposes and research.[7]

As mentioned previously in this chapter, President Bush designated William Bennett as a "drug czar" with wide-ranging powers to coordinate the prevention, treatment, and law enforcement aspects of drug abuse. The 1989 Congress passed a bill allocating $9.4 billion to fund all aspects of the struggle against drugs. It was hoped that the high visibility of this cabinet position, the extra money, the President's sanction, and an aroused society would produce positive results. The Clinton administration is continuing the effort to address drug abuse by increased funding for drug prevention programs and by giving an economic boost to poverty families and their children in the form of new job opportunities. President Clinton is trying to develop a sense of hope and self esteem in vulnerable families throughout the country. He believes that this plan will address the causes of substance abuse.

Facilities already established—schools, social services, health organizations, and law enforcement agencies—form the basis for a community's program. Special clinics that focus on drug treatment are necessary and are described later in this chapter.

Programs involving social work can be classified according to the following general categories: (1) to head off abuse before it begins, (2) to treat the victims and their families, and (3) to alleviate social conditions that breed abuse.

### Education

To solve the drug problem, emphasis must be given to prevention. Social workers in schools and social agencies need to be alert to conditions that make for potential drug abuse, and take necessary steps to correct these circumstances.

Social workers help in the prevention and education program that includes, but is not limited to, the following:

Teaching about drug abuse in the classroom, beginning in elementary grades.
Arranging for groups to hear credible speakers.
Sponsoring adult education classes.
Helping business and industry take advantage of educational opportunities.
Training professionals and paraprofessionals who work with drug abusers.
Making information readily available to the public.

Changes that might be made in high schools to make schooling more appealing than drugs are: providing credit for students who work on community projects, greater involvement in their own learning and school administration, make vocational education programs relevant, and provide recreational facilities for leisure time. An effective preventive tool used in many high schools is the work of peer self-help groups. Students from a wide range of social and economic groups are taught how to reach all the students—with emphasis on those who appear to be vulnerable—to help them remain drug free.

Recognizing that drug abusers are people with personal problems, and that these problems often originate in the family interaction, many school districts are developing family life education programs that extend from kindergarten through high school. Successful programs relate drug abuse to self-understanding, interpersonal and family relationships, and the role of the family in society.

Just as young people like to talk with their peers, so do parents appreciate opportunities for talking with other parents. In groups they learn about drugs and also have the supportive contact of other parents who may have problems similar to their own. With imagination, leaders, who are often social workers, use role playing, small discussion groups, films, and lectures.

## Treatment

Community programs generally give high priority to treatment facilities for drug abusers. Social and psychiatric services have been combined with medicine in treatment. Therapeutic services include psychotherapy, family therapy, medical and chemical treatment, and individual and group counseling.

Because there are differences in the treatment approach to the different drugs used, a variety of modalities have been developed for abusers. A method of treatment that works well for one may not be effective for another. Treatment centers for drug abusers include emergency care, inpatient services, outpatient clinics, chemical therapy, therapeutic communities, and referral services. Social workers are important members of the teams of professionals who staff these services.

## Emergency Care

Provisions for emergency medical and nonmedical help need to be provided. Social workers in drug crisis centers and Hotlines, maintained on a twenty-four-hour basis, deal with many emergencies.

## Inpatient Services

An essential in any drug treatment program is a facility to detoxify narcotic and barbiturate addicts who are in crisis situations. Individuals who have become dependent on drugs or who have serious illnesses connected with their drug use need hospital care. Because of frequent psychotic and paranoid reactions by users of barbiturates and amphetamines, it is usually preferable to detoxify them on an inpatient basis. Withdrawal from these drugs requires constant care because of the many physical and psychological complications that may arise.

## Outpatient Services

Many agencies provide outpatient therapy, including established mental health centers and social agencies in addition to the clinics or treatment centers established exclusively for drug abusers. They may offer short- or long-term therapy, combine methadone or other chemical therapy, or offer group sessions. Outpatient clinics are often the first contact an abuser has when seeking help.

Some cities use outpatient clinics to detoxify patients, and most hospitals stabilize methadone patients on an ambulatory basis. Psychotherapy, vocational and educational assistance, and help in solving personal problems are services that are available to support addicts who have been detoxified and are seeking help on an outpatient basis.

## Methadone Maintenance

The use of methadone to "cure" heroin addiction is a controversial solution to the problem. Those who oppose its use maintain that methadone itself is addictive and should not be used to cure narcotic addiction. Those who favor its use say it is orally effective, nontoxic, and safe to use over a long period of time. It is used in both inpatient and outpatient clinics where the staff usually includes a psychiatrist, a physician, nurses, social workers, and paraprofessionals.

After a patient has worked through personal, family, and employment problems, and is successfully living a normal life, the methadone is gradually decreased until he or she is drug free. The time involved varies but many are able to achieve a drug-free state in about nine months. This method has helped thousands of hardcore addicts to become law-abiding citizens.

## Narcotic Antagonists

Narcotic antagonists are drugs that work against opiates, and when they are used, narcotics cannot be felt. Two antagonists commonly used are cyclazocine and naloxone. They have been effective with well-motivated and well-integrated persons, and are also used with younger users.

## Therapeutic Communities

Self-help therapeutic communities have generated great interest. Across the nation hundreds of facilities offer residential experiences, small group therapy, and participation in vocational rehabilitation preparatory to living "outside" again.

Admission requirements and living rules generally stress the need for the user to come to grips with his or her problem, and accept the help offered. Many depend heavily upon paraprofessionals, usually ex-addicts who serve as counselors and role models. Long-term surveillance and after-care attention, plus the closeness of the group, are basic ingredients of the treatment program.

## Therapeutic Communities for Young Users

Since many young abusers are unable to get the help they need from outpatient facilities, some workers in the drug abuse field recommend therapeutic communities especially adapted to youth. They often need vocational and on-the-job training as well as high school classes needed for graduation. Work with their families is often indicated.

## Treatment for Alcohol Abuse

Alcoholics Anonymous (AA), using the self-help approach, has been the outstanding source of help for the alcoholic in the past. Its auxiliaries, Al-Anon and Al-Ateen, have helped spouses and children. Alcoholics, as other addicts, show a history of emotional deprivation, feelings of inferiority, depression, anxiety, and difficulties with parents and family. Social workers are seeing more alcoholics and their families in mental health clinics, family counseling centers, and in industry-sponsored clinics.

## Integrating Approaches to Treatment

Having a number of approaches to treatment makes it possible for drug abusers to choose the type of treatment best suited to their needs. Outpatient services are the least expensive. Long-term inpatient services are expensive, and many are not able to commit themselves to staying on the program long enough to be rehabilitated.

In making plans with an individual for treatment, social and family ties, job opportunities, and personal strengths need to be assessed before deciding which facility would best suit his or her needs. With their knowledge of community resources, social workers are helpful in providing information to patients of the types of facilities available. They also aid in coordinating the efforts of those who work with this problem.

To combat this widespread use and abuse of drugs, it would help to: (1) strengthen parent-child relationships, (2) stress positive aspects of the parent role in the home, (3) make clear and articulate to children the value system of parents, (4) make the school experience socially and emotionally rewarding and supportive for youth, and (5) program all social institutions in their efforts on behalf of youth to achieve a growth-promoting, psychological, therapeutic, and educational experience.

The teen years are difficult for most youngsters. Some who have not had strong relationships with their parents and have no close family ties, who have had difficulties in school, or who have had conflict with the law turn to drugs for relief of anxieties, to help them acquire status with a group, to achieve sociability, or to defy authority. Social work is one of the professions that can help. Teenagers often seek help from social workers when life is threatening and difficult.

## Preventing Alcohol and Other Drug Abuse

Treatment and rehabilitation of drug addicts and alcoholics is expensive as well as unpredictable as to its ultimate success. Therefore, programs to alleviate conditions that breed drug abuse should be given high priority.

Although drug abuse most often starts in adolescence, the climate that precipitates it may start many years earlier. Teachers and social workers in the schools can be alert for problems of children in elementary grades, and institute education, counseling, or therapy.

Adolescents who have a variety of interests and ways of using their leisure time are less likely to become involved in the drug culture. A community drug abuse council can generate action to provide alternatives and new and appealing programs for youth.

## Research

Research is being conducted covering many phases of drug abuse, including medical factors, law enforcement problems, industrial losses, and social implications. Research plays an important part in the understanding of this problem and likely will continue.

Parents, as role models for their children, need to examine the effect of their own use of legal and illegal drugs. Parents who use legal psychoactive or mood-altering drugs (such as sedatives, depressants, stimulants, or sleeping pills) should examine honestly their reasons for doing so. In consultation with their spouse, adult friends, and physicians, they should decide whether they can do without these prescription drugs; if they cannot, they should be extremely cautious not to abuse medical permission to use them. Parents also should tell their children why they use the drug, that it is a legally controlled substance, that it should never be mixed with other drugs or alcohol, and that it should never be used "for fun." It is medicine, not a "recreational drug."

Parents who use illegal drugs might wish to reevaluate their behavior. Not to use legal or illegal drugs may not prevent their children from using them. It will however increase their credibility when trying to intervene or prevent their children's abuse of drugs.

Most young people learn about illicit drug use from their peers. Blum conducted a lengthy study to find out why some youngsters become drug users and others do not.[8] This study has significance to social workers. Blum and associates studied 101 white middle-class families, classified according to the drug use of their children. All families lived in the same area, both parents lived at home, one child was in college and younger children were at home. All members of the families participated.

Conclusions from this study are that children from homes where parental love and concern are evident, where teachings against use of mind- or mood-altering substances are stressed, and where emotional needs are met are less likely to become drug users.

The families in this study where there was no drug abuse were alert, flexible, firm, polite, self-confident, honest, and forgiving. These qualities can be learned, and if they are not learned through the family, they can be learned through other group experiences. Priority needs to be given to action programs that help families develop responsible citizens. Peer groups will become the primary force in a young person's life only if parents relinquish their position as head of the family.

Blum's research points to an association between drug abuse and home influences. Other studies reveal similar associations between drug abuse and the school, employment, the widespread use of prescription drugs, and the drug culture. As with most major social problems, there are many influences within and outside the individual that contribute to the misuse and abuse of drugs.

Harrison evaluated an alcohol- and other drug-prevention demonstration project that was funded by the National Office for Substance Abuse Prevention.[9] The project was designed to reduce risk factors for alcohol and other drug abuse by improving family communication skills.

Harrison found that families who participated in the project significantly increased family cohesion, family time together, and decreased family conflicts. The parents showed increases in their parenting abilities and mental health, and the youth exhibited less problem behaviors, better social skills, and engaged in more appropriate behavior.

The Johnston et al. study has indicated that after several years of significant decline in illicit drug use, high school seniors are beginning to use more drugs. Hopefully, the 1993 increases in drug use will not signify a new upward trend. The Johnston study points out the following facts to indicate the magnitude and variety of substance-use problems which remain among American young people:

- By the end of eighth grade, one-third (32 percent) of American secondary school students have tried an illicit drug (if inhalants are included as an illicit drug). Almost two-fifths of tenth graders have done so (39 percent), and nearly one-half of twelfth graders (47 percent).
- By their late twenties, over 75 percent of America's young adults today have tried an illicit drug, including over 50 percent who have tried some illicit drug other than marijuana. These figures do not include inhalants.
- By age 28, about one-third of young Americans have tried cocaine; and as early as the senior year of high school 6 percent have done so. Roughly one in every forty seniors (2.6 percent) have tried the particularly dangerous form of cocaine called crack; in the young adult sample one in twenty-five (4.3 percent) have tried it.
- One in forty (2.4 percent) of high school seniors in 1993 smoke marijuana daily, as is true among young adults aged 19 to 28 (2.4 percent). Among seniors in 1993, 9.6 percent had been daily marijuana smokers at some time for at least a month, and among young adults the comparable figure is 12.8 percent.
- Some 28 percent of seniors had five or more drinks in a row at least once in the prior two weeks, and such behavior tends to increase among young adults one to four years past high school. The prevalence of such behavior among male college students reaches 49 percent.
- Some 30 percent of seniors are current cigarette smokers and 19 percent already are current daily smokers, and these numbers are rising. In addition, many of the lighter smokers will convert to heavy smoking after high school.

Thus, despite the improvements in recent years, it is still true that this nation's secondary school students and young adults show a level of involvement with illicit drugs which is greater than has been documented in any other industrialized nation in the world. Even by longer-term historical standards in this country, these rates remain extremely high. Heavy drinking also remains widespread and troublesome; and certainly the continuing initiation of a large and growing proportion of young people to cigarette smoking is a matter of the greatest public health concern.

- Finally, we note the seemingly unending capacity of pharmacological experts and amateurs to discover new substances with abuse potential that can be used to alter mood and consciousness, as well as the potential for our young people to "discover" the abuse potential of existing products, like Robitussin™, and to "rediscover" older drugs, such as LSD. While as a society we have made significant progress on a number of fronts in the fight against drug abuse, we must continually be preparing for, and remaining vigilant against, the opening of new fronts, as well as the re-emergence of trouble on older ones.
- The drug problem is not an enemy which can be vanquished, as in a war. It is more a recurring and relapsing problem which must be contained to the extent possible on a long-term, ongoing basis.[10]

## Role of Social Work in Treatment

Social work is becoming more involved in the treatment of drug abusers. As in the case with the abuse of alcohol, the families of drug abusers are almost always affected; they need help to understand the problem, to allay fears, anxieties, and guilt feelings; to help solidify the family unit; and at the same time learn to give support to the abuser.

Social workers are called upon to help in a variety of traditional social work settings—juvenile courts, adult probation and parole, mental health clinics, hospitals, family counseling centers, schools, university health and counseling centers, and in private practice. In addition, drug treatment centers are employing social workers. In many, social workers are the administrators as well as the therapists, and work with the psychiatrist, physician, psychologist, and often ex-addicts who may, or may not, have had professional training as counselors.

Most addicts and abusers have serious personality problems, suffer from social maladjustment, or have disruptive home influences before they start using drugs. Treatment cannot be complete until these earlier problems are faced and worked through. Social workers provide these services.

Working with addicts presents many problems that social workers have not heretofore encountered, and new methods of approach and new thinking are needed to cope with the situations they are facing.

One of the big problems in traditional casework methods is that attempting to substitute acceptable satisfactions for drugs does not appeal to the addict because there is nothing else that creates the euphoria with its accompanying feeling of "all's right with the world." Casework should not be abandoned, but must become flexible enough to bend with the client, who possibly has little motivation to give up drugs. Drug users seek help if they are financially unable to support the habit, if they are worn out from evading the police, are physically ill, if they have had a close friend die of an overdose, or if they have to choose between going to jail or seeking treatment.

For many addicts, it is unrealistic to assume that the only goal is to be drug free. With the use of chemotherapy many who have been unable to continue in drug-free treatment centers are finding their way back into productivity. Social workers may set the ultimate goal of total abstinence, but must realize that this may be achieved only after numerous relapses, if at all. It is important for workers to realize that any period of abstinence is a step forward, and has important aspects to the user, family, and to the community. Addicts often return to the use of drugs when crises occur.

Some of the ways that social workers are involved in the treatment of drug and alcohol abusers and their families are illustrated by the following examples.

## Treating Preaddictive Adolescents

Treating preaddictive adolescents is difficult. The results of most studies indicate that a total-family approach is necessary. Parents and adolescents have to agree to a set of ground rules. There should he no drugs available in the home, and the parents have to be committed to this condition. Parents have to enforce the rules by providing constant vigilance, parental prohibition, and love.

Most parents have an underlying concern to be good parents. Through the enforcement of the rules, parents begin to feel respected. Parents also begin to see themselves as positive forces in the lives of their children. Many times adolescents will respond to the more positive atmosphere in the family and feel that their parents really do care about their successes and about them.

When the family atmosphere begins to improve, the social worker should give both the parents and adolescent positive feedback and reinforcement. The worker can play an important role in sustaining the family improvement.

## Social Work with Alcoholics

Social work has been slow to reach out to the alcoholic to offer therapy, leaving this large group to get help from Alcoholics Anonymous and Salvation Army programs. With an estimated annual increase of 200,000, alcoholics and their families are greatly in need of the service of social workers, who have much to offer with traditional and new methods of therapy. As with other addicts, no one method of treatment is successful with all, and a variety of approaches greatly increases the likelihood that one will find the treatment that fits his or her particular needs. Treatment centers and trained personnel have not kept pace with the demands.

Social workers must increase their knowledge and skills in working with alcoholics. As Kane states:

> For social workers in alcoholism clinics, inpatient alcoholism treatment centers, halfway houses, court-affiliated "drunk driving" programs, the prevention and treatment of alcohol problems in some form or other are the primary focus of their work. But for many other social workers (and perhaps, unfortunately, to a greater

extent than they appreciate) some form of problem drinking is an intervening variable complicating the achievement of professional goals with a client. Problem drinking, for instance, often contributes to child and wife abuse, delinquent behavior, marital friction, economic dependence, and noncompliance with medical regimens. As one article illustrates, alcohol abuse by one or more parents may even be an unsuspected contributor to the poor performance in school of children in the caseload of a school social worker. Taken together, we social workers are in frontline positions to identify problem drinking in a family constellation and to make appropriate referrals for special help or to incorporate goals on drinking practices into our own work with clients.[11]

Working with the alcoholic presents different problems from working with other clients, and requires understanding of the disease as well as of the individual. Workers who reject alcoholics will not be successful with them, for they are usually very sensitive people with low self-esteem and, having experienced rejection by their families, friends, and employers, look for it in social workers. It is important for the worker to understand that clients will have relapses, but this does not mean failure.

It is important to understand that family support is essential in the treatment of alcoholics. In almost all families, there is disorganization and distress over the alcoholic's problems. The extent to which families suffer from the effects of alcoholism is difficult to describe. Not only do they often suffer monetary privations, but also have to endure rejection by neighbors and friends; anxiety and guilt feelings; and humiliation, abuse, neglect, and failure. Clearly, the problem of alcoholism in one individual cannot be separated from its effect on all the members of a family. The whole family needs to recover from this family disease.

## Treating a Heroin Addict on an Outpatient Basis

Charles, a heroin addict, was successful in becoming drug free by the use of methadone, coupled with intensive therapy and vocational assistance.

---

Charles came into the clinic every morning at 6:45 to be checked, and to drink his daily supply of methadone on his way to work. He chatted amiably with the fellow in back of him in line, commented to his social worker on the music at the symphony concert he had attended the night before, and went whistling out the door.

Eleven months earlier when Charles first dragged into the clinic, he was burned out, in poor health, and in the depths of despair. He had been caught in a burglary, and the judge had given him the alternative of seeking help or going to jail.

In his early twenties, Charles was married and had one son. He was always broke, had mountains of unpaid bills, was suspicious and depressed. In the home there was constant conflict over his addiction, lack of respect, indifference to his family obligations, and unlawful activities. He spent most of his time hustling money to buy a fix, and often turned to burglarizing to obtain cash or property to pawn to supply his heroin.

At the clinic, he was made to feel comfortable and helped to accept the treatment offered. He suffered during the first few weeks, and would certainly have dropped out if he could have done so without going to jail. But after he had been stabilized on methadone he was helped to find a job as a bricklayer, which he enjoyed.

He was given help with his personal problems in therapy sessions during the evening, and his wife came with him for group therapy where they both were given support and understanding of the drug problem.

Several times conflicts, anxieties, and feelings of helplessness made him reach out for the euphoria of heroin. But he would start over again. To help him through the evening hours, the clinic frequently provided him with tickets to symphony concerts, plays, and ballets, which afforded new experiences for him. During the summer one of the counselors, a former addict, took him hiking and fishing on weekends.

After seven months of treatment, Charles and his wife had paid off their most pressing debts and were able to move into their own apartment, being alone for the first time in four years. When family life became more stable, his job secure, and his finances adequate, the team of workers at the clinic decided to cut down on his daily doses of methadone, a little at a time, until he was drug free.

Charles was one of the relatively few who did become drug free. Unfortunately, all cases are not this successful.

## Social Work with Addicts in an Inpatient Facility

Some heroin addicts have such serious personal problems that they are unable to maintain themselves or benefit from help offered in outpatient clinics. For them, inpatient services are needed. Linda, who needed constant support on a twenty-four-hour basis, is a case study in a community-sponsored clinic.

Linda, age 23 and pregnant, voluntarily came to the clinic optimistic about kicking her addiction. She had tried a drug-free therapeutic community, but had been unable to maintain their strict requirements.

She had started using marijuana at age 18, and had tried barbiturates, amphetamines, and tranquilizers. She had been addicted to heroin for about three years. Those years had been permeated with a succession of affairs, a brief marriage, the births of two infants, and continual involvement with the criminal justice system for theft, prostitution, drugs, and traffic violations.

Linda was bright, resourceful, manipulative, and highly motivated to become drug free one day, but lacking in motivation another day. Her two children had been placed in foster care, and the judge had decreed that she could not have them back unless she was totally drug free within six months. She wanted to have her children, and this was the chief source of motivation.

In therapy she was rarely able to handle insightful kinds of efforts, fleeing either mentally, physically, or both from any attempt to examine the psychodynamics of her personality. She related only to crisis intervention or task-centered therapeutic approaches. Her only concern was with immediate solutions to currently pressing problems directly affecting her. She responded to such problems with a sense of panic, despair, or urgency. Avoidance was typically preferable to having to deal with the problem. Once a problem was solved, she saw no value in learning how it had developed or how it could have been handled in less anxiety-provoking ways.

By virtue of her membership in the drug culture, she had successfully learned habits, values, attitudes, and lifestyle modes of behavior with which she could function well in that subculture. She could efficiently function in aspects of the larger social system that were important to her lifestyle, for example, the criminal justice system and the social welfare system. When necessary, she could function in the "straight" labor market to meet her immediate needs.

In a therapeutic-helping relationship the social worker set a specific goal to build a foundation of trust and confidence that would enable Linda to feel comfortable in asking for help with her day-to-day problems. A longer range goal was to deepen that trust and confidence.

She was able initially to communicate that she recognized her emotional difficulties, but had previously discovered that the fear of risking oftentimes had become too great to handle, so that she felt unable or unwilling to delve into her feelings any further than just the initial cry for help. She withdrew from the risk, hurt, and fear of explaining her feelings by running away, either physically, mentally, or both. She would curl up, face away, leave the room, go to sleep, or decline to talk.

Several weeks before the birth of her child, she became completely drug free, hoping the baby would not be addicted. But three days after birth, the infant began to show withdrawal symptoms. This necessitated finding a foster home where the foster parents would have the patience and understanding and stamina necessary for the close vigilance of this child. Having the baby addicted was defeating to Linda, who felt she had tried hard to save it from this difficulty. She was very depressed and in the next few weeks needed constant support.

In seeking support and then not being able to utilize it fully, Linda nevertheless received valuable reinforcement through the meaningful testing of loyalties that she felt capable of initiating. She learned that help was really there, that promises were fulfilled, and that the relationship remained intact regardless of the problems encountered. The decision of the judge that she be drug free within six months was not realistic in terms of her extremely precarious history. It was apparent that he was imposing his values on her, and that she would not be able to respond, not within the time limit he set. Many people lead a "normal" life, maintain a home, and work steadily on methadone maintenance. Perhaps using these guidelines, a more realistic goal could have been set for Linda, one that she possibly could have attained.

## Summary

Narcotics, marijuana, and alcohol have been used from the earliest recorded times, and are likely to be used for years to come. Add the enormous number of new drugs that have been put on the market since World War II, and it is easy to see that the drug-abuse problem is one that will not easily be eradicated. Almost daily it is discovered that another drug has the potential for abuse.

Most drug abuse begins with teenagers who are influenced by their peers to try something new and exciting. Some of them continue to experiment until it is too late to turn back without help. The extent of drug addiction and dependence is enormous, and extremely costly both in terms of personal loss and the monetary loss to society as a whole.

No single agency or small group of agencies can handle this problem. A total community effort is necessary, using education, preventive measures, various treatment modalities, and rehabilitative services to those who are the victims of drugs.

Because of the almost insurmountable difficulties to treatment of many addicts, emphasis needs to be given to programs of prevention among the coming generations. Factual information alone will not do this. Efforts are needed to strengthen the family, and to make family relation-

ships a dominant force in the lives of young people, to help children develop positive attitudes,
communication skills, and provide satisfying
experiences in their school activities. It is important to find recreational and leisure time activities
that will turn young people to worthwhile endeavors, instead of having them turn to drugs.

A herculean task is presented by drug abuse,
and it is becoming increasingly clear that little
short of a total community effort is needed to make
inroads into what was once considered hopeless.
Social work can help.

## Selected References

BECK, AARON T., *Cognitive Therapy of Substance Abuse,* New York: Guilford Press, 1993.

BLUM, RICHARD H., and ASSOCIATES, *Horatio Alger's Children: The Role of the Family in the Origin and Prevention of Drug Risk.* San Francisco: Jossey-Bass, 1972.

CHASNOFF, IRA, "Cocaine, Pregnancy and the Growing Child," *Current Problems in Pediatrics,* August 1992.

COHEN, SIDNEY, *The Substance Abuse Problems,* vol. 2. New York: The Haworth Press, 1985.

GRANT, MARCUS, and BRUCE PITSON, *Alcohol: The Prevention Debate.* New York: St. Martin's Press, 1983.

JOHNSTON, LLOYD D., PATRICK M. O'MALLEY and JERALD G. BACHMAN, *National Survey Results on Drug Use from the Monitoring the Future Study, 1975–1993.* Washington, DC: National Institute on Drug Abuse, NIH Publications No. 94–3809, 1994.

KNOTT, DAVID H., *Alcohol Problems: Diagnosis and Treatment.* Elmsford, NY: Pergamon Press, 1986.

NATIONAL INSTITUTE ON DRUG ABUSE, *Let's Talk About Drug Abuse.* Washington, DC: U.S. Department of Health, Education, and Welfare, DHEW Publication No. (ADM) 78-706, 1979.

NATIONAL INSTITUTE ON DRUG ABUSE, *Drug Abuse and Drug Abuse Research: The Third Triennial Report to Congress.* Washington, DC: U.S. Department of Health and Human Services, 1991.

ROBINSON, DAVID, *Talking Out of Alcoholism: The Self-help Process of Alcoholics Anonymous.* Baltimore, MD: University Park Press, 1979.

STEPHENS, RICHARD C., *The Street Addict Role: A Theory of Heroin Addiction.* Ithaca: New York State University Press, 1991.

TURNER, FRANCIS J., ed., *Adult Psychopathology.* New York: The Free Press, 1984.

TURNER, FRANCIS J., ed., *Child Psychopathology.* New York: Free Press, 1989.

VAILLANT, GEORGE E., *The Natural History of Alcoholism: Causes, Patterns and Paths to Recovery.* Cambridge, MA: Harvard University Press, 1983.

WITTERS, W., and P. VENTURELLI, *Drugs and Society,* 2nd ed. Boston: Jones and Bartlett Publishers, 1988.

## Notes

1. Richard H. Blum and Associates, *The Dream Sellers* (San Francisco: Jossey-Bass, 1972), p. 4.

2. Utah State Representatives Craig Moody and Nolan Karras, as quoted in *Deseret News,* Salt Lake City, UT, June 20, 1989, B–1.

3. Lloyd D. Johnston, Patrick M. O'Malley, and Jerald G. Bachman, *National Survey Results on Drug Use from the Monitoring the Future Study, 1975–1993* (Washington, DC: National Institute on Drug Abuse, NIH Publication no. 94–3809, 1994), pp. 23–24.

4. Morton A. Stenchever, Terry J. Kunysz, and Majorie A. Allen, "Chromosome Breakage in Users of Marijuana," *American Journal of Obstetrics and Gynecology,* 118 (January 1974), 109, 111.

5. Channing L. Bete Co., Inc., "What Everyone Should Know About Alcoholism," a scriptographic booklet (South Deerfield, MA: 1985), p. 5.

6. Karol L. Kumpfer, "Prevention Approaches to Adolescent Substance Use/Abuse," presentation to the American Academy of Child Psychiatry Institute on Substance Abuse and Adolescence (San Antonio, TX: October 23, 1985).

7. Bureau of Narcotics and Dangerous Drugs, *Fact Sheets* (Washington, DC: U.S. Department of Justice, n.d.), pp. 1–1, 1–2.

8. Richard H. Blum and Associates, *Horatio Alger's Children* (San Francisco: Jossey-Bass, 1972).

9. Steven R. Harrison, *Final Evaluation Report: Community Youth Activity Project,* Social Research Institute, Graduate School of Social Work, University of Utah, Salt Lake City, 1992.

10. Johnston, *National Survey Results on Drug Use from the Monitoring the Future Study, 1975–1993,* pp. 6–7.

11. Rosalie Kane, "To Our Health!... Social Work and Alcohol Problems," *Health and Social Work,* 4 (November 1979), pp. 6–7.

# Chapter *18*

# *Services with Minorities*

*Joe and Ron, 17-year-old high school seniors, celebrated graduation by participating in drinking parties that resulted in each stealing an auto. Both were picked up by the police the next day, but Ron was released to his parents; Joe, who was black, was put in jail. Although they had both been in* *trouble with the law a few times, when they were brought before the juvenile court judge, Joe was sent to the Youth Development Center and Ron was placed on probation. People who knew them both observed that they should have been treated the same.*

Social work has a deep tradition in social reform. Part of that early effort was in working with minorities and addressing such issues as immigration laws, relocation, and work with individuals.

With the civil rights movements of the 1960s, social work became more sensitive to the pressing problems of minorities as affected by various social institutions. Social work is attempting to strengthen and broaden its approach in its effort to bring about institutional change that will benefit minorities in America. At the present time many new forces are appearing that may change the direction of the country in addressing the social structures needed to deal with minority problems. In 1995 California took a strong stand against affirmative action, and their governor attempted to use that stand as a national platform on which to launch his presidential campaign. California also voted for Proposition 187, which denied most public services to illegal immigrants. NASW News reported:

> Six states—California, Texas and Florida among them—have sued the federal government to recoup billions the states contend they have spent for public services, education, health care and prison costs for illegal immigrants. In 1993, Florida started denying foster care to illegal immigrant children, a policy that also is being challenged in court, according to news reports.[1]

It has become clear that if social work is to assist minorities effectively, it must mediate the strong forces that seem to be returning the blame of minority problems to the victims themselves. Social workers must not forget both the subtle and overt discrimination in our society that deprives minority groups from accessing rewarding social roles such as good jobs and good education.

## Minority Problems

Racial discrimination is real. A vivid example is given in the *Autobiography of Malcolm X*. When Malcolm told his eighth-grade teacher that be wanted to be a lawyer, she advised him:

> Malcolm, one of life's first needs is for us to be realistic.... A lawyer, that's no realistic goal for a nigger.... You are good with your hands—making things.... Why don't you plan to become a carpenter?[2]

*Racism* is the word used to reflect prejudices and mistreatment of those from minority groups, particularly blacks, American Indians, and Spanish-speaking Americans. Two kinds of racism—individual and institutional—are described by Carmichael and Hamilton:

> Racism is both overt and covert. It takes two closely related forms: individual whites acting against individual blacks, and acts by the total white community against the black community. We call these individual racism and institutional racism. The first consists of overt acts by individuals, which cause death, injury, or the violent destruction of property. This type can be recorded by television cameras; it can frequently be observed in the process of commission. The second type is less overt, far more subtle, less identifiable in terms of *specific* individuals committing the acts. But it is no less destructive of human life. The second type originates in the operation of established and respected forces in the society, and thus receives far less public condemnation than the first type.
>
> When white terrorists bomb a black church and kill five black children, that is an act of individual racism, widely deplored by most segments of the society. But when in the same city—Birmingham, Alabama—500 black babies die each year because of the lack of proper food, shelter, and medical facilities, and thousands more are destroyed and maimed physically, emotionally, and intellectually because of conditions of poverty and discrimination in the black community, that is a function of institutional racism.[3]

Jones underlined the potency of racism when he wrote: "Institutional racism is comparable to a runaway vine. Often it is difficult to find its root. And as with the vine, you can kill as many branches as you choose, but if you fail to destroy the root, the vine continues to grow."[4]

There have been important gains in the lifestyles of minorities since the Civil Rights Act was passed on June 29, 1964. No longer would a public school teacher suggest openly that "... a lawyer, that's no realistic goal for a nigger."

Ethnic minorities are a large and important segment of our society. According to the 1990 Census, the three largest racial or ethnic minorities in the United States (total population 248.7 million) are blacks (29.9 million, 12.1 percent); Hispanics (22.4 million, 9 percent); and Asian Americans (7.3 million, 2.9 percent). Hispanics added the greatest number of people between 1980 and 1990, but the Asian group gained approximately 108 percent during the decade, making it proportionately the fastest-growing ethnic minority group.

The total nonwhite population in the United States increased from 23.3 percent in 1980 to 28.7 percent in 1990.

The structure and culture of the United States are continually attempting to accommodate and assimilate people from all over the world. Historically the "melting-pot" theory was established as the answer for new immigrants coming to the United States. This theory suggests that all kinds of people are brought together, and a superior breed results from the assimilation of the new members. Glasgow suggests that "the melting-pot ideal was never viewed as encompassing black Americans or any other nonwhites."[5] Many believe that cultural diversity and ethnic reaffirmation are important and enriching aspects of the American way of life, that values and opportunities inhere in multiethnic diversities.

Even though gains have been made by ethnic minorities in this country, discrimination is still a real problem. Minority groups have never been offered the full scope of the reward structures of our society. Wilson states:

> It is no secret that the social problems of urban life in the United States are, in great measure, associated with race.
>
> While rising rates of crime, drug addiction, out-of-wedlock births, female-headed families, and welfare dependency have afflicted American society generally in recent years, the increases have been most dramatic among what has become a large and seemingly permanent black underclass inhabiting the cores of the nation's major cities.
>
> And yet, liberal journalists, social scientists, policy makers, and civil-rights leaders for almost two decades have been reluctant to face this fact. Often, analysts of such issues as violent crime or teenage pregnancy deliberately make no reference to race at all, unless to emphasize the deleterious consequences of racial discrimination or the institutionalized inequality of American society.[6]

The black underclass is struggling in the inner cities, but other blacks have made significant progress. Puckrein reports that the proportion of all black families earning an annual income of $25,000 or more (in 1982 dollars) grew from 10.4 to 24.5 percent between 1960 and 1982. Puckrein also notes that between 1970 and 1980 the number of blacks annually enrolled in American universities doubled from 522,000 to over one million. Also, blacks have moved into white-collar and professional occupations as well as owning some 230,000 businesses (according to 1977 figures).[7]

In addition to blacks, Hispanics, Asian Americans, American Indians, and other minority groups display a scenario of both continuing problems and progress. However, anyone looking at the total picture must admit to the critical, growing gap between the majority and minority populations.

Two years before the racially motivated riots in Los Angeles, one author, Hugh Davis Graham, warned:

> As the United States approaches the year 2000, special studies are accumulating that describe our entry into the 21st century with a tone of alarm. In *LA 2000: A City for the Future,* a blue ribbon panel of civic leaders assisted by the Rand Corporation warned that "Los Angeles is rapidly becoming a bimodal city." The city's

high school class of 2000, which was just entering kindergarten when *LA 2000* was released was more than 72% minority (51.4% Hispanic, 12.4% Black, 6.9% Asian). In 1988, 38% of these students were classified as limited-English proficient (LEP), and a third of them (approximately 25% of the Black students and 40% of the Latino students) were expected to drop out of school. Almost half of the applicants for entry-level jobs in Los Angeles County, the report observed, were currently rejected because of inadequate skills in reading, writing, and basic computations.[8]

Graham further concludes:

> The growth of a two-tiered society in 21st century America suggested an Orwellian future—of class warfare deepened by racial, ethnic, and generational strife. . . .[9]

In another study, sponsored by the U.S. Department of Labor, the authors state:

> If the policies and employment patterns of the present continue, it is likely that the demographic opportunity of the 1990s will be missed and that by the year 2000, the problems of minority unemployment, crime and dependency will be worse than they are today. Without substantial adjustments, blacks and Hispanics will have a smaller fraction of the jobs of the year 2000 than they have today, while their share of those seeking work will have risen.[10]

Social workers responded quickly to the 1992 Los Angeles rioting by going "into school, disaster centers, and communities, offering crisis counseling, delivering food and clothing, and confronting ethnic tensions, racism and bigotry."[11] Hiratsuka states:

> Few were surprised by the violence that exploded this spring after a jury acquitted four white police officers of nearly all charges in the beating of Rodney King, a black motorist whose ordeal was captured on videotape.
>   Social workers traced the roots of the crisis to a society that refuses to acknowledge race and class division, denies opportunities to those at the bottom and often pits struggling ethnic groups against each other. Many despaired of making U.S. leaders understand the seriousness of the problems that led to the nation's deadliest riot—and could do so again.[12]

More than any other profession, social work has tried to address the problems of discrimination. In 1978 the Council on Social Work Education published *The Dual Perspective: Inclusion of Ethnic Minority Content in the Social Work Curriculum.* The Dual Perspective model was actually mandated by the social work profession to sensitize both social work faculty and students to the special problems and needs of minorities. De Hoyos and colleagues describe the dual perspective model as follows:

> The model suggests that individuals develop two self-images: a personal self-image (through the individual's family and immediate community—the nurturing

system) and a social self-image (through the society's political, economic, and educational systems—the sustaining system). It further suggests that whether minority group members acquire a good or poor self-image within the family unit, they usually develop a poor "social," or "major," self-image because of the prejudice and discrimination typically found in social institutions.[13]

De Hoyos and co-workers further state that although the dual perspective has been an important sensitizing tool in social work, they believe that two other perspectives are utilized much more in social work literature to explain the problems of minorities. These two perspectives are cultural dissonance and institutional racism.[14] Traditionally, cultural dissonance has been thought to be created by the differences between the culture of the minority group and the culture of the majority group. Cultural dissonance can be illustrated by the following case history:

Jane was an 18-year-old Indian girl who finished her high school education on one of the larger southwest reservations. She went to college in another state. She had a struggle in getting registered and getting adjusted to the large impersonal college system. Three weeks into the semester one of Jane's aunts died unexpectedly and, as was the custom or culture of her family, Jane immediately left for the reservation. She did not think it was appropriate to mention her family situation to any of her teachers. When she returned to school, she was critically behind in much of her work. A few of her teachers were understanding, but most of them required her to make up the class work quickly and under pressure. Jane panicked and left the college without even taking the time to withdraw formally.

The culture of Jane's family had required her to leave to attend her aunt's funeral. The college culture required her to get her work in on time and to produce even though she was under stress. The cultural dissonance created so many problems that she could not cope and left abruptly for home.

The second perspective of institutional racism was popularized in the mid1960s. Institutional racism deals with minority problems in terms of discrimination practiced in social structures. The most glaring institutional racism is found in the employment structures of the United States. There are far fewer employment opportunities for minorities. The following case history illustrates the impact of institutional racism:

Jim, a 17-year-old black high school junior moved from the west coast to a Midwestern semirural community. He needed a job, and so he made applications all over the community. He was constantly turned down by the local businessmen and went the whole summer without a job. His divorced mother was working at a dry-cleaning establishment and tried to give him some spending money, but it was a continual strain on the family.

Jim began to interact with other boys who were defined by the community as undesirables. Soon he was picked up for stealing hubcaps and gas. The juvenile authorities established a record on him, and by the time he entered school for his senior year, he had been labeled as a troublemaker. Jim had never been a top student, but now his grades really began to suffer. The combination of his increased truancy and more involvement with his "gang" caused the school officials to ask him to leave. They sent him to an alternative program which he did not complete. After three more arrests he was placed in a juvenile correction facility.

Jim's case history illustrates how subtly institutional racism works. While no one can predict what would have happened to Jim if he had been given a good summer job, the chances of his making it in our society seemingly would have been much better. Society has to reward its members, and the economic system is unfortunately one of the most powerful reward systems.

## *Social Work Intervention with Minorities*

Two recent theoretical models seem to hold promise for systematic social work intervention into the problems of minority groups. The first model is a three-stage model proposed by De Hoyos[15] and others, who utilize the stages of (1) individual intervention, (2) interactional intervention, and (3) social-cultural intervention as their basic framework (see Figure 18.1). They make the point that social workers have utilized stages 1 and 2 with both nonminority and minority clients rather effectively. However, they state that, "Although this

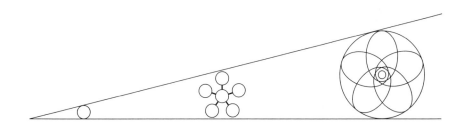

| Individual Intervention | Interactional Intervention | Sociocultural Intervention |
|---|---|---|
| Neo-Freudian theory Cognitive theory, etc. | Ecological systems, General systems, etc. | Structural functionalism |
| Psychoanalysis, Traditional casework, Existential therapy, etc. | Structural, functional, family, ecological, amd communication therapies, etc. | Sociocultural therapy |

**FIGURE 18.1    Three-stage Model**

*Source:* Genevieve De Hoyos, Arturo De Hoyos, and Christian B. Anderson, "Sociocultural Dislocation, Beyond Dual Perspective," *Social Work,* 31 (January–February 1986), 63.

two-level approach may be sufficient with nonminority clients a third stage of intervention—the sociocultural approach—is needed."[16]

At the sociocultural level, social workers know that without conditionally rewarding roles individuals can only remain forever unrewarded, marginal, and alienated. On the basis of this understanding, professionals can objectively and openly help minority clients to identify goals by choosing to:

- accommodate to the majority structure so as to share in its social rewards
- reject the accommodation to the majority structure and build separate majority institutions
- strike a compromise between accommodation to and rejection of the majority structure.

The authors suggest that, by using sociocultural intervention skills with minority clients, social workers can be:

- more objective and insightful in their assessment of cases
- more understanding, supportive, and nonjudgmental
- better informed regarding sociocultural issues
- more effective in problem solving
- more effective in interpreting and teaching middle-class values and behavior
- more effective in interpreting and teaching values and behavior of minority groups
- better negotiators between majority and minority persons, as advocates, and as peacemakers
- more realistic, rational, and pragmatic in their role as sounding boards.[17]

By utilizing this three-stage model, social workers can conceptualize their practice with minorities in a more meaningful way. The social worker can be effective with minority clients by methodically considering each of the three stages to see where intervention needs to take place. Perhaps intervention in only one of the stages can be helpful, but more often than not, intervention needs to occur in two or three of the stages at the same time. For instance, a client's self-image (stage 1) problem can be helped immensely if the social worker can arrange a job (stage 2). However, the social worker who can help the client begin to negotiate between his or her minority value system and the majority value system (stage 3) will be helping the client learn to deal with both cultural dissonance and institutional racism. It should be obvious that stage 3 also requires social workers to try to intervene in the structure of society to ensure that minorities can seek out and find rewarding roles to prevent a sense of hopelessness and alienation.

The second model entitled biculturalism was effectively presented by de Anda in 1984.[18] Her thrust was to propose a model that would help social workers conceptualize minority people living and being socialized in two cultures simultaneously. De Anda believes that dual socialization is made possible because there is, generally speaking, an overlap between the minority and majority cultures that provides for shared values and norms. De Anda's model of biculturalism is illustrated in Figures 18.2 and 18.3.

De Anda further addressed six factors that play an important role in helping a member of an ethnic minority group to become bicultural. These six factors are seminal for the social work profession. De Anda states:

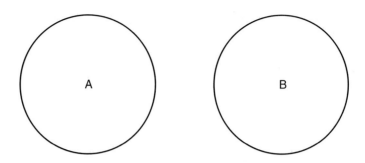

A = Majority Culture
B = Minority Culture

**FIGURE 18.2    Two Separate Cultures**

*Source:* Diane de Anda, "Bicultural Socialization: Factors Affecting the Minority Experience," *Social Work,* 29 (March–April 1984), 102.

To foster the development of behavioral repertoires for dealing with the demands of both the majority and minority cultures, the worker needs to examine the impact of the six factors previously discussed to determine whether they are serving to facilitate or impede the process of bicultural socialization for the client. The components of this complex task include:

1. Determining areas of interface between the two cultures that can serve as "doorways" between them.
2. Noting the major points of conflict between the two cultures and the negative consequences for the client.

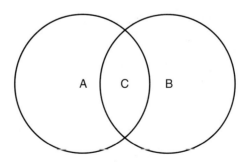

A = Majority Culture
B = Minority Culture
C = Shared Values and Norms

**FIGURE 18.3    Biculturalism**

*Source:* de Anda, p. 102.

3. Searching out and providing translators, mediators, and models who can offer guidelines for dealing with such conflicts and offer critical experiential information.
4. Arranging when possible for increased corrective feedback for the client in the environment.
5. Working to expand the client's repertoire of problem-solving skills, particularly those that are the least context bound, and helping to develop a larger repertoire of context-specific problem-solving skills.
6. Educating people of the majority culture about the significant characteristics, values, and needs of minority cultures, as well as serving as an advocate of greater flexibility and adjustment in the mainstream culture's institutions.[19]

The concept of biculturalism is being tested with several different minority groups throughout the country. Szopocznik studied biculturalism with Cuban American families and states that both rejection of the culture of origin and failure to interact with the majority culture causes maladjustive behavior.[20] Schiller is studying the effects of biculturalism in the adjustment of American Indian students enrolled at Northern Arizona University.[21] Her work is an attempt to link success of bicultural adjustment to success in adapting to a university setting.

The biculturalism framework provides another conceptual tool for the profession of social work to continue to help minority clients realize their full potential in the American culture.

## Social Services

A controversial issue is whether or not social workers need to be of the same color and race to be effective in working with clients and their problems. Numerous differing opinions and positions exist. Some claim it is essential for blacks to work with blacks; others disagree and propose that individual problems and competencies, not race, are the important factors.

Ozawa suggests that in implementing social welfare programs "separatism should be used selectively to make social services more effective," and then adds:

> For example, it makes sense to assign a black social worker to black families because this adds cultural affinity to the client-worker relationship. But it does not make sense to hire an inadequately trained black man to run a computer program just because he is black or to insist that a black teacher be hired to teach chemistry when all the qualified chemistry teachers are white.[22]

Kadushin reports various studies indicating that social workers can cross color boundaries effectively in some situations, although in others racial similarity is definitely advantageous. He concludes:

> ...although nonwhite workers may be necessary for nonwhite clients in some instances and therapeutically desirable in others, white workers can work and

have worked effectively with nonwhite clients. They seem to say that although race is important, the nature of the interpersonal relationship established between two people is more important than skin color and that although there are disadvantages to racially mixed worker-client contacts, there are special advantages. Conversely, there are special advantages to racial similarity and there are countervailing disadvantages. In other words, the problem is not as clear-cut as might be supposed.[23]

In providing services for and with persons of a different ethnicity, two factors seem to be particularly important. One is the need for the workers to understand the differences, culturally and otherwise, that exist, and be accepting of these. The other is to be selective in regard to who does what; in other words, in working with some individuals and problems it would be essential for the worker to be of the same race; in other situations it might make no difference or could even be advantageous to have a worker of a different ethnic group.

Illustrative of cultural differences that need to be kept in mind are those listed by Locklear regarding the American Indian:

1. Generosity is still the paramount virtue among most Indians. . . .
2. Many Indians continue to hold the old concepts of time. For them, time is circular rather than horizontal. Past, present, and future are all one. . . .
3. For most Indians, work must be more than a steady job. . . .
4. Family and interpersonal relationships have priority over all else. . . .
5. The extended family system continues to operate in many tribes, thus providing an enlarged sphere of family relationships as well as family responsibilities. . . .
6. Many Indians are basically noncompetitive in their relationships to non-Indians. . . . [24]

Because of language barriers and cultural differences, it is maintained by many that Chicanos, for example, should work with Chicanos. Others suggest that non-Chicanos may be just as effective if they understand the cultural differences and have language skills. Mizio agrees that oftentimes a person of the same ethnic origin may be most effective; then adds, "But it is also true that some white workers can establish viable working relationships with minority clients, some minority workers do not work well with minority clients, and the majority of social workers are white."[25]

Van Soest has suggested several seminal guidelines for social work practitioners who work in our multicultural society. The guidelines are:

- Honor each person's value, dignity, and right to self-determination.
- Use effective communication, listening, empathy, and negotiating skills.
- Avoid attacking others and their views as a way of validating one's own position.
- Recognize the pervasiveness of oppression in society, and encourage examination of the residues of racism, sexism, and homophobia on both individual and organization levels.
- Maintain the interests and welfare of clients as the priority. . . .[26]

## Educational Developments

The history of social work reflects differential services, often limited or isolated, for ethnic and racial groups. Individuals and families from minority groups have been assisted by social workers in various ways. Concomitant with these services have been attempts to provide special emphasis and direction in the training of social workers so they could become more sensitive and effective in providing these services. Across the past several decades only a minimum of effort has been expended in this direction. Since the 1960s numerous thrusts have emerged, pinpointing the need for more understanding of ethnic differences and special needs in working with minority clients.

Schools of social work and undergraduate social work programs have inaugurated, in various degrees and ways, programs and curricula tooled to improve services to minority peoples. These efforts have gained in momentum, culminating, at least standardwise, with the official pronouncement of the accreditation standard approved by the Council on Social Work Education, that schools of social work must demonstrate in a positive manner a program to recruit more minority students and faculty and to change and alter their curricula to incorporate more understanding and training for working with minorities.

Three important parts of the educational venture relevant to minorities are students, faculty, and curriculum. Positive movements regarding all three are taking place in most schools of social work and in undergraduate social work programs.

### Minority Students

Minority student enrollments are on the upswing. In the 1950s many schools of social work enrolled no minority students and the numbers in the other schools were minimal. Since the late 1960s enrollments of minority students have increased considerably. Social work educators have conscientiously recruited minority students. In November of 1994, 27.3 percent of the 24,536 juniors and seniors in baccalaureate social work programs were ethnic minority students. Minorities comprised 21.5 percent of the 21,312 full-time MSW students and 23.1 percent of the 11,432 part-time students. Minorities comprised 21.6 percent of the 1,102 full-time doctoral students and 19 percent of the 995 part-time students.

Most schools of social work have adopted specific recruitment and training programs, which usually offer scholarships and other financial aid to increase the number of minority students in training, who may then become available to provide services for their own people and others. For example, one western school, through several grants and planned emphasis, has sponsored special programs to aid the American Indians.

In addition to financial assistance needed for minority students, other assistance is often provided to offset educational and cultural limitations experienced by some minority students wishing to enter schools of social work. Many schools have faculty and others who provide special counseling and assistance for minority students before coming to school, and while there, to insure competency upon graduation.

Substantial efforts are in operation to recruit and train more minority students in the undergraduate social work programs. The standards for accreditation for baccalaureate degree programs in social work, which have as their primary stated educational objective "preparation for beginning professional social work practice," state that major positive efforts are to be carried out in recruiting and training of minority students, encompassing additional minority faculty and significant alterations in curricula. The standards are explicit: "Preparation for effective social work practice requires curriculum content that develops in the student an understanding of and appreciation for ethnic, racial, and cultural diversity in a pluralistic society."

## Minority Faculty

A second major thrust has been in relation to the increase of minority faculty. In November 1967, fifty-nine schools of social work in the United States reported[27] a total of 212 full-time minority group faculty members for all ranks, which amounted to 12.3 percent of the total of 1,718 faculty. By November 1994, increases had taken place with minority faculty members in all social work programs. Of the 454 programs reporting their statistics to the Council on Social Work Education, 24 percent of the 5,395 full-time faculty members were ethnic minorities. It is also important to note that 60 percent of the full-time faculty members were women. Social work education is committed to opening its system to women.

Not only has there been considerable increase in the number of minority faculty in schools of social work, but there has been a major development toward helping other faculty to understand more about minorities, and to increase their abilities to teach minority content and practice. Workshops, classes, consultations, and other staff development activities have been inaugurated to increase knowledge and teaching skills, and improve attitudes toward minorities.

Turner suggests there are two major issues confronting social work education in relation to minorities: "(1) how to equip social workers with the knowledge, skills, and attitudes that will enable them to improve the status of minorities and (2) how to attract more minority-group students into social work education."[28]

Turner also proposes that schools of social work respond with the following, specifically:

1. Developmental recruitment.
2. Willingness to pay a significant part of the cost of preparing teachers.
3. Willingness to employ minority persons at senior as well as junior levels.
4. Employment of more than token numbers of minority faculty.
5. Reeducation of existing faculty members about their roles.
6. Developing university administration support for hiring of minority persons.[29]

## Curriculum Minority Content

In addition to increasing the number of minority students and faculty, it is imperative that the curricula of the schools of social work be altered and enriched to include pertinent materials regarding content, attitudes, and skills of practice. The current standards of the Council on Social Work Education state that positive attempts must be made in this direction for accreditation to be approved, both on undergraduate and graduate levels.

Turner suggests that the curriculum must deal with three distinct educational needs:

(1) the need of the minority student to have a systematic and in-depth knowledge of his own group, (2) the need for all students to have basic information about the major ethnic and racial groups in America today, and (3) the need of the minority-

Native American student receiving her MSW degree.

majority problem specialist for more in-depth knowledge about any minority group he expects to work with.[30]

It is clearly apparent that there is a bona fide need to incorporate into the curricula of graduate and undergraduate programs the knowledge, attitudes, and skills that bring the minority peoples, their problems, and solutions within the scope of social work practice. Turner suggests that these developments are tied in with social justice, and that:

Tradition and history have made problems of ethnic and racial justice an inextricable part of the more general problem of social justice. The curriculum must make this connection clear to the student, for he who fights for one must be committed to fight for both.[31]

Turner summarizes action all social workers should be able to perform in the minority arena:

1. Recognize racist policies and acts, individual or institutional.
2. Bring racist practices to the attention of those who have responsibility and power to stop them.
3. Commit resources they have to change or redesign policies that are racist.
4. Respond constructively to efforts to eliminate racism.[32]

## Summary

*From this brief presentation it is apparent that social work is in the process of developing an increased interest in minorities and enriched services that cope with some of the problems related to ethnic and racial diversity. That many debilitating and unfair racial prejudices exist is obvious; that attempts are being made to meet some of these problems is encouraging.*

*Minority persons are aided by social workers in nearly all of the traditional social agencies; in fact, they constitute unduly large clientele percentages in public welfare, corrections, and other community services. Two major concepts used to define minority problems are cultural dissonance and institutional racism. The social work profession is acutely aware of these phenomena and is working to mitigate them in our society.*

*Two new major theoretical concepts of sociocultural intervention and biculturalism are adding new insights to the practice of social work. These models give specific guidelines for working with minorities.*

*A beginning has been made in recruiting and training more minority students, to provide more minority social workers. Increased numbers of minority faculty are teaching in graduate and undergraduate educational programs. Curricula of schools of social work and undergraduate social work programs have been and are being altered to help all students understand more about working with minority clients, and to give special emphasis to many in becoming more competent in providing professional services to all ethnic groups.*

## Selected References

BROWN, EDDIE F., and TIMOTHY F. SHAUGHNESSY, eds., *Education for Social Work Practice with American Indian Families.* Tempe: School of Social Work, Arizona State University, 1979.

CROMPTON, DON W., "Minority Content in Social Work Education—Promise or Pitfall?" *Journal of Education for Social Work,* 10 (Winter 1974), 9–18.

GRAHAM, HUGH DAVIS, "Race, Language, and Social Policy: Comparing the Black and Hispanic Experience in the U.S.," *Population and Environment* 12(l), 43–58.

GREEN, J. W., *Cultural Awareness in The Human Services.* Englewood Cliffs, NJ: Prentice Hall, 1982.

JACKSON, JACQUELYNE JOHNSON, *Minorities and Aging.* Belmont, CA: Wadsworth Publishing Co., 1980.

JOHNSON, H. C., "Human Behavior and Social Environment: New Perspectives," *Culture, Organizations and Macrosystems: How They Affect Behavior.* New York: Curriculum Concepts, 1983.

LONGRES, JOHN F., *Human Behavior in the Social Environment.* Itasca, IL: F. E. Peacock Publishers, Inc., 1990.

MCADOO, HARRIETTE PIPES, *Black Families.* Newbury Park, CA: Sage Publications, 1988.

PROCTOR, ENOLA K., and LARRY E. DAVID, "The Challenge of Racial Difference: Skills for Clinical Practice," *Social Work,* 39 (May 1994), 314–323.

ROTHMAN, JACK, *Issues in Race and Ethnic Relations, Theory, Research and Action.* Itasca, IL: F. E. Peacock Publishers, 1977.

SCHRIVER, JOE M., *Human Behavior and the Social Environment: Shifting Paradigms in Essential Knowledge for Social Work Practice.* Boston, MA: Allyn and Bacon, 1995.

SCOTT, CARL, ed., *Ethnic Minorities in Social Work Education.* New York: Council on Social Work Education, 1970.

SOTOMAYOR, MARTA, ed., *Cross-Cultural Perspectives in Social Work Practice and Education.* Houston: Graduate School of Social Work, University of Houston, 1976.

SOTOMAYOR, MARTA, and PHILIP D. ORTEGO Y GASCA, eds., *Chicano Content and Social Work Education.* New York: Council on Social Work Education, 1975.

WASHINGTON, ROBERT O., "Social Development: A Focus For Practice and Education." *Social Work,* 27 (January 1982).

# *Notes*

1. John Hiratsuka, "Immigration Cost, Compassion Collide," *NASW News,* 40 (January 1995), 3.

2. Quoted in William G. Mayfield, "Mental Health in the Black Community," *Social Work,* 17 (May 1972), 110.

3. Stokely Carmichael and Charles V. Hamilton, *Black Power: The Politics of Liberation in America* (New York: Random House, 1967), p. 4.

4. Terry Jones, "Institutional Racism in the United States," *Social Work,* 19 (March 1974), 221.

5. Douglas Glasgow, "Black Power Through Community Control," *Social Work,* 17 (May 1972), 61.

6. William Julius Wilson, "The Black Underclass," *Wilson Quarterly,* 7, no. 2 (Spring 1984), 88.

7. Gary Puckrein, "Moving Up," *Wilson Quarterly,* 7, no. 1 (Spring 1984), 74–76.

8. Hugh Davis Graham, "Race, Language and Social Policy: Comparing the Black and Hispanic Experience in the U.S.," *Population and Environment,* 12, no. 1 (Fall 1990), 44.

9. Ibid., p. 44.

10. W. B. Johnston and A. E. Packer, *Workforce 2000: Work and Workers for the Twenty-First Century* (Indianapolis: Hudson Institute, 1987), p. 114.

11. John Hiratsuka, "L.A. Burning: Social Workers Respond," *NASW News,* 37 (July 1992), 3.

12. Ibid., p. 3.

13. Genevieve De Hoyos, Arturo De Hoyos, and Christian B. Anderson, "Sociocultural Dislocation: Beyond the Dual Perspective," *Social Work,* 31 (January–February 1986), 61.

14. Ibid., p. 61.

15. Ibid., p.62.

16. Ibid., p.62.

17. Ibid., p. 65.

18. Diane de Anda, "Bicultural Socialization: Factors Affecting the Minority Experience," *Social Work,* 29 (March–April 1984), 101–107.

19. Ibid., pp. 106–107.

20. J. Szopocznik, D. Santisteban, W. Kurtines, P. Vidal, and D. Hervis, "Bicultural Effectiveness Training: A Treatment Intervention for Enhancing Intercultural Adjustment in Cuban American Families," *Hispanic Journal of Behavioral Sciences,* 6 (1984), 317–344.

21. Phyllis M. Schiller, *Biculturalism and Psychosocial Adjustment among American Indian University Students.* Unpublished DSW Dissertation, Graduate School of Social Work, University of Utah, June 1987.

22. Martha N. Ozawa, "Social Welfare, the Minority Share," *Social Work,* 17 (May 1972), 41–42.

23. Alfred Kadushin, "The Racial Factor in the Interview," *Social Work,* 17 (May 1972), 98.

24. Herbert H. Locklear, "American Indian Myths," *Social Work,* 17 (May 1972), 77–78.

25. Emelicia Mizio, "White Worker-Minority Client," *Social Work,* 17 (May 1972), 83.

26. Dorothy Van Soest, "Multiculturalism and Social Work Education: The Non-Debate about Competing Perspectives," *Social Work Education,* 31 (Winter 1995), 64.

27. Carl Scott, ed., *Ethnic Minorities in Social Work Education* (New York: Council on Social Work Education, 1970), pp. 45–46.

28. John B. Turner, "Education for Practice with Minorities," *Social Work,* 17 (May 1972), 112. Reprinted with permission of the National Association of Social Workers.

29. Ibid., p. 113.

31. Ibid., p. 117.

32. Ibid., p. 116.

33. Ibid., p. 115.

$$C \quad h \quad a \quad p \quad t \quad e \quad r \quad \textit{19}$$

# Social Work in Rural Areas

*John sat, quiet and withdrawn, gazing out of the car window as they traveled the country road toward the county seat. The "voices" were calling to him, as they so often did, and he became increasingly restless, which was also happening more and more frequently. In the two years since he graduated from high school, things just hadn't been going well. He had imagined as he grew up that he would be a help to his dad on the farm, but now he could do little because of the insistent "voices."*

*His parents watched in disbelief as he changed. They tried to understand what was happening. They had never known anyone to behave as he did. He became agitated over nothing. He couldn't concentrate for more than a few minutes. They knew he needed help, and it was for this help*

*that they were making this trip to town. They had an appointment for him to see the traveling mental health professionals who came only once a month to their remote area.*

*As they drove on, they wondered what the recommendations would be. They feared he would need to be hospitalized, which would mean he would be 240 miles from home. Now that the haying season was here, it would be almost impossible for them to visit the hospital. They hoped they would be able to care for him at home, and that his medication would not be too complicated for them to manage. But most of all, they hoped their son would be able to get some help so he could be a normal, happy person who could lead a productive life again.*

Social work services are needed in the rural areas of the United States. Ginsberg states that "the social and economic problems faced by the people of nonmetropolitan America are often as severe or even more serious than those faced by their metropolitan fellow citizens."[1] The rural population of the United States is difficult to define, but demographic experts place the rural population between 55 million and 87 million, depending on the definition that is used for rural. Ginsberg graphically makes the point that "it is larger than the populations of all but a few of the world's nations and nearly equals the population of France or England."[2] A recent study by the National Center for Social Policy and Practice found a shortage of mental health professionals in the rural areas of six selected states.[3] The report graphically outlines the difficulty rural people have in obtaining services. The shortages found in mental health workers is only a tip of the iceberg. Professional social work services are lacking in many rural social service delivery systems.

In addition to a lack of rural social work services and personnel, rural areas are under tremendous stress. In the past thirty years some rural communities have been emptied of most of their people and are now faced with a crumbling social infrastructure. Other small communities have had to withstand the effects of proportionately enormous growth when a manufacturing plant has located nearby. In addition to these major population shifts, rural communities are in the throes of economic recession. The "farm crisis" is real, as across the nation farmers and their families are uprooted by bankruptcy.

All of these combined forces have taken their toll on the traditionally stable farm family. One recent rural study identified urgently needed services in the following areas: (1) job and economic problems; (2) alcohol and drug problems of adults and youth; (3) lack of constructive leisure-time programs and facilities; (4) marriage and family problems; and (5) personal stress, anxiety, and depression.[4]

At a hearing of the House Select Committee on Children, Youth, and Families in April 1989, it was noted that 16.9 percent of the population living in rural areas had incomes below the poverty line.[5] The poverty line was defined as $9,056 annual income for a family of three. The 16.9 percent in rural areas is almost equal to the 18.6 percent poverty rate found in the central city areas of our large cities. It is alarming to note that between the years 1978 and 1987 poverty rates rose from 13.5 percent to 16.9 percent. The report also indicates that rural poor families are more likely than urban families to live in households headed by two parents who both work. Rural poor are somewhat more likely to be elderly and white.

In the 1980s and 1990s, rural communities have continued to change. Ruff contends that some rural communities have combined "rural" and "urban" to become "rurban."[6] She states that a rurban community is somewhere on a continuum between rural and urban and meets the following four criteria:

1. *Population size.* The U.S. Census Bureau uses 2,500 or less as a population size to define rural. The author suggests a population between 2,500 and 10,000 to define a rurban community.
2. *Economic base.* Moving from dependence on a primary source of occupational income to a diversity of occupations causes the community to shift from rural into a rurban status. Some residents may live in the rurban community and work outside, but the community does not necessarily become a suburb or a purely residential area.
3. *Availability of services.* The rurban community moves from being isolated or completely removed from services to a situation where services become more accessible either because of improved transportation, or because services physically move into the geographic area.
4. *Homogeneous cultural mores.* In the traditional rural community, the majority of the population is in tune with communally accepted mores and behavior. As populations grow and newcomers move in, these dynamics change and diverse groups with different expectations and social behavior mores appear, and the community moves to a rurban status as opposed to a rural status.[7]

Regardless of whether a community is a traditional "rural" community or a "rurban" transition community, it is frequently underserved by human service professionals. Social work educators must continue to train social workers to meet the needs of rural communities.

## *Beginnings in Rural Social Work*

The beginnings of rural social work practice can be traced to the Country Life Commission of 1908 appointed by President Theodore Roosevelt and the National Conference of Charities and Correction of the same year. The Great Depression and New Deal philosophy of the 1930s gave impetus and a broadening to the practice of rural social work.

Interest in rural social work waned during World War II and the 1950s. A resurgence of interest began to develop in the late 1960s as a result of the War on Poverty philosophy and also important social work leadership by Leon Ginsberg and others. In 1969 Ginsberg, dean of the West Virginia School of Social Work, delivered a major address on rural social work at the Council on Social Work Education Annual Program Meeting. Other leaders joined the rural social work movement and created organizations and meetings called the Rural Caucus and the Annual Institute of Rural Social Work. A professional journal called *Human Services in the Rural Environment* was initiated in 1976 at the University of Wisconsin at Madison.

At the Tenth National Institute on Social Work in Rural Areas held in 1985, one of the presenters, Mike Jacobsen, observed:

> It has been demonstrated that the years 1969 to 1985 mark a rapid growth in the scholarly activities of rural social work educators and practitioners in the United States. A qualitative analysis of this development suggests that this scholarly productivity has had the effect of providing a history for rural social work in the United States, specified useful arrangements for field and continuing rural education, detailed many professional and community changes in rural human services, demonstrated the nature of competence in rural practice, and provided the context for further scholarly development of rural social work topics.[8]

Rural America.

## *Rural Social Work Practice*

A rural social worker is described as a generalist who brings to bear a broad range of methodologies and skills in practice. The generalist rural social worker must have a good background in community development and organization and must also be able to work with individuals or groups. He or she must have the skills to analyze community systems and decide on effective intervention levels within the total system. The rural social worker also needs to be a good administrator and a resource specialist. Rural social work requires a strong sense of independence and the ability to work in an unstructured environment. Ginsberg states:

> The special characteristics of rural settings require most workers to practice in ways that differ from their urban counterparts. Social workers in rural communities require skills in all the social work methods and must be able to use themselves effectively with social institutions of all sizes—from the individual and his family to the total community. The need for social workers who are generalists in rural communities is confirmed by social work theoreticians and practitioners of both the past and the present.[9]

The rural social worker needs to understand both the positives and negatives of working in small rural communities. Some important positive elements are: (1) open communication systems, (2) interagency cooperation, and (3) a sense of community. The rural community has perhaps the most open communication system in our society today. News travels quickly, and residents can respond readily. Even though services are minimal in many areas, the positive interagency cooperation can help to mitigate the lack of resources. Agency personnel reach out to one another on a personal, informal level to provide resources to clients. The sense of community is pervasive, and community residents are willing to take care of "their own." An example of this sense of community was demonstrated recently in a rural community when a large barn filled with hay burned down. Before the embers were completely cooled, neighbors came with their equipment and had the mess cleaned up within hours. Many brought loads of baled hay to enable the burned-out family to feed their stock until other arrangements could be made.

Some negative elements of working in a rural area are: (1) geographic isolation, (2) personnel isolation, and (3) service isolation. When a client who lives 150 miles away calls for an appointment, care must be taken to coordinate times and efforts so that valuable time and energy will not be wasted. Geographic isolation is also demonstrated when it takes a rural social worker two or three hours to return children to their homes following an after-school self-esteem group session. Personnel and service isolation can cause the rural social worker to feel great pressure of being the "only one" available. The rural social worker needs to be able to reach out frequently for consultation and support systems to prevent worker burnout.

Two authors have developed the argument for the need to develop a curriculum for "advanced generalist" in social work education. They acknowledge that there continues to be a disparity between social work education and rural social work practice. They believe that MSW programs should allow for a rural advanced generalist concentration that includes the following:

> This program attempts to build upon the generic core of social work education essential to students training to be rural practitioners. In developing practitioners who can work with all segments and institutions of the rural community and who are prepared to adopt a variety of roles, this disparity between the promise of social work and its practice can be reached.
>
> Students must both be prepared with the technical expertise of micro, mezzo, and macro intervention skills, and instilled with a guiding philosophy which leads them to look for opportunities to intervene at multiple levels.
>
> The task of preparing advanced generalist practitioners who are able to intervene with individuals suffering from the effects of social problems, as well as the systems from which the social problems themselves are generated, is not simple. This, however, is the task to which rural social work educators must commit themselves.[10]

## Roles of the Rural Social Worker

As mentioned earlier, the rural social worker is a generalist who must have the ability to work with individuals, families, and groups, as well as with the total community. A more specific listing of roles follows:

> *Direct Service Role—with Individuals, Couples, Families and Groups:* Rural social workers need to convey to the community the fact that social work is a valuable resource to every community member. Working directly with individuals and families to help them function more effectively is central to rural social work practice.
>
> Rural communities that are faced with population change or economic downturn require increased social work services to individuals and families. With these additional stresses comes an increase in problems such as family violence, substance abuse, and depression. Many rural social service agencies have established 24-hour-a-day crisis lines where individuals and families can call for help.
>
> *Resource Specialist:* One of the most difficult roles the rural social worker assumes is that of assisting in the optimal utilization of the limited resources available in many rural areas. It requires imagination and creativity to put resources together in a different configuration in order to serve human needs effectively.
>
> The rural social worker must find ways to keep up with all the programs being funded through the states and federal government. For instance, if a couple has a newborn child who is blind, the social worker needs to know what resources are available and how the couple can make proper contact with the appropriate program. Since programs are continually changing, the rural social worker must keep up with the changes.

*Social Service Administrator and Community Organizer:* Most rural communities have few professional people, and rural social workers usually find themselves in the role of trying to coordinate all the social services in the community. For instance, one rural social worker initiated monthly meetings with the public health nurse, school teachers, probation officer, and several local church leaders to insure that community social service activities were coordinated and effective.

The rural social worker may also be called upon to develop new funding sources to meet unmet needs in the community. The administrative function of raising money can be a real challenge to a social worker who wants to serve the community well.

The rural social worker needs to be able to relate to the power structure of the community. Rural communities have an informal power structure of leaders who operate unofficially but often have greater power than elected officials. These leaders reflect local values and may play an important role in determining how money is spent and whether or not the community will give new programs their support. Local government officials and funding sources must also be informed about the total agency operation. Rural social work agencies get into trouble when they fail to develop meaningful linkages with their governing bodies. Rural social workers need to be able to relate to both the informal and the formal power structure of the community and to orchestrate agency support, which in turn facilitates important services to rural clients.

The following case is an example of the work done by a rural social worker that incorporates all of the roles described above.

---

The social worker was informed of a problem that was developing in a rural junior high school. A group of popular, well-known girls were making it difficult for new students to be accepted in the school. They went out of their way to make newcomers feel they were not wanted. The situation was exacerbated when the group of girls began to victimize a brain-damaged youngster.

The social worker decided to mobilize the school system and the PTA to remedy the situation. The social worker, the principal, and the president of the PTA planned a series of five lectures entitled "A Community that Cares" to be given at the PTA meetings during the school year. The lectures were developed around the themes, "Individualizing and Accepting Each Child" and "Understanding the Feelings of New People Moving into the Community."

The community accepted the lecture series very well. The PTA president had strong ties with the dominant religious group and received the backing of the community from several different power bases.

The initial meeting was cordial, and PTA members were pleased to consider problems of new and different children. The second meeting turned out to be the key meeting. The social worker talked of the importance of individualizing each child and the constant need to reinforce the child's feeling of self-worth.

A newcomer to the community, a father, asked if he could tell his story. He, his wife, and a daughter who had been brain-damaged at birth had purposely moved into a rural community so that their child would have greater opportunities to interact with other children and the school system.

With some feeling, he said that they had been extremely disappointed because this community had rejected them. The hardest thing they had to deal with was the rejection of their daughter by other children, some teachers, and even adults in the community. In a parent-teacher conference, one teacher had insisted that the only thing wrong with their daughter was that they had spoiled her so that she acted like a baby. He related incidents where the "in" group of girls seemed to delight in hitting her every time they passed her. And perhaps hardest of all was that he had heard some parents actually told their children not to play with her because she was different.

As the parents and teachers listened to the father, they could sense the beginning of an attitude change in the community. The social worker quickly followed up with interviews with involved teachers and PTA officers to keep the lines of communication open.

The remainder of the lecture series reinforced important attitude changes in a community that was willing to listen. There was marked improvement in the system. The community became more sensitive to the needs of the newcomers. Some of the children invited the brain-damaged girl to their homes. The social worker continued to work with the family and the girl throughout the school year. Relationships became much more positive.[11]

## Positive Aspects of Social Work Roles in Rural Communities

Even though rural social work is challenging, there are many positive aspects of serving in smaller communities. Ginsberg has identified five areas that offer the rural social worker significant rewards:

- *Independence.* Social workers in metropolitan areas frequently are responsible to a fairly complex administrative and supervisory structure. They may find their work closely monitored. They may have extensive reporting requirements in the organization. Social workers in rural communities are more likely to be autonomous and to work with little or no supervision because there are simply fewer social workers in the agency. A metropolitan social services agency, for example, might have hundreds of social work employees. The rural office of the same agency might have only a handful of workers. Therefore, those who are ambitious to work independently or prefer setting their own courses and critiquing their own performances may find it much more satisfying to work in a smaller community.
- *Rapid Advancement.* Social workers in smaller communities can often expect relatively rapid advancement. Workers may move from direct worker to supervisor and to administrator or manager in a relatively short time because other workers find smaller communities to be unattractive locations for their work. The competition for promotion or other opportunities is often not nearly as great in smaller communities as it is in metropolitan areas.

  Most American social workers, like most other Americans, come from metropolitan areas. Their family and social ties are in such communities, and, therefore, many are reluctant to relocate in rural communities. Such attitudes and behaviors only enhance the opportunities for workers who enjoy life in smaller communities.

- *Tangible Results.* Social workers in smaller communities often find that they can see tangible results from their efforts. That is, they can see the impact of their efforts on the lives of the people in the community. Being able to see the difference one makes is one of social work's rewards in all settings and in communities of all sizes. In a rural community, one can make a difference at the micro as well as the macro level. One can see changes made in individuals and families, as well as changes made in the larger community and in the social system.

- *Personal Rewards.* Great personal rewards are possible for human services professionals in many small communities. Because they are independent and can make a difference in the lives of many people, rural workers may find themselves being thanked for the work they do. A small-community physician, Dr. Michael Watson (1992), reported at a recent meeting that some of his clients tell him they "love" him for what he has done to help them. A nurse practitioner, who serves with him and who performs some of the primary health care tasks that might be done by physicians in larger communities, receives similar kinds of comments from her patients. Another nurse, who is also a midwife in Dr. Watson's community, has delivered many of the children in that small community. This nurse-midwife is a good example of what can happen to the rural professional. She is relatively autonomous and works under the direction of only one physician, who provides her with consultation more than supervision. She practices a skill that is not as frequently used by nurses in metropolitan communities. She has special relationships with her clients and has won their respect and affection.

- *Recognition.* While many people prefer anonymity, there is a special joy for many in being well-known and recognized in the community. The social worker who is known to everyone, who is spoken to by everyone on the street, in the grocery store, and in the post office, has the special satisfaction of being an important person in the rural community. Rarely are social workers in metropolitan areas accorded the same kinds of respect that social workers are often given in nonmetropolitan communities. The social worker may be a frequent speaker at major civic clubs or a consultant to local government who is quoted regularly in the local newspaper. In many ways, rural social workers establish stronger and broader relationships than their metropolitan counterparts might have.[12]

## Rural Social Service Agencies

Rural social service agencies are going to play an important role as the United States tries to redirect some of its resources to meet the growing needs of rural areas. This will result in opportunities for new social workers to begin their professional careers in rural agencies.

The rural agencies are unique in the social welfare system. They are usually small, informal, and have a strong personal, direct link to the community they serve. The typical agency has one to three workers plus an agency director, who often doubles as a supervisor.

The agency's service area is likely to include several small towns as well as isolated residents distributed over hundreds of square miles.

In the last few years the National Institute of Mental Health has encouraged the development of community mental health centers in rural areas. These centers and the public welfare agencies provide most of the services to individuals and families. Other service providers such as corrections, substance abuse, vocational rehabilitation, and education may establish a one- or two-person agency in a rural county.

Whatever system the state employs to deliver social services to its rural residents, the social worker actually "becomes the agency." The personal visibility of rural practitioners is so great that residents will quickly equate both their professional and personal behavior with the agency. In one rural area the mental health agency was highly respected because of the work of one social worker who was sincerely committed to his clients. People in the area made use of the agency because they knew and respected the social work practitioner.

## Summary

*Rural areas of the United States are facing difficult times. Boom and bust cycles—coupled with high inflation and lower land prices—have created a great deal of stress and unhappiness for rural residents. Rural social workers are actively attempting to mitigate the problems of individuals, families, and communities.*

*Rural social work practice requires skills in all social work methods, and individual social workers must be able to adapt themselves effectively to social institutions of all sizes, from the individual to the total community. Rural social workers also need to understand the functioning of a rural community and must be able to work within the values and structures of that community. There are many positive rewards for social workers choosing to practice in rural areas.*

*Social work education is an ideal curriculum for rural practice. The emphasis on the interaction of the individual and the environment prepares the rural social worker to provide important leadership in the area of social services. Although social workers may not be able to effect an upturn in the rural economy or create new jobs, they can help cushion the negative effects and help individuals, families, and communities cope with the problems and find workable solutions.*

## Selected References

ALLEN, BARBARA, and THOMAS J. SCHLERETH, eds., *Sense of Place: American Regional Cultures.* Lexington: University Press of Kentucky, 1990.

COPPEDGE, ROBERT O., and CARLTON G. DAVIS, eds., *Rural Poverty and the Policy Crisis.* Ames: Iowa State University Press, 1977.

FARLEY, O. WILLIAM, KENNETH A. GRIFFITHS, REX A. SKIDMORE, and MILTON G. THACKERAY, *Rural Social Work Practice.* New York: The Free Press, 1982.

FITCHEN, J. M., *Endangered Spaces, Enduring Places: Change, Identity and Survival in Rural America.* Boulder, CO: Westview Press, 1991.

GINSBERG, LEON, *Social Work Almanac.* Washington DC: National Association of Social Workers, 1992.

GINSBERG, LEON H., ed., *Social Work in Rural Communities,* 2nd ed. Alexandria, VA: Council on Social Work Education, 1993.

Herbers, John, *The New Heartland: America's Flight beyond the Suburbs and How It Is Changing Our Future.* New York: Times Books, 1986.

Krout, John A., *The Aged in Rural America.* Westport, CT: Greenwood Press, 1986.

McNeil, John S., and Stanley E. Weinstein, eds., *Innovations in Health Care Practice.* Washington, DC: National Association of Social Workers, Inc., 1988.

## Notes

1. Leon H. Ginsberg, ed., *Social Work in Rural Communities,* 2nd ed. (Alexandria, VA: Council on Social Work Education, 1993), p. 4. Reprinted with the permission of the Council on Social Work Education.

2. Ibid., p. 4.

3. *NASW News,* 8 (September 1988), 1.

4. O. William Farley, Kenneth A. Griffiths, Mark Fraser, and Lou Ann Jorgensen, "Rural Social Work: Addressing the Crisis of Rural America," in *Innovations in Health Care Practices,* John S. McNeil and Stanley E. Weinstein, eds. (Washington, DC: National Association of Social Workers, 1988), p. 64.

5. Kathryn H. Porter, *Poverty in Rural America: A National Overview* (Washington DC: Center on Budget and Policy Priorities, 1989), p. 3.

6. Elizabeth Ruff, "The Community as Client in Rural Social Work," *Human Services in the Rural Environment,* 14 (Spring 1991), 21.

7. Ibid., p. 21.

8. Mike Jacobsen, "Scholarship and the Rural Social Work Movement," in *Social Work in Rural Areas: Proceedings of the Tenth National Institute on Social Work in Rural Areas,* Anne Summers, Joe M. Schriner, Paul Sundet, and Roland Meinert, eds. (Bateville, AR: Arkansas College, 1987), p. 21.

9. Leon H. Ginsberg, "Social Work in Rural Areas," in *Social Work in Rural Areas: Preparation and Practice,* Ronald K. Green and Stephen Webster, eds. (Knoxville: University of Tennessee, 1977), p. 7.

10. James A. Campbell and Melanie Shepart, "Social Work Education for Rural Practice: The Advanced Generalist," *Human Services in the Rural Environment,* 14 (Summer 1990), 24.

11. O. William Farley, Kenneth A. Griffiths, Rex A. Skidmore, and Milton G. Thackeray, *Rural Social Work Practice* (New York: The Free Press, 1982), pp. 227–228.

12. Ginsberg, *Social Work in Rural Communities,* pp. 12–13.

$$Chapter\ 20$$

# Case Management

*Joyce is a 33-year-old white married female who spent the majority of her life between the ages of 16 and 27 in state mental hospitals. During her late teenage years she was diagnosed as having paranoid-type schizophrenia. In addition to her psychosis, Joyce also struggled with substance abuse. Staff from a rural community mental health center responded to requests from Joyce's family to see if she could be released from the hospital and returned to the community where she would have a better quality of life. State hospital personnel were worried about discharging Joyce and predicted dire consequences.*

*Joyce returned to the community, and the mental health center initiated case management to assist her in being able to live out of the hospital. Even though Joyce suffered from hallucinations and suicidal ideation, the case management staff helped her through these episodes. Joyce also had a family that was interested and supportive of her. In 1989 Joyce and another mental health client were married.*

*Joyce worked at numerous jobs but always tried to do more than she was capable of doing, which resulted in her becoming overwhelmed and unable to work. The rural community was also limited in job opportunities, and Joyce usually ended up in menial cleaning jobs. Joyce continued to need short hospitalization periods to keep herself under control. However, the short periods of hospitalization were in the community where she lived and where she could receive continuous support from her case manager, husband, and family. With this support she could return to independent living within a few days.*

*Even though Joyce continues to struggle with recurring episodes of illness, the case management intervention has helped sustain her in an environment where she has the opportunity to develop independence and a quality lifestyle. Joyce is adamant that case management services were very important in her attempt to adjust to the community. She has remained out of long-term state hospitalization for six years.*

Case management is a newly emerging human service designed to deliver services to individuals and their families with complex, multiple problems or disabilities. Social work and other helping professions have often utilized case management as part of their service delivery systems, but now it is becoming a discrete, independently reimbursed, primary service. Barker has defined the general parameters of case management as:

> A procedure to plan, seek, and monitor services from different social agencies and staff on behalf of a client. Usually one agency takes primary responsibility for the client and assigns a case manager, who coordinates services, advocates for the cli-

ent and sometimes controls resources and purchases services for the client. The procedure makes it possible for many social workers in the agency, or different agencies, to coordinate their efforts to serve a given client through professional teamwork, thus expanding the range of needed services offered. Case management may involve monitoring the progress of a client whose needs require the services of several professionals, agencies, health care facilities, and human services programs. It typically involves case finding, comprehensive multidimensional assessment, and frequent reassessment. Case management can occur within a single large organization or within a community program that coordinates services among agencies.[1]

Renewal of interest in case management as a separate service delivery system has been brought about by our increasingly complex and diverse society, which has created a fragmented, complicated, and depersonalized social service system. Many of the most vulnerable people—who need services the most—do not receive timely, meaningful, and preventive assistance because they cannot effectively apply for needed services or negotiate the conflicting eligibility requirements of social service agencies. The purpose of case management is to assist clients to receive the services they need by linking clients to both the formal and informal helping-service networks within a community and then to follow up to ensure that the client has actually received the resources and social services required.

The new appeal of case management has also been based on the belief that this service could assist with cost-effectiveness and cost-control. The skyrocketing costs of health care have provided the impetus for much of the case management movement. Winn and Sierra address case management in the health care context as follows:

> Medical cost containment, of which case management is a part, is estimated to be a $7 billion industry in the United States. While case management provides no direct care, it serves to facilitate appropriate, cost-effective access to finite health care resources. Private, state, and federal payers are ever vigilant to find creative ways to coordinate care and contain costs for high-risk populations.
>
> Case managers act as gatekeepers, resource managers and decision makers for billions of dollars worth of care annually. Various professions vie for leadership because case management is such a growing and important function due to increased demand for services and the need to reduce and manage costs. Each discipline perceives theirs as uniquely suited to manage complex cases. Those professions include physicians, social workers, nurses, and vocational rehabilitation specialists.[2]

Whether case management will be able to fulfill its mandate of being able both to personalize and coordinate services and to make them cost-effective is yet to be determined. However, the following case history illustrates that case management can be effective.

---

Mrs. J. is a 35-year-old divorced woman with two children (ages 7 and 10). Her husband left her six years ago. For the first four years she was supported by the Aid to Families with Dependent Children program (AFDC) of the state welfare department. During those four years, her life was spent trying to find housing, obtaining food stamps, trying to get medical care for her children or mental health counseling for herself. Much of her energy was spent in going from agency to agency filling out forms and meeting with workers from different agencies. She had no direction and little hope,

Two years ago she was assigned a case manager in a pilot project developed by the state welfare department. The case manager was assigned a very small caseload of 20 clients, which allowed her the opportunity of making contact with each of her clients on a weekly basis. After making an assessment of Mrs. J.'s total situation, the case manager and Mrs. J. developed, jointly, a treatment plan that was workable. During this process, the case manager used counseling skills to help Mrs. J. resolve some painful emotional dilemmas that had in the past impeded her from making sound decisions.

Mrs. J.'s treatment plan was focused on her obtaining a marketable job skill. Before being able to obtain any training, Mrs. J.'s family needs had to be addressed. The case manager assisted Mrs. J. in obtaining public housing and child care for her children. In addition, the case manager helped Mrs. J. obtain special funding to pay for tuition at a local community college.

The first year of college work was not easy for Mrs. J., and the case manager had to be very supportive; however, the second year was much less traumatic. Mrs. J. is now in her third year of schooling and is looking forward to fulfilling her prenursing requirements.

---

The case history of Mrs. J. illustrates that case managers must deal with both "concrete" services such as finding a client a place to live, making sure clients have food and proper medical care, and "counseling" services to help individuals resolve emotional blocks to making effective decisions. The luxury of a small caseload allowed the case manager to individualize the treatment plan for Mrs. J. and to conduct follow-up when personal problems emerged from time to time. Mrs. J's continuing therapeutic relationship with the case manager allowed her to obtain a sense of hope, which in turn motivated her to develop a more satisfying, functional, and productive lifestyle.

The profession of social work has been in the forefront of designing case management systems throughout its history. Case management is one of the most important treatment interventions that social workers have at their disposal. The entire profession of social work is based on "person-in-the-environment" interaction. Most schools of social work have utilized an ecosystems approach to help students conceptualize the interaction between society and the individual and to assess problems based on that interaction. From this assessment, the treatment plan is formulated and includes both individual counseling and attempts to impact the social system—which may be part of the problem.

Professional social workers are entering a job market in the 1990s that is clamoring for case management expertise. Almost all social service agencies are designing case management systems to help long-term clients who are dysfunctional because of problems in such areas as health, child welfare, juvenile justice, mental health, aging, and developmental disabilities. Many patterns of case management are developing throughout the country, but regardless of the pattern chosen, the social work profession needs to play a major role in this treatment intervention. Social workers are professionally well equipped to design, manage, and provide case management services.

## *Historical Developments*

Case management was identified as early as 1863 when the commonwealth of Massachusetts established programs under the Board of Charities to coordinate public services as well as to conserve public funds.[3] Case management has also been linked to the Mary Richmond era and the early settlement house developments.

Much of the focus of the current case management had its origins in the rehabilitation-focused workers' compensation programs of the 1940s. Case management programs did not receive a lot of attention until the early 1970s when the federal government identified social service coordination and service integration as a priority and began funding demonstration projects of service coordination systems. Various federal laws were passed between 1970 and 1987 that included components of case management services. The Consolidated Omnibus Budget Reconciliation Act (Cobra), which was passed in 1985, encouraged states to provide case management as an optional Medicaid service. The Special Education Legislation of 1987 (P.L. 99-457) and the Family Support Act of 1988 (P.L. 100-485) included case management provisions. These laws expanded the use of case management in many social service areas.[4]

The Family Support Act (FSA) of 1988 also provided new impetus for case management. The Job Opportunity and Basic Skills Training Program (JOBS) by which the FSA seeks to increase the economic self-sufficiency of AFDC recipients contains provisions for case management. The goal of case management under this program is to ensure that needy families with children obtain education, training, and employment to help them avoid long-term welfare dependence. Hagen observed:

> The most obvious direct practice role for social work is in case management provided for by the JOBS legislation. States have the option of using case managers to assist recipients in participating in the JOBS program. The models for case management and roles of case managers will be developed at the state and local levels. Social work could have an instrumental role in developing models that build on the participants' strengths, empower AFDC mothers, and broker services and advocate on the client's behalf for necessary support services. These services may extend beyond the education and training provision of JOBS to include the other social services that families may need.[5]

Various case management models are currently in use. In some instances, case management is viewed as monitoring of client progress on paper only, a function sometimes performed by specially trained clerical staff. In other instances, personnel are drawn from other vocational education and training programs. In Iowa's program to serve multiproblem families, family development specialists are used. To date, there is not much social work presence in the development of case management models.

The JOBS program also requires state welfare agencies to develop individualized employment plans and services for participants based on an initial assessment of their education, work experience, employment skills, family circumstances, and supportive services needs including child care. At state option, the assessment may also include the needs of the children. To develop meaningful employability plans, these assessments must be comprehensive and must involve the client as a mutual partner. Complex decisions must be made about such issues as child care arrangements and what family circumstances will constitute deferral from the JOBS program. Social workers are well prepared to conduct a thorough psychosocial assessment.

## Case Management Defined

Obviously, the profession of social work is vitally interested in the case management movement. In 1984 the board of directors of the National Association of Social Workers (NASW) published *Standards and Guidelines for Social Work Case Management for the Functionally Impaired.* In June 1992 NASW's board of directors approved new standards for social work case management, which described the intervention as "a method of providing services whereby a professional social worker assesses the needs of the client and the client's family, when appropriate, and arranges, coordinates, monitors, evaluates and advocates for a package of multiple services to meet the specific client's complex needs."[6]

Greene defines the key elements of case management practice, which are shown in Table 20.1.[7]

Rothman suggests that case management basically incorporates two central functions: "(1) providing individualized advice, counseling, and therapy to clients in the community and (2) linking clients to needed services and supports in community agencies and informal helping networks."[8]

Vourlekis and Greene define case management by describing the following practice functions:

### Client Identification and Outreach

In this initial stage of the case management process, consultation with potential consumers provides information on potential barriers and obstacles to service utilization and access. . . .

At the service system or community level, the case manager provides input into policy and program plans, helping to define the scope and shape of services. . . .

### TABLE 20.1    Key Features of Social Work Case Management Practice

**Social Work Case Management Practice**

- is a process based on a trusting and enabling client–social worker relationship
- utilizes the social work dual focus of understanding the person in the environment in working with populations at risk
- aims to ensure a continuum of care to clients with complex, multiple problems and disabilities
- attempts to intervene clinically to ameliorate the emotional problems accompanying illness or loss of function
- utilizes the social work skills of brokering and advocacy as a boundary-spanning approach to service delivery
- targets clients who require a range of community-based or long-term care services, encompassing economic, health/medical, social, and personal care needs
- aims to provide services in the least restrictive environment
- requires the use of assessment of the client's functional capacity and support network in determining the level of care
- affirms the traditional social work values of self-determination and the worth and dignity of the individual and the concept of mutual responsibility in decision making.

### *Individual and Family Assessment and Diagnosis*

The case manager uses systematic data-gathering skills to answer critical questions about needed improvements in the fit between the person and family, and the relevant environment.... The case manager assesses the service system resources and deficits at the same time....

### *Planning and Resource Identification*

The case manager mobilizes client problem-solving capacity to develop jointly a care plan that is workable. Negotiation—requiring contracting skills—among client, family, and other providers concerning goals and expectations may be necessary before a realistic plan can be determined....

At the service system level, the case manager searches for appropriate resources, including those that are culturally sensitive. Resource gaps are identified as well....

### *Linking Clients to Needed Resources*

At this point, accessing, acquiring, and even creating needed resources is a central concern. In working with the client, the case manager addresses any of the client's specific concerns or perceived obstacles to using a resource....

### *Service Implementation and Coordination*

With some clients, the case manager must draw upon advanced clinical skills to assist the client throughout the process of using services to reach desired goals....

Clients may need practical assistance from the case manager as well. Emergency transportation, assistance with making a move, coffee and danish, and a chance to get outside—these requests might be made of a case manager....

### *Monitoring Service Delivery*

It is at the case level that the case manager makes sure that the system is accountable to the client, and that the client meets agreed-upon expectations. The case manager works actively to make things go as they should, and reports and intervenes when things go wrong....

### *Advocacy to Obtain Services*

This function involves the case manager in implementing a planned strategy of power to obtain specific services or resources for a client (case advocacy) or perhaps for the total group of clients (cause advocacy)....

### *Evaluation*

The involvement of the direct-practitioner case manager in evaluating the quality, appropriateness, and effectiveness of the case management services provided takes place on two levels as well...at the level of the individual client...at the delivery system level....[9]

The eight "practice key skills" developed by Vourlekis and Greene are included because they represent a comprehensive definitional statement and explanation of social work case management. However, all of these helping skills are to little avail if the case manager is asked to work with more than fifteen or twenty clients at one time. Case management intervention is only effective when caseloads are kept small. Again, it should be noted that the case management movement has been created to individualize the treatment process and to empower dysfunctional individuals by being able to assist them to better utilize resources that are available to them.

## Case Management Research

More research is needed in case management. Regardless of its growing acceptance, case management is not a well-defined service intervention. Almost every agency tailors the intervention to meet its own needs. The measure of outcome is especially troublesome in many case management projects. Rothman states that the major foci in case management measurement attempts are: "(1) social functioning or quality of life, (2) intrapsychic status, and (3) behavioral indicators of experience with key institutions."[10] All three of the measurement foci are rather difficult to put into operation. In addition to measurement problems, case management takes place in service environments that "are turbulent, with shifting funding levels, policies, and client priorities, as well as turnover of staff, cross-professional rivalries, and political pressures."[11]

Regardless of the many methodological problems, researchers continue to try to validate the intervention of case management. For example, one recent study of a semirural community mental health center in Utah has produced some significant findings on case management effectiveness. Funded by the National Institute of Mental Health, this research project was actually able to maintain an experimental design that included a control and experimental group over a two-year period. Also, the case management team was well trained in the Strengths case management model advocated by Rapp and Wintersteen.[12] The following research report summarizes the effective work accomplished by case managers:

A year after full implementation of an experimental case management program in Logan, Utah, case management consumers reported significantly better mental and physical health, fewer problems with mood or thinking, greater competence in daily living, and higher psychological well-being in comparison to a control group of consumers who received only psychosocial rehabilitation services. Case management family members also reported lower consumer psychiatric symptomatology and felt less burdened by their consumer's illness than the control group's family members. In addition, primary care providers assessed case management consumers as less depressed, more rational, and more productive than control group consumers. These group differences in consumer, family member, and service provider reports were obtained in spite of group equivalence in pre-intervention level of functioning, level of help received, social support, family cohesiveness, and a variety of personal liabilities (e.g., chronic pain or poor work history).

A 36-month longitudinal analysis of hospitalization and crisis center records substantiated these interview reports. Following full program implementation, case management consumers showed a decrease in rate of hospitalization and frequency of crisis center contacts; control group consumers did not. The co-occurrence within the case management group of fewer hospitalizations and crises, together with family member reports of lower emotional burden, is of particular relevance to mental health policy. Although researchers warn that planned reductions in consumer hospitalization often increase family burden (e.g., Olfson, 1990), family member reports in Logan suggest that case management can simultaneously reduce hospitalizations and lower family burden by providing continuous emotional support to consumers and consultation to family members. That is, when a reduction in hospitalization is brought about through a decrease in consumer symptomatology, reductions in family burden can accompany consumer community retention.[13]

Continued research efforts must be made to define case management empirically and to test its effectiveness as a social work intervention. Social service personnel who have worked in the case management arena are convinced that the intervention works and that individuals are helped to be more functional.

## *Summary*

*The emphasis being placed on case management at the present time is the result of a number of forces in our society. There has been a recognition that many people cannot negotiate our complicated and fragmented social service systems without help. The federal government has recognized this need and has legislated requirements for case managers for various programs.*

*The profession of social work has traditionally been concerned with the interaction of the individual and society and is in an excellent position to provide leadership in this field. Professional social workers are entering a job market in the 1990s that is clamoring for case management expertise. Social workers are well-equipped professionals with the skill and competency to design, manage, and provide case management.*

*The definition of case management is still rather unclear. However, researchers are continuing to define and measure case management tasks in an empirical fashion. Some studies have demonstrated impressive results, but many questions remain regarding research methodologies.*

*The key roles that case managers accomplish are: (1) client identification and outreach; (2) individual and family assessment and diagnosis; (3) planning and resource identification; (4) linking clients to needed resources; (5) service implementation and coordination; (6) monitoring service delivery; (7) advocacy to obtain services; and (8) evaluation.*

*The renewed interest of case management in social work has been created by a recognition that social service systems must return to an individualized/coordinated/follow-up approach if we are to help and empower dysfunctional individuals in our society.*

# Selected References

BIGELOW, D. A., and D. J. YOUNG, "Effectiveness of a Case Management Program," *Community Mental Health Journal,* 25 (1991), 115–123.

CHAMBERLAIN, R., and C. A. RAPP, "A Decade of Case Management: A Methodological Review of Outcome Research," *Community Mental Health Journal,* 27 (1991), 171–188.

GOERING, P. N., D. A. WASYLENKI, M. FARKAS, W. J. LANCEE, and R. BALLANTYNE, "What Difference Does Case Management Make?" *Hospital and Community Psychiatry,* 39 (1988), 272–276.

MACIAS, CATHALEENE, RONALD KINNEY, O. WILLIAM FARLEY, ROBERT JACKSON and BETTY VOS, "The Role of Case Management within a Community Support System: Partnership with Psychosocial Rehabilitation," *Community Mental Health Journal,* 30, no. 4 (1994), 323–339.

MODRCIN, M., C. A. RAPP, and J. POERTNER, "The Evaluation of Case Management Services with the Chronically Mental Ill," *Evaluation and Program Planning,* 11 (1988), 307–314.

MOORE, STEPHEN, "Case Management and the Integration of Services: How Service Delivery Systems Shape Case Management," *Social Work,* 37 (September 1992), 418–423.

RAPP, C. A., and R. WINTERSTEEN, "The Strengths Model of Case Management: Results from Twelve Demonstrations," *Psychosocial Rehabilitation Journal,* 13 (1989), 23–32.

ROTHMAN, JACK, *Guidelines for Case Management.* Itasca, IL: F.E. Peacock Publishers, Inc., 1992.

SOLOMON, P., "The Efficacy of Case Management Services for Severely Mentally Disabled Clients," *Community Mental Health Journal,* 28, no. 3 (1992), 163–180.

STEIN, L., and M. A. TEST, "Alternative to Mental Health Hospital Treatment. A Conceptual Model, Treatment Program, and Clinical Intervention," *Archives of General Psychiatry,* 37 (1980), 392–397.

VOURLEKIS, BETSY S., and ROBERTA R. GREENE, eds., *Social Work Case Management.* New York: Aldine de Gruyter, 1992.

# Notes

1. Robert L. Barker, *The Social Work Dictionary,* 3rd ed. (Washington, DC: NASW Press, 1995), p. 33.

2. Judy Winn and Ramona Sierra, "Case Management: Cooperation Among Disciplines," *Journal of Insurance Medicine,* 28 (Winter 1991), 258.

3. Karen Orloss Kaplan, "Recent Trends in Case Management," in Leon Ginsberg et al., *Encyclopedia of Social Work,* 18th ed., 1990 supplement (Silver Spring, MD: National Association of Social Workers, 1990), p. 61.

4. Ibid., p. 61.

5. Jan L. Hagen, "Women, Work and Welfare: Is There a Role for Social Work?," *Social Work,* 37 (January 1992), 11.

6. National Association of Social Workers, "Case Manager's Role Clarified by Guidelines," *NASW News,* 37 (September 1992), 7.

7. Roberta R. Greene, "Case Management: An Arena for Social Work Practice," in Betsy S. Vourlekis and Roberta R. Greene, eds., *Social Work Case Management* (New York: Aldine de Gruyter, 1992), p. 3.

8. Jack Rothman, *Guidelines for Case Management* (Itasca, IL: F. E. Peacock Publishers, Inc., 1992), p. 3.

9. Betsy S. Vourlekis and Roberta R. Greene, eds., *Social Work Case Management* (New York: Aldine de Gruyter, 1992), pp. 183–188.

10. Rothman, *Guidelines for Case Management,* p. 11.

11. Ibid., p. 11.

12. Charles A. Rapp and R. Wintersteen, "The Strengths Model of Case Management: Results from Twelve Demonstrations," *Psychosocial Rehabilitation Journal,* 13 (1989), 23–32.

13. Cathaleene Macias, Ronald Kinney, O. William Farley, Robert Jackson, and Betty Vos, "The Role of Case Management within a Community Support System: Partnership with Psychosocial Rehabilitation," *Community Mental Health Journal,* 30, no. 4 (1994), 335–337.

Chapter *21*

---

# Social Work: A Maturing Profession

*Two college students were discussing their goals in life. One turned to his friend and queried, "When I'm all through working and about to retire, I wonder what I will have accomplished in life?"*

*He and his friend talked about various professions and jobs, and then the first student observed, "I've decided to become a social worker. As I've thought about it, I feel I can make a great contribution to people, as well as obtain real satisfactions for myself."*

Social work is regarded by most people as a profession. Many say it is a recognized profession; others believe it is an emerging one. The United States Census Bureau includes, among others, the following as professions: accountant, architect, artist, attorney, clergyman, college professor, dentist, engineer, journalist, judge, librarian, natural scientist, optometrist, pharmacist, physician, social scientist, social worker, surgeon, and teacher. Is social work really a profession? Has it emerged or is it still maturing? What are the characteristics of a profession? These and related questions are considered in this chapter.

## Criteria of a Profession

William Wickenden, while president of Case School of Applied Science, gave a pioneering address before the Engineering Institute of Canada in which he described the characteristics of the professional person. He mentioned four distinctive marks. The first is a *"type of activity,* which carries high individual responsibility and which applies special skill to problems on a distinctly intellectual plane." Second, he said "is a *motive of service,* associated with limited rewards as distinct from profit." The third is "the *motive of self-expression,* which implies joy and pride in one's work and a self-imposed standard of excellence." And fourth is "a conscious *recognition of social duty* to be fulfilled among other means by guarding the ideals and standards of one's profession, by advancing it in public understanding and esteem, by sharing advances in technical knowledge, and by rendering gratuitous public service, in addition to that for ordinary compensation, as a return to society for special advantages of education and status."

Wickenden went on to describe the attributes that mark off the corporate life of a group of persons as professional in character:

> We may place first a *body of knowledge* (science) and of *art* (skill) held as a common possession and to be extended by united effort. Next is *an educational process* based on this body of knowledge and art, in ordering which the professional group has a recognized responsibility. Third is a *standard* of personal qualifications for admission to the professional group, based on character, training, and proved competence. Next follows *a standard of conduct* based on courtesy, honor, and ethics, which guides the practitioner in his relations with clients, colleagues, and the public. Fifth, we may place a more or less formal *recognition of status,* either by one's colleagues or by the state, as a basis for good standing. And finally, there is usually *an organization* of the professional group, devoted to its common advancement and its social duty, rather than to the maintenance of an economic monopoly.[1]

Greenwood[2] canvassed the sociological literature on occupations and came to the conclusion that there are five distinguishing attributes of a profession: (1) systematic theory, (2) authority, (3) community sanction, (4) ethical codes, and (5) a culture. He discusses each of these characteristics and then concludes:

> Social work is already a profession; it has too many points of congruence with the model to be classifiable otherwise. Social work is, however, seeking to rise within the professional hierarchy, so that it, too, might enjoy maximum prestige, authority, and monopoly, which presently belong to a few top professions.[3]

In regard to a systematic body of knowledge or theory, social work is getting a good start. In comparison to some professions it has a long way to go. Nevertheless, if one studies carefully the research being accomplished and the theories now extant in social work, it is clearly evident that there is a beginning systematic body of knowledge that serves as a foundation for this helping profession.

The social worker today possesses a professional authority. He or she is respected by other disciplines and, in the main, by clients who come for help. Although the social worker honors the freedom of choice and the right of self-determination of the client, he or she possesses an authoritative demeanor that builds confidence in the client and helps, through the use of a relationship, to bring about desired changes. The client derives a sense of security from this assumption of authority by the professional social worker.

As Greenwood points out, the social worker also has the sanction of the community. It is evident that society in general approves of social work and respects it—as indicated by the number of social workers who are hired for positions in public and private agencies. More and more people are asking, "Where can I find a social worker?"

In 1960 the social work profession developed a code of ethics that replaced earlier preliminary codes sponsored by local and national groups in social welfare. The code was revised in 1967, in 1979, and again in 1990 by the Delegate Assembly of NASW.

The fifth characteristic, that of a professional culture, is certainly existent in social work today. Social work has its own professional organizations, such as the National Association of Social Workers and the Council on Social Work Education. It has a characteristic jargon, and has a unique focus on certain values, norms, and symbols. It stresses the importance of social work as a career and the necessity of dedication and interest in mankind and society as personal prerequisites for the individual who plans to go into this field.

If we look at some of the distinguishing characteristics of social work, we find amplification of the uniqueness of social work as a profession. Social work considers the total person in the total social environment, and is usually within an agency that has structure. It sponsors the use of casework, group work, community organization, social research, and administration in unique combinations of problem-solving methodologies. It places particular stress upon self-determination and helping the client to help him- or herself, adhering particularly to the democratic process. Social workers are the only persons in the professions who are called *workers.* They use and coordinate agency and community resources. They specialize on the interplay of all relevant knowledge and facts. Social workers have helped to develop and utilize the teamwork approach. Their research has certain distinguishing characteristics. Money is used as a tool in service and training. The social worker stresses the importance of the family. The supervisory process is a unique characteristic of the social work profession. It has a differential educational training program as well as unique literature and professional organizations. All of these factors—and others—set social work apart from the other helping professions.

## Historical Background

A profession includes an approved training program, a professional organization, related organizations and activities, and a body of skilled workers. If we turn the pages of history, we find social work has substantial professional underpinning. Several organizations and developments have played significant roles in relation to social work.

### Schools of Social Work

Within the past several decades social work has been developing rapidly, and the importance of the training process is evident. Its roots go far back, particularly in relation to the efforts in England and the United States of more than a century ago when welfare agencies were created to help families and individuals, especially financially, and also to provide some psychological support. As these services began to increase and become formalized, the need for training became apparent.

By 1898 the New York Charity Organization Society "took the initial steps in the direction of a professional school by holding a six weeks' training course, designed primarily to increase the efficiency of social workers already in the field."[4] This was the beginning of the New York School of Social Work. (The name was changed in 1963 to Columbia University School of Social Work.) Soon other training centers were established in different parts of the country. Before 1910 there were schools of social work in the five largest cities in the United States.

Professional schools of social work increased in number so that by 1994 there were 112 programs in the United States offering appropriate master's education. Most of these programs are integral parts of universities and have become recognized as important centers for providing graduate, professional training in higher education. Many universities also offer undergraduate training programs in social work.

Enrollments in these schools, involving only a few persons at the turn of the century, have increased so that in 1961–62 there were 6,666 full-time students enrolled in graduate schools of social work, and in June 1962, a total of 2,476 students graduated with the Master of Social Work degree.

In November 1994, there were 21,622 full-time students in the social work master's program, along with 11,590 part-time students, based on data provided by CSWE. For the academic year 1993–94, there were 12,856 master's degrees awarded by these programs, an all-time high. In 1993–94, degrees in baccalaureate social work education were awarded to 10,511 students.

## *Council on Social Work Education*

Established in 1952 through a merger of three organizations with related functions, the Council on Social Work Education (CSWE) gives leadership in the United States and throughout the world to the efforts of the "total social work profession and to citizens interested in the welfare of their own families and their communities to increase the number of professionally qualified social workers, and at the same time improve the quality of their education for social work." The basic aims of the council are to support, strengthen, and improve social work education and to increase the number of qualified social workers.

The CSWE sponsors a unique partnership of citizens, social work practitioners, agency executives, and educators who work together.

A council brochure explains that it is responsible for assuring the quality of social work education and is the only accrediting body for social work education in the United States. It is authorized by the Department of Education, and the National Commission on Accrediting.

Membership is open to institutional members, which include graduate and undergraduate programs of social work in the United States, major public and voluntary national state and local social agencies, the National Federation of Student Social Workers, and professional membership organizations. Individual members include practitioners, educators, and anyone interested in social work education.

The council sponsors or assists with the following: standards, curriculum development, continuing education, research, services to minority groups, fellowships, consultation services, publications, and an annual program meeting.

The twenty-fifth annual program meeting was held in Boston in March 1979, with 2,487 social work educators, students, and practitioners in attendance. Trends and key issues were discussed in 239 sessions, with an overall theme of "Pursuit of Excellence in Education and Practice."

The 1995 annual program meeting of CSWE was held in San Diego, California, with the underlying goal of improving the quality of social work education and practice, and with a general theme of "Empowerment: Building for Strength." Announcement was made that the 42nd annual program meeting of CSWE would be held in Washington, DC, in 1996 with the theme of "Public Policy Challenges for Social Work Education."

The Commission on Accreditation, authorized by the council, accredits new schools of social work, as well as periodically conducts on-campus reviews of all the graduate schools of social work with the goal of improving social work training and strengthening academic standards. Also, since 1974 the commission has had the authority and responsibility to accredit undergraduate social work programs.

One of the most valuable services of the council is to provide publications that help schools of social work, agencies, and individuals to improve educational facilities and social work practice. Current catalogues include pages of available publications related to the social work educational endeavor.

## National Association of Social Workers

For a discipline to become a profession, it is imperative that a professional organization be established. This has happened in social work. The first basic professional organization was the American Association of Social Workers, established in 1921, and which by 1954 had a membership of about 13,500 located in 132 local chapters. Six other professional organizations, built around social work specialties and with memberships totaling more than 7,500, had also furthered the profession. In the 1950s representatives of these seven organizations met and established a single integrated organization, the National Association of Social Workers, which is open to all trained and qualified social workers. This association was officially organized on July 7, 1955, at a special meeting of representatives of the seven predecessor organizations.

This association has grown in numbers and prestige so that by 1995 it had a membership of 154,000 and is respected among professionally trained people in the various helping disciplines. The association has a code of ethics, and has issued policy statements on salaries, on the goals of public social policy, and on standards for social work personnel practices. It has made tremendous strides in helping with the recruitment of qualified personnel for social work training and practice. In 1986 the association had 55 chapters (each state, plus New York City, Los Angeles, Puerto Rico, the Virgin Islands, and Europe). By 1995, a few changes had taken place with 55 chapters remaining.

The seven associations that participated in the formation of the National Association of Social Workers were the American Association of Group Workers, American Association of Medical Social Workers, American Association of Psychiatric Social Workers, American Association of Social Workers, Association for the Study of Community Organization, National Association of School Social Workers, and the Social Work Research Group. Actually, the main activities of most of these groups have been absorbed by the National Association of Social Workers. The various group members have been able to maintain some of their specialized interests, at the same time fusing into a united organization that is benefiting all social workers, social work education, and social work practice.

According to its bylaws, amended in August 1990, the association, to achieve its aims, "shall at all times recognize and carry out a threefold responsibility: (1) to promote activities appropriate to strengthening and unifying the social work profession as a whole, (2) to promote the sound and continuous development of the various areas of social work practice whereby the profession contributes to the meeting of particular aspects of human need, and (3) to promote efforts in behalf of human well-being by methods of social action."

A major development sponsored by NASW has been the establishment of the Academy of Certified Social Workers (ACSW). Through careful planning and good public relations, 18,500 social workers became certified on December 1, 1961, when this program officially began. Today there are more than 58,000. This is a significant step in raising the status of social workers and, in particular, in improving standards of practice in this field. Moreover, a new NASW credential has been established for social workers who have bachelor's degrees—the Academy of Certified Baccalaureate Social Worker (ACBSW). More than 2,000 qualified by passing the first BSW credential exam, which was given in June 1991.[5]

A new development in professional social work has been the emergence of the NASW Diplomate Exam,[6] which may lead to a credential properly referred to as the NASW Diplomate in Clinical Social Work, the NASW Diplomate, or the DCSW. Some 2,000 social workers in November 1994 completed the first examination administered in the new NASW Diplomate in Clinical Social Work credential program.

The National Association of Social Workers has a delegate assembly that meets every three years to consider issues, policies, and social action. The Delegate Assembly is the ultimate policymaking body for NASW. In February 1995 its president, Ann A. Abbott, issued a call to launch the process that will culminate August 14–18, 1996, in convening this Assembly, comprising 300 elected delegates who represent NASW's members, and who "will determine organizational policy, set program priorities and take stands on social and professional issues to guide NASW for three years."[7]

Another area of interest to NASW is licensing. Certification and licensing in social work began with the legal regulation of the profession of social work in Puerto Rico in 1934, by an act that established compulsory certification, or licensing. In 1945 in California the first voluntary registration for MSWs in social work was enacted. In the 1960s, eight state laws were passed to expand legal regulation of the profession. Additional laws were passed in three states in 1972 and two more in 1974, bringing the total to 14 states with some form of legal regulation. By 1985 there were 36 states and U.S. territories with social work licensure or registration laws.[8]

In 1969 the delegate assembly adopted a position favoring licensure, and since then NASW has given considerable guidance and support for licensing.

In 1973 NASW, according to a news release, "incorporated the requirement for ACSW certification—the MSW degree plus two years' experience, together with a written examination—into its model licensing statute. This statute is being used as a guideline in promoting state licensing and regulation of social work practice. NASW is negotiating with states that have licensing laws to accept ACSW membership as an alternative to the states examination processes."

By 1988, forty-four states, the District of Columbia, the Virgin Islands, and Puerto Rico had some form of regulation, such as licensure or certification. This meant there were only six remaining states without social work regulations. It was anticipated that by the

1990 Delegate Assembly there would likely be at least an initial form of regulation in all states.[9] Through the efforts of NASW and others the social work profession gained its goal of legal regulation throughout the United States when, in April 1992, Governor Tommy Thompson of Wisconsin signed a social work certification act for that state.

NASW plays an active role in establishing and maintaining standards for social work practice. Illustrative of this function are the standards for the practice of clinical social work, approved by the NASW Board of Directors, June 1984, revised April 1989, which state that clinical social workers shall:

> Function in accordance with the ethics and the stated standards of the profession, including its accountability procedures.
>
> Have and continue to develop specialized knowledge and understanding of individuals, families, and groups and of therapeutic and preventive interventions.
>
> Respond in a professional manner to all persons who seek their assistance.
>
> Be knowledgeable about the services available in the community and make appropriate referrals for their clients.
>
> Maintain their accessibility to clients.
>
> Safeguard the confidential nature of the treatment relationship and of the information obtained within that relationship.
>
> Maintain access to professional case consultation.
>
> Establish and maintain professional offices and procedures.
>
> Represent themselves to the public with accuracy.
>
> Engage in the independent private practice of clinical social work only when qualified to do so.
>
> Have the right to establish an independent private practice.

Another indication of the professional vitality of NASW was the plan announced in 1988 for a new building to house the association. It was to be located in the nation's capital and would likely cost about $36 million when completed.[10] NASW moved into its new headquarters in February 1992 at 750 First St., N.E., Washington, D.C.

## Social Work Today

Another way to view the maturing of social work as a profession is to consider some of the major characteristics and activities of social work and social workers in the present era.

### Code of Ethics

A major breakthrough in the development of social work as a profession occurred when the delegate assembly of the National Association of Social Workers adopted an official code of ethics for the association on October 13, 1960, and amended on April 11, 1967, with a philosophical introduction as follows:

Social work is based on humanitarian, democratic ideals. Professional social workers are dedicated to service for the welfare of mankind, to the disciplined use of a recognized body of knowledge about human beings and their interactions, and to the marshaling of community resources to promote the well-being of all without discrimination.

Social work practice is a public trust that requires of its practitioners integrity, compassion, belief in the dignity and worth of human beings, respect for individual differences, a commitment to service, and a dedication to truth. It requires mastery of a body of knowledge and skill gained through professional education and experience. It requires also recognition of the limitations of present knowledge and skill and of the services we are now equipped to give. The end sought is the performance of a service with integrity and competence.

Each member of the profession carries responsibility to maintain and improve social work service; constantly to examine, use, and increase the knowledge on which practice and social policy are based; and to develop further the philosophy and skills of the profession.

The 1990 Delegate Assembly revised the Code of Ethics adapted by the 1979 Delegate Assembly and specified the professional relationships and standards as follows:

## *1990 NASW Code of Ethics— Summary of Major Principles*[11]

I. THE SOCIAL WORKER'S CONDUCT AND COMPORTMENT AS A SOCIAL WORKER
   A. *Propriety.* The social worker should maintain high standards of personal conduct in the capacity or identity as social worker.
   B. *Competence and Professional Development.* The social worker should strive to become and remain proficient in professional practice and the performance of professional functions.
   C. *Service.* The social worker should regard as primary the service obligation of the social work profession.
   D. *Integrity.* The social worker should act in accordance with the highest standards of professional integrity.
   E. *Scholarship and Research.* The social worker engaged in study and research should be guided by the conventions of scholarly inquiry.

II. THE SOCIAL WORKER'S ETHICAL RESPONSIBILITY TO CLIENTS
   F. *Primacy of Clients' Interests.* The social worker's primary responsibility is to clients.
   G. *Rights and Prerogatives of Clients.* The social worker should make every effort to foster maximum self-determination on the part of clients.
   H. *Confidentiality and Privacy.* The social worker should respect the privacy of clients and hold in confidence all information obtained in the course of professional service.
   I. *Fees.* When setting fees, the social worker should ensure that they are fair, reasonable, considerate, and commensurate with the service performed and with due regard for the clients' ability to pay.

III. THE SOCIAL WORKER'S ETHICAL RESPONSIBILITY TO COLLEAGUES
   J. *Respect, Fairness, and Courtesy.* The social worker should treat colleagues with respect, courtesy, fairness, and good faith.
   K. *Dealing with Colleagues' Clients.* The social worker has the responsibility to relate to the clients of colleagues with full professional consideration.

IV. THE SOCIAL WORKER'S ETHICAL RESPONSIBILITY TO EMPLOYERS AND EMPLOYING ORGANIZATIONS
   L. *Commitments to Employing Organizations.* The social worker should adhere to commitments made to the employing organizations.

V. THE SOCIAL WORKER'S ETHICAL RESPONSIBILITY TO THE SOCIAL WORK PROFESSION
   M. *Maintaining the Integrity of the Profession.* The social worker should uphold and advance the values, ethics, knowledge, and mission of the profession.
   N. *Community Service.* The social worker should assist the profession in making social services available to the general public.
   O. *Development of Knowledge.* The social worker should take responsibility for identifying, developing, and fully utilizing knowledge for professional practice.

VI. THE SOCIAL WORKER'S ETHICAL RESPONSIBILITY TO SOCIETY
   P. *Promoting the General Welfare.* The social worker should promote the general welfare of society.

This code of ethics gives the social worker a societal compass. It helps the worker realize that he or she is a person who should have responsible interest and compassion regarding people, their problems, and their relationships with others.

A bright light on the ethical horizon is the introduction of ethics committees in social work. Reamer suggests that this movement is bringing significant changes in human service agencies, and that such committees assist in educating staff, formulating policies, and reviewing cases that contain complex ethical issues.[12]

## *Schools of Social Work*

Social work education is provided on both undergraduate and graduate levels. The Council on Social Work Education by 1994 had accredited the programs of 382 undergraduate departments of colleges and universities offering social work training. Many persons who complete their undergraduate training go on to graduate social work schools or take social work positions in agencies. Another aim of this program is to provide social welfare content in the liberal education of students to aid in promoting good citizenship.

The 112 graduate training programs for the master's degree in the United States ordinarily take two years and combine classes in instruction with actual fieldwork practice in agencies. Since 1971 the council has authorized "advanced standing" for students who have

Social work enters the computer world.

completed approved undergraduate social work programs, and some schools of social work have established various plans that make it possible for such students to obtain their master's degrees in less than two years, some requiring only one year of graduate work.

Most graduate schools operate on the concurrent plan wherein they offer academic classes and field work training simultaneously. Several schools use the *block* plan, which provides for academic training at the beginning of the total program, followed by intensive five-day-a-week field instruction for several months, and finally culminates in additional academic seminars and other integrative instructional activities. Nearly all of the health and welfare agencies are utilized for field instruction, including psychiatric, medical, school, correctional, settlement, public welfare, child welfare, and group work agencies.

The basic program for the master's degree includes the three core areas of human behavior and social environment, social services and social policies, and the methods courses. Earlier, considerable emphasis was placed on *specialization* in certain fields such as psychiatric social work, medical social work, and school social work. Since the 1960s the training has been mainly on a generic base, with students taking the two-year training program to become social workers qualified to work in various agencies. In addition to the three core areas there is considerable work offered in research, and schools require either an individual or group thesis, a research project or completion of research classes for graduation. Elective courses provide a well-rounded program for the person who is going to practice as a professional social worker.

There is again a focus and emphasis on "specialization." Schools of social work have one or more "concentrations" involving methods and/or fields or problems for practice—casework, group work, micro or macro approach, social planning, drug abuse, health care. In addition, most schools have one or more "special emphases," which again bring added support to cope with specific problems in specific ways.

Some schools offer a third-year program, which provides for a deepening and intensification of study regarding casework, group work, administration, research, community organization, or some other aspect of the total service program.

Fifty-one graduate schools have introduced doctoral programs. In 1962 there were 17 schools (two in Canada) offering post-master's programs, either a third-year or doctoral program, or both. Enrollment during 1962–63 amounted to 176 full-time students. In November 1987 there were 703 full-time and 820 part-time students enrolled in doctoral programs, based on data provided by CSWE from 42 of the 47 existing programs. For the academic year 1993–94, doctoral degrees were awarded to 294 students by 55 graduate programs. A current movement exists to change DSW programs to Ph.D. programs.

## Research

Since the 1960s social work has blossomed in the area of research, which is basic to professional development. Most schools of social work have one or more research projects or grants they are sponsoring. Grants are awarded not only from federal and state government sources, but also from foundations and from private business and other corporations. More and more people are coming to social workers, requesting help to study human social behavior, the helping processes, and related activities.

A development that is augmenting research in social work is that many agencies, public and private, are sponsoring research projects of their own. Various kinds of studies are being financed from regular agency budgets to ferret out facts regarding social problems and what might be done about them. A concrete example of this trend is the allocation of $17,000 by one state welfare department to a community services council to conduct a study of working mothers—with the aim of ascertaining the pertinent facts and implications related to family problems and their solutions.

Another contribution, as it applies to research, is the work being done by the more than 10,000 students who graduate each year with their MSW degrees. Many participate in a research study, individually or in groups. About 250 doctoral dissertations are being completed each year. These studies are making contributions toward new knowledge about human behavior and social work education and practice.

## Private Practice

One of the key developments in recent years has been the increase in the amount of private practice by persons with training in social work. Many social workers have joined forces with doctors or psychiatrists in providing services for patients. Others have set up their "shingles" in offices by themselves. Numerous questions have arisen and some leaders in social work have wondered about this development. However, the fact is that many qualified social workers are in private practice, and recent articles and studies reflect that this development seems to be another move toward professionalism. A study in 1968 of NASW members indicated fewer than 1,000 full time private practitioners, with an estimated 15,000 doing some private counseling on a part-time basis.[13]

In 1975 a review of the NASW Data Bank indicated 8,500 members were in full-time or part-time private practice. Gabriel estimated, using these data and adding those not reporting and those not members of NASW, that there were from 10,000 to 20,000 social workers in private practice.[14] In 1992 Barker reported it is likely "there are more than 28,000 social workers in private practice."[15] He also suggested that private social work is growing not only in the United States but in many other countries, especially in Australia, India, Israel, Great Britain, and Canada.

Since then there has been a considerable and gradual increase in private practice, both full-time and part-time, so that today social-work students are seriously considering these career choices. In fact, in a study of students in a New York State Master's of Social Work program, two-thirds (63 percent) thought they would enter private practice sometime during their careers.[16]

In December 1962, a workshop on private practice was held in Cleveland, Ohio, immediately prior to the 1962 delegate assembly of the National Association of Social Workers. Considerable difference of opinion was presented, but the overall conclusion was that, with certain safeguards, private practice does seem to fit into the total realm of professional social work. Following hours of debate, the delegate assembly adopted interim minimum standards for NASW members engaged in private practice of social work. They agreed that no NASW member may enter private practice unless:

1. He is a graduate of a school of social work accredited by the Council on Social Work Education or its predecessor organizations.
2. He is a member of the Academy of Certified Social Workers.
3. He has five years of acceptable full-time experience in agencies providing supervision by professionally trained social workers, of which two years were in one agency consecutively under such supervision, while giving direct service and using the method or methods to be used in the practice contemplated.[17]

The assembly, in adopting these standards and recommendations, pointed out that the qualifications should "not be construed as an endorsement of the competence of any individual member who meets the standards but rather be viewed as minimum criteria under which the form of practice would be sanctioned." The NASW Board of Directors modified these standards in 1971[18] stipulating that membership in ACSW was the profession's sole standard for self-regulated practice, in agency or private practice.

Social workers differ about the desirability of private practice. Of course, there are advantages and disadvantages in this challenging endeavor. Barker[19] suggests that the actual and anticipated rewards of private practice are: freedom from bureaucratic limitations found in agency employment, flexibility in work, opportunity to remain in direct practice, financial considerations, the challenge, opportunity to work with more motivated clients, and greater control over one's own work environment. He also suggests there are three main hazards in private practice: financial difficulties facing most private practitioners, malpractice and other legal difficulties, and problems centering in professional and public accountability, licensing, and qualifications for practice.

Numerous attempts have been made, some successfully, in the past few years to gain status for social workers for third-party payments for their services. NASW, many local chapters, and many individuals are working to gain further recognition in this regard. Acceptance of third-party payments for social workers is a step that will undoubtedly greatly strengthen and increase private social work practice. The 1984–85 annual report of NASW highlights its philosophy and current developments regarding third-party payments, as follows:

> Vendorship, the term sometimes applied to the practice of payment by a third party (an insurance carrier) to an individual who has provided services to another (the first and second parties), is an important issue for the profession. Only 15 states now have laws that require insurance carriers to extend vendorship rights to clinical social workers. While it seems illogical and unjust to deny such rights to the profession that provides the bulk of mental health services in the United States, the chief impact of such a policy is to deny millions of citizens access to the services of qualified practitioners, who generally charge less for the same services than other mental health professionals granted vendorship rights.
>
> Universal vendorship is one of the organization's highest priorities. Through arduous work by chapter leaders, two states, Montana and Tennessee, passed vendorship bills in the fiscal year 1985.[20]

In 1984 vendorship was listed as the highest priority goal of the National Association of Social Workers Delegate Assembly in the area of professional standards. It is of interest that many state legislatures are considering legislation to provide for third-party payments for professional social workers. Such action resulted in a social work licensure bill containing a vendorship clause becoming law in New Mexico, effective July 1989.

Reimbursement demands and treatment decisions related to vendorship and third-party payments, according to Strom in 1992, are producing a growing dilemma for social workers. Strom reports that as "health costs have increased, so have the number of restrictions placed by insurers on reimbursement for mental health services" and "with the growth in vendorship for social workers, professionals in the mental health field are increasingly challenged to provide appropriate services within the parameters of what will be reimbursed by the third party.[21]

Kelley and Alexander made a questionnaire study of clinical social workers and concluded that private practice has become an accepted form of social work in recent years, and that most who conduct private practice provide services on a part-time basis.[22] The advantages of such private practice included the following: provides a professional independence for agency practitioners, additional income, contact for supervisors and administrators with clients, educators can maintain skills and enrich teaching, and social workers who are parents can keep their schedules flexible and choose hours of work. The disadvantages related to these broad areas are: generating referrals, practical business issues, time management, professional development and quality control, and interaction between the agency and the private practitioner.

## Publications

Another criterion of a profession is that it produces professional publications. *Social Work,* introduced in 1955, is published bimonthly by the National Association of Social Workers and is recognized as a respectable professional journal. It has a current circulation of more than 160,000. This same organization publishes *NASW News,* a monthly that keeps professional social workers up-to-date on current developments, and includes personnel information, which lists job openings. NASW publishes the *Encyclopedia of Social Work.* This has become the standard reference work for social work education and practice.

NASW also publishes *Social Work Abstracts,* a quarterly that has brief descriptions of current articles and other materials relevant to social work practice, research, and education. Three newer quarterly journals, *Health and Social Work, Social Work in Education,* and *Social Work Research,* are offered for health care practitioners, school social workers, and those interested in research, respectively.

The Council on Social Work Education publishes the *Journal of Social Work Education,* which first appeared in July 1965, and is published three times a year. It is concerned with education for the fields of social work and social welfare, which includes materials on trends, new developments, issues, and problems at the undergraduate, master's, and post-master's levels.

Numerous professional books are appearing in social work and many articles written by social workers are published in professional and scientific journals, particularly those related to social functioning and the treatment of human interactional problems.

## Salaries and jobs

One of the first official activities of NASW was to establish a policy regarding salaries. The association recommended in 1957 that the beginning salary be a minimum of $5,400 per annum and suggested that social workers should be able to look forward to receiving $10,000 per annum after ten years' experience. In 1974 NASW recommended that the graduate of an approved baccalaureate social work program should receive $10,000 annually and the inexperienced master's graduate should receive a minimum of $12,500. Since then salaries have increased considerably. Present salaries for most MSW graduates would be in the range of $20,000 to $28,000 a year and for those who have been in practice about ten years, $30,000 to $50,000. Some social workers in private practice now make $75,000 to $150,000 annually. The 1995 *Social Work Almanac* reports a NASW sample study of its members which showed that in 1993 the average salary of those in direct service was $31,729 and the median salary was $29,000.

An NASW study in 1987 indicated that the average salary earned by social workers amounted to $27,800. This was based on salaries of administrators, direct service workers, experienced therapists, and the new BSW, and those in private practice as well as salaried workers.[23]

One of the fascinating aspects of social work practice is that it can take place in a variety of settings or agencies. Job opportunities are available in almost every kind of endeavor for helping people individually, or on a family or community basis. Positions are offered in settings such as comprehensive mental health centers, medical hospitals, business and industry, schools, prisons, YMCAs, public welfare, child welfare, suicide prevention centers, and adoption agencies.

The contributions of social work as a profession are being recognized in today's world. For the first time in history the U.S. Congress, in 1984, declared March as National Social Work Month. President Reagan signed the resolution, Public Law 98-232, which affirmed appreciation to the many thousands of social workers who dedicate their lives to helping those in need. The resolution recognized that "professional social workers are in the vanguard of the forces working to provide protection for children and the aged, the reduction of racism and sexism, and the prevention of the social and emotional disintegration of individuals and families."

Alice Stratton, deputy assistant secretary of the Navy, was an example of a social worker making significant contributions in a high position in government. In 1988 she was making policies on issues affecting the quality of life of Navy and Marine Corps families throughout the nation and abroad, especially about 400,000 active-duty personnel who were married or single parents.[24]

In addition, social worker Patricia A. E. Rodgers, in 1990, was director of VISTA, guiding the efforts of more than 3,000 volunteers in this "domestic Peace Corps." In 1993 five social workers were nominated by President Clinton to fill high-level posts as assistant secretaries[25] directly under Cabinet members who were heads of federal departments, as follows: Fernando Torres-Gill, assistant secretary for aging at the Department of Health and Human Services; Wardell Townsend, assistant secretary of agriculture at the Department of Agriculture; Wendy Sherman, assistant secretary for legislative affairs at the Department of State; Ada Deer, assistant secretary for Indian Affairs at the Department of the Interior; and Augusta Kappner, assistant secretary for vocational and adult education at the Department of Education. Prior to these appointments only one social worker had served as an assistant secretary in the federal government at any one time. Currently, social workers serve in the U.S. Congress, in numerous state legislatures, and in other important government and community positions.

## Summary

*Social work is a rapidly developing profession. Its charity and social welfare roots reach back for many centuries. The history of civilization reflects a sincere attempt to provide welfare services for people, families, and communities with problems. Particularly since the turn of the twentieth century, there have been more formalized programs to professionalize the social welfare helping process.*

*To train qualified social workers, many schools of social work and related programs have been established, providing appropriate social work degrees at the baccalaureate, master's, and doctoral levels. Professional organizations were created to help dedicated, welfare-minded individuals to join forces and support each other in providing humanitarian services. These associations provided effective services over a period of years. In 1955 came the uniting and integration of seven professional social work organizations into the unified National Association of Social Workers. This organization has made significant contributions within its first years of existence.*

*In the field of education, the Council on Social Work Education, established in 1952, has likewise made important strides in upgrading standards of education, in furthering recruitment, in offering* consultation services, and in interpreting to the public what social work really is and can be.

Research, publications, and private practice all point to an ongoing, significant profession of social work. The code of ethics outlines the "right" goals of this helping profession and pre-sents worthwhile guidelines for the dedicated persons who join. Advanced educational programs beyond the master's degree are on the increase, and they are providing opportunities for further education, greater knowledge, better skills, and mature professional attitudes.

## Selected References

ABBOTT, ANN A., "Professional Conduct," in *Encyclopedia of Social Work,* 19th ed., Vol. III. Washington, DC: NASW Press, 1995, pp. 1916–1921.

ARCHES, JOAN, "Social Structure, Burnout, and Job Satisfaction," *Social Work,* 36 (May 1991), 202–206.

BARKER, ROBERT L., "Private Practice," in *Encyclopedia of Social Work,* 19th ed., Vol. III. Washington, DC: NASW Press, 1995, pp. 1905–1910.

BARKER, ROBERT L., *Social Work in Private Practice,* 2nd ed., Silver Spring, MD: NASW Press, 1992.

BERLINER, ARTHUR K., "Misconduct in Social Work Practice," *Social Work,* 34 (January 1989), 69–72.

BUTLER, AMY C., "The Attractions of Private Practice," *Journal of Social Work Education,* 28 (Winter 1992), 47–60.

COHEN, BEN-ZION, "The Ethics of Social Work Supervision Revisited," *Social Work,* 32 (May–June 1987), 194–196.

FARLEY, O. WILLIAM, BOYD E. OVIATT, REX A. SKIDMORE, and MILTON G. THACKERAY, "Social Work—Professional Mediocrity or Maturation," *Social Casework,* 58 (April 1977), 236–242.

HART, AILEEN, "Training Social Administrators for Leadership in the Coming Decades," *Administration in Social Work,* 12, no. 3 (1988), 1–11.

HOLLAND, THOMAS P., and ALLIE C. KILPATRICK, "Ethical Issues in Social Work: Toward a Grounded Theory of Professional Ethics," *Social Work,* 36 (March 1991), 138–143.

HOPPS, JUNE GARY, and PAULINE M. COLLINS, "Social Work Profession Overview," in *Encyclopedia of Social Work,* 19th ed., Vol. III. Washington, DC: NASW Press, 1995, pp. 2266–2282.

JACOBS, CAROLYN, and DORCAS D. BOWLES, eds., *Ethnicity and Race: Critical Concepts in Social Work.* Silver Spring, MD: National Association of Social Workers, 1988.

JAYARATNE, SRINIKA, MARY LOU DAVIS-SACKS, and WAYNE A. CHESS, "Private Practice May Be Good for Your Health and Well-being," *Social Work,* 36 (May 1991), 224–229.

MAYPOLE, DONALD E., "Sexual Harassment of Social Workers at Work: Injustice Within?" *Social Work,* 31 (January–February 1986), 29–31.

REAMER, FREDERIC G., "Ethics Committees in Social Work," *Social Work,* 32 (May–June 1987), 188–192.

SAXTON, PAUL, M., "Vendorship for Social Work: Observations on the Maturation of the Profession," *Social Work,* 33 (May–June 1988), 197–201.

## Notes

1. William E. Wickenden, "The Second Mile," address delivered before the Engineering Institute of Canada, 1941.

2. Ernest Greenwood, "Attributes of a Profession," *Social Work,* 2 (July 1957), 45–55.

3. Ibid., p. 54.

4. Esther Lucile Brown, *Social Work as a Profession* (New York: Russell Sage Foundation, 1942), p. 29.

5. NASW *News,* 36 (July 1991), 7.

6. NASW *News,* 40 (March 1995), 11.

7. "Call to Delegate Assembly," NASW *News,* 40 (March 1995), 2.

8. "In Retrospect: Three Decades of Progress," NASW *News,* 30 (October 1985), 16.

9. "Social Work Regulation Gaining Support in Six Remaining States," NASW *News,* 33 (October 1988), 11; NASW *News,* 37 (June 1992), 10.

10. NASW *News,* 33 (November 1988), 1.

11. *Code of Ethics* (Silver Spring, MD: National Association of Social Workers, n.d.), pp. 1–2.

12. Frederic G. Reamer, "Ethics Committees in Social Work," *Social Work,* 32 (May–June 1987), 188.

13. Patricia W. Soyka, "Unlocking Human Resources: A Career in Social Work," *Public Affairs Pamphlet* No. 458 (1973), p. 10.

14. Estelle Gabriel, "Private Practice in Social Work," *Encyclopedia of Social Work,* 2 (Washington, DC: National Association of Social Workers, 1977), 1056.

15. Robert L. Barker, *Social Work in Private Practice,* 2nd ed. (Washington, DC: National Association of Social Workers, 1992), p. 13.

16. Amy C. Butler, "The Attractions of Private Practice," *Journal of Social Work Education,* 28 (Winter 1992), 52.

17. NASW *News,* 8 (February 1963), 5.

18. Estelle Gabriel, *Encyclopedia of Social Work,* 2, 1055.

19. Robert Barker, op cit., pp. 28, 38.

20. National Association of Social Workers, *Annual Report,* 1984–85, p. 6.

21. Kimberly Strom, "Reimbursement Demands and Treatment Decisions: A Growing Dilemma for Social Workers," *Social Work,* 37 (September 1992), 398–403.

22. Patricia Kelley and Paul Alexander, "Part-time Private Practice: Practical and Ethical Considerations," *Social Work,* 30 (May–June 1985), 254–257.

23. *Salaries in Social Work* (Silver Spring, MD: National Association of Social Workers, 1987), p. 3.

24. "Social Worker Carves Niche at Pentagon," NASW *News,* 33 (April 1988), 5.

25. NASW *News,* 38 (September 1993), 1, 14.

# Chapter *22*

# *Social Work Prevention and Enrichment*

*Police officials report that most automobiles that are stolen by teenagers have the keys in the ignition and a few even have the engines running. If something were done to educate adults to remove the keys from their automobiles and to lock their cars when they park, the number of auto thefts would likely decrease. In thinking about human behavior, and especially about social problems, is*

*it not possible to reduce and prevent problems? Social work is very much interested in this approach. For example, social work now provides "home-based family care" in which a social worker may be attached to a family in crisis with its children for 24 hours a day, helping to prevent family breakup or other problems.*

Prevention is a word used in many different ways. It indicates action that staves off something from happening. Stated positively, it is the process of action taken so that antisocial behavior or personal, family, or community problems are minimized or do not arise at all. Theoretically, it means the doing of something so that personal and social pathology will not develop. The National Commission on Social Work Practice of the National Association of Social Workers defined prevention in social work as "activities which have merit in averting, or discouraging the development of, specific social problems, or in delaying or controlling the growth of such problems after they have presented beginning symptoms."

Broadly speaking, prevention in relation to social work may be regarded in two ways: first, proper action taken so that the personal, family, or community problems do not arise at all; and secondly, action taken so that personal, family, and community problems are not repeated even though such problems existed at the outset. Prevention is concerned with keeping the vase intact, rather than trying to repair the broken pieces. It is interested in keeping human personalities and human interrelationships operating on an integrated and mature level, rather than in gluing together human parts that may have been cracked, broken apart, or splintered.

The field of public health in medicine has offered many helpful concepts and specific terminology in regard to prevention, and social workers have borrowed from this field several ideas and principles. Five levels of prevention in public health, commonly accepted in

**359**

preventive medicine, are: (1) health promotion, (2) specific protection, (3) early diagnosis and treatment, (4) disability limitation, and (5) rehabilitation.[1]

The field of public health also describes the levels of prevention as primary, secondary, and tertiary. Leavell and Clark[2] explain that primary prevention includes health promotion and specific protection, that secondary prevention encompasses early diagnosis and prompt treatment, and that tertiary prevention includes disability limitation and rehabilitation. Health promotion concerns the general health and well-being of the population and is not directed at any particular disease or disorder. Health education and motivation are particularly important on this level of prevention. Examples of this level would include promotion of adequate housing, selective periodic health examinations, and health promotional activities that aim toward the realization of optimal personality development. Specific protection would include such measures as immunization, sanitation, and sound nutrition.

In regard to secondary prevention, early diagnosis and prompt treatment are particularly important. This level stresses case findings and handling of disruptive problems. The aim, of course, is to relieve distress and to shorten duration of the illness, minimize contagion, and reduce symptoms. Tertiary prevention is focused mainly on the chronic and serious illnesses and includes attempts to reduce pain and suffering. Disability limitation includes delaying the consequences of clinically advanced diseases. The preventive measures are primarily therapeutic and are directed toward the patient in order to arrest the disease process and to prevent further complications. Rehabilitation is "more than stopping a disease process; it is also the prevention of complete disability after anatomic and physiologic changes are more or less stabilized. Its positive objective is to return the affected individual to a useful place in society and make maximum use of his remaining capacities."[3]

Rapoport claims that the concept of prevention, evolved largely from the public health field, is often used in "a distorted and confusing manner in the social work framework."[4] Wittman, a pioneer in social work prevention, observed that we are devoting our main effort to areas of secondary and tertiary prevention and are doing very little on the primary level.[5] We need to become more interested in and focused upon enhancing the well-being of individuals, families, and communities and helping to bring about an enrichment in daily living. Social workers need to look at the socially healthy people as well as the disabled. To assist on the broad basis of health promotion, we need to do more on the positive side by working with normal people and increasing the long-range values of social work to the community. We need to consider the "points of entry" where preventive social work may be particularly effective. Social work may help especially in relation to obstetrics, the nursery school, kindergarten, with adolescence, and at time of marriage. "All can provide points of departure for constructive preventive social services."[6]

Wittman suggests that until there is some extension of service coverage to the total population, rather than to the present social work clientele as we now know it, we must remain committed mainly to the secondary and tertiary levels of prevention. The major concern for the near future should be "to develop adaptations of current practice which will reach more of the healthy segment of the population and may thereby retard the rising incidence of social pathology."[7]

Dr. Stephen Goldston, at a pilot national conference on primary prevention in mental health in April 1976, presented the following definition, which also has meaning for social work:

Primary prevention encompasses those activities directed to specifically identified vulnerable high-risk groups within the community who have not been labeled as psychiatrically ill and for whom measures can be undertaken to avoid the onset of emotional disturbance and/or to enhance their level of positive mental health. Programs for the promotion of mental health are primarily educational rather than clinical in conception and operation with their ultimate goal being to increase people's capacities for dealing with crises and for taking steps to improve their own lives.[8]

Hazelkorn recognizes that social work has a long way to go in regard to prevention both in relation to training and practice. She concludes, however, that "there is the obligation to prepare graduates for a future that will undoubtedly include preventive social work alongside preventive medicine and preventive psychiatry."[9] She also indicated many approaches being experimented with by social workers that have a preventive emphasis, such as genetic counseling, activities in family planning, prenatal and well-baby clinics, family life education, work with tenant groups, and epidemiological approaches in public assistance.

A general, current definition of prevention is found in *The Social Work Dictionary:*

Actions taken by social workers and others to minimize and eliminate those social, psychological, or other conditions known to cause or contribute to physical and emotional illness and sometimes socioeconomic problems. Prevention includes establishing those conditions in society that enhance the opportunities for individuals, families, and communities to achieve positive fulfillment.[10]

## Social Work Focus on Prevention

At present there is considerable interest in prevention in social work practice, and this interest is filtering into the educational process. Some individuals think this emphasis is entirely new to social welfare and social work; history shows otherwise.

At the Twelfth Annual Session of the National Conference of Charities and Correction, held in Washington, D.C., June 1885, a considerable amount of the conference was devoted to *preventive work.* In fact, more than sixty pages of the proceedings were concerned with various papers and discussions in this area, which included such topics as: "Thirty Years' Experience in Nursery and Child Hospital Work," "The Shady Side of the 'Placing-Out System'," "Methods of Industrial Training for Girls," "The Kindergarten as a Character Builder," and "Compulsory Education." Indicative of pioneer thinking was a report of one discussion in this field.

Mr. Caldwell thought the method of trying to get rid of crime by attacking the adult criminal was like trying to restore a tree to health by binding up the branches, when the real trouble was in the root. The way to get rid of pauperism and crime is to take care of the children, and to begin with them as early as possible. As John Plowman says about breaking a colt, "The work will thrive, if you start before he's five." Not only the children, but the homes need reforming.[11]

Within more recent years social work educators and practitioners have developed considerable interest in prevention and have conceptualized some of their ideas. Boehm, in a paper on the nature of social work, describes the functions of social work as threefold: (1) *Restoration*—which seeks to identify, control, or eliminate factors in the interactional process that cause breakdown or impairment of social relationships; (2) *Provision of resources*—which is concerned with the creation, enrichment, improvement and coordination of social resources; and (3) *Prevention*—which consists of early discovery, control, and elimination of conditions that could hamper effective social functioning.[12]

This same classification was presented in the Curriculum Study, Council on Social Work Education, which gives emphasis to the importance of prevention in the total field of social work.

The National Association of Social Workers has been very much interested in the whole area and process of prevention. In 1962, a pioneering report on "Prevention and Treatment" contained a pertinent statement with an introduction as follows:

> The basic concern of social work with prevention arises out of the profession's service commitment. If the social pathology with which most social workers deal could be prevented, then many individuals would be spared destructive experiences and society would benefit. This in itself is important enough to justify greater efforts toward the further development of effective prevention. If, for example, it is possible to prevent the disintegration of families rather than merely aiding members of the disintegrated family group to deal with affects of separation, who would deny the worthiness of the preventative effort?[13]

After considerable discussion of some of the issues and problems related to prevention, the report concluded that "NASW, as the single professional membership association with the authority and responsibility to speak for social work, needs, through the democratic process, to evolve its position concerning the issue of prevention and then implement that position in communities throughout the nation."[14]

Roskin suggests that we need to integrate primary prevention into social work practice more. He indicates that there are three treatment approaches that are readily adaptable to a primary prevention focus with groups, families, and individuals. These include the (1) behavioral, (2) task-focused, and (3) variations in psychodynamic ego psychology.[15]

Wittman recalls that the 1960s was the period for the emergence of beginning theory dealing with prevention in social work and that the 1970s produced demonstrations in class and field experiences.[16] In February 1980, there were four schools offering concentrations in prevention and eight schools with elective courses in preventive social work. The four schools offering a concentration in prevention with a combination of class and field experiences were George Warren Brown School of Social Work, Simmons College, University of North Carolina, and University of Connecticut.

Several developments on the political and economic scene have given additional interest and emphasis to the area of prevention. President John F. Kennedy, in the first presidential message wholly on the subject of welfare, in 1962, told Congress, "Public welfare must be more than a salvage operation, picking up debris from the wreckage of human lives. Its emphasis must be directed increasingly toward prevention and rehabilitation." In 1961, the

U.S. Congress passed a law for the prevention and control of juvenile delinquency, which provided $10 million annually to encourage demonstrations, experimentations, and training activities that would help to meet this problem and prevent it. Twenty years later seven cabinet-level departments and two federal agencies provided direct financial assistance to forty-five delinquency-related programs. Olson-Raymer suggests that today's practitioners and theorists question the effectiveness of individualized treatment in preventing delinquency but "they have good reasons to believe preventive school, family, community, and peer group programs aimed at modifying negative institutional policies and practices may help prevent juvenile crime."[17]

In February 1963, President Kennedy, in the first presidential address to Congress specifically on mental health, asked lawmakers to consider this disastrous national problem and to appropriate money to increase facilities, particularly community mental health centers for reducing and preventing mental illness. He suggested that we must first "seek out the causes of mental illness and of mental retardation and eradicate them." He warned that we need to prevent thousands of new cases of mental illness and mental retardation, and recommended appropriations of several millions of dollars to help establish additional community mental health centers and provide staff and other activities that would help in this total preventive and rehabilitative movement.

The 1962 amendments to the Social Security Act included a new emphasis on prevention as well as protection and rehabilitation. Legislation and proposals by the Johnson, Nixon, Ford, Carter, Reagan, Bush, and Clinton administrations have emphasized reduction and prevention of many social problems, such as delinquency, drug abuse, alcoholism, and child abuse.

Both social work education and practice are putting more emphasis on primary prevention. For example, the CSWE project on Prevention in Social Work Education held a two-day conference in Louisville, Kentucky, in October 1979, with a major focus on primary prevention for curriculum development. It was the "first major forum for faculty development in primary prevention in social work education.[18]

In December 1985, a Governor's Conference was held in New York on "Healthy People." Steven E. Katz, State Commissioner of Mental Health, said, "The theme of this conference reinforces the conviction that Governor Cuomo shares with us: Prevention is a critical element in human services and as such deserves serious attention."[19] Topics covered at the three-day conference represented some of the most critical prevention problems facing health and human services today, including: Alzheimer's disease, depression, teenage suicide, developmental disabilities, alcohol abuse, substance abuse, rural mental health, child abuse, sex abuse, family violence, stress, and emotional problems in children.

Another indication of the importance of prevention in social work and related services was the introduction of a journal in this area of study and practice, *Prevention in Human Services,* begun in 1982 and published biannually.

## Problems Involved

Several factors cloud the preventive scene. First is the complexity of human behavior. Final answers have not been acquired regarding what causes social problems or the best solutions. Thus, it is very difficult to plan action and to predict what the outcome will be in regard to a specific personal or social situation. A legitimate question arises: If we do not know the precise causes of a social problem, can we prevent the problem? In medicine and other fields, even though we do not know the exact causal relationships of phenomena, we are able to produce situations that seem to bring about desired results. We do not know for sure what electricity is, but we are able to control it. In medicine, we are not aware of the exact cause of the common cold, but there are precautions and activities practiced that seem to prevent colds and reduce the number. Handwashing helped to prevent surgical deaths before anyone knew about germ theory.

Another problem is that our knowledge and skills in relation to human behavior and social functioning are just in the beginning stages. We can ask many more questions than we can answer. Thus, it becomes a genuine challenge to increase and utilize knowledge and skills in the prevention of social malfunctioning.

McMurtry reviewed the literature and research studies about the effectiveness of prevention related to child maltreatment. He suggested that secondary prevention of child maltreatment involves identifying potential abusers and treating them before the abuse takes place. He concluded that although accurate identification of parents at risk may eventually be possible, more research is needed to establish identifying criteria and to determine effective means of intervention to prevent abuse.[20]

Another problem is the difficulty of evaluation. How do we know for sure that the action we have taken has brought the results we desired? With so many factors involved in human behavior, it is especially difficult to be objective in evaluating what takes place and why.

## Examples of Prevention

Several examples of prevention are presented to illustrate some of the possibilities and potentialities involving social work.

### Premarital Counseling

Premarital counseling is illustrative of an attempt at primary prevention on the part of social workers and other counselors. Within family service agencies, marriage and family counseling bureaus on university campuses, and in private marriage counseling clinics many individuals are interviewed by professionally trained social workers in an attempt to help them to understand themselves better in relation to marriage and their mates. Theoretically, this is an attempt to help them to gain the most from marriage, to prevent problems that might arise, and to guide them toward meaningful positive relationships on the marital journey. A record taken from a university setting illustrates some aspects of this process.

Mr. C, age 26, majoring in biology, and Miss T, age 23, majoring in English, came to the Bureau in the spring of the academic year and stated that they planned to marry in June, after Mr. C had received his master's degree and Miss T had completed her undergraduate studies. They said they had come to the Bureau because they had heard that marriage counseling would provide an opportunity for them to learn more about each other and about marriage. They had no major problems. Although they had differed on many things during the two years of courtship, they had been able to work through their disagreements to the satisfaction of each.

A caseworker interviewed each of them three times and then saw them together for one final interview. Each was given an opportunity to take the Marriage Prediction and the Personality Inventory tests. The results of these tests were favorable and indicated that each had a mature personality.

In the individual interviews with the marriage counselor, Miss T discussed a few of her fears about marriage, particularly in relation to childbearing. She also indicated some concern about the differences in religious belief and activity between herself and Mr. C, although both belonged to the same denomination. She had many other questions related to courtship and the future marital relationship. She talked about how she and Mr. C might improve their ability to communicate with each other and to solve differences that seemed to arise. Mr. C also raised several questions that he seemed anxious to discuss with the worker. He, too, was worried about religious differences, but felt that these could be worked out satisfactorily. He was concerned about money management, and he wondered whether he was being fair and realistic in going ahead with marriage at this time in view of his desire to continue graduate work.

In the joint interview, Miss T and Mr. C's religious differences, their financial planning, and other matters were discussed, and the couple seemed to develop greater understanding of each other and some helpful insights regarding their relationship. They felt definitely that they would like to go ahead with their plans for marriage. At the close of this interview Mr. C said, "I feel that counseling has helped us to understand ourselves, each other, and what marriage is all about as we never have before." Miss T added, "Talking to the worker has removed some fears I have had. I think it has opened the door for us to know each other better, to communicate with each other better, and to learn how to solve problems that are bound to come up in marriage."

---

A summary of functions by three marriage counselors who work in a university agency further describes the emphasis on and the methods of prevention through premarital counseling:

1. Through interviewing, provide an opportunity for prospective marriage partners to discuss concerns regarding their approaching marriage. Questions frequently focus on personality differences, wedding plans, the honeymoon, physical adjustment, housing plans, religious differences, money and its management, emancipation from family, adjustment to new friendships, and in-laws.
2. By giving factual information directly or by suggesting appropriate reading material.
3. Through the use of personality tests, inventories, and other tools.
4. By giving counselees an opportunity to ventilate fears, doubts, and wishes regarding marriage and each other, so that they recognize how important inner feelings are in a marital relationship.
5. By encouraging the couple to go to a physician for medical examination and conference, which includes a pelvic examination for the woman.
6. By referral, if indicated, to other specialists or agencies for needed assistance.

**7.** Through the counselor's conferring, if the situation warrants, with other counselors or consultants in his own agency, or with other specialists in the community regarding the problems of the counselees.

**8.** By acquainting the couple with the resources of marriage counseling so if later they are confronted with problems they feel unable to handle alone they will seek professional help.

**9.** By assisting the couple to build and strengthen a realistic, positive philosophy toward marriage. The counselor encourages the couple to discuss their basic goals and values; he or she aids them to realize that no marriage is perfect, all have conflicts, and all require effort, compromise, and adjustment. The counselor helps the couple to leave the counseling situation with "eyes open" to the somewhat uncertain path ahead but with a firm conviction that a happy and successful marriage is worth working for.

In Family Service Societies, many activities are sponsored to assist on a preventive level. Staff members give talks before service clubs, P.T.A. groups, Family Life Institutes, and other groups of people. Their purpose is to help members of society to understand marriage and family relationships better and to adjust more adequately in these relationships.

## Preventive Mental Health

From 1964 to 1968 a pioneering demonstration-research project, supported in part by the Department of Health, Education, and Welfare in cooperation with both labor and management, took place in the men's garment industry in New York City.[21] The project involved several hundred blue-collar workers with mental health problems.

During the life of the project, 718 persons (from about 20,000 workers) were referred to the program, of which 442 were evaluated and serviced, mainly on a short-term basis. The initial interview was shared by a psychiatrist and a social worker.

Probably the most significant conclusion of this mental health program was that mentally ill individuals can work and produce on the job successfully if the total work community, bolstered by professional workers, understands, accepts, and utilizes mental health care and its benefits.

An innovative example of preventive services is the InstaCare Center, sponsored by a local hospital in a suburb of a metropolitan area. A licensed clinical social worker in 1996 was providing individual and marital counseling services, with considerable emphasis on prevention of personal, emotional, and social problems. The worker also was teaching classes, again in the preventive realm, on Pain and Stress Management, Imaging and Weight Management, Creating Your Own Self-Esteem, and Saying What You Really Mean.

## Family Counseling

An additional example of the preventive aspects of social work comes from the files of the Family Service Association of America. The following case glimpse was presented in an interpretive publication to illustrate its procedures and services, and was taken from the files of a southern family service agency.

Mr. Wilson, an airline pilot, came to Family Service stating he was at the end of his rope. For the last six months he had been struggling to find a way to help his wife control her drinking. He felt she was becoming an alcoholic and he feared not only what she was doing to herself, but also what might happen to their son. *He found himself, he said, "pushing his plane on the home journey."*

There had been no apparent problem for either of the Wilsons until about a year before. The trouble started when Mrs. Wilson always wanted "just one more" at parties and "just one more" after she got home. Mr. Wilson began to lose his temper because she didn't stop drinking until she passed out. He wasn't sure how much drinking she did while he was away, but she was almost always in a bad state when he arrived home. When he tried to talk to her about it, she just became quieter and more depressed. Then she would say, "get the divorce you want and leave me alone." He couldn't get across to her that he didn't want a divorce—he wanted her as his wife—the wife she had been—not the one she was now. Both Mr. and Mrs. Wilson received family counseling for a period of six months.

Strangely enough, Mrs. Wilson's pattern of drinking was related to her husband's presence in the home. While he was away—she did not drink—but as his return became imminent, she began to drink heavily. This pattern was further related to a major source of friction—Mrs. Wilson's almost irrational involvement with her younger brother and sister, their resentment of her, and their dislike and criticism of Mr. Wilson.

Mrs. Wilson was the oldest of the three children in her family. The parents had died when the children were quite young and the family was divided. Mrs. Wilson had tried desperately to meet her own needs for a family by attempting to care for the other children. As soon as she began working, she had sent money to the next oldest. She assumed more responsibility than was appreciated, and her strivings and ambitions for her brother and sister were not met by them. Currently, Mrs. Wilson's superior financial, educational, and social status, and her constant effort to "help" them achieve more, were further irritants to them.

They felt that Mr. Wilson, too, saw himself as better off than they were. They were openly critical and suspicious of him, and they insinuated to Mrs. Wilson that her husband probably was paying attention to other women on his trips out of town. She began to believe this.

Mr. Wilson was impatient and concerned about the way in which Mrs. Wilson was continually frustrated in her attempts to "mother" her younger brother and sister, because they were irritated rather than appreciative of her help. He had been openly critical about this and he had been increasingly critical of Mrs. Wilson's housekeeping, her care of their child, and her unwillingness to be his wife. He said if she didn't straighten out—the marriage couldn't continue.

In the course of family counseling, Mrs. Wilson was helped to give up her attempted control over her brother and sister. She became more independent of them and allowed them to be themselves. As she was able to separate herself from her assumed "mother role," she was better able to view her own marriage and her role as a wife and mother.

When Mr. Wilson was able to face the fact that her drinking was related to the relationship between himself, his wife, and her relatives, and to realize that it did not represent a hopeless alcoholic pattern, he was able to relax some of the pressures he had placed on Mrs. Wilson.

Although the beginning of success in talking together and listening to each other came in the caseworker's office, later on they were more truly "communicating" with each other when they were alone, and at home. Mr. Wilson became more accepting of his wife's need to talk out her frustrations about her brother and sister, and he was better able to let her manage his life in little ways. Mrs. Wilson, who has gained a better understanding of herself and a truer self-concept, doesn't need to escape by drinking.[22]

## *Religious Leaders*

A social worker was invited to meet with religious leaders in a rural community. He talked for some time about understanding parent-child relationships and behavior of people. Questions were invited to help the people to gain understanding and some insights regarding what causes personal and social problems and what might be done about them. The whole focus was to assist these people in a positive manner to understand more about human relationships and how they can assist in preventing problems. The first session was considered to be so profitable by all the participants that they agreed to hold a series of six more meetings in which the social worker was the enabler, assisting these religious leaders to increase their knowledge and skills and, consequently, to aid them in working with their clientele to prevent personal and social problems.

## *Delinquency Prevention*

In a metropolitan community in the eastern United States was a dilapidated area with poor housing and a high degree of social disorganization. Delinquency rates were very high. Some enterprising, dedicated community leaders decided to take action. Through the efforts of public-spirited citizens and professional helpers who involved the youth, a recreational center was established. In the next year, only three arrests were made among the teenagers in comparison with more than 150 the year before. What had happened? Had this concerted action helped prevent delinquency? The answer is yes. The introduction of a recreational center brought about a significant change in this slum community. It was staffed by trained and interested personnel providing services, including counseling and group involvement of the youth in this part of the city.

In 1993 there were numerous attempts by police officers, aided by social workers, to prevent "runaway children" (about 10,000 daily in the United States) and to reduce child abuse from relatives and others, which has become a major personal and social problem in our high tech society. Experience reflects that most victimized children are uneducated on methods of self-protection and that positive programs for child education and parental education can make a difference. Numerous programs are being established, with the assistance of social workers, to help prevent and reduce both runaways and child abuse.

## *Families in Crises*

A very exciting prevention idea that has appeared recently is called Family Preservation Services (FPS). Its purpose is to have social workers or other FPS workers provide immediate and intense services to families in crisis. The workers carry small caseloads of two to six families and are on call at all times, providing twenty-four-hour-a-day coverage. All services are provided in the family's natural environment—primarily the home—and are directed toward maintaining children in their own homes. The workers provide a wide range of counseling, advocacy, training, and concrete assistance.

The theory behind this comprehensive family approach is basically prevention. If a chaotic family environment can be modified, then parents and children may have a chance to increase their level of functioning and prevent critical problems that result from family breakdown. The following case illustrates the preventive efforts of family preservation services.

The Clark family was referred to a FPS worker when their infant daughter was released from the hospital. A nurse had referred the Clarks because she was concerned with the family situation. The Clarks' three-year-old son had recently been diagnosed as hyperactive, and Childrens Protective Services was concerned about three concussions the boy had been treated for over the last year.

When the FPS worker arrived at the home, she found complete chaos. It was filthy and had a strong odor of gas. Mrs. Clark was thin, pale, and weak. She had lost her front teeth due to poor health. Mr. Clark worked as an insurance salesman but had not sold a policy for five months. Mrs. Clark told the worker that they had many conflicts. She did not know how to handle her three-year-old son and expressed total frustration.

The FPS worker helped Mrs. Clark deal with the gas leak. Together they called the landlord and had the furnace repaired. Each day the worker concentrated on concrete ways to help this family, which eventually built a strong relationship between both Mr. and Mrs. Clark and the worker. The worker assisted Mrs. Clark with her dental problems and encouraged Mr. Clark to enroll in a job training program. During this time the worker helped both parents learn to treat their children in a less abusive manner.

This treatment intervention took place over several weeks, with the FPS worker seeing the family each day. Toward the end of the intervention the worker helped the family move to a better apartment and arranged marital counseling for Mr. and Mrs. Clark. The parents were feeling better about themselves and had not hurt their two children in any way. The intense day-to-day intervention of an FPS worker had prevented major problems and had offered the Clark family a sense of hope.[23]

Social workers with child developing enriching skills.

## Suicide Prevention

In most populous centers throughout the United States, social workers are playing significant roles in suicide prevention centers. Their understanding and skills have helped "save" lives of many men, women, and youths.

Many "hotline" calls have helped disturbed or distraught persons to handle personal crisis situations and to make contact with people or agencies that can make a difference in their lives. Rape crisis centers are now available in many cities to assist with this difficult problem and its damaging results. Social workers are helping provide treatment and preventive services on a twenty-four-hour basis.

## Social Work Practice in the Workplace

Social work practice in the workplace is emerging on the cutting edge of prevention. Within the past two decades innovative developments have appeared on the industrial scene involving social workers. Enough demonstrations have taken place to indicate that preventive social work can make a difference in human problems and their solutions in business and in labor unions.

Social workers were hired in 1969 to provide counseling and other services to 8,000 employees and their families at Kennecott Copper Corporation, Utah Copper Division. The results were impressive.[24]

Another example of a positive preventive program took place in a large telephone company in a metropolitan city that invited a school of social work to train students in their head office. Counseling was provided and a series of bimonthly noon-day lectures were presented to employees who wished to attend. The voluntary response was substantial and many who attended observed that the lectures had been helpful. Sample topics, presented by experts, were: "Family Patterns of Communication," "Human Sexuality," "Stress Management," and "The Empty Nest Syndrome."

Anderson and Stark[25] suggest another service for social work prevention, related to employment and geographic relocation. They recommend that Employment Assistance Programs (EAPs) be increased in industry to reduce stress-related problems for workers and their families as they move from one position to another area.

## Implications of Prevention

With the current interest and emphasis on social work, it is apparent that considerable time and talents must be spent in thinking through the relationship of professional social work to the preventive process. Several implications stand out.

If social workers are really going to tap the resources of prevention, they must spend more time and effort in creative thinking and activity. They will need to go beyond and extend the present boundaries and activities of practice. What can be done by social workers to prevent personal, family, and community problems is one of the great challenges of today.

It is apparent that practice in working with individuals, groups, and communities will need to be utilized, as well as the process of research and administration, if prevention is to become more effective. The caseworker, the group worker, and the community organizer can all play important roles in the preventive process. Through working together, they can assist each other in accomplishing desired goals. One challenge seems to be a closer cooperation and coordination among workers who are skilled in different techniques and methodologies.

One great need is for objective research and evaluation of activities and projects related to prevention. We need to quantify and objectify procedures. We need to know in advance what we are doing, what we hope to accomplish, and then to be able to measure afterward what has actually taken place.

A step forward came with the appearance of Bloom's *Primary Prevention: The Possible Science.*[26] He studies primary prevention theoretically and also presents illustrations of empirical studies of preventive programs in social work and related areas. He presents selected examples, related to a developmental framework, such as school dropout, substance abuse, delinquency, divorce, child abuse, heart disease, and widowhood. He suggests that complete preventive solutions have not been achieved in any of these areas, but illustrates important advances in each. He views "primary prevention of many social and medical problems as possible, not as a dream, but as a possible science, a systematic and creative enterprise that identifies probable future states among currently neutral events and acts to promote desired configuration among them while at the same time attempting to obviate undesired combinations."

There should be special focus on the *before* in relation to prevention. In other words, if social workers can utilize professional knowledge and skills to prevent problems from arising on the horizon of daily living, this seems to be particularly important. The educational and consultation processes are especially significant in this area of social work.

To anticipate problems that might arise in advance of their occurrence calls for greater understanding of human behavior, interrelationships, and social phenomena.

Experimentation is needed as never before. Social workers must try new techniques, skills, and plans to see if they will work in preventing personal and social problems. In the educational field, additional interest in prevention will necessitate increased offerings regarding this process in the curriculum of the professional schools. Principles regarding prevention and case examples will need to be introduced into the core areas and specific classes, and probably diffused directly and indirectly throughout the total curriculum. A few schools already offer separate classes on prevention, and there will undoubtedly be more in the future.

Social work practice needs to be broadened to include more emphasis on consultation, family life education, and related activities. Social workers must become more community-minded and more family-minded. They need to ferret out the principles and knowledge that will help families and communities to anticipate problems and to prevent them. They need to broaden their skills so that they can utilize a variety of techniques and methods to help bring about desired prevention-based results.

## Social Work Enrichment

The newest process utilized by social workers is enrichment. Traditionally social work has provided services for individuals, families, and communities; offered counseling/therapy for persons and families in trouble; and advanced its interest and services with prevention. All these processes are relevant to relationship problems or the reduction or prevention of them. Enrichment has a different focus, aimed especially at the quality of life. It encompasses attempts to help people go on from where they are, to add positive experiences and values to living.

Enrichment not only includes working with the handicapped and disadvantaged but also is available to all people, recognizing that all people have problems in human relationships and also have room for growth and improvement of their abilities and activities.

Most of the materials in this chapter relate to the enrichment process, directly or indirectly. Solving relationship problems can not only relieve pain and tension, but can enhance satisfactions in living.

Social work enrichment is the process of helping people improve their relationships with others, bringing increased satisfactions and enjoyments. For example, a married couple may be getting along satisfactorily, but with increased knowledge and improved abilities in their relationship they may be able to taste of life in positive ways they have never experienced before. The social worker helps couples to increase their knowledge and improve abilities to move ahead. All of the social work methods may be utilized in enrichment: casework, group work, and community organization. Research may provide evaluative data on what is effective. Administration may be used in staff development and in providing community enrichment programs.

Premarital counseling is an example of enrichment that can make a difference. Couples with no major problems may talk with a social worker and gain increased knowledge and improved abilities to benefit from marital relationships on a higher level of satisfaction. They may gain insights about self-esteem, decision making, communication, solving conflicts and the loving process that can deepen their life together in many ways. They may learn how to build each other rather than psychologically bruise each other, resulting in a genuine maturity of living.

Classes taught by social workers on parenting for the general public are another example of the enrichment process. Discussion of various topics can bring deeper meanings and satisfactions for parent-child relationships, such as accepting your children, loving your children, building self-esteem, and listening to your children.

The whole area of enrichment has hardly been touched, even though some social workers question it. Creative social workers may encourage all kinds of positive developments in this innovative, qualitative arena.

## Summary

*The old adage of "An ounce of prevention is worth a pound of cure" is emphasized as never before in the helping professions. In particular, medicine has led with its public health programs.*

*Within the past few years, prevention has come to the fore in social work and is now recognized as a major function. There is still consider-* *able uncertainty and lack of clarity regarding the roles of social work in relation to prevention. Nevertheless, various demonstrations and experiments indicate that the social worker can anticipate social problems and can help to avert them. Additional study, experimentation, and research are much needed in this area.*

*The enrichment process is just beginning to take hold in social work. Almost unlimited potentials seem available for introducing practical services that will increase knowledge of people about human relationships, and enhance their social abilities bringing deeper, positive satisfactions.*

## Selected References

ANDERSON, CHARLENE, and CAROLYN STARK, "Psychosocial Problems of Job Relocation: Preventive Roles in Industry," *Social Work,* 33 (January–February 1988), 38–41.

BALLEW, JULIUS R., "Role of Natural Helpers in Preventing Child Abuse and Neglect," *Social Work,* 30 (January–February 1985), 37–41.

BARKER, ROBERT L., *Social Work in Private Practice,* 2nd ed. Washington, DC: National Association of Social Workers, 1992.

BLOOM, MARTIN, *Primary Prevention: The Possible Science.* Englewood Cliffs, NJ: Prentice Hall, 1981.

BRACHT, NEIL, "Prevention and Wellness," in *Encyclopedia of Social Work,* 19th ed., Vol. III. Washington, DC: NASW Press, 1995, pp. 1879–1887.

DALEY, DENNIS C., "Relapse Prevention with Substance Abusers: Clinical Issues and Myths," *Social Work,* 32 (March–April 1987), 138–142.

HARRISON, W. DAVID, "Community Development," in *Encyclopedia of Social Work,* 19th ed., Vol. I. Washington, DC: NASW Press, 1995, pp. 555–562.

KEEFE, THOMAS, "Stress-Coping Skills: An Ounce of Prevention in Direct Practice," *Social Casework,* 69 (October 1988), 475–482.

MEYER, CAROL H., ed. *Preventive Intervention in Social Work.* Washington, DC: National Association of Social Workers, 1974.

ROSKIN, MICHAEL, "Integration of Primary Prevention into Social Work Practice," *Social Work,* 25 (May 1980), 192–196.

SCHWARTZ, IRA M., "Delinquency Prevention: Where's the Beef?" *The Journal of Criminal Law and Criminology,* 82 (Spring 1991), 132–140.

SPUNGEN, CAROL A., SUSAN E. JENSEN, NORMA W. FINKELSTEIN, and FREDDA A. SATINSKY, "Child Personal Safety: Model Program for Prevention of Child Abuse," *Social Work,* 34 (March 1989), 127–131.

STANTON, GRETA W., "Prevention Intervention with Stepfamilies," *Social Work,* 31 (May–June 1986), 201–206.

WODARSKI, JOHN S., and PAMELA HARRIS, "Adolescent Suicide: A Review of Influences and the Means for Prevention," *Social Work,* 32 (November–December 1987), 477–484.

## Notes

1. Hugh R. Leavell and E. Gurney Clark, *Preventive Medicine—For the Doctor in His Community* (New York: McGraw-Hill, 1958), p. 31.

2. Ibid., pp. 21–39.

3. Ibid., p. 27.

4. Lydia Rapoport, "The Concept of Prevention in Social Work," *Social Work,* 6 (January 1961), 3.

5. Milton Wittman, "Preventive Social Work: A Goal for Practice and Education," *Social Work,* 6 (January 1961), 23.

6. Ibid., p. 24.

7. Ibid., p. 27.

8. Donald C. Klein and Stephen E. Goldston, eds., *Primary Prevention: An Idea Whose Time Has Come* (Rockville, MD: National Institute of Mental Health, 1977), p. 27.

9. Florence Hazelkorn, "An Ounce of Prevention . . . ," *Journal of Education for Social Work,* 3 (Fall 1967), 70.

10. Robert L. Barker, *The Social Work Dictionary,* 3rd ed. (Washington, DC: NASW Press, 1995), p. 292.

11. *Proceedings of the National Conference of Charities and Correction,* Twelfth Annual Session, held in Washington, DC, June 4–10, 1885 (Boston: Press of Geo. H. Ellis, 1885), p. 462.

12. Werner W. Boehm, "The Nature of Social Work," *Social Work,* 3 (April 1958), 16–17.

13. Bertram M. Beck, "Prevention and Treatment," based on the work of the subcommittee on Trends, Issues and Priorities of the NASW National Commission on Social Work Practice, 1962, p. 1 (mimeographed).

14. Ibid., p. 31.

15. Michael Roskin, "Integration of Primary Prevention into Social Work Practice," *Social Work,* 25 (May 1980), 194.

16. Milton Wittman, "Preventive Social Work: What? How? Where?" Educational Symposium, Preventive Social Work, Graduate School of Social Work, University of Utah, Salt Lake City, Utah, April 17–18, 1980.

17. Gayle Olson-Raymer, "The Role of the Federal Government in Juvenile Delinquency Prevention," *The Journal of Criminal Law and Criminology,* 74 (Summer, 1983), 600.

18. National Conference on Primary Prevention in Mental Health Convened," *Social Work Reporter* 28 (January 1980), 7.

19. New York State Office of Mental Health, *This Month in Mental Health,* 9 (January 1986), 1, 3.

20. Steven L. McMurtry, "Secondary Prevention of Child Maltreatment: A Review," *Social Work,* 30 (January–February 1985), 42.

21. Hyman, J. Weiner, Sheila H. Akabas, and John J. Sommer, *Mental Health Care in the World of Work* (New York: Association Press, 1973).

22. "An Airline Pilot Who Was Pushing His Plane," *Family Service Highlights,* Family Service Association of America, 21 (September–November 1960), 114–115.

23. This case was shared by Dr. Mark Fraser, former Professor of Social Work, University of Utah.

24. Rex A. Skidmore, Dan Balsam, and Otto Jones, "Social Work Practice in Industry," *Social Work,* 19 (May 1974), 282.

25. Charlene Anderson and Carolyn Stark, "Psychosocial Problems of Job Relocation: Preventive Roles in Industry," *Social Work,* 33 (January–February 1988), 38–41.

26. Martin Bloom, *Primary Prevention: The Possible Science* (Englewood Cliffs, NJ: Prentice Hall, 1981).

$$C\ h\ a\ p\ t\ e\ r\ \ \ 23$$

# Social Work
# and the Future

*Naisbitt and Aburdene, in their challenging book,* Megatrends 2000, *observe that the year 2000 is "operating like a powerful magnet on humanity, reaching down into the 1990s and intensifying the decade. It is amplifying emotions, accelerating change, heightening awareness, and compelling us to reexamine ourselves, our values, and* our institutions."[1] *They discuss ten likely new directions for the 1990s, which include a global economic boom, women in leadership, global lifestyles and cultural nationalism, and triumph of the individual. What might these and other anticipated developments and changes mean to the profession of social work in the years ahead?*

We live in a rapidly changing world that idolizes speed and automation. Newspapers, TV, and radio flash the latest scientific inventions, and satellites encircle the globe. As television and other broadcasts are transmitted worldwide, many questions arise regarding the part that people and human relationships play in the total scheme of things.

Indicative of the prospects of the future and the rapidly changing world was a suggestion of Mortimer Adler that the most important cabinet position in the United States government in the future could well be the "Secretary of the Future."[2] He then suggested that two major problems face future generations. First, "Can the masses obtain the intellectual, cultural, and comfortable levels which in the past were held only by a few aristocrats?" Second, "Could it be that man isn't up to enjoying too much free time, power, comfort and wealth, which technological advances will undoubtedly realize in the next thousand years?"

In 1970 Toffler's startling book, *Future Shock,*[3] was published, in which he dramatically described ways in which people are becoming overwhelmed in responding to change. He claimed that future shock is no longer "a distantly potential danger, but a real sickness from which increasingly large numbers already suffer," and also suggested that "unless man quickly learns to control the rate of change in his personal affairs as well as in society at large, we are doomed to a massive adaptational breakdown."[4]

Although Toffler describes realistically some of the specific effects of drastic, accelerated change upon individuals, families, and communities, he is basically optimistic that we can do something about these things, illustrated by his concluding statement:

... by making imaginative use of change to channel change, we cannot only spare ourselves the trauma of future shock, we can reach out and humanize distant tomorrows.[5]

Naisbitt in *Megatrends* outlines where our sophisticated technology is taking us, stressing that we are moving from an industrial society to an economy based on the creation and distribution of information. He describes basic trends affecting our political, social, and economic life that will shape our future. He suggests that while we are moving in dual directions of high tech/high touch, matching each new technology with a human response, human relations are becoming even more important. In conclusion he observes that "as we move from an industrial to an information society, we will use our brainpower to create instead of our physical power, and the technology of the day will extend and enhance our mental ability.... Yet the most formidable challenge will be to train people to work in the information society."[6]

In this fast-moving uncertain age, where is social work likely to find itself? In the years ahead, how will social work fit into the total scheme?

If it were possible to look into a crystal ball and to see exactly what is ahead, we would likely be surprised in many ways. Since this is impossible, the next best action is to look at the past and the present and to make projections and predictions based upon available knowledge regarding what is likely to happen. This chapter is an attempt to consider some of the likely developments in social work in the years ahead.

## Professional Maturation

Social work education and practice are churning and in a state of turmoil in many ways. Educators and practitioners differ considerably in their thinking, and opinions range along a continuum from the disappearance of social work as a profession to professional maturation and enrichment encompassing an increase of skilled professional delivery of services. A few leaders, in a pessimistic vein, talk about the demise of social work. Others claim that we are on the horizon of really blossoming and that the doors are open to improved services and innovative opportunities for the social work profession.

Most social workers feel that although there are critical problems and pressures, numerous opportunities are available for the social work profession to move ahead on a sound basis, strengthening current delivery of services and innovating services that have been practically untouched to date. An example is the growth of social work in private industry, which is being accepted and accelerated by several large corporations and smaller businesses, providing much-needed services for their employees and families relating to personal and family problems.

Social work is relatively new, surfacing as a beginning profession at the end of the nineteenth century. It is bound to face some critical problems. When one realizes it is only since the 1950s that the National Association of Social Workers and the Council on Social Work Education came into existence, it seems almost phenomenal what has happened in the development of social work. Many leaders anticipate that the current divergencies of opinion regarding training and practice are healthy and will bring about a balanced combination of generic principles and skills in practice, accompanied by specializations providing skills and knowledge for working with various social problems and with groups of people with particular needs. Another positive factor is America's service commitment for competent personnel for its institutions. What happens in the years ahead will depend upon the leaders in social work education and practice and how they act and react with other social workers, related professions, and political leaders. Philosophically, social workers would agree with the Chinese, who have two definitions for the word crisis—danger and opportunity.

## Increase in Services

Based on data supplied by the U.S. Department of Labor, it was estimated there were 385,000 social workers in the United States in 1978. Since then there has been a steady increase in social workers (more than 600,000 in 1996), and indications are that this will continue even though there have been federal and state curtailments in various social service programs. On the other hand, new services continue to be developed, both in public and private sectors, requiring the skills and knowledge of qualified social workers. Also, private practice continues to expand.

On the cutting edge of growth and innovation in social work is practice in industry. As mentioned before, numerous industrial firms and businesses are instituting various personnel and human services, which hire social workers to help employees and their families. Such workers are employed in the delivery of social services in a variety of kinds of industrial and business settings, including steel companies, banks, tobacco companies, insurance firms, and many others.

"Shadow consultation" is a recent innovation offered by social workers with many potentialities for the future. This involves a qualified social worker spending a typical day with a business manager, observing everything he or she does from specific planning to telephone calls, and interviews. At the end of the day, the social worker and manager discuss what has gone on during the day, how it has gone on, and specific ways in which improvement may take place in the "manager's effectiveness in relating to and directing his or her associates and team."[7]

Problems in human relationships in many other areas are reaching for social workers. Drug abuse is of great concern in the sports world, and social workers are being hired to help. All four major sports (football, baseball, basketball, and hockey) now have league-wide policies prohibiting use of drugs by athletes. The National Football League and the NFL Players Association have involved the Hazelden Foundation in Minnesota, since 1982, to operate a program to help players to end their drug problems, including alcohol. *NASW News* reports that "Tim Plant, a social worker who counsels football players at Hazelden, says services include outpatient and inpatient care or a combination. An aftercare program also is provided to support the work done during initial counseling."[8]

Symour and Marston report an innovative development in social work practice, evolving in a vision care clinic, where optometric students and graduate and undergraduate social work students in field placements are working together offering opportunities in interdisciplinary cooperation. The social workers help with understanding of psychosocial factors and in assisting patients to make effective use of treatment and rehabilitation programs that are available. The authors conclude: "The relationship between visual functioning and non-visual factors such as stress offers opportunities for a new role for social workers in the field of vision care."[9]

Another door is opening for social work, this time with architecture. Meenaghan describes a three-year collaboration between the School of Architecture and the College of Social Work at Ohio State University that has focused on specific content areas within the social work curriculum that were found to be functional to some architectural programs. Nearly 300 students had taken part in collaborative courses, and Meenaghan concluded, "Selected social work curriculum can be utilized in attaining a social perspective in architecture."[10]

## *Professional Identification and Visibility*

One of the challenging problems of the emerging profession of social work has been the need to develop a stronger professional identification. A few decades ago there were many dedicated social workers and several independent, semiprofessional associations, all of which at times seemed to be striking out in different directions. A significant step took place in 1955 with the creation of the National Association of Social Workers, which has made major contributions to the development of professional interest and identification. Through its staff and various committees, it has helped practitioners, educators, lay citizens, and students to realize that social work is an important profession calling for the best in people, including integrity, maturity of personality, and specific professional training. The association has helped considerably to assist social workers to identify with their profession, and to interpret to nonsocial workers the role of social work.

Graduate and undergraduate students are encouraged to become members in this association and to identify with its purposes and activities prior to embarking upon practice. They have an opportunity to study the code of ethics and to understand its professional implications. They also have opportunities for association with professional persons, self-expression, and professional identification. Although some social workers are critical of NASW and have left its ranks, and many uncertainties exist, in the years ahead it is generally anticipated that this association will continue to bolster, build, and strengthen the profession, both on a national and a local level. Its membership is increasing each year. In 1961 the membership totaled 34,494, by 1981 had mounted to 86,000, and by 1995 had reached 154,000.

On a local chapter basis, it is probable that members of NASW will devote more of their time and talents to strengthening their profession, improving practice, expanding recruitment, and participating in other professional activities.

The Council on Social Work Education, with its special emphasis on training, has been another major force in leading social workers to a stronger professional identification. Its annual conference has increased in stature in the past few years. For the 1989 conference in Chicago participants came from colleges and universities with graduate training programs in social work, from undergraduate programs in preparation for social work, as well as from various fields of practice. More than 3500 participants joined together with serious intent to understand social work better and to improve the training programs resulting in more effective practice in social work. Various projects and activities of the council are providing many opportunities for strengthening the total profession at all levels—paraprofessional, undergraduate, master's, and doctoral.

Some questions have been raised about the effectiveness of social work practice, particularly in relation to the one-to-one method. Research studies differ somewhat on outcomes. However, Rubin reviewed twelve research studies with controlled experimentation between July 1978 and June 1983 and reported that the overall conclusion was, "Recent experiments have provided more grounds for optimism regarding the development of effective forms of direct social work practice."[11] He also suggested we need more methodologically credible experimental research evaluating effectiveness of social work direct practice.

## *Licensing*

Since the 1960s several steps have been made toward licensing in social work. For a field to become a full-fledged profession, it is almost imperative that some kind of official control and licensing be in operation. Doctors must pass examinations and be issued licenses in the states in which they practice. Lawyers qualify by taking state bar examinations to become properly licensed. Until a few years ago, there was little attempt to control social work standards and practice. However, there have been assertive activities in several states related to certification or licensing.

In 1961 the National Association of Social Workers inaugurated a movement to strengthen social work practice. Provision was made for a voluntary system of registration, resulting in *certified social workers.* An Academy of Certified Social Workers was established and practicing workers were invited to apply for membership. Membership was contingent upon a person's having had two years of paid social work employment and two years of NASW membership. Stipulations were that future applicants must not only have a master's degree in social work, but also at least two years of experience in social work under qualified supervision by a member of the Academy of Certified Social Workers. This plan has been approved with considerable enthusiasm by professional social workers as a major step toward licensing. In 1963 there were more than 20,000 persons who had applied for certification and who had been awarded membership in the Academy; in 1980 the number had increased to 46,300 and today there are more than 58,000. As a result of this movement, social workers everywhere now add *ACSW* after their names on letters, just as those of other professions give designations that display professional meaning.

In November 1974, the National Association of Social Workers reported fourteen states with some form of regulation of social work, including nine that had acts providing title protection only, and six that licensed social work practice or part of it. In legislative sessions in early 1974, Kansas and Kentucky passed laws for licensure. In 1980 the Oklahoma legislature passed a law making it the fourteenth state to formally license social workers. By 1988 forty-four states, the District of Columbia, the Virgin Islands, and Puerto Rico had some form of regulation, such as licensure or certification. Through the efforts of NASW and others the social work profession gained its goal of legal regulation throughout the United States when, in April 1992, Governor Tommy Thompson of Wisconsin signed a social work certification act for his state.

## *Spirituality in Social Work Practice*

In keeping with the social work philosophy of working with the total person in the total environment, a current development is the increase in consideration of spiritual factors in social work practice. We are beginning to recognize that spiritual components need additional study for helping with personal or family problems. Spirituality, according to *The Social Work Dictionary,* 1995 edition, is "devotion to the immaterial part of humanity and nature rather than worldly things such as possessions; an orientation to people's religious, moral, or emotional nature."[12]

Sermabeikian suggests that "the spiritual perspective is an important but relatively unexplored area in social work practice."[13] Obviously, we need more research to understand its significance in human behavior, especially as it relates to meeting basic needs of clients. We also need to improve our skills in utilizing spiritual resources in bringing positive behavioral changes.

A significant event related to the spiritual component and social work's use of it was the First National Conference for the Society for Spirituality and Social Work, held in Salt Lake City, July 7–11, 1995. More than 400 participants were present.

## *Changing Continuum in Social Work Education*

Social work education is churning; changes are developing rapidly. There is, however, an emphasis on a "social work continuum," which encompasses training on the paraprofessional, undergraduate, master's, and doctoral levels.

The Council on Social Work Education has assumed leadership in providing guidance and direction for community colleges and other educational institutions offering training for paraprofessionals (many of whom are indigenous persons) on the freshman, sophomore, or special levels of education not involving regular college work. The number of such programs is on the increase.

On the undergraduate level there is a major thrust toward strengthening the social work curriculum, in moving toward the BSW degree, or providing a substantive major on the undergraduate level. In 1971 the council authorized the establishment of undergraduate programs that could be approved by the council (which now may be accredited by the council) and provide the "first professional level of practice," for its graduates. Consequently there has been a surge to strengthen undergraduate programs in social work and to help qualify the graduates of these programs to perform competently in the delivery of social services.

The MSW program provides a professional course of study that builds upon beginning level undergraduate offerings. It also includes one area of concentration or more. In May 1982, the Board of Directors of the CSWE adopted a new Curriculum Policy Statement for the MSW and BSW programs—a pioneering statement that included both programs together for the first time. This statement provided ample opportunities for individual programs to be creative and innovative, but also required basic educational levels for attaining core knowledge and practice skills needed for successful social work practice. The CSWE 1992 Curriculum Policy Statement reaffirms the basic relationships between the undergraduate and graduate programs in social work and further defines differences and resources of each program.

A development in social work education that will likely increase is the doctoral program. These programs vary considerably, and so far there have been no specific standards established by the Council on Social Work Education regarding them. However, within a few years there will probably be some recommendations and minimum requirements formulated.

Most of the doctoral programs in social work require the students to take courses taught by the social work faculty and also to enroll in related graduate departments, which can help them to enrich their understanding of human behavior and of the helping processes. Some of them offer additional fieldwork experience.

In all probability, most of those who obtain a doctoral degree will go into schools of social work and become teachers themselves. Some will enter practice in key administrative

Homelessness—a major social work challenge.

positions in hospitals, community mental health centers, or other social work agencies; others will accept research positions. A current trend is to replace the DSW degree with the PhD degree with the goal of strengthening academic research and advanced graduate study.

## Development of the Role of Consultant

Within the past years, social workers have not only used consultants from the disciplines of psychiatry, psychology, medicine, and other areas, but have become consultants themselves. Many social workers spend full time in the role of the consultant. For example, in one school district in California, two social workers spend their entire working day, every day, in a consultative capacity. They talk with teachers, principals, counselors, and other professional people about their problems in working with the boys and girls and their families. The basic aim is to help teachers, counselors, and others to understand themselves better and what they are doing in relation to assisting the youngsters with personal or family troubles.

Social workers are used as consultants in a variety of settings, and are likely in the future to be used by additional agencies. They are hired as consultants not only in schools and in comprehensive mental health centers, but also in family service societies, in YWCAs and YMCAs, in Girl Scout groups, in hospitals, in business enterprises, and in numerous other kinds of agencies or settings.

In the role of consultant, the social worker acts mainly as a catalyst who unlocks the door to bring about better understanding, information, and procedures that may be helpful to other professional people. In this capacity the social worker does not instruct the others as to what to do, but helps them to understand what different lines of action are possible and then leaves the choices to them. As a consultant, the social worker does not have authority over those with whom he or she consults. The social worker acts as an advisor and one who assists them to understand more about social dysfunctioning and what can be done about it.

## Status of the Social Worker

The future may portend higher status for the social worker than the past or present. When social work was coming into its own during the early decades of the twentieth century, many people were very critical of it. Some claimed social work was all wrong because it abolished independence. Others declared social work was synonymous with socialism. A minority thought of social work as merely the process of handing out a dole to the poor and transient.

In the last few decades major shifts in attitudes have taken place. While community leaders were previously sometimes critical of social work and its practices, today some of these same leaders are referring members of their families and close friends to social work agencies. The general attitude has changed so that most citizens today look upon social work as a profession with many *solid* services to perform. These changes are evident in the demand for social workers, not only in regard to well-established social work services, but in the creation of new agencies and services.

A major reason for the favorable shift in attitude has been that millions of individuals, families, and numerous communities have benefited from social work services. As people have been helped with their personal and family problems, to face them, work them through, and go on to an enrichment of living, they have usually become exponents of social work and its services.

Although according to some studies there are several professions that have higher prestige and status ratings than does social work, movement seems to be gradual and substantial toward an elevation of its position. Increased salaries and improved working conditions, along with fringe benefits, are indicative of this development. In the last two decades salaries for social workers have increased considerably, so that current salaries for most MSW graduates are in the range of $20,000 to $28,000 a year, and for those with practice experience of about ten years, $30,000 to $50,000. Higher incomes will likely attract more men and women of excellent backgrounds and dedicated interests in people. This, again, will provide an effective chain reaction for improving the status and prestige of the profession. As salaries increase, better people apply for training, which results in more effective social work services. More effective services help to bring about increases in income. From nearly every direction the prospect looks encouraging for higher salaries in social work.

Today social workers are being appointed to key administrative positions in government, education, business, and private endeavors, adding to their status. Another example of the increased status of social work is that since the middle of the 1980s social workers have been invited to appear in court hearings as expert witnesses. They are asked to state their opinions and often influence the judgment or verdict. Their professional understanding of people and their behavior is respected as never before.

## Administration Shifting

Historically, administration in social work agencies included a director, assistant directors, supervisors, and staff. Concentration of power was at the top with a lessening of authority and increase of staff in the lower echelons. Messages, decisions, and plans were passed downward to the caseworkers on the lower base of agency operation.

In recent years much shifting has taken place, with power being shared among three groups: administration, staff, and clients. A sound sharing of authority, planning, and decision-making has been developing among these three groups intertwined in structure and actions. There has been a definite shift from authority at the top to participation among all levels. Suggestions and decisions have been shared among the three groups, all existing in an interactional circle. Staff and client satisfactions and expressions are becoming powerful forces in social work practice.

## Private Practice

In the years ahead there is likely to be an increase in private practice. Since NASW has given its approval to private practice, more practitioners are moving into this area, either on a full-time or part-time basis. Economic emoluments, clinical challenges, and opportunities for service seem to be primary motivating factors. In 1968 a study of NASW members revealed fewer than 1,000 full-time private practitioners, with an estimated 15,000 doing part-time private counseling.[14] By 1995 there were more than 28,000 social workers in private practice.

Currently, private practice has become a major component of social work practice, involving both full-time and part-time patterns. A study of students in a New York State Master's of Social Work program indicated that more than half of them (57 percent) said they thought they would enter private practice within ten years after obtaining their MSW degree.[15]

Beginnings have been made in authorization of third-party payments to social workers by corporations and some governmental programs. At the same time, this battle, basically, has yet to be won in many ways and places.

## Case Management

Although the social work profession has always utilized case management as one of its effective treatment interventions with individuals and families having complex problems, during recent years it has been identified and used increasingly as a discrete service that will likely grow in popularity in the years ahead. Case management has gained so much attention because it is a process that requires a case manager to have a small number of clients (usually fifteen to twenty) and to individualize treatment by assessing the client's needs, setting jointly agreed upon goals, linking the client to necessary resources, and following through so the client receives the needed services.

As our society becomes more complex and sophisticated, the need for case management will undoubtedly increase. Severely dysfunctional individuals and families are usually unable to negotiate all the complicated social service systems available to them. Social work will likely play a major role in the development, management, and provision of case management in the future. Social work educators throughout the country should develop a special curriculum focus to prepare practitioners to give direction to the strong emphasis being placed on case management intervention. Newly graduating social work professionals will likely enter a climate that is clamoring for case management expertise.

## Advocacy Role

Numerous social workers and agencies employing social workers assume a social action role encompassing advocacy for their clients. It is likely in the future that this role will be increased. Social workers assume the role of helping individuals, alone and in groups, but also help them in relation to the societal context in which they live.

On a broad base, more social workers are becoming active in political movements and politics and are sharing their goals and ideas with others, to help bring about changes in the political, social, and economic arenas, as well as to assist clients clinically.

## Improved Public Relations

Many believe that one of the major weaknesses of social work is its inadequate public relations. Especially in the past, social work has done very little to paint a favorable public image. Today there is considerable interest in this kind of activity, and many social workers and agencies are spending time and energy in improving their public relations policies and activities.

The strengthening of public relations is arising through two main avenues. The first involves increased interest and activity among the social workers themselves. There is additional interest in studying knowledge and skills of public relations in the graduate schools of social work. There are also more social workers "on the firing line" who feel that they must take more interest and participate more fully in improving their public image.

A second approach is one that will probably be tapped more in the future. This is the hiring of public relations experts as consultants to social work agencies and social workers. Social workers are beginning to recognize that they are not experts in public relations and that if they are going to obtain the best professional services available, they will need to pay for these services, to employ those who are especially trained. Why should not social workers hire experts in public relations just as they hire consultants in psychiatry, psychology, and other related disciplines? There are many examples to indicate that this procedure has been most effective in improving the public image of social work and social work agencies and programs. This trend likely will continue in the future.

Lobbying is being recognized as another important development in social work. The Council on Social Work Education and the National Association of Social Workers have full-time lobbyists in Washington, D.C., who have become highly effective in helping to influence federal legislation relevant to social work education and practice. Mahaffey maintains that social workers need to understand the lobbying process and suggests actions and techniques that might be utilized. She quotes the late Whitney M. Young, Jr., who said in his closing remarks to the 1969 NASW delegate assembly: "I think that social work is uniquely equipped to play a major role in the social and human renaissance of our society," and then concluded, "There *are* social workers who are successfully influencing the political process. The profession needs more of them."[16]

## Rural Social Work

In recent years, movement has brought more social work services to the sparsely populated areas of the United States.

Two major efforts have been taking place in bringing social work services to less populated communities: (1) traveling teams of professional workers, including social workers, have made regular visits to outlying areas, offering nearly the whole gamut of health and welfare services, (2) individual social workers with inclination toward the rural way of life have accepted positions and moved to smaller communities.

Rural social work has many limitations, but also many advantages. Professional isolation, limited resources, and minimal cultural opportunities exemplify the limitations. Positives include an openness and a personal and informal way of life, along with many opportunities for recreational and social activities. Rural social work services are likely to increase in the years ahead.

## Expansion of Leadership Roles

During the past few decades social workers have been rather quiescent in terms of leadership. Today the situation is changing, and tomorrow augurs well for increased leadership positions for social workers.

Social workers are gaining positions as directors of mental health centers, state hospitals, state training schools, youth development centers, and in many other agencies and organizations. It is recognized that social workers have a breadth of knowledge and skill in regard to the larger community that is positive and can be meaningful in leadership positions. Also, more social workers are playing leadership roles in agencies in directing staff development for all professionals, and in acting as team coordinators and planners.

On the political scene social workers are moving into elected positions and are gaining status in governmental councils and legislative bodies. In recent years social workers have been elected to the United States Senate and House of Representatives as well as to state legislatures and many other governmental positions. In educational circles social workers are beginning to become presidents of colleges and universities, vice presidents, and deans for student affairs. It is likely these trends will continue.

An example of a top educational appointment was that of Leon H. Ginsberg, former social work dean and commissioner of the West Virginia Human Services Department, who was named chancellor in 1984 of the West Virginia Board of Regents, which administers the state's sixteen colleges and universities.

According to Brilliant, insufficient attention has been given to training in leadership for students in schools of social work. She recommends the following:

> Students should study theories of leadership and the role of social work leadership; they should be given practice in leadership role playing and in field situations; and they should be presented with stimulating models of leadership behavior by teachers and mentors in school and in fieldwork.[17]

## Increase in International Social Work

Social work knowledge and skills have little concern for national boundaries. Numerous social workers are traveling to countries around the world, acting as consultants for government agencies and social work leaders, both public and private. This movement is a two-way process with social workers in countries abroad being used as consultants in the United States and in other New World countries.

An example of active international cooperation and collaboration in human relations is the Alliance of Universities for Democracy, a consortium of 94 universities from central and eastern Europe and the United States. It was established in 1990 to enhance the role of universities in promoting democratic institutions, economic development, education, philanthropy, and human rights in the newly established democracies of central and eastern

Europe. The alliance promotes collaborative work among universities, drawing on social workers for expert participation.

The International Federation of Social Workers is an organization that is doing much to further the cause of social work throughout the world. NASW president, Ann A. Abbott, attended their meeting in Sri Lanka on July 4, 1994 and reported more than 70 countries sent representatives to this biennial conference, with a challenging theme, "The Social Work Profession: A Family United in Troubled Times." She recalled that half a world away she "experienced in a highly personal way the power of social work's commitment to embrace rather than reject diversity."[18]

## Prevention

The Curriculum Study of 1959, of the Council on Social Work Education, stressed prevention as one of the three basic functions of social work practice, which gave added impetus to the preventive movement. Recent professional conferences and meetings have nearly all included one or more papers and discussions on the importance of prevention in social work.

Certainly in the years ahead there will be more stress placed upon prevention. Is it not really better to try to prevent personal, family, and community problems from happening in the first place, rather than to cure or treat them? Is it not more effective to spend time and talents in action that will prevent problem situations from taking place? Many believe that the intrinsic powers and contributions of social work in the years ahead lie in preventive approaches.

## Enrichment

Traditionally, social work has been concerned with helping the poor and the handicapped, working with emergency and long-range problems in human relationships. Two decades ago a major thrust appeared on the helping scene to prevent social problems for both individuals and society. Social work moved ahead with a variety of programs and methods to meet this challenge. In more recent years, another social focus has come to the fore—enrichment in living.

Enrichment in living involves working with all classes of people, the rich, middle-class, or poor—with the aim of assisting them to experience a fuller, more meaningful life. Millions of individuals, couples, and families are getting along satisfactorily but are not tapping positive resources that are inherent in them and their relationships. They may enrich their lives by utilizing qualitative resources, knowledge, and skills that are available. Marriage enrichment groups are an example of a pattern that is developing rapidly. Social workers often act as leaders of such groups and assist seven or eight couples to look at who they are, where they are, where they would like to be, and help them reach their goals. Many such programs call for a weekend marathon in which group members stay at a hotel and are accessible for group sessions, individual discussions, and other activities that help extend their paths to fuller living. The future is wide open for expansion of enrichment programs.

## Movement for Higher Quality

Traditionally, social work has provided services for the disadvantaged and others with inadequate social relationships. In the past, report after report has been collected to emphasize numbers of interviews, group conferences, testing, and other indicators of work accomplished. Efficiency and effectiveness have been tabulated in many different ways to reflect agency services. Today there is a growing emphasis to provide not only quantity of services, but, in particular, to reach for quality.

According to Martin, top-quality management (TQM) is rapidly shaping up as today's new managerial wave. Many corporations have initiated TQM programs in recent years. Martin also suggests that it is just a matter of time "before this new management wave washes over human service organizations. In anticipation of this eventuality, human service administrators may find it in their best interest to begin exploring the concept of TQM."[19] And a major element in this new approach is its emphasis on quality as a primary organizational goal.

## Summary

*We live in a fast-changing world, which has many implications for the rapidly developing profession of social work. In the years ahead, what pathways will social work be likely to follow?*

*Several trends and developments are emerging as projections are made into the future of social work: innovative services, increased status, higher salaries, growth of private practice, spirituality considerations in practice, curriculum modification, greater use of case management,* *increased advocacy role, improved public relations, growth in international social work, more leadership roles, additional emphasis on prevention and enrichment, and movement for higher quality in social work education and practice.*

*The potentialities seem generally favorable for social work and social workers. Some rough spots lie ahead, but professional training and services are likely to be consolidated, increased, and improved.*

## Selected References

CORNETT, CARLTON, "Toward a More Comprehensive Personology: Integrating a Spiritual Perspective into Social Work Practice," *Social Work,* 37 (March 1992), 101–102.

COWLEY, AU-DEANE S., "Transpersonal Social Work: A Theory for the 1990s," *Social Work,* 38 (September 1993), 527–534.

FORTUNE, ANNE E., and LOU LOENTAL HANKS, "Gender Inequities in Early Social Worker Careers," *Social Work,* 33 (May–June 1988), 221–226.

HART, AILEEN, "Training Social Administrators for Leadership in the Coming Decades," *Administration in Social Work,* 12, no. 3 (1988), 1–11.

HOKENSTAD, M. C., S. K. KHINDUKA, and JAMES MIDGLEY, eds. *Profiles in International Social Work.* Washington, DC: National Association of Social Workers, 1992.

JACOBS, CAROLYN, and DORCAS D. BOWLES, eds., *Ethnicity and Race: Critical Concepts in Social Work.* Silver Spring, MD: National Association of Social Workers, 1988.

MACAROV, DAVID, *Certain Change: Social Work Practice in the Future.* Silver Spring, MD: National Association of Social Workers, 1991.

NURIUS, PAULA S., and WALTER W. HUDSON, "Computer-Based Practice: Future Dream or Current

Technology?" *Social Work,* 33 (July–August 1988), 357–362.

PROCTOR, ENOLA K., and LARRY E. DAVIS, "The Challenge of Racial Difference: Skills for Clinical Practice," *Social Work,* 39 (May 1994), 314–323.

REESER, LINDA CHERREY, and IRWIN EPSTEIN, *Professionalization and Activism in Social Work: The 60's, the 80's, and the Future.* New York: Columbia University Press, 1990.

RESNICK, HY, and JOSEPHINE KING, "Shadow Consultation: Intervention in Industry," *Social Work,* 30 (September–October 1985), 447–450.

RUBIN, ALLEN, "Practice Effectiveness: More Grounds for Optimism," *Social Work,* 30 (November–December 1985), 469–476.

SERMABEIKIAN, PATRICIA, "Our Clients, Ourselves: The Spiritual Perspective and Social Work Practice," *Social Work,* 39 (March 1994), 178–182.

## Notes

1. John Naisbitt and Patricia Aburdene, *Megatrends 2000, Ten New Directions for the 1990's* (New York: William Morrow & Company, Inc., 1990), p. 11.

2. Lecture by Dr. Mortimer Adler at the University of Utah, February 18, 1963.

3. Alvin Toffler, *Future Shock* (New York: Random House, 1970).

4. Ibid., p. 2.

5. Ibid., p. 487.

6. John Naisbitt, *Megatrends, Ten New Directions Transforming Our Lives* (New York: Warner Books, 1982), pp. 249–250.

7. Hy Resnick and Josephine King, "Shadow Consultation: Intervention in Industry," *Social Work,* 30 (September–October 1985), 447.

8. "Therapists Tackle Drug Abuse in Sports," *NASW News,* 30 (September 1985), 7.

9. B. J. Symour and Beverly Marston, "Social Work and Optometry: A New Partnership," *Social Work,* 29 (November–December 1984), 540.

10. Thomas M. Meenaghan, "Using Social Work Curriculum in Socially Oriented Architecture Programs," *Journal of Education for Social Work,* 20 (Spring 1984), 76.

11. Allen Rubin, "Practice Effectiveness: More Grounds for Optimism," *Social Work,* 30 (November–December 1985), 469.

12. Robert L. Barker, *The Social Work Dictionary,* 3rd ed. (Washington, DC: NASW Press, 1995), p. 363.

13. Patricia Sermabeikian, "Our Clients, Ourselves: The Spiritual Perspective and Social Work Practice," *Social Work,* 39 (March 1994), 178.

14. Patricia W. Soyka, *Unlocking Human Resources: A Career in Social Work* (New York: Public Affairs Committee, 1971), p. 10.

15. Amy C. Butler, "The Attractions of Private Practice," *Journal of Social Work Education,* 28 (Winter 1992), 52.

16. Maryann Mahaffey, "Lobbying and Social Work," *Social Work,* 17 (January 1972), 11.

17. Eleanor L. Brilliant, "Social Work Leadership: A Missing Ingredient?" *Social Work,* 31 (September–October 1986), 329.

18. *NASW News,* 39 (September 1994), 2.

19. Lawrence L. Martin, "Total Quality Management: The New Managerial Wave," *Administration in Social Work,* 17, No. 2 1993), 1–2.

# Name Index

# Subject Index

**Photo Credits**

The photos on pages 5, 24, 29, 45, 83, 106, 132, 149, 200, 217, 237, 277, and 381 © Robert Harbison.

The photos on pages 169, 182, 320, 325, 351, and 369 courtesy of the University of Utah Photo Archives, Special Collections, University of Utah Library; also University of Utah Public Relations Department.